PROXY WARS

PROXY WARS

Suppressing Violence through
Local Agents

**Edited by Eli Berman
and David A. Lake**

CORNELL UNIVERSITY PRESS   ITHACA AND LONDON

The authors are grateful for funding from the Office of Naval Research awards #N00014-14-1-0843 and #N00014-16-1-2516. Any opinions, findings, and conclusions or recommendations expressed in this material are those of the author(s) and do not necessarily reflect the views of the Office of Naval Research.

First published 2019 by Cornell University Press

Library of Congress Cataloging-in-Publication Data

Names: Berman, Eli, editor. | Lake, David A., 1956– editor. | Macdonald, Julia. South Korea, 1950–1953.
Title: Proxy wars : suppressing violence through local agents / edited by Eli Berman and David A. Lake.
Description: Ithaca : Cornell University Press, 2019. | Includes bibliographical references and index.
Identifiers: LCCN 2018029903 (print) | LCCN 2018032286 (ebook) | ISBN 9781501733093 (pdf) | ISBN 9781501733109 (epub/mobi) | ISBN 9781501733055 | ISBN 9781501733055 (cloth) | ISBN 9781501733062 (pbk.)
Subjects: LCSH: Proxy war—History—20th century—Case studies. | Proxy war—History—21st century—Case studies. | United States—Foreign relations—20th century—Case studies. | United States—Foreign relations—21st century—Case studies.
Classification: LCC JZ6385 (ebook) | LCC JZ6385. P76 2019 (print) | DDC 355.02—dc23
LC record available at https://lccn.loc.gov/2018029903

Contents

Conclusion
Eli Berman and David A. Lake

Tables

Figures

Acknowledgments

This volume is the product of a multiyear effort by a diverse group of scholars. Our debts are wide and deep, as is our gratitude. One of our greatest debts is to David Laitin, the intellectual godfather of this project, who challenged us to try the method and helped devise the template we have used for the case studies. We are also grateful to Gerard Padró i Miquel and Pierre Yared for their intellectual leadership in developing the theory, and then tailoring it when we discovered the need to account for capacity building as an alternative. They also advised us in ways large and small on the case studies as those progressed.

We have benefited not only from the authors of the chapters included in this volume but also from the contributions of other UC San Diego graduate students who participated in our initial discussions and workshops, including Derek Bonett, Garrett Bredell, Shannon Carcelli, and Liesel Spangler. John Powell contributed to a miniconference at UC San Diego in June 2016. We are especially grateful to our colleagues from the policy community who took time from their busy schedules to "ground-truth" our studies in September 2016 at a conference generously hosted at George Washington University. Conrad Crane, Luke Hartig, Ethan Hollander, Daniel Kurtzer, Daniel Markey, Natan Sachs, Abbey Steele, David Ucko, and Kael Weston all provided detailed and extremely useful commentary on the draft chapters. We appreciate the contributions of our academic colleagues who attended that conference as well, including Charles Glaser, Marc Grinberg, Yonatan Lupu, Rennah Miles, Harris Mylonas, and Elizabeth Saunders. Finally, two anonymous reviewers for Cornell University Press provided excellent comments on the penultimate version of the manuscript, seeing value in what we had accomplished to that point but challenging us in ways that greatly improved the final volume. Roger Haydon was, as always, the consummate editor. Lynne Bush worked wonders in compiling, formatting, and editing the manuscript under severe time constraints created only by our usual inefficiencies. Eric Levy copyedited the volume and Ken Bolton prepared the index. None of the above bears responsibility for our errors of commission or omission.

This book is part of a larger "Deterrence with Proxies" research project funded by the Minerva Research Institute through the Office of Naval Research award #N00014-16-1-2516. Any opinions, findings, and conclusions or recommendations expressed in this material are those of the author(s) and do not necessarily reflect the views of the Office of Naval Research. We have benefited from the comments and advice of numerous Minerva scholars and program managers, most notably Erin Fitzgerald and David Montgomery, and especially our own program manager Harold Hawkins. The critical logistical capacity of the Deterrence with Proxies project has been provided by Katherine Levy and Nicole Daneshvar of the University of California Institute on Global Conflict and Cooperation, whom we thank for their cheerful efficiency and creative problem solving.

Finally, and most important, we thank our devoted spouses, Linda and Wendy, for their patience and support.

PROXY WARS

INTRODUCTION
Principals, Agents, and Indirect Foreign Policies

Eli Berman, David A. Lake,
Gerard Padró i Miquel, and Pierre Yared

After invading Iraq and removing Saddam Hussein from power in 2003, the United States raced to build a new government in Baghdad that would, in the hopes of the administration, be an ally in the global war on terror. As the civil war subsequently raged out of control, and Islamist fighters poured into the country to defeat the American "infidels" and establish a base of operations for global jihad, the United States sought to "step up" an Iraqi army that would allow its own forces to "step down." It handpicked a new leader, Prime Minister Nouri al-Maliki, who it hoped would create a broad-based government representing all factions of Iraqi society and rob the insurgency of its fuel. Concerned about his own political survival, however, al-Maliki quickly formed a coalition dominated by Shia, deepening the sectarian cleavages that were feeding the flames of civil war. Only after the United States seized control of the conflict in 2007 with the "surge," bolstered the Sunnis in the Anbar Awakening, and began withholding supplies from the Shiite militias allied with al-Maliki did the prime minister moderate his sectarianism. As the civil war ebbed, and with the Americans still eager to return home as soon as possible, al-Maliki held out for terms in the Status of Forces Agreement that he knew the United States would reject, leading to the withdrawal of U.S. troops in 2011. With the United States once again dependent on al-Maliki to accomplish its aims in Iraq, he returned to his earlier sectarianism, deepened ties to Iran, and further alienated the Sunnis. Despite billions of dollars in aid and extensive training of Iraqi forces, the still-weak state crumbled when ISIS invaded western Iraq in the summer of 2014. Although the United States tried to build up a local proxy (or agent—a subordinate charged with some task) in what was to become the most important front in the global war on terror, it was ultimately unable to control the Iraqi government, its agent.

The most common image of world politics is states negotiating, cooperating, or sometimes fighting with one another: billiard balls bouncing around on the global pool table. Yet working through local proxies has always been a central tool of foreign policy.[1] To stabilize countries in the region as a prophylactic against renewed European imperialism, and to suppress local peasant movements that might demand land reform, the United States promoted local strongmen in the Caribbean and Central America in the early years of the twentieth century, and then turned a blind eye to their repressive rule. As President Franklin D. Roosevelt once quipped about Gen. Rafael Leonidas Trujillo y Molina of the Dominican Republic, "He may be an SOB, but he's our SOB."[2] The sentiment, however, applies more broadly. The United States also promoted pro-Western leaders in Europe after World War II, recruiting them as allies against the Soviet Union, and supported anti-Communist leaders and rebel factions globally during the Cold War. It supported the shah of Iran as its regional partner under the Nixon Doctrine of the 1970s, and then expanded this strategy to include other conservative regimes in the Middle East in the pursuit of a "new world order," including the regimes of President Hosni Mubarak of Egypt and, after an interlude in the Arab Spring, President Abdel Fattah el-Sisi. To varying degrees, in South Korea (chapter 1), Colombia (chapter 3), El Salvador (chapter 5), and elsewhere, the United States has effectively managed these proxy relationships to accomplish many of its foreign policy goals.

This reliance on local proxies is not unique to the United States. Historically, European empires, and especially the British, typically operated through local, collaborating elites. Germany allowed Denmark to retain its nominal sovereignty for much of World War II, expecting its leaders to suppress the local resistance. As Germany's probability of victory in Europe declined, the collaborationists stopped enforcing Berlin's will—ultimately prompting Hitler to take over the country and govern it directly (chapter 2). The Soviet Union created its own proxies in Eastern Europe after 1945, and paralleled U.S. efforts to promote sympathetic leaders in the developing world during the Cold War. In similar ways, Israel sets incentives for the Palestinian Authority to control violence emanating from the West Bank (chapter 7) and for Hamas to limit rocket attacks from Gaza (chapter 4).

Understanding indirect control, how to motivate local leaders to act in sometimes costly ways—and when and how it succeeds—is essential to effective foreign policy in today's world, especially for managing violence and illicit activities by nonstate actors operating from the territory of other states. Countries such as the United States reserve the right, and sometimes undertake direct action, to fight transnational terrorists, insurgents, or drug lords. More often, however, they rely on local agents to suppress these threats. For instance, although the United States intervened directly in Afghanistan to overthrow the Taliban and pursue al-Qaeda, even there it quickly reverted to indirect control in creating, supporting, and operating through the government of President Hamid Karzai, and now that of Ashraf Ghani. Working through local agents to accomplish U.S. foreign policy goals is likely to become even more common in the years ahead. After long and unsuccessful wars in Afghanistan and Iraq, the American public has soured on direct military interventions. President Donald J. Trump has espoused a more isolationist foreign policy, and is seeking to induce allies and partners to take more responsibility for their own defense, at home and abroad. If the United States does less, it must rely on others to do more. The question is, then, how do we motivate proxies to do what the United States wants?

The Argument in Brief

To answer this question, we use a theory-driven investigation of case studies. One goal is to determine when it makes sense for a principal—a superior power—to engage in indirect control to deal with issues of counterterrorism, counterinsurgency, and counternarcotics operations, three areas where private actors within fragile states threaten global order and the interests of other states. In that sense, we test the limits of this strategic approach to transnational threats. A second goal, when indirect control makes sense, is to investigate how to manage that relationship successfully, at minimum cost to the principal.

We first develop a theoretical framework in which a principal can choose different courses of action in addressing what we generically call a disturbance, such as terrorism emanating from a neighboring country. It can take direct action, such as military strikes. At the opposite extreme, it can disengage and endure continuing attacks. Alternatively, and this is our focus, it can engage in indirect control, that is, the principal promises rewards and punishments to the proxy, which compel the latter to act to suppress the disturbance. The principal might additionally, or alternatively, bolster the suppressive capacity of the proxy by, for instance, supplying it with weapons or training.

The theory suggests that in making the right strategic decision, the alignment of interests, or objectives, between the principal and the agent is of paramount importance. Interests might diverge because of preferences—disturbances trouble the principal more than they do the proxy—or because the proxy has higher priorities or higher costs, perhaps dictated by domestic political pressures. If those interests strongly diverge, that is, if the principal is much more interested in threat suppression than the local proxy is, it will be extremely costly for the principal to apply sufficient rewards and punishments to make the agent comply. To provide capacity in this case is also self-defeating, as weapons and training will be diverted by the proxy to its own purposes rather than to suppressing the disturbance that threatens the principal. Hence, in this case, the only feasible options for the principal are direct action or disengagement.

In contrast, for a medium range of interest divergence, the principal can tailor punishments and rewards to compel the agent more or less successfully to address the disturbance. By success, we mean the compliance of a proxy with the goals of the principal. This may fall short of absolute success—completely defeating an insurgency, eliminating the drug trade, and so on—since the principal itself may not want to expend the resources necessary to reduce disturbances to zero. Rather, the theoretical prediction that we aim to assess is whether one state, the principal, can induce actions it desires by another state, the proxy, with suitably chosen rewards and punishments.

Finally, only when the interests of principal and agent are very closely aligned will the principal choose a strategy of unconditional capacity building, through increased aid, military training, and other forms of assistance necessary to achieve their shared ambition. This was largely the case in postwar Europe, for instance, where both the United States and local allies saw the Soviet Union as a threat.

Having outlined this theory, we use it to guide our reading of the case studies developed in subsequent chapters. From these analytical narratives (a method we explain below), we derive three main findings. First, when principals use rewards and punishments tailored to the agents' domestic political context, proxies typically comply. This finding follows from comparisons across our nine cases. In South Korea (chapter 1), for instance, immediately after World War II, the United States and President Syngman Rhee were at loggerheads. The United States sought to build a professionalized army able to defend the country from North Korea and its Communist allies. Rhee was more concerned with securing his hold on office, so he "coup-proofed" his military, stacking it with loyalists. Invasion from the north largely aligned Rhee's interests with those of the United States, and when those interests did diverge, relatively small rewards and punishments were effective in prompting Rhee to professionalize his officer corps.

Conversely, when the principal fails to use appropriate incentives, the local proxy shirks, failing to act to suppress disturbances, as desired by the principal. Iraq (chapter 9) is a clear example of principal failure. When the administration of President George W. Bush refused to make its rewards to al-Maliki contingent on behavior, the new leader ignored U.S. pleas to build a large coalition representative of all segments of Iraqi society. Instead, he formed a highly sectarian Shia-only coalition, which was ultimately dependent on Iran for support.

Second, we find that when the salience of the disturbance to the principal or the costs of effort (interest divergence) for the agent increase and the principal responds with higher-powered incentives—larger rewards and punishments—the proxy responds as expected with greater effort. This within-case comparison holds in all cases in which incentives are applied fairly consistently (five of nine) and often in the other four as well. Even in Iraq, for instance, where the United States did eventually impose small punishments on al-Maliki during the surge, the otherwise uncooperative prime minister responded by cracking down on his Shia coalition partners, as demanded by Gen. David Petraeus and Ambassador Ryan Crocker. The clear lesson: agents do respond to incentives.

Third, we also find examples in which indirect control is not attempted, or only partially implemented. Given its dependence on Pakistan to supply troops in Afghanistan, the United States lacked sufficient leverage to induce Islamabad's cooperation in the war on terror, or even in hunting down Osama bin Laden, ultimately taking direct action to capture the al-Qaeda leader. Similarly, Israel has tried rewards and punishments with the Palestinian Authority to control terrorism, but has been unwilling, for domestic political reasons, to grant the "big" reward of significant autonomy (or even sovereignty) desired by Palestinian leaders. Ultimately, as predicted by our theory, if interests diverge too much, the principal must either undertake direct action—as in the case of the surge in Iraq or the capture of bin Laden—or simply admit that indirect control is too costly to meet its ambitions.

Our case studies also demonstrate a finding at odds with our theory. As a principal, the United States too often assumes that its interests are closely aligned with those of its proxy, and funnels unconditional aid and support to the proxy's leader—ostensibly to build greater capacity—failing to use the levers it possesses to induce appropriate effort. This was the case in relations with Yemen after 2003, where the Bush administration, absorbed by the war in Iraq, abandoned a previously effective proxy (chapter 8), and of course in Iraq, where the administration failed to wield the incentives available to it (chapter 9). We examine these and three other cases (El Salvador, Pakistan, and the Palestinian Authority) in which the principal fails to incentivize as much as the model predicts it would, and ask why. Without appropriate incentives, self-interested proxies use the flow of resources for their own opportunistic ends, diverting aid to favored constituencies, using foreign-trained troops to fight sectarian battles, or otherwise benefiting their own political agendas. The proxy then fails to achieve the goals desired by the principal, such as suppressing terrorism, insurgency, or drug trafficking.

Indirect control is above all a political strategy. The interests of the principal and proxy are rarely aligned, differing at least at the margin and sometimes significantly. The greater the divergence in interests with its proxy, the larger the incentives the principal must use to induce desired behaviors. So, incentives to the agent must be conditional either on proxy effort or, since those efforts are typically not fully observed, on the level of disturbances. Indirect control is therefore effective only under limited conditions.

In the remainder of this introductory chapter, we outline a general principal-agent theory tailored to the problem of indirect international control. We first describe the strategy of indirect control in more detail. Then we identify conditions enabling effective indirect control and the relationships between the costs and benefits of alternative strategies. The third section outlines our research design and the organization of this volume.

Indirect Control of Political Violence

The problem of private, nonstate actors projecting violence across national borders has waxed and waned over time and by region. The principle of national sovereignty is one of the great innovations of international society and provides the context within which transnational violence occurs today. Although often misunderstood, sovereignty is merely a statement about how political authority should be organized within and between states. As now conceived, sovereignty asserts that public authority is indivisible and culminates in a single apex in each territorially defined state.[3] Two corollaries are especially important: the first raises the costs of direct action, while the second reinforces a reliance on indirect control.

If to be sovereign means that the state is the ultimate authority in a single, hierarchically ordered domain, it necessarily implies that no other state or ruler can exercise authority in that same area or over the same people. By extension, no foreign state can intervene legitimately in the internal affairs of a sovereign state. The norm of nonintervention was first articulated in the writings of Christian von Wolff (1748) and Emmerich de Vattel (1758), but the first serious attempts to establish it originated in Latin America, in the Calvo and Drago Doctrines, articulated in 1868 and 1902, respectively. The first doctrine holds that jurisdiction in international investment disputes lies with the country in which the investment is located. The second declares that no foreign power can use force against a Latin American country to collect debt. Both doctrines were subsequently recognized as customary international law, as well as embodied in several national constitutions and treaties. Opposed by the United States until 1933, the principle of nonintervention was finally included in the Convention on Rights and Duties of States, which stated that "no state has the right to intervene in the internal or external affairs of another." Elaborating further, the Charter of the Organization of American States, signed in 1948, declares that "no State or group of States has the right to intervene, directly or indirectly, for any reason whatever, in the internal or external affairs of any other State." That idea was universalized in article 2 (7) of the United Nations Charter, which states that "nothing contained in the present Charter shall authorize the United Nations to intervene in matters which are essentially within the domestic jurisdiction of any state or shall require the Members to submit such matters to settlement under the present Charter."[4]

The principle of nonintervention is, of course, frequently violated in practice. Indeed, so frequent are exceptions to the principle that Stephen Krasner has labeled the entire idea of sovereignty an "organized hypocrisy."[5] Nonetheless, it has the effect of declaring as "unlawful" direct military interventions into other sovereign states except in extraordinary circumstances, such as preventive attacks. As with any law, states may choose to ignore the rule, as they do, but they pay a price in reputation, in balancing behavior by other states, or even in armed opposition. Direct action aimed at suppressing violent subnational groups remains possible under the parallel principle of self-defense, but it is now a practice that attracts international opprobrium as a violation of sovereignty.

If states are the ultimate authorities within their realms, it follows as a second corollary that they are responsible for all violence emanating from within their borders. States are permitted to use violence—wage war—against one another, but they are expected to suppress private actors from using their territories to project violence against other states. In turn, any violence that springs forth from their territory is presumed to be permitted or approved by the state, and thus a possible casus belli. This norm of public responsibility for private violence did not fully emerge until the end of the nineteenth (and the beginning of the twentieth) century, with the outlawing of privateering, mercenaries, and "freebooters" of all sorts.[6] Like the norm of nonintervention, it has been fairly robust only since the early twentieth century. Eventually, though, violence from any source originating in one country against a second came to be interpreted as intentional, and thus an act of aggression. While states might deny knowledge of, or responsibility for, forces operating from within their borders, this is no longer an acceptable excuse. States are responsible, whether they like it or not, and hold each other to account for violence suffered in all forms.

This second corollary somewhat offsets the first. If states are prohibited from intervening in the internal affairs of others, the failure of a state to fulfill its responsibilities and prevent transnational violence originating in its territory permits others to invoke the right of self-defense, regardless of whether the attack arose from a lack of will or capacity by the state. Tellingly, few states contested the right of the United States to invade Afghanistan and overthrow the Taliban after the terrorist attacks of 9/11, because the regime allowed or at least acquiesced in al-Qaeda's use of its territory as a headquarters and for training bases. Equally important, state responsibility for transnational violence implies and even affirms the use of indirect control. States should regulate violence originating within their territories, and other states can—and should, when necessary—reward or sanction them accordingly. If a state consistently fails in this responsibility, more-over, it may be appropriate for a country like the United States to induce compli-ance, invest in state capacity, or even support the removal of a local leader. More-over, even when direct action is permissible for self-defense, indirect control that attempts to assist leaders in controlling violence—or incentivizes leaders to meet their responsibilities—is possible, and potentially less costly than direct action.

Although indirect control as foreign policy dates back at least to the Roman Empire, three changes in the world today have made it more salient.[7] First, pri-vate violence has gone global. New technologies, along with economic integra-tion, have empowered even small private groups to wage war against states or other opponents from anywhere around the world. The ready availability of automatic weapons and the ease of assembling "suicide vests" allow committed individuals to carry out attacks against soft targets pretty much anywhere at will, as demonstrated repeatedly in recent years in Paris, Brussels, Orlando, Istanbul, New York, and more places than anyone cares to name. Communications tech-nologies and open borders allow insurgents to learn from the internet and one another, coordinate their activities more easily, and recruit new members. The very globalization that so many violent groups now oppose has also allowed ter-rorists to carry out attacks on an unprecedented, worldwide scale. Where perhaps in the past the problem of transnational violence affected only neighbors, today it is a global scourge.

Second, more states now lack the capacity or will to police their own nonstate groups. Despite their nominal sovereignty, fragile and failed states do not—almost by definition—control all of their territory.[8] Prior to 1945, in order to be recog-nized by their peers, states needed to demonstrate effective sovereignty, including the ability to prevent private violence from spilling across national borders. Since the formation of the United Nations and the movement to decolonization, states have adopted the notion of juridical sovereignty, which does not require that states actually control all of their territory or residents.[9] Many countries today contain extended unpoliced peripheries, whose occupants are poorly served and whose international neighbors are at risk of violence and refugee flows. The number of such failed or fragile states has escalated in recent years. Other states are more or less willing to let transnational insurgents operate from within their borders, for their own political reasons or out of opposition to particular great powers. Some governments are actually supported by (and deeply integrated with) private violence-wielding groups, as in the case of drug cartels or al-Qaeda in Afghanistan before the U.S. intervention. Increasingly, states either cannot or choose not to regulate violent nonstate groups that operate within their borders.

Third, the United States and other Western states have become frequent targets of transnational terrorists and drug cartels. In part, this is because they create and enforce a liberal international order that violates traditional values and social structures in countries increasingly integrated into the global economy. Under the "new world order," and no longer checked and balanced by a near-equal superpower as in the Cold War, the United States has aggressively sought to expand the liberal international order into new regions, successfully in the case of Eastern Europe and less so in the Middle East, where there has been a violent backlash. It has also reached more deeply into societies in Latin America, Central Asia, and elsewhere to eradicate the drug trade at its source. At least some of the violence now directed at the United States and other Western states is "blowback" from the attempt to expand the Pax Americana to new areas.[10] Related, and likely more important, is U.S. and European support for the repressive and autocratic governments that often serve as their proxies, especially in the Middle East today. Opponents in Saudi Arabia, Afghanistan, and even Jordan now understand that the road to reform or revolution at home often runs through Washington, DC. Rather than just focusing on the "near enemy"—their local and perhaps apostate regimes—opponents turn their violence toward the "far enemy" and its allies that, as in the case of recent attacks in Europe, can be targeted easily.[11]

These changes combine to create new and unique threats to global leaders such as the United States and Europe, and to regional powers. Transnational terrorists can now hide in the interstices of state authority and rise up to wield significant force at the time and place of their choosing. Although not unprecedented, the scale and possibility of private violence have greatly increased in recent decades. In an age when interstate war has become increasingly unlikely, transnational insurgencies have emerged as the most potent and existential threat to some states and citizens and have radically disrupted the lives and politics of even those not directly targeted.

How has the United States responded to terrorism from abroad? The primary approaches—putting aside massive defensive efforts—have been direct control (as discussed above) and capacity building. Capacity building is also an indirect foreign policy, but one that relies on building up a local agent so that it can more effectively counter the perceived threat to the principal. That is, the problem is conceived as one in which the proxy lacks only the ability to suppress the disturbance, not the will. Under this assumption, it makes sense for the principal to expand the suppressive capacity of the proxy. As threats grow, the failure of that policy leads proponents to argue for providing even greater resources to the proxy.

Our theory implies, however, that when the assumption is wrong—that is, when the policy objectives or the interests of the principal and proxy are highly dissimilar—resources provided by the principal will not be used by the proxy to suppress threats to the former, but rather to pursue the priorities of the latter. Foreign aid may simply be used to repress the leader's political opponents (or enlarge his Swiss bank account) rather than to fight the insurgents or win the hearts and minds of the civilian population. Indeed, as long as the problem is conceived as inadequate capacity, then the more the proxy fails in fighting groups wielding transnational violence against the principal, the more resources it might expect to receive. If so, why would the leader ever seek to succeed? This problem of incentives severely limits the conditions under which capacity building should be pursued.

The main alternative to capacity building, and the focus of our volume, is the strategy of indirect control, characterized by the use of rewards and punishments (that is, tailored incentives) by the principal to motivate local proxies to suppress disturbances of concern. By making rewards and punishments contingent on success in reducing threats, the principal induces the proxy to engage in actions to suppress the disturbance. The further apart the interests of the principal and proxy, the larger the rewards and punishments must be to induce effort by the latter.

Beyond some threshold of divergence in policy interests, this strategy becomes too costly for the principal. In that case, the principal may choose to take action directly, since the proxy cannot be induced to do so, or may abandon the effort completely and simply accept some level of threat and violence. It is precisely in this circumstance, however, that capacity building will be particularly worthless, and perhaps counterproductive. When the principal and the proxy disagree on the purpose to which resources are to be directed, a strategy of capacity building will simply mean that the principal is throwing good money after bad.

In the wake of long and unsuccessful wars in Afghanistan and Iraq, and anticipating the need for more "small footprint" operations around the globe, which effectively require operating through local agents, understanding how to use indirect control to better counter transnational threats is an urgent priority. We are not, of course, the first to recognize these trends, or the first to use principal-agent theory to understand their dynamics and effect.[12] The need to work through local proxies, and the difficulties of doing so, is increasingly recognized.[13] The value of our approach lies in its more rigorous specification of the alternatives to indirect control and the ways in which the size of the threat, which we call the disturbance, and the divergence in interests between the actors, which we capture as the costs of effort to the proxy, condition the choice of principals to work through local agents. By more clearly specifying the alternatives—capacity building, direct action, or doing nothing—we can better explain why some principals continue to choose indirect control even though it does not appear on its face to succeed, if one defines success as the total suppression of disturbances. The threat may not be large enough to warrant sufficiently rewarding or punishing the proxy to bring about perfect suppression, or the costs of direct action—dealing with an insurgency itself, for instance—may be so high that working through a "poor" agent with very different policy interests may still be preferred. In short, nothing in our theory suggests that disturbances will be (or even should be) reduced to zero. But we can identify when a strategy of capacity building is possible, when indirect control is likely to be more effective, and when direct control or doing nothing are the only viable alternatives. We can also draw out comparative static predictions on the relationship between the disturbance, the costs of effort, and the use of incentives, all of which influence whether indirect control is likely to be more or less effective.

A Principal-Agent Framework

Our framework for analyzing conditions and strategies for indirect control consists of two players.[14] First, there is a principal, a relatively powerful actor interested in minimizing the occurrence of some disturbance. A disturbance might be a terrorist attack, noncooperation on diplomatic goals, nuclear weapons tests, human rights abuses, flows of drugs, or lawlessness, for example. Depending on the setting, the principal might be a counterinsurgent, the government of a neighboring country, or the government of a great power interested in minimizing disturbances arising from another country. Second, there is an agent (or proxy), a subordinate whose actions the principal might influence, and who can suppress disturbances at lower cost than the principal can (when acting directly). This agent can serve as the principal's proxy in minimizing disturbances. The agent in our analyses varies across cases but is usually the leader of the country from which the disturbance originates. Our analysis focuses on characterizing the interaction between a principal and an agent in an environment in which both players act rationally subject to constraints, anticipating the behavior of the other player.

The principal can (1) do nothing, and live with the disturbance; (2) act directly to suppress the disturbance, which we call direct control; (3) provide unconditional assistance to the proxy, which we refer to as capacity building; (4) replace the proxy; or (5) use rewards and punishments contingent on the occurrence of disturbances, which we term indirect control. The proxy responds to the strategy of the principal by choosing whether to reduce the disturbance and how much effort to exert in doing so. Critically, the proxy's actions (or, equivalently, the costs of taking those actions) are not fully observed by the principal.

Key parameters in our theory and cases are the expected size and frequency of the disturbance—which determine the principal's interest in dealing with it—and the costs of effort by the proxy. The latter summarizes two elements. On the one hand, these costs capture how difficult it is for the agent to deal with the disturbance. Dealing with a transnational terrorist group that is popular at home is more costly to the agent, for instance, than dealing with a reviled one. On the other hand, these costs capture how divergent are the interests of principal and agent with regard to the disturbance. Indeed, a situation in which the agent is intrinsically interested in addressing the problem (that is, well aligned with the principal) is captured in the model by low effort cost. At the limit where the agent would, when unprompted, do exactly what the principal wishes it to do, the effort cost would be nil. This would be the case of a perfectly aligned agent.

The first step in our analysis specifies the empirical scope of the theory by highlighting the baseline assumptions of the theoretical model. The second step describes the structure of the implicit contract between the principal and the agent and the optimal use of the incentive tools by the principal. The third step analyzes how the contract changes in response to changes in the environment. The final step derives predictions from an extension of the model in which we consider the principal's investment in the agent's capacity to deal with disturbances.

Scope Conditions

Our framework applies to a large number of principal-agent relationships in which the following three conditions hold. First, relative to the principal, the agent has a natural advantage at controlling the disturbance, due to a particular level of expertise, familiarity with the problem, or simply a lower cost of dealing with it. However, there is divergence in interests between the principal and the agent: the agent in isolation would exert less effort at suppression than the principal would like it to. Indeed, the agent may even benefit from the realization of the disturbance, so it might not exert any effort at all if left alone. This local advantage is essential: if it did not exist, the principal would never choose indirect control. Typically, the advantage of the agent derives from knowledge of local conditions that would be costly for the principal to acquire. This is the main source of local advantage in our cases.[15]

Second, the agent is subordinate, in the sense that the principal has tools that it can use to compel the agent to exert effort in minimizing disturbances. The principal can reward the agent through diplomatic concessions, military aid, or economic investments. As opposed to capacity-building resource transfers, discussed later in this introduction, rewards are of private benefit to the agent and are contingent on the agent's cooperation. The principal can punish the agent through withheld economic aid, diplomatic or military confrontation, or even engagement in actions that debilitate the agent. If the agent is a leader, the principal can have the agent removed, either directly by regime change or indirectly by supporting the agent's opponents. The principal uses these tools to incentivize the agent and thus address the divergent interests. This scope condition excludes from the purview of our theory instances where the agent can exert enough influence (or counterinfluence) over the principal to negate these rewards and punishments (other than by not suppressing disturbances).[16] The case of Pakistan (chapter 6), in which the United States needed Islamabad's cooperation to resupply its troops in Afghanistan, is one in which this subordinacy condition may be violated.

Finally, there is private information on the side of the agent that hampers the principal's ability to perfectly provide incentives. This private information can take the form of unobserved effort (hidden action) or unobserved costs (hidden information). For example, it may be the case that the principal cannot observe perfectly how much effort is being exerted by the agent. That is, the agent claims it is exerting effort but it is instead shirking—the principal does not observe exactly what the agent is doing, so who is to say the agent is lying? Alternatively, it may be hard to determine the correct kind of effort, that which is most effective in suppressing disturbances. An agent might be observed bolstering his own private Praetorian Guard, but when confronted about it, might claim that building elite forces is the best way to defeat terrorist cells. Not knowing exactly what is going on in the country, the principal has a difficult time assessing this claim, which might or might not be correct.

Alternatively, it may be the case that the principal can observe fully what the agent is doing and knows exactly what should be done. What the principal does not observe, however, are the full costs that the agent would incur if it exerted the right level and type of effort. For example, this cost of effort could be the threat of an internal coup, greater domestic resistance to the agent's rule, or the collapse of a critical patronage network; the principal may not be able to assess the extent of these threats. In this case, the right interpretation is that the agent can always claim that it is doing the maximum that could reasonably be expected from it, and the principal cannot properly assess or audit this claim. For ease of exposition, we will eschew this version of imperfect information in what follows, and focus on the case where the principal cannot observe either the level or the kind of effort that the agent is exerting. This problem of unobserved costs produces predictions identical to those that follow.

In reality, we often see the principal investing in monitoring the agent, to reduce private information. A larger contingent of military advisers, for instance, or directing intelligence collection and analysis at the proxy, may provide more information about the agent effort. Such investments, however, are typically costly to the principal, of diminishing marginal value, and imperfect. In our analysis, we assume that despite the principal's monitoring, the agent still holds private information.

Complicating the principal's problem is that disturbances have a random element; they may occasionally occur even when the agent is fully cooperating, and sometimes no disturbance occurs even when proxy effort is absent. For example, even if the agent exerts the correct kind and amount of unobservable effort, a disturbance may occur due to circumstances beyond the agent's control. In this situation, because of the presence of private information, the principal would not be able to tell if the disturbance was due to low effort exerted by the agent or instead to a fully complying agent's being unlucky. Given the principal's lack of information, an agent always has an incentive to claim that it cooperated but suffered bad luck, even if the agent's low effort is in fact at fault. That is, disturbances do not fully reveal proxy effort to the principal, so the principal's rewards and punishments will sometimes be allocated unfairly (and punishments will be even more frequently protested).

To summarize, indirect control describes a situation in which a principal compels an agent to deal with a potential disturbance. Because of divergent interests between the two parties, the principal must provide incentives to the agent, the provision of which is complicated by asymmetric information. In designing incentives, the principal recognizes that the agent may pretend to cooperate and make excuses if disturbances occur. The principal must react to the realized disturbances (rather than to reported effort), so as to provide ex ante incentives for the agent.

The Implicit Contract between Principal and Agent

A principal facing an agent can structure an implicit contract in which it commits to a specific set of actions as a function of what is observable to it. Because effort is unobservable to the principal, actions cannot be contingent on agent effort. Instead, the principal must commit to a level of rewards, a level of punishments, and a probability of replacement that depend on the realization and size of a disturbance, the outcome that the principal can perfectly observe.[17] The agent is assumed to know the implicit contract in advance, and it privately chooses an effort level. After this happens, a potential disturbance is realized; after observing the disturbance and its size, the principal follows through on the terms of the contract. Given that the principal cannot observe the agent's effort, and the disturbance is stochastic, rewards and punishments following disturbances are not a contract violation, or "out of equilibrium," but are required by the contract.

We focus on the optimal contract from the perspective of the principal: the contract that minimizes the size and number of disturbances subject to the cost of incentivizing the agent. Importantly, rewards and punishments to the agent are costly for the principal, so the principal will minimize their use. That is, other things equal, the principal would rather not transfer monetary or in-kind resources to the agent, and would prefer not to expend valuable diplomatic, reputational, or military capital punishing it. Replacement, on the other hand, while costly for the agent, need not be costly to the principal.[18] This depends on the quality of the likely replacement agent: if the incumbent agent is worse than possible replacements, the principal benefits, but if the incumbent is better than the replacements, then replacement is costly.

Predictions of the Model

The evidence base of this book is a set of cases, which we use to test the main propositions that follow from the theory outlined above. These are summarized in table 0.1.

The cost of effort to the agent is crucial in determining the optimal implicit contract between principal and agent. It is therefore important to understand the nature of the agents' effort cost. As we discussed above, these costs are related to two factors. The first is the direct cost of disturbance suppression, which is a function of the competence of the agent. Some agents are simply better at, say, counterinsurgency or counternarcotics operations than others, because they have better equipment, more experience, or better relationships with sources of operational intelligence.[19]

The second factor that raises costs is divergent preferences over the disturbance. As already noted, the principal seeks to reduce disturbances to some cost-effective level, but the agent might not share those priorities. For instance, the agent may share the principal's desire to suppress terrorists or the drug trade, or it may feel that its coercive resources are better spent defending the borders, deterring warlords, or collecting taxes, for example. Indeed, the agent may actually benefit from the disturbance, perhaps receiving bribes from drug lords, as in the case of Colombia (chapter 3), or gaining political support from citizens diametrically opposed to the policies of the principal, as in the case of Denmark seeking to overthrow Nazi control (chapter 2). Agents themselves may also have independent policy preferences, which differ from those of their constituents, or they may be dependent on different constituencies, with some latitude about

TABLE 0.1 Predictions of the theory

Basic predictions

H_1: The higher the cost of effort to the agent, the more likely the principal will be to engage in direct control or do nothing.

H_2: The smaller the disturbance, the more likely the principal is to reward the agent.

H_3: The larger the disturbance, the more likely the principal is to punish the agent.

H_4: Rewards and punishments will never be observed simultaneously.

H_5: The larger the disturbance, the more likely the principal is to replace the agent.

H_6: When interests are not fully aligned, and the principal does not offer contingent rewards and punishments, the agent is not likely to exert effort. Conversely, when the principal offers larger contingent rewards and punishments, the agent is more likely to exert effort.

Comparative static predictions

H_7: Conditional on indirect control being preferred to either direct control or doing nothing, as the cost of effort to the agent increases, the principal will be more likely to reward, punish, or replace the agent.

H_8: Conditional on indirect control being preferred to either direct control or doing nothing, as the cost of rewards to the principal increases, the principal will be more likely to punish or replace the agent.

H_9: Conditional on indirect control being preferred to either direct control or doing nothing, as the cost of punishment to the principal increases, the principal will be more likely to reward or replace the agent.

H_{10}: Conditional on indirect control being preferred to either direct control or doing nothing, as the cost of replacement to the principal increases (possible replacements are less competent), the principal will be more likely to reward or punish the agent.

H_{11}: As the cost of disturbances increases (the principal's goal becomes more important), the principal will be more likely to engage in indirect control, and the more likely it will be to reward, punish, or replace the agent.

Capacity-building predictions

H_{12}: The lower the agent's indirect costs of effort (the more aligned the agent's interests are with those of the principal), the more likely the principal will be to invest in capacity building.

where they draw their support from. As is frequent in our cases, the agent may share the principal's general goal (political stability) but differ dramatically in how it prefers to suppress the disturbance (attention to civilian casualties, degree of democratization, emphasis on reducing corruption, and so on).

We will refer to all of these differences in objectives and costs between principal and proxy as divergent interests, or misaligned interests. Differences across settings in the degree of interest alignment are a source of variation that is key to understanding our case studies. The higher the cost of effort to the agent, the more powerful the incentives the principal must employ to induce high effort—that is, the larger the rewards for effort and punishments for lack of effort. How do these costs affect the nature of the optimal implicit contract between principal and proxy?

High-Cost Agent. Rewards and punishments are costly to the principal. The higher the costs of effort are to the agent, the stronger the incentives that the principal must use in order to compel the agent to act. It follows that there is some level of effort cost so high that indirect control is precluded. Even if the agent is better at accomplishing the task than the principal is, the agent requires such massive incentives to overcome its distaste for suppression that the principal will choose to engage in some other strategy. There are three possibilities: First, the principal might decide on direct control and itself attempt to control the disturbance, through deployment of forces, air strikes, or drone strikes, for example. Second, the principal might give up entirely, doing nothing to address the disturbance. In practice, this can involve temporarily or permanently withdrawing from the troubled territory or, alternatively, waiting for a change of leadership, when a lower-cost agent might emerge as a proxy. Or the principal could replace the agent, perhaps using a temporary episode of direct control to do so. This logic is reflected in hypothesis H_1, in table 0.1.

Low-Cost Agent. If the agent has sufficiently low costs of effort, then it is worthwhile for the principal to engage in indirect control, since incentives are not too costly. The optimal implicit contract under indirect control takes the following form, as illustrated in figure 0.1, which graphs rewards and punishments on the vertical axis against the level of damage from disturbances on the horizontal.

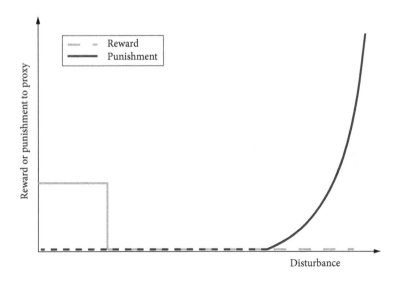

FIGURE 0.1. Rewards and punishments as a function of disturbances

1. *The principal reacts to zero or small disturbances with rewards.* The better the observed outcome for the principal (i.e., low damage from disturbances), the larger or more likely the reward prescribed by the contract (H_2). Note that the reward does not need to serve a purpose other than increasing the agent's incentives to exert effort. In other words, our prediction holds if the reward is a pure resource cost to the principal as well as if the principal partially benefits from the reward (if it serves the purpose of capacity building for the future, for example).

2. *The principal reacts to large disturbances with punishments.* The larger the disturbance, the larger the punishment (H_3). As in the case of rewards, this punishment does not need to serve any purpose other than increasing the agent's incentives to exert effort (for example, it need not be linked to controlling or targeting insurgents). The gradation of punishments in response to worse outcomes is not derived from any sense of fairness but is due to the efficient provision of incentives: large disturbances are associated with large punishments because such large disturbances are more likely to occur if the agent did not exert effort. Punishments may even seem to the agent and outside observers to be disproportionate to the disturbance, engendering criticism from the international community, for instance, for "overreactions" to any particular disturbance. This occurs because the principal is not reacting to any known level of effort by the agent but is attempting to condition the agent's incentives to exert high effort (now and in the future).

3. *The principal does not use rewards and punishments simultaneously in response to a disturbance* (H_4). This is because both are costly to the principal and they work against each other in incentivizing the agent. As a consequence of this insight, we may see inaction by the principal for intermediate-size disturbances; these are not small enough to elicit a reward and not large enough to elicit punishment. As shown in figure 0.1, at low levels of disturbance the principal uses rewards, at high levels of disturbance the principal uses punishments, and at intermediate levels the principal uses neither.

4. *The principal reacts to larger disturbances by increasing the likelihood of replacing the agent* (H_5). Agents with low suppression costs are more likely to endure. A principal may be eager to replace a high-cost agent with one that has lower costs. In this case, replacement can be observed for a wide range of disturbances and may occur simultaneously with punishment as well as rewards. In contrast, a principal will hesitate to replace an agent with low costs, since any replacement agent with higher effort costs will be less compliant. Therefore, replacement of low-cost agents is

only observed after large disturbances. In this case, replacement is used, together with large punishments, as a disciplining mechanism (even if the replacement is likely to be higher cost).

5. *Agent compliance:* When interests are not fully aligned and the principal does not offer contingent rewards and punishments, the agent is not likely to exert effort (H_6). As we will see, this case is often relevant. Proxies with consistently aligned interests trivially satisfy the scope condition, so we ignore such cases. Principals often generate variation within cases over time in their willingness (or perhaps ability) to offer high-powered incentives, so we will have plenty of evidence with which to test this prediction.

How the Implicit Contract Responds to Changes in the Environment

Having described the structure of the optimal contract, we can now discuss how the contract evolves in response to changes in the environment. These are comparative statics predictions.

Changing Agent Effort Cost. The costs of effort to the agent may change. For example, the agent may lose influence with his or her population, making suppression more difficult. Alternatively, the agent may be replaced through an election process by another agent with higher costs. How does the implicit contract adapt? Our earlier discussion applies. If the agent's cost of effort becomes sufficiently high, the principal may choose to forgo indirect control altogether, either engaging in direct control or doing nothing. If, instead, the agent's effort cost remains low enough that indirect control is not abandoned, then the principal will respond with more high-powered incentives (H_7). This means that the principal becomes more responsive to disturbances; it will reward the agent more following small disturbances and it will punish the agent more following larger disturbances (a vertical stretch of the curves in figure 0.1). Intuitively, the agent's effort cost has increased, so larger carrots and larger sticks are required to induce it to act. This increases the cost to the principal of providing incentives.

Changing Principal's Cost of Incentives. The cost of utilizing different incentive tools for the principal can evolve over time, which changes the structure of the optimal contract. When the cost of rewarding the agent with concessions increases (or, equivalently, the benefit that the agent derives from these concessions declines), the principal responds by reducing its use of rewards and increasing its use of the other incentive tools (H_8). In particular, it will punish more often and more severely and will replace the agent more often in response to large disturbances. In some circumstances, this change can make incentive provision by the principal so difficult that it may choose to forgo indirect control altogether.

Analogous reasoning applies if the cost of punishment rises. For instance, punishments may become more costly for the principal if there is a greater public backlash by the principal's own constituents about their use, if the agent becomes immune to their pain, or if other, more pressing proxy relationships elsewhere in the world increase the opportunity costs of punishment. Increased cost of punishment will result in the principal's punishing less often and utilizing rewards and replacement incentives more (H_9). Again, incentive provision by the principal may become so costly as a consequence of such a change in the environment that indirect control is abandoned altogether.

Finally, the same argument holds if the cost of replacement rises—for example, because the expected costs of effort by the replacement agent increase. In this case, replacement is used less often by the principal, who shifts to using rewards and punishments more often (H_{10}). In short, the optimal incentive contract is driven by the relative costs and benefits of the three incentive tools. Increasing the cost and reducing the effectiveness of one tool leads to greater use of the other two, and vice versa.

Changing Importance of the Principal's Goal. As a final comparative static, consider what happens if the benefits of indirect control increase for the principal. For example, this occurred for the United States after 2001 when sensitivity to attacks increased, and again as the Iraq war dragged on and public support for direct action declined (see chapter 9). In this case, using the agent to prevent these attacks becomes significantly more important to the principal, who will deploy higher-power incentives to induce agent effort (H_{11}). This might seem counterintuitive: the more important disturbances become to the principal, the more eager the principal is to delegate their suppression to the agent. To understand, recall that, with the right incentives, the agent is more efficient at dealing with the disturbance than is the principal. This means that a less competent agent who might otherwise be too costly to engage through indirect control may become a worthwhile agent if the disturbance becomes more salient to the principal. In such a circumstance, because the agent has high costs of effort, high-powered incentives will be utilized: bigger (or more likely) rewards and punishments.

Capacity Building

At one level, and as practiced by the United States before and after the end of the Cold War, building proxy capacity is conceived as an alternative strategy to indirectly controlling threats: the principal expands the ability of the agent to suppress disturbances through noncontingent flows of resources. We can incorporate capacity building into our principal-agent model, and identify conditions under which it is likely to be effective. The relationship between principals and agents is dynamic: a principal can choose to incur investment costs in the present that increase the agent's future effectiveness of suppressive effort. (Almost equivalently, the principal can invest in the political survival of a low-cost proxy.) This is, in terms of theory, what we mean by capacity building.

After an investment in proxy capacity, since the proxy's effort becomes more effective at suppressing disturbances, the probability of large disturbances diminishes, which benefits the principal. This can be achieved through military training, logistic support, material support, and institution building. Capacity building may also increase public support for the agent and thereby make it easier to control the disturbance. This investment is costly to the principal but differs from the rewards considered above in three ways: (1) it takes place before the agent's decision to exert effort, (2) it does not provide any (direct) personal benefit to the agent, and (3) it is not contingent on the agent's level of effort in the current period. In its pure conceptual form, capacity building only increases the agent's effectiveness at controlling the disturbance.

Crucial to the discussion is that capacity building is complementary to the agent's effort decision. In other words, if the agent exerts the required effort, the principal reaps the benefits of investing in an increased effectiveness of effort. If the agent does not exert effort, capacity building has a muted effect on the insurgency and might even be counterproductive, enabling the agent to engage in actions that the principal finds positively undesirable, such as using better-trained military forces against internal political rivals—perhaps including innocent civilians—or rivals supported by the principal.

For this reason, in the optimal contract the principal only transfers resources to build capacity when agents have sufficiently aligned interests so that indirect control is the principal's optimal strategy—in other words, if there is a cost-effective contract that can induce the agent to exert effort after capacity building. If the cost of effort is so high that it is very expensive to induce the agent to exert effort with the incentive tools considered above, the principal has no reason to invest in capacity. Such investments would be wasted since the benefits are only realized if the agent actually exerts effort within a situation of indirect control.

This is an important implication of the theory for contemporary policy, as we will see in the chapters to come. If the interests of the principal and agent are sufficiently misaligned (i.e., the agent's effort cost is so high that it exerts no effort), capacity building by the principal is wasted. Therefore, the greater the interest misalignment between principal and agent, the less likely is capacity building by the principal. Stated positively, only if the preferences that underlie interests are sufficiently aligned should the principal invest in capacity (H_{12}).

Possible Objections

One possible criticism of our approach is the notion of a "contract" between principal and agent. Above, we define an implicit contract, which we mean quite literally. Principal and agent need not sit down and agree on a schedule of rewards and punishments contingent on disturbances. Rather, given (our second scope condition) that the proxy is subordinate, the principal can impose a schedule of rewards and punishments for effort. At no time is it likely in the cases we consider that a complete schedule is dictated—or that a discussion occurs at all. Although we do not model it explicitly, the real-life principal need not announce a complete schedule of rewards and punishments. Through repeated interactions, the agent will eventually learn the schedule of rewards and punishments the principal is using, and respond accordingly. All that is necessary for our model is that the agent knows the relationship between disturbances observed by the principal and the rewards or punishments that will be imposed in response.

A second critique is that actors we treat as agents might not think of themselves as such, and would reject our analytical characterization of them as proxies. One such case is Hamas, as an agent of Israel, investigated in chapter 4. In the theory, any actor can be understood as a proxy for the principal, though they vary in their costs of effort—by which we mean, again, the cost to the agent of suppressing disturbances. The further apart the policy interests of the principal and the agent, the higher the cost of effort. With diametrically opposed preferences, Israel-Hamas might seem to take on an extreme value on this dimension; indeed, it is one of the few cases we examine where the agent may actually gain from the disturbance that hurts the principal and that the principal wants suppressed. In fact, some of the disturbances in question are surely rockets launched by Hamas.

We do not often observe principal-agent relationships of this nature. By analogy, we do not normally hire lawyers to defend us who actually benefit from seeing us go to jail. But, as noted above, the theory can accommodate exactly this situation and predicts that the principal must use very large rewards and punishments to overcome the high cost to Hamas, in this case, of complying with Israel's demands. Because the costs to the principal of rewards and punishments are very large, there is usually a better alternative, and thus we do not observe many cases of principals choosing indirect control over agents whose stated intention is to destroy them.

To understand the Israel-Hamas case, and possibly others like it, the agency relationship is best placed in context—and this context actually reveals some of the power of our model and its explicit consideration of policy alternatives. In the theory, principals have five options: (1) do nothing, and suffer the cost of the disturbance—terrorism, in the case of Israel-Hamas; (2) directly suppress the disturbance, which is enormously costly for Israel, as it would require invading and permanently governing Gaza; (3) provide direct capacity assistance to Hamas, which is unlikely to be utilized to achieve Israel's ends given interest misalignment; (4) replace the agent, which is also prohibitively costly for Israel; or (5) try to manipulate the incentives of the proxy as much as possible, which is what Israel has done. It is not that Israel wants Hamas as an agent. It would greatly prefer a proxy with preferences more aligned with its own. But given that Israel cannot tolerate continued terrorist attacks, and either suppressing terrorism itself or invading Gaza and overthrowing Hamas is prohibitively costly, Israel is stuck with a proxy it dislikes but tries to push in the "right" direction through selective rewards and punishments. It is precisely because the alternatives are so unfavorable that Israel must—despite its reluctance and the problems of dealing with a stated enemy as its agent—nonetheless try as much as possible to use incentives to induce Hamas to restrain attacks.

Does indirect control work well in this instance? No. Attacks from Gaza against Israel still occur. But does it work better than the alternatives? There the answer is unfortunately yes, and not just for Israel but for Hamas as well. Faced with the alternatives of direct Israeli control, or some other entity acting as Israel's proxy, Hamas, like Israel, chooses the least bad option in pursuing a proxy strategy. This case is useful in illustrating the limits of agency relationships in reducing violence. It also helps demonstrate the value of a theory that forces us to consider all the parameters and options simultaneously in order to explain a surprising equilibrium as the result of constrained choices of strategy, as Israel and Hamas have had to do in this case.

Case Studies

The case studies in this volume illustrate the theory in action, using propositions derived from a common theory (H_1 through H_{12}) to elucidate important events. The case studies are "analytic narratives" structured as the examination of specific events from the point of view of a single general theory.[20] We draw two different kinds of comparisons from our cases. First, we compare across cases. Because we lack comparable data from different countries and time periods, we reach only tentative conclusions at this level.[21] Most important, we can examine whether the principal used incentives keyed to the agent's local political context, and whether these incentives moved the agent's behavior in the expected direction. We can think of this most appropriately as a test of the noncontingent capacity-building approach versus our indirect-control approach. The finding is in that sense quite clear: when principals use incentives, agents respond accordingly, complying when rewards or punishments are sufficiently large, and shirking when rewards and punishments are small or not used at all. The cases are ordered from the simplest that clearly fit the expectations of the theory (Korea) to the most complex that are more problematic for the theory (Iraq), leading the reader through successively more challenging examples. The first four chapters explore cases where the principal successfully uses incentives in strategic ways to control the agent's actions. The next five chapters examine cases where the principal often fails to use incentives fully, and faces the consequence of an agent shirking.

Second, we compare within cases over time, structuring the narrative around significant changes in the parameters of the model, especially changes in the agent's cost of effort or the costs of the disturbance to the principal. With each case as its own best control, we can assess whether changes in parameters produce the changes in behavior by the principal or agent predicted by the theory.[22] We find that changes in key variables nearly always correlate with changes in behavior as expected. This holds even in the latter cases where the principal often fails to use available incentives fully. For example, sanctions were eventually employed even in Iraq, where the Bush administration was reluctant to punish Prime Minister al-Maliki for his obvious noncompliance with U.S. goals, as the disturbance and the cost of that disturbance to the president increased. In response, al-Maliki altered course, at least in the short run. These within-case comparisons strongly support the theory and highlight the efficacy of indirect control.

Case studies are most useful and appropriate when key variables in the theory are difficult to operationalize or code systematically (and sample sizes are thus necessarily small). In our case studies, a key factor is the agent's costs of effort. Precisely because the agent's level of effort is observed only imperfectly, if at all, the principal bases the implicit contract on actual disturbances. If levels of effort by agents are difficult for principals to know—despite all their incentives for acquiring additional information so as to induce high effort by the agents—it is equally difficult for outside analysts like ourselves to know, even ex post, whether effort was exerted. Indeed, retrospective accounts by decision makers are likely to be biased to justify their actions, given the available information, and are thus flawed measures of their interim knowledge. Nor can a theory of asymmetric information be assessed by observing outcomes and then reasoning backward to what the effort "must have been" or how it must have been perceived at the time. Such retrospective histories may provide an account of how events unfolded, but not why. Due to the inherent unobservability of key factors in the theory, the case studies draw on diverse sources of information that differ from one to the other and rely on context and case-specific knowledge in interpreting the available information. The case studies also engage in disciplined counterfactual reasoning to render the best assessments of the agent's costs of effort and other variables in the theory.

Case selection required a disciplined application of scope conditions. In particular, we required that (1) the agent possess some advantage in suppressing disturbances, typically local knowledge; (2) the agent be subordinate, that is, that the principal is powerful enough to wield rewards and punishments effectively and, in some cases, even to replace the agent; and (3) the agent possess private information about its own actions (or costs). Those three conditions create an "agency problem," at least potentially.

In addition, cases were chosen because they were salient, by which we mean that the disturbance was sufficiently costly to the principal that we might expect it to seek a proxy relationship or, at an extreme, to engage in direct control. In the case of very small disturbances, our theory predicts that the principal will not react, as long as both direct action and indirect control are costly. Though non-response by a principal to some small disturbance would support the theory, it is more challenging to code the parameters in such "non-events" and, in any case, does not make for a very interesting or compelling study. Conversely, in cases of very large disturbances—such as the 9/11 attacks on the United States—direct action is likely necessary, with the option of fighting a perpetrator through proxies left unconsidered. All of this implies that there are many more cases that would support the theory than the range of salient agency relationships we focus on here.[23]

It is useful to note cases not studied. Peer relationships such as the United States and Russia are characterized by rewards and punishments, but both countries have the ability to influence the actions of the other (other than through shirking), so subordination is absent. We also rejected as uninteresting subordinate relationships among allies, in which interest alignment is so close that capacity building is the obvious choice and rewards and punishments would be redundant.

Finally, our cases were not selected with foreknowledge of whether or not they would support the theory. One advantage of such difficult-to-assess variables is that they make (inadvertently) drawing a biased sample unlikely, since considerable research into a case is necessary before drawing even tentative conclusions about the theory's success in predicting outcomes. We discuss our analytical narrative approach more fully in the conclusion.

As a check on coding and analysis of cases, preliminary drafts were circulated internally among the group, and discussed critically with principal investigators in team meetings over a period of almost three years. In addition, to check again that cases were not being shoehorned to fit into a common theoretical framework, more developed drafts were circulated among subject experts and discussed by those experts—who included academics and practitioners—in a conference in Washington, DC, in September 2016. We summarize our thoughts on that process in the conclusion as well.

No case illustrates the theory perfectly. In nearly every instance, the principal or proxy deviates in some way from the spare and parsimonious expectations of the theory. However, in most cases there is strong congruence. In South Korea, existential threats to the domestic regime and the U.S. battle against global Communism forced an alignment of interests with the United States, which in turn provided assistance with building capacity and threats of punishment that brought a reluctant regime to the bargaining table. In Denmark, Colombia, and Gaza, the interests of agents deviated dramatically from those of principals over time, and greater rewards and punishments were necessary to induce sufficient effort. We then turn to El Salvador, where the United States as principal used inexplicably weak incentives on a noncompliant proxy. We follow with two cases where the high costs of punishments and rewards severely restricted the principal's ability to manage its proxy, namely, the United States with Pakistan and Israel with the Palestinian Authority. We close with two further cases of a problematic principal: Yemen, where the United States expanded its demands while cutting its rewards, and Iraq, where the United States mostly failed to condition its rewards and punishments on the behavior of its proxy. We summarize the results of the cross-national and especially the within-case comparisons in more detail in the conclusion.

NOTES

1. On proxy relationships in foreign policy, see Ladwig 2016, 2017. On client states more generally, see Carney 1989 and Sylvan and Majeski 2009. For an empirical study, similar to ours, that finds that only contingent rewards and punishments work to motivate proxies, see Macdonald 1992.

2. Quoted in Lowenthal 1995, 24.

3. On sovereignty, see Glanville 2014; Krasner 1999; Osiander 2001; and Ramos 2013. For a more developed discussion of the ideas here, see Lake 2016, chap. 2.

4. Although the principle was stated here in very general terms, there is now a large corpus of General Assembly resolutions, meeting records, reports, letters, and official documents clarifying the meaning of the principle and its specific applications (Onuf 1998, 151). The most important documents are General Assembly resolutions 2131 (XX), December 21, 1965; 2625 (XXV), October 24, 1970; and 36/103, December 9, 1981. For other documents, see article 2 (7) at http://www.un.org/en/sc/repertoire/principles.shtml.

5. Krasner 1999.

6. Thomson 1994.

7. On indirect control by Rome, see Padró i Miquel and Yared 2012.

8. Risse 2011.

9. Jackson 1990.

10. On blowback, see Johnson 2000.

11. Gerges 2009.

12. Ladwig 2016, 2017.

13. See Karlin 2017a, b; Watts et al. 2014; Watts 2015.

14. For a rigorous version of the theory sketched here, see Berman, Lake, Padró i Miquel, and Yared 2018. Our framework builds on the work of Yared (2010) and Padró i Miquel and Yared (2012), who formally analyze such situations using a framework of repeated games with private information. For principal-agent theories of international politics, see Hawkins et al. 2006a. In the language of game theory, a player is an actor who pursues an objective by making strategic choices, aware that her opponents are doing the same, and capable of calculating the outcome that may result. Game theory began with John von Neumann's 1928 paper *"Zur Theorie der Gesellschaftsspiele,"* available in English as "On the Theory of Games of Strategy." The assumption of unitary principal and unitary agent is an abstraction. Obviously, the U.S. government, for instance, is not a strict hierarchy in which only the president, as the ultimate decision maker, matters. It is empirically possible—indeed, we can think of examples of this—that branches of the government will work at cross-purposes with one another, with Defense, for instance, rewarding the agent, and the State Department punishing it. The same for the agent: the quasi-civilian leaders and the intelligence agencies in Pakistan, for instance, do not always work in tandem. When referring to the principal and agent in our cases, we refer to the aggregate of all decisions made by the parties constituting each entity.

15. This does not imply that the proxy can always manage the disturbance alone, especially when it lacks capacity. As in the South Korean case (chapter 1), the agent might lack the ability to suppress the disturbance entirely on its own but nonetheless have a cost advantage in doing so because of its knowledge of local conditions.

16. On the "big influence" of sometimes small allies, see Fox 1959; Rothstein 1968; Keohane 1969, 1971; Handel 1990.

17. Equivalently, in the case of unobserved costs, the principal responds to the direct observation of the agent's effort.

18. There may be some fixed costs to the principal of replacement in stimulating a coup, subsidizing the opposition at the time of the next scheduled election, and so on. Regime change need not take only the level of cost suffered in Iraq in 2003. The higher these fixed costs, the less likely the principal is to select replacement relative to the other strategies, but this does not affect any of the other predictions of the model.

19. For evidence on how counterinsurgents improve their sources of operational intelligence through improved governance, development assistance, and other means, see Berman, Felter, and Shapiro 2018.

20. On analytic narratives, see Bates et al. 1998.

21. Because we cannot observe key factors, cross-case comparisons are difficult to make, though we do so to the extent possible and have made considerable efforts as a group to challenge one another's conclusions on this score. Although we cannot claim certainty in our cross-case comparisons, a common theory and deep collaboration among the authors allow some degree of calibration across variables in the several studies. The main exception is the chapter by Matthew Nanes (chapter 4), which compares relations between a single principal (Israel) and two agents (Lebanon and Hamas) with very different costs of effort. With this most similar case design, Nanes can draw more focused assessments.

22. On within- versus cross-case comparisons, see Goertz and Mahony 2012, chap. 7. Comparative static assessments differ slightly from the process-tracing approach advocated by qualitative-methods theorists; see George and Bennett 2005.

23. In truncating the range of variation in one of our key parameters, we increase the uncertainty over but do not bias our inferences. See King, Keohane, and Verba 1994, 137.

1

SOUTH KOREA, 1950–53

Exogenous Realignment of Preferences

Julia M. Macdonald

The U.S. relationship with South Korea (also the Republic of Korea, or ROK) during the Korean War (1950–53) provides substantial evidence supporting a principal-proxy approach, and shows the benefits that can flow from the principal's effective use of incentives.[1] In particular, this chapter shows how the use of carefully calibrated rewards and punishments by the United States was able to effectively induce the South Korean government to exert high levels of effort in addressing the North Korean Communist threat, ultimately bringing an end to the Korean War.[2]

During this timeframe, the nature of the disturbance facing the U.S. and South Korean governments shifted from the suppression of a small-scale Communist insurgency to the defense of the South Korean government from a full-scale Communist attack from the north. The magnitude of the North Korean invasion created an acute crisis for both South Korea and the United States and produced an unusual degree of interest alignment between the two governments. Prior to the outbreak of war, South Korean president Syngman Rhee had faced a complex internal threat environment: a Communist insurgency as well as elite opposition to his rule. In order to address these challenges to his regime, Rhee employed coercive and corrupt practices to ensure the loyalty of the ROK armed forces, placing him at direct odds with U.S. efforts to create a professional and disciplined army. The North Korean invasion quickly altered Rhee's calculations. The existential threat unified the South Korean government in its objective of survival, lowering the costs to Rhee of cooperating with the United States.

The high costs to the United States of losing South Korea to a growing Communist threat, combined with the low capacity of the South Korean army to meet the North Korean invaders, led the United States to deploy a large contingent of U.S. troops to the peninsula and take direct action against the North Korean forces. Motivated by early successes on the battlefield, the United States and the ROK pushed northward with the shared goal of unifying the Korean Peninsula under a non-Communist regime. These hopes were quickly dashed, however, by the Chinese invasion of October 1950, which threatened a dangerous expansion of the war. Facing a second existential crisis in a matter of months, the U.S. and ROK governments' chief concern once again became the prevention of a full-scale collapse of the South.

Having rendered a swift victory elusive, the Chinese invasion led to a sharp change in U.S. policy toward the peninsula. The United States quickly retreated to more limited war aims focused on restoring the status quo ante bellum and developing a professional ROK army capable of defending the South from future attacks. Yet this change in policy placed the United States in conflict with President Rhee, who was less concerned with army discipline than he was with maintaining a loyal, patronage-based armed force that would protect him from internal political threats. As the war progressed and domestic pressures on Rhee continued to mount, his cost of effort increased and U.S.-ROK preferences diverged.

To induce Rhee's cooperation in building a more professional, well-trained armed force, the United States resorted to incentives. More specifically, the United States made the continued provision of military equipment and training to the ROK armed forces—assistance that Rhee desperately needed—contingent on observed improvements in the performance of the ROK military. Detecting improvement was made possible by the large U.S. footprint on the ground in South Korea and by the increasing number of military advisers able to monitor units. Information provided by these advisers helped the United States effectively tailor its rewards and punishments to incentivize high levels of effort. By 1953, the continued severity of the Communist threat combined with the effective use of U.S. incentives resulted in rapid improvements in the performance of the ROK military, and secured Rhee's agreement to an armistice that ended the Korean War.

Historical Background

At the end of World War II, the Korean Peninsula was divided into two halves, with the Soviet Union occupying the North and the United States the South. In an effort to avoid maintaining troops in Korea indefinitely, the United States and the Soviet Union agreed to divide Korea temporarily along the thirty-eighth parallel. This division became effectively permanent in 1948 when Kim Il Sung organized a Communist government in the North. The United States responded by establishing a democratic regime in the South and handing over control to South Korea's first president, Syngman Rhee, on August 15, 1948.[3]

Rhee faced two key challenges upon assuming power: a growing Communist insurgency in the South and elite political opposition to his rule. By the time the U.S. military government transferred control to Rhee, Communist guerrillas controlled large areas of South Korea, most notably in the Southwest, where farmers had suffered the most from exploitation.[4] The size of the threat became clear when a series of mutinies carried out by Communist sympathizers within the ROK Army (ROKA) swept through the Southwest in late 1948.[5] Rhee also faced an increasingly hostile domestic political environment. Although many of his conservative opponents shared his anti-Communist ideology, the new Korean president faced a prerogative-conscious National Assembly that was faction ridden and beholden to various political interest groups within Korea. As Rhee attempted to expand his executive powers, the assembly sought to check his desire for political dominance.[6]

Rhee addressed the challenges to his rule by punishing his opposition. For example, he responded to the mutinies in late 1948 by weeding out subversive elements within the armed forces. More than two thousand people were killed in the wake of the October Yosu rebellion, and an additional eight thousand were arrested on the suspicion of Communist affiliation.[7] Rhee authorized the Korean intelligence staff to arrest participating officers and enlisted men, charging them with treason, subversion, and other similar crimes. By the end of the year, almost five thousand officers and soldiers had been purged in this way.[8] Approximately ninety thousand civilian police arrests had been recorded in South Korea by April 1949.[9]

Political rivals received similar treatment. Rhee made political appointments according to demonstrated loyalty and subservience to his regime, and frequently removed officials who expressed (or were suspected of expressing) any dissent.[10] Vocal opponents who refused to be bribed into submission were removed. In 1949, Rhee arrested thirteen members of the National Assembly for "disturbing the tranquility of the nation" by expressing opinions critical of him, calling for the withdrawal of U.S. troops, and opposing his goal of invading North Korea.[11] Rhee's fiercest enemies were often assassinated under mysterious circumstances. This was the fate of Kim Koo, Rhee's chief rival in the 1948 election, who had maintained a significant and worrisome following. Koo was not alone, however, as Rhee sought to systematically bribe or eliminate all opposition to his regime.[12]

U.S. support for Syngman Rhee had been a decisive factor in his rise to power in 1948. Rhee's hostility to Communism, his significant power base, and, perhaps most important, his seeming willingness to cooperate with the United States made him the least objectionable candidate to the U.S. military government at the time of independence. Rhee's strong nationalist ambitions and his desire to see a unified Korean Peninsula were known by U.S. officials and caused some consternation in Washington. Nevertheless, his procapitalist credentials, combined with the lack of alternatives, made Rhee the one and only U.S. choice.[13]

Prior to the outbreak of the Korean War, the U.S. objective was to help Rhee establish a small, professional South Korean military that would be capable of eliminating the Communist insurgent threat and defending the northern border.[14] To assist the new ROK government in building this force, the United States created the U.S. Military Advisory Group to the Republic of Korea (KMAG) on July 1, 1949.[15] In addition to providing five hundred advisers, the United States shipped supplies and equipment to furnish an army of fifty thousand men, and established a small military school system.[16]

However, the United States' interest in a small, well-trained army ran counter to the political realities in South Korea at the time. Personal control over the armed forces was central to Rhee's ability to suppress internal rebellions and to protect himself against rival elites. The U.S. objective of a small, politically neutral military was therefore directly at odds with Rhee's desire to build a large, politically loyal force that he could use to crush internal challenges to his regime. A politicized officer corps that could be swayed through bribery and the spoils of office was far more important to the Korean president than was developing a meritocratic, autonomous army that might remove him from power or be co-opted by rival elites.[17] When KMAG inspected the implementation of American military aid to South Korea in 1948, the advisers were horrified at the levels of corruption they found: more than half of the aid had been wasted or had simply disappeared.[18] Rhee's political involvement also meant that U.S. military assistance and emphasis on basic tactics and marksmanship failed to have much of an effect on the performance of the fledgling South Korean forces. KMAG advisers wrote scathing after-action reports and noted serious defects in ROK training and leadership.[19]

By early 1950, the United States was reducing its commitment to South Korea.[20] Progressive land-reform measures combined with slight improvements in the performance of the ROK Army had led to a reduction in the number of Communist guerrillas, thereby reducing the Communist threat to the United States.[21] In addition to the relatively low cost of the disturbance, the United States was preoccupied with domestic political priorities, and President Harry S. Truman was under pressure to cut the military budget. There was little desire in Washington to channel more military assistance to suppress an insurgency that did not pose an existential threat to South Korea, nor was there interest in grant-ing more aid to a regime that was behaving contrary to U.S. interests.[22]

This situation changed abruptly on June 25, 1950, when North Korean forces crossed the thirty-eighth parallel and invaded South Korea. Faced with the pos-sibility of losing a democratic ally to Communist forces, the United States quickly deployed a large contingent of troops, taking direct action to repel the North Korean forces. After the Chinese invasion of late 1950, the United States supple-mented its direct participation in the war with a strategy of indirect action focused on developing a professional, well-trained ROK armed force.[23] From 1951 to 1953, the United States rapidly increased both the number of advisers and its military aid to South Korea, with the goal of ending the war and withdrawing its troops. President Rhee remained the effective decision maker in South Korea throughout the period of the war and thus was the proxy that the principal (the United States) was trying to control. Table 1.1 summarizes these key events from 1945 to 1953.

TABLE 1.1 Timeline of key events

DATE	EVENT
May 1945	Korean Peninsula is divided into two parts: Communist North and anti-Communist South
August 15, 1948	Syngman Rhee becomes the first president of South Korea
June 25, 1950	North Korea invades South Korea
June 28, 1950	Communist forces take Seoul
July 1, 1950	First U.S. infantry unit arrives in South Korea
July 7, 1950	The United Nations Security Council passes a resolution recommending a unified U.S.-led command
July 8, 1950	Gen. Douglas MacArthur is appointed commander of the UN command
July 14, 1950	President Rhee places all ROK forces under the U.S.-led UN command
September 11, 1950	NSC 81/1 makes unification of Korea a U.S. war aim
September 15, 1950	Inchon landing; UN forces retake Seoul
October 7, 1950	UN authorizes MacArthur to enter North Korea
October 25, 1950	Chinese Communist forces launch their first-phase offensive
January 4, 1951	Communist forces recapture Seoul
March 14, 1951	UN forces retake Seoul
April 11, 1951	President Truman relieves General MacArthur for insubordination
May 17, 1951	NSC 48/5 formalizes limited U.S. war aims in Korea
July 10, 1951	Korean War truce talks begin
November 27, 1951	Thirty-eighth parallel agreed to as a line of demarcation
November 4, 1952	Dwight D. Eisenhower is elected president of the United States
June 18, 1953	President Rhee releases 27,388 prisoners of war
July 27, 1953	Armistice signed ending the Korean War

Theoretical Expectations

The model developed in the introduction offers a series of predictions about U.S. and South Korean behavior during the period of the Korean War. These predictions primarily relate to the agent's changing cost of effort, which includes the direct costs of suppressing the disturbance as well as the indirect political costs of doing so. During this period the disturbance relevant to the United States was the threat of Communism spreading globally, which manifested in North Korea's 1950 invasion of South Korea, followed soon thereafter by the invasion of Chinese Communist forces. The direct costs of suppressing this disturbance were extremely high at the onset of the war, and decreased over time in accordance with improvements in the ROK military. At the time of the North Korean invasion, a poorly trained and equipped ROK force faced ninety thousand well-trained North Korean troops, soon to be joined by the formidable Chinese armed forces. KMAG reports just prior to the outbreak of the war clearly state that ROKA units were poorly trained, lacked basic marksmanship and fire discipline, and were largely devoid of any heavy equipment.[24] By contrast, at the end of the war the ROKA was a well-equipped force of some 576,000 men, the large majority of whom had received division-level training.[25]

President Rhee's indirect costs of effort were low in the early stages of the war and rose sharply thereafter. The existential threat of the North Korean invasion, followed quickly by the Chinese intervention, suspended politics as usual in South Korea and effectively subdued the domestic political opposition that had previously imposed high costs on President Rhee for cooperating with the United States. Since all South Korean elites faced a unifying external threat that exceeded their domestic interests, cooperating with the United States to achieve its goal of military professionalization became a less costly strategy for Rhee.

As the front began to stabilize in early 1951, opposition to Rhee's autocratic rule resurfaced, and domestic pressure mounted to push past the thirty-eighth parallel and overthrow the northern regime. In light of growing internal threats, the United States' desire to build a smaller, professionalized army to defend more limited objectives became politically costly for Rhee in an environment where a large, well-equipped, and loyal armed force would serve his interests better. The key factor that kept Rhee's costs from soaring was a large U.S. footprint that could protect the ROK leader from the threat of a coup. Thus, from 1951 onward, though both the U.S. and ROK governments shared the ultimate goal of an independent South Korea, they differed in important ways over how they preferred to suppress the disturbance.

The cost of disturbance to the United States throughout the majority of the Korean War remained high. The large-scale invasion, initially by North Korea and then by China, threatened the survival of a key democratic partner in the fight against Communism. As a result, the United States was concerned not only about the survival of South Korea itself, but also about the consequences of U.S. actions for relationships with other allies, as well as with the Soviet Union and China in the future. The war in Korea thus became the main front in a global war against Communism. As the war dragged on and the front stabilized, the cost of the disturbance to the United States remained relatively high due to domestic political support for a swift victory against a Communist enemy, and Dwight D. Eisenhower's election promise to achieve it.

The U.S. footprint in South Korea and the high costs of the disturbance to the United States meant that direct action was a credible threat. In fact, the footprint was large throughout the war, increasing over time with the arrival of more ground troops and military advisers. By 1953, the United States had more than three hundred thousand troops stationed in South Korea.[26] The number of U.S. military advisers increased in kind, from five hundred in early 1950 to almost three thousand by the end of the war, with many advisers embedded in ROK military units.[27]

Finally, the cost of replacement of the agent to the United States was high during this period. The United States had been heavily involved in the selection of Syngman Rhee as leader. His hostility to Communism, combined with his pro-American attitude, made him a rarity in South Korea at the time. Alternatives to Rhee were considered too politically extreme and could not be relied on to cooperate with Washington. This lack of a reasonable substitute during the wartime period served to limit the range of options available to the United States.[28]

According to the theory developed in the introduction, the high cost of disturbance to the United States, combined with low levels of initial ROK capacity, implies that the United States should prefer direct to indirect control in the early stages of the Korean War. One of the key scope conditions of the principal-agent theory is that the agent must have a natural advantage at controlling the disturbance due to a particular level of expertise, familiarity with the problem, or lower cost of dealing with the problem relative to the principal. Without this local advantage, the principal will always prefer direct action to suppress the disturbance to desired levels (H_1). In this case, the North Korean invasion in June 1950 was a large-scale conventional military assault directed at a poorly trained South Korean armed force. The comparative advantage at controlling the disturbance lay with the United States and its large, conventionally trained army. The United States should therefore view the high level of disturbance observed during the first phase of the war as a function of low ROK capacity, rather than as an indication of low levels of effort. Rhee's low costs of effort in the wake of the North

Korean invasion—and therefore his high level of interest alignment with the United States—means that we should also expect to see investment in capacity building (that is, unconditional military assistance) by the United States in this early stage of the war (H_{12}).

The theory further predicts that as the front stabilized and the ROK's costs of effort increased, Rhee would exert less effort in controlling the disturbance of concern to the United States. Recognizing this, the United States should respond by resorting to higher-powered incentives to motivate Rhee (H_7). More specifically, we should see the United States placing conditions on military aid in order to punish Rhee when he exerts lower levels of effort, and rewarding him with contingent aid when levels of effort are higher (where levels of effort are observed directly but imperfectly by U.S. troops and indicated indirectly by the size of disturbances). Finally, since the cost of replacing the proxy is high, the United States should resort to punishments over replacement when ROK levels of effort decline. Overall, if the United States behaves as the theory expects, the use of incentives should induce high levels of ROK effort and the United States should be able to effectively suppress the disturbance through its ROK agent (H_6). See table 1.2 for a summary of these theoretical expectations.

TABLE 1.2 Theoretical expectations and summary results, South Korea

PERIOD	KEY PARAMETER(S)	THEORETICAL EXPECTATION	OBSERVED ACTION
Pre–June 1950	Agent's level of capacity low; agent's cost of effort high; principal's cost of disturbance low	Principal will engage in direct control or do nothing (H_1)	Principal chooses to gradually withdraw support; agent exerts low levels of effort
June 1950–spring 1951	Agent's level of capacity low; agent's cost of effort low; principal's cost of disturbance high	Principal will engage in direct control (due to extremely low agent capacity) (H_1) and capacity building (H_{12})	Principal chooses direct control; no conditions placed on military assistance; some capacity building
Spring 1951–spring 1953	Agent's level of capacity increases; agent's cost of effort increases; principal's cost of disturbance decreases slightly (moderate-high)	Principal will use larger punishments while disturbances increase, then smaller punishments and greater rewards as disturbances decrease (H_7); proxy will respond with greater effort (H_6)	Principal uses punishments after observing higher levels of disturbance and rewards when disturbances decrease; agent responds to incentives by exerting more effort

(Continued)

TABLE 1.2 (Continued)

PERIOD	KEY PARAMETER(S)	THEORETICAL EXPECTATION	OBSERVED ACTION
Spring 1953	Agent's level of capacity increases; agent's cost of effort increases; principal's cost of disturbance remains moderate-high	Principal will use larger punishments while disturbances increase, then smaller punishments and greater rewards as disturbances decrease (H_7); proxy will respond with greater effort (H_6)	Principal uses punishments after observing higher levels of disturbance and rewards when disturbances decrease; agent responds to incentives by exerting more effort

South Korea, 1950–53

This section presents empirical evidence across three distinct time periods in order to evaluate the predictions of the principal-agent model: (1) June 1950–spring 1951, (2) spring 1951–spring 1953, and (3) spring 1953.[29] This periodization reflects key changes in the principal-agent relationship between the United States and South Korea.

June 1950–Spring 1951

The North Korean People's Army invaded South Korea on June 25, 1950, with approximately ninety thousand men. By the end of June, these forces held all the territory north of the Han River and had forced the ROK Army into a rapid retreat. The North Korean troops captured Seoul on June 28, and by mid-August ROKA and allied forces had been driven into a small perimeter in the southeastern corner of South Korea around the port city of Pusan.[30] Just one month after the initial attack, North Korea was close to achieving its goal of placing a unified Korean Peninsula under the Communist banner.

The ROK Army was entirely unprepared to deal with the scale of the North Korean attack. In June 1950, no ROKA unit had progressed beyond regimental training, and the army lacked heavy equipment to use in its defense. KMAG advisers had reported numerous deficiencies in small-unit training and basic marksmanship in 1949, just one year prior to the war.[31] When the Communists attacked, the ROKA units fled, abandoning their positions and equipment.[32] Within the first month, an estimated 70 percent of ROK supplies and equipment, together with all technical service installations in and around Seoul, were seized or destroyed, and the army's supply system was practically nonexistent.

Almost half of the South Korean army—forty-four thousand out of ninety-eight thousand—were killed, captured, or missing.[33]

While the arrival of U.S. troops and assistance provided a brief respite for the South Korean soldiers, the ROKA collapsed again when confronted by Chinese forces. From October 25 onward, Chinese troops attacked successive regiments of the ROK Army, leading soldiers to abandon all vehicles and artillery and retreat in complete disarray. In some ROK regiments, three-quarters of all ROK advisers and soldiers were killed or captured in battle.[34] This pattern of Chinese attack followed by ROKA collapse continued into the early months of 1951.[35]

The invasion and corresponding collapse of the ROKA created an existential shock for Rhee and the South Korean elites, eliminating political infighting. Just prior to the outbreak of the war, Rhee had faced an increasingly hostile domestic political environment, having parted ways with the Korean Democratic Party (KDP) in 1949 over charges of patronage and corruption. Later that year, Assembly Speaker Shin Ik-hi and National Police Director Cho Byong-ok merged the KDP with other conservative factions to form an anti-Rhee Democratic Nationalist Party. The new party called for a constitutional amendment to make the cabinet responsible to the assembly and moved to curb Rhee's presidential powers. In addition to this nationalist coalition, independents were appalled by Rhee's excessive campaign against the political Left and called for placing checks on the executive.[36] When the parliamentary elections in May 1950 saw Rhee's support base in the assembly drop from fifty-six seats to twelve, his rivals immediately sought to introduce their amendment.[37]

The threat posed by the scale of the North Korean assault led all politicians to abandon their parochial concerns and focus on the survival of the South Korean state. The North Korean rulers had made no secret of their total war aims and their desire to "liberate" the South. Prime Minister Kim Il Sung had written to the United Nations in October 1949, declaring the right to unify Korea by force. In June 1950, Pyongyang broadcast a proposal to establish a single government by August 15, 1950, the fifth anniversary of Korea's liberation from Japan.[38] In addition to being aware of North Korea's political objectives, the South Korean government had recently witnessed the fate of Chiang Kai-shek in the Chinese Civil War. When Communist forces seized Seoul in July 1950 and forced the South Korean government to flee south to Pusan, North Korea seemed closer than ever to achieving its goal. In response, South Korean domestic political factions united in their desire to preserve their lives and defeat the Communist North, shifting their focus toward meeting this external threat. As one author notes, "The invasion brought a respite in Rhee's political wars; politics was put aside," even if only temporarily.[39]

As the year progressed and military prospects improved, South Korean elites remained unified in their desire to push north of the thirty-eighth parallel, thereby lowering Rhee's costs of cooperating with the United States.[40] A victory in the North promised Rhee's allies a larger portion of the political pie, with Rhee already appointing governors to rule in his name over liberated regions. Rhee's rivals also viewed unification as a means of increasing their overall political power, but for these individuals there was a bonus. The UN General Assembly had decreed that the government of a united Korea should be determined by UN-supervised elections throughout Korea—a decision that Rhee vociferously opposed.[41] Nonetheless, the liberated areas of North Korea were kept under military administration in accordance with the UN directive, and Rhee's opponents hoped that the conclusion of the war would bring new elections that could challenge his hold on power.[42] These hopes were dashed, however, when Chinese forces invaded in the late fall of 1950. By December 1950, Communist troops were closing in on Seoul, re-creating the existential crisis of June and uniting Rhee and his political opponents in a bid for survival.[43]

The cost of losing South Korea to the Communist North was high for the United States throughout this period. The American public was still reeling from the loss of China to the Communists. Displaying strength in the face of another attack was thus popular domestically for President Truman, who was being criticized for his alleged weakness in confronting Communism at home and abroad.[44] In addition to domestic political pressure to take action against the global Communist threat, the United States also feared that the loss of South Korea would negatively affect its reputation internationally, both in terms of its commitments to other democratic allies and also with regard to its relations with the Soviet Union and China moving forward.[45] The fact that the invasion came in the wake of a successful Soviet atomic bomb test, a Communist victory in China, and the Sino-Soviet mutual defense pact made the risk of losing a democratic ally in Asia even greater.[46] As the State Department's inaugural director of policy planning, George Kennan, noted at the time, "The symbolic significance of [South Korea's] preservation is tremendous, especially in Japan."[47] President Truman commented to a group of legislators that "if we let Korea down, the Soviets will keep right on going and swallow up one piece of Asia after another."[48] He was convinced that even if the Communist invasion did not signal Moscow's readiness to risk full-scale war with the United States, it represented a challenge to U.S. resolve that had to be met.[49]

These same reputational and domestic political concerns led Truman to seize on U.S. battlefield successes in August 1950 and advocate for a shift in U.S. war aims: from defending the prewar status quo to "liberating" the North from the Communists—an objective shared by the ROK government.[50] The decision to expand war aims to include the unification of Korea was codified in NSC 81/1, and signed on September 11, 1950.[51] The UN was supportive of the official change in objectives and quickly pushed a resolution through the General Assembly.[52] The Chinese invasion in November 1950, however, dashed all U.S. hopes of a swift victory against the North and raised the possibility of full-scale defeat once again.[53] Foreshadowing a change in U.S. policy, Gen. Douglas MacArthur commented that China's involvement meant that any possibility of quickly ending the conflict and unifying Korea was now gone.[54]

The United States responded to the North Korean (and subsequent Chinese) invasion by assuming direct control of South Korean forces and providing substantial, unconditional military assistance to the ROK government. The initial U.S. commitment came from the Seventh Fleet in the Taiwan Strait and included one carrier fleet, one cruiser, and eight destroyers.[55] Realizing the poor state of the ROK military and the real possibility of South Korean collapse, the United States quickly followed this commitment with the deployment of U.S. ground forces on June 30 as part of a broader U.S.-led (UN) force. On July 10, Truman appointed General MacArthur as the new Far East commander and supreme commander, Allied powers. By the end of July, U.S. and ROK forces outnumbered the North Korean army on the front line by ninety-two thousand (of which forty-seven thousand were Americans) to seventy thousand.[56] On July 15, with more troops and equipment arriving, President Rhee agreed to place all ROK armed forces under the direct operational control of MacArthur's UN Command.[57]

In addition to deploying combat troops, the United States also made a commitment to increase its advisory mission to improve the competency of the ROK Army—again, with no conditions attached. However, the operational tempo during this stage of the conflict severely limited the ability of KMAG to perform its advisory duties. During the retreat to the Pusan Perimeter, many advisers were forced to abandon their roles, fight alongside the Korean forces, and take command of ROK Army formations.[58] KMAG, faced with the need for a drastic increase in manpower, reopened training centers in Taegu in mid-July and in Pusan in August, stationing a U.S. adviser at each. The plan was to turn out 150 recruits per day, with each group receiving at least a full week of basic training. Unfortunately, the exigencies of the battlefield and the urgent need for replacements on the front lines meant that most trainees received only a few days of brief instruction. The schools were further limited by a lack of facilities and equipment. Since the United States expected a quick victory, moreover, KMAG received no permanent increase in manpower at this time.[59]

In sum, the shock of the North Korean invasion to the south and the high costs of the disturbance to the United States aligned the U.S. and ROK governments in their desire to defeat the Communist threat. These aligned preferences led to high agent effort, with Rhee granting the United States direct control of ROK forces. The United States also increased its capacity-building efforts during this period, although these efforts were limited by the high operational tempo of the war. As a result, the chief contribution of U.S. assistance during this initial phase was its large-scale troop deployment and its direct control of combat operations.

Stalemate: Spring 1951–Spring 1953

China's entrance into the war forced some rethinking in Washington in early spring 1951. NSC 81/1 of September 1950 formally supported the use of force to cross the thirty-eighth parallel and unify North Korea, with the caveat that such actions should not provoke Soviet or Chinese intervention.[60] Yet that is precisely what had happened. The possibility of an expanded war with China was an unacceptable risk for the United States and pushed officials to agree on a more modest resolution to the Korean conflict. As soon as the front stabilized in January 1951, U.S. officials indicated that military action north of the thirty-eighth parallel was no longer feasible and that the new goal would be to seek a cease-fire. The new U.S. objectives in Korea were formalized on May 17 in NSC 48/5. The policy document clarified that Chinese entry into the war made a military strategy for Korean unification impossible and called for a negotiated settlement.[61] Washington's immediate goal in South Korea was now to support the development of a well-trained, professional ROK armed force capable of restoring the status quo ante and defending the ROK border at the thirty-eighth parallel.[62]

The decision to revert to limited war aims took place in the midst of mounting domestic political pressure in the United States to bring about a swift and favorable victory in Korea. Despite a decline in direct battlefield costs to the United States during this period,[63] frustration with the Truman administration grew in light of General MacArthur's dismissal for seeking an expansion of the war, failed cease-fire negotiations in July 1951, and the emergence of a stalemate on the battlefield.[64] The American public had been rallied in support of a proactive, offensive war against Communism. Lack of progress on the battlefield thus produced widespread dissatisfaction, as did the idea of a protracted, limited war in Asia.[65] Truman's approval rating dropped as low as 23 percent at the end of 1951, largely as a result of his handling of the Korean War (see figure 1.1). In light of his poor public-opinion ratings and mounting political opposition, Truman announced on March 29, 1952, that he would not run for reelection.[66] In November 1952, Eisenhower was elected president and pledged to bring a quick, favorable end to the Korean conflict.[67]

The diminished U.S. war aims created difficulties for President Rhee, who had shored up his anti-Communist base on the promise of a unified Korea.[68] This

FIGURE 1.1. Gallup poll of Truman's job approval ratings. Presidential Approval Ratings—Gallup Historical Statistics and Trends, http://www.gallup.com/poll/116677/presidential-approval-ratings-gallup-historical statistics-trends. aspx

support grew in importance as the battlefield stalemate enabled a reemergence of domestic political rivalries. Rhee's presidential term was due to expire in 1952, and his opponents in the National Assembly were determined to overthrow him in the next election. Stories of corruption and Rhee's penchant for autocratic rule had hardened the political elites' desire to oust him from power.[69]

Rhee's increased domestic political costs during this timeframe created tensions in the U.S.-ROK relationship, especially over military issues. The South Korean leader argued that a lack of soldiers and poor equipment were the key obstacles to a more effective ROKA. He continued to lobby the United States to provide more equipment for a larger South Korean armed force that would remain loyal to him, protect him from internal threats, and carry out his objective of northward expansion.[70] In March 1951, the ROK foreign minister informed U.S. officials that the South Korean government was eager for the United States to give full consideration to effectively utilizing the Korean manpower reserves and continuing past the thirty-eighth parallel to unite the peninsula.[71] In response, the United States emphasized the need for leadership training and military discipline before expanding the size of the South Korean army, an argument for which Rhee had little time.[72]

For its part, the ROKA continued to perform poorly against the Chinese during the 1951 spring offensive, revealing low levels of effort by Rhee to professionalize the military. During the second defense of Seoul, ROK forces broke in a wave of panic in the face of a Communist assault. The ROKA was ordered to resume its position the next day, only to dissolve in the face of a second Chinese attack and abandon all equipment. This pattern recurred across the ROK front line as South Korean soldiers left their positions to flee south.[73]

In light of the ROKA's poor performance, the United States placed conditions on its military aid, in order to compel Rhee to comply with its objective of professionalizing the armed forces.[74] In response to the collapse of ROKA divisions during the Communist spring offensive, KMAG commander Gen. James Van Fleet removed all ROK divisions from combat and warned the ROK chief of staff, Maj. Gen. Lee Jong-chan, that if the army could not make reliable progress toward military effectiveness he would not return ROK units to the front at all.[75] He further limited the functions of the ROKA staff to manpower induction, training, and administration.[76] Van Fleet emphasized that responsibility for building a professional army belonged to President Rhee and his government, and he refused to furnish any more valuable equipment and weapons to South Korea until the ROK military demonstrated leadership and training worthy of that support.[77] Finally, Van Fleet ordered KMAG to take control of the ROK Army's budget and personnel policies, and to promote officers based on merit.[78]

President Truman also responded to Rhee's requests to arm additional divisions of the ROK Army, stating,

> Any program of increasing the strength of the armed forces of Korea must, of course, depend on the availability of trained and competent leadership without which newly created units would be unable to withstand a seasoned foe. This was demonstrated by the evident weakness of certain Korean contingents in recent combat. I believe, therefore, that immediate efforts must be concentrated upon the rapid development of such leaders in order to lay the sound basis for increasing the strength of your armed forces.[79]

The United States also issued threats in 1952 when Rhee expressed his early opposition to peace negotiations. In February 1952, Truman warned Rhee that unless he moderated his public statements against a cease-fire, South Korea would lose American support. Truman informed Rhee that the degree of military assistance that he could expect from the United States in the future would be contingent on "the sense of responsibility demonstrated by [his] government, its ability to maintain the unity of the Korean people, and its devotion to democratic ideals."[80] These threats were always issued in private to senior officials in the ROK government, while a constant facade of U.S. public support for Rhee was maintained.

The South Korean leader relented and acquiesced to U.S. demands, placing his troops under complete U.S. control and agreeing to the purge of his crony officers. Rhee's need for U.S. military assistance to counter the Communist threat outweighed the costs of implementing U.S. policies—costs that were mitigated in part by a large U.S. troop presence that could deter internal threats to his regime. In return for Rhee's cooperation, the United States increased its flow of military aid. The number of advisers increased from 1,308 in September 1951, to 1,815 by January 1952, to 2,866 by mid-1953.[81] This increased capacity enabled KMAG to establish five replacement training centers (RTCs), to resume officer schooling as soon as the operational environment permitted, and perhaps most important, to directly monitor the ROK's level of effort.[82] KMAG also sent ROK officers to attend U.S. service schools starting in late 1951. By 1952, the pattern of KMAG training operations for the remainder of the war was in place. The school and instruction programs handled large groups of students and trainees, the field training camps provided refresher instruction, and combat and service support forces were available to strengthen the offensive and defensive capabilities of the ROK Army.[83] In late 1952, a program to expand the ROK Army to twenty divisions and six corps allowed for the replacement of U.S. divisions in South Korea by ROKA divisions. The ROK Army grew from 273,000 in June 1951, to 376,000 in June 1952, to 576,000 by July 1953.[84]

By mid-1952, the ROKA's combat capabilities had improved appreciably, with the South Koreans holding their own against routine Chinese and North Korean probes, patrols, and limited attacks.[85] In October 1952, for example, one ROK division, while suffering more than 3,500 casualties, held its ground against a ten-day attack by more than twenty-three thousand Communist soldiers.[86] By 1953, all ROKA forces had received division-level training, and combat proficiency had increased accordingly. The South Korean army performed well against Chinese attacks in the spring and summer of 1953, exhibiting greater tactical flexibility across all measures than it had in 1950.[87]

In sum, the Chinese invasion of late 1950 and the subsequent reversal of U.S. war aims created interest divergence between the U.S. and ROK governments. The increased costs to Rhee of pursuing U.S. interests resulted in lower levels of effort and poor ROK military performance—an outcome observed directly by U.S. advisers and troops on the ground, and indirectly through the increased frequency of (successful) Communist assaults. In response to low agent effort, and with a growing interest in withdrawing from the peninsula, the United States placed conditions on military aid in order to incentivize Rhee's increased cooperation, all the while continuing its capacity-building efforts. The U.S. strategy proved effective: the quality of the ROK armed forces improved drastically from spring 1951 through spring 1953.

Resolution: Spring 1953

Pressure from the American public to end the war on favorable terms and with-draw from Korea remained strong during this final stretch, as evidenced by the fact that Eisenhower had been elected on a promise of removing U.S. troops from the peninsula.[88] In addition, the United States faced pressure from its allies to deal with the intransigent South Korean leader. London told Washington that it had become difficult to remain silent while the United States let Rhee undermine the truce agreement with the North.[89] On the battlefield, a renewed Chinese offensive struck across the ROK front line, throwing South Korean forces into disarray. Facing the heaviest Communist attacks in two years, UN forces suffered seven-teen thousand casualties in just twenty days.[90] Battlefield losses, combined with mounting political pressure, thus created a strong desire in the United States to end the war.

However, the prospect of a cease-fire settlement that permanently divided the peninsula and permitted the continued presence of a Communist threat in the North ran counter to Rhee's wartime objectives. The South Korean leader had built his support base on the promise of unification, and anything less risked his political future. "Any so-called 'peace plan' which involves [a] division of this nation along any artificial border is entirely unacceptable to [the] people of Korea, north and south," Rhee stated publicly on June 26, 1951, adding that "any proposal which leaves aggressors in possession of any part of Korea would be an insult to this nation."[91] Rhee's position, which held constant throughout the course of the war, received widespread domestic political support. In spring 1953, anti-American rallies erupted around the country, and opposition politi-cians in the National Assembly joined with Rhee in a condemnation of American behavior.[92] Given the level of public opposition to a cease-fire, absent a complete victory Rhee needed something big from the negotiations that he could use to bolster his hold on power in the postwar period.[93]

To scuttle the peace talks and place the United States on the wrong foot, Rhee reverted to old habits and interfered in military affairs. In April 1953, Rhee told Eisenhower that if the United States signed the armistice with North Korea, it would have to withdraw all of its troops from the peninsula, and the ROK Army would continue to fight alone against the Chinese, North Koreans, and Soviets.[94] Rhee called on the South Korean people to reassert South Korea's right to fight on to a decisive end, with or without the U.S. coalition.[95] On June 7, Rhee imposed security restrictions around the country and ordered all ROK officers on duty in the United States to return home.[96] On June 18, violating an agreement on a prisoners-of-war (POW) exchange program—a key sticking point through-out the war—Rhee ordered the army to release 27,388 North Korean prisoners who refused to be repatriated to the North.[97] This act was designed to sabotage the peace talks and to coerce the United States into granting the South Korean government greater concessions. Ignoring several threatening letters from the Eisenhower administration, Rhee took a tough line and outlined three key conditions that he wanted met before South Korea would adhere to the U.S. plan: (1) withdrawal of Chinese forces, (2) conclusion of a mutual defense pact, and (3) a guarantee of continued U.S. military and economic aid.

The United States issued a number of private warnings to Rhee to incentivize his compliance with the terms of the armistice. On May 25, UN Allied commander Gen. Mark Clark and U.S. ambassador Ellis Briggs met with Rhee and made it clear that the United States would take a strong stand against action that undermined its policy in the Far East. They further warned that U.S. assistance after the war was contingent on Rhee's assurance that South Korea would cooperate with UN troops. The United States insisted that Rhee refrain from sabotaging the agreement and leave his forces under the operational control of the UN Command. If South Korea acted unilaterally, however, the United States would take "all necessary measures" to safeguard the security of its forces.[98] Deputy Secretary of Defense Roger Kyes advised that the United States threaten its withdrawal:

> It is probable that Rhee will continue to bluff and to temporize so long as he thinks there is [a] chance of wringing from us any [additional] concessions [or] forcing [a] change in our [position]. Most promising line of action now open seems to be to cause Rhee and his advisers to believe that we will withdraw from Korea in event he sabotages [armistice]. If no change results in Rhee's attitude, it would be our hope that influential ROK [political] and [military] elements would themselves take steps to bring about [situation] in ROK Gov which will assure ROK cooperation with [armistice].[99]

Rhee's continued intransigence even led the United States to consider a coup (Plan Everready) if Rhee removed South Korean troops from the U.S.-led command.[100] This possibility was dismissed, however, for lack of a suitable replacement.[101]

After Rhee released the POWs, Eisenhower intervened directly. The U.S. president wrote a strong note to Rhee, stating that unless Rhee was "prepared immediately and unequivocally to accept the authority of the UN command to conduct the present hostilities and to bring them to a close, it will be necessary to effect another arrangement."[102] This letter was followed by a personal visit from Assistant Secretary of State Walter Robertson to make clear Washington's determination to conclude an armistice with or without the South Korean government.[103] Rhee capitulated on July 9, pledging not to make any further attempts to obstruct the armistice agreement.[104] In return, South Korea was rewarded with a mutual security treaty, $200 million in immediate aid as part of a longer-term assistance package, and a U.S. commitment to the expansion of the South Korean military.[105] In order to keep a check on Rhee's nationalist goals, the United States sought written guarantees from Rhee that he would not act independently to provoke hostilities in the North, and that the United States would retain operational command authority over all ROK military forces upon the conclusion of the armistice.[106]

Thus by mid-1953, ROK and U.S. interests, aligned at the beginning of the war in 1950, had diverged almost completely over how to conclude the conflict. The United States wanted South Korea to sign an armistice that maintained the status quo ante bellum, while Rhee wanted to push north to unify the peninsula. In response to low levels of agent effort and the ROK government's continued intransigence, the United States employed a combination of rewards and punishments to incentivize Rhee to end the war.

Alternative Explanations

This chapter has argued that the United States, through the use of rewards and punishments, successfully influenced Rhee's behavior and brought about an end to the Korean War in line with U.S. interests. There are no clear alternative explanations for Rhee's behavior during the course of the conflict other than as a response to U.S. incentives. The one exception may be during the final stages of the war, when it is possible that Rhee had his own reasons for agreeing to the cease-fire, independent of U.S. actions. Personal and/or domestic political pressures other than those accounted for here may have convinced Rhee to sign the armistice. This seems unlikely, however. First, it is clear from his public and private statements that Rhee was an ardent nationalist with a true desire to unite the Korean peninsula. Furthermore, as documented earlier in the chapter, the South Korean public and the National Assembly were opposed to the armistice, increasing domestic pressure on Rhee to refuse—not concede to—U.S. terms.[107] Rhee thus had strong personal and domestic political reasons to continue resisting U.S. demands, and it seems unlikely that he would have changed course absent external pressure to do so.

Second, the timing of Rhee's behavior indicates that the United States' threat of abandonment was key to his decision to agree to the armistice. Rhee continued to obstruct negotiations until it became clear that the United States was willing to withdraw from the peninsula without guaranteeing military assistance and security to South Korea. This fear became most acute after Rhee released the POWs, which resulted in a clear warning by President Eisenhower and the deployment of Assistant Secretary of State Robertson to convey Washington's displeasure.[108] During this time, the United States also undertook a series of military measures to indicate its preparedness to withdraw, including meetings of high-level U.S. commanders, movements of U.S. forces, and a slowdown of supplies and equipment to Korea.[109] This was accompanied by a radio announcement on July 7 that the Eighth Army commander was making separate plans for the withdrawal of American and British divisions from South Korea if a truce was signed with the Communists, with or without the cooperation of the ROKA.[110] Given Washington's determination to sign the armistice, Rhee concluded that a world with a U.S. security guarantee was better than one without, and he agreed to cooperate in ending the war.

This chapter shows how the effective use of incentives by a principal can induce high levels of effort from an agent, resulting in the suppression of a disturbance (H_6). In the prewar period, President Syngman Rhee's concern with internal regime threats made it highly costly to implement U.S. military reforms, leading to a low level of ROK effort. The exogenous shock of the North Korean invasion served to override Rhee's domestic political concerns and unified the ROK government in its quest for survival. The lack of domestic political infighting in the initial phase of the war lowered the costs to Rhee of cooperating with the United States. As the war continued, however, and the United States retreated to more limited war aims, the interests of the ROK and U.S. governments diverged. As political opposition and pressure to invade the North and overthrow the regime mounted, contingent incentives became necessary—and were used—to induce higher levels of ROK effort.

This case offers empirical support for a number of the theory's predictions. First, it provides strong support for the expectation that as agent costs of effort increase, the principal will be more likely to reward or punish the agent to induce higher levels of effort. More specifically, U.S. behavior comports with the expectation that larger disturbances will be punished, while smaller disturbances will be met with rewards. Second, this case supports the expectation that as the cost of replacement increases, the principal will be more likely to reward or punish the agent. Third, while not a formal expectation of the theory, the Korea case also shows the benefits of monitoring in revealing information about levels of agent effort and providing the principal with the means to create more targeted incentives. The large U.S. footprint in South Korea in the form of KMAG advisers and combat troops enabled the U.S. government to observe the ROK military's level of effort more directly than is the case in many principal-agent relationships. Fourth, this case provides further justification for one of the theory's key scope conditions.

In the early phase of the war, the low level of ROK capacity and the ROK's lack of natural advantage at controlling the disturbance removed any benefit of indirect action; as a result, the United States preferred to exert direct control.

Finally, the South Korea case demonstrates that when the interests of the principal and agent are relatively aligned, and the agent lacks the ability to fulfill the wishes of the principal, the latter will provide resources to build capacity, thereby enabling the agent to act more effectively in the future. Interestingly, however, the case fails to find support for the prediction that the principal's investment in capacity building is always larger earlier rather than later in a relationship with an agent. In the case of South Korea, the investment appeared to increase incrementally over time, and became larger later in the relationship after Rhee complied with U.S. demands. This may be due to the unusual condition of direct U.S. command over ROKA forces.

The length of the Korean War, and especially the extended period of stalemate, raises some additional questions. First, why did the United States choose to stay in the war for so long, even after the front had stabilized in mid-1951? One possible answer is that the United States, having built up so much domestic support for the war against Communism, could not pull out of Korea prematurely and risk losing another key ally to China. Since the South Korean armed forces were not capable of mounting a strong defense in mid-1951, withdrawing posed too great a risk. The question remains, however, as to why the United States did not apply more pressure on Rhee to obtain a cease-fire agreement during the long stalemate from 1951 to 1953. Why did the United States settle on this amount of conditionality, and not push for more? Here it is plausible that U.S. officials were aware of the limits of ROK capacity and the risks of domestic instability if Rhee were pushed too hard, too quickly. As in Iraq and other cases in this volume, the very weakness of the agent appears to limit the principal's ability to inflict punishments large enough to induce full compliance.

NOTES

1. "Incentives" here refers to the use of both rewards and punishments by the principal.

2. The Korean War was a complex event involving a number of international actors. While many parties were involved in the conflict, this chapter focuses explicitly on the U.S.–South Korean relationship in order to evaluate the principal-agent theory developed in the introduction.

3. Sawyer 1962, 45.

4. Birtle 2009, 86. By 1949, the South Korean Labor Force had several thousand guerrillas backed by ten thousand party members, six hundred thousand active followers, and up to two million supporters in affiliated front organizations.

5. Millett 2005, 142–48, 166–75.

6. Allen 1960, 108–10, 142.

7. Ibid., 108.

8. Gibby 2012, 64.

9. Hastings 1987, 42.

10. Allen 1960, 102.

11. Cumings 2005, 218.

12. Allen 1960, 110.

13. Hastings 1987, 33, 35; Millett 2005, 61–62. The alternative candidates were considered either too left leaning or too far to the right. The few who appeared to share U.S. progressive ideals lacked leadership skills or a power base from which to rule.

14. Schnabel and Watson 1998, 22.

15. KMAG allocated more than $10 million in military aid to South Korea for the 1950 fiscal year. This was subsequently raised to $10,970,000 on March 15, 1950. Ibid., 98; Rearden 1984, 101–3.

16. Appleman 1992, 16; Sawyer 1962, 88–89, 100.

17. Gibby 2012, 67; Millett 2005, 172. On this point more generally, see North, Wallis, and Weingast 2009, e.g., 20.

18. Na, 64–65. Corrupt officers frequently appropriated money and materiel without permission from KMAG.

19. Gibby 2012, 64.

20. Lowe 1986, 9.

21. The number of Communist guerrillas fell from three thousand in September 1949 to approximately four hundred by May 1950. Ibid., 67; Millett 2005, 221; You 2013, 300.

22. Hastings 1987, 42–43; Millett 2005, 215.

23. The U.S. armed forces in Korea remained in direct control of the ROKA throughout the war. However, in conjunction with its direct combat participation, the U.S. military also carried out a separate military-assistance mission. The U.S. government began attaching conditions to this assistance from mid-1951 onward in order to compel Rhee to address the North Korean threat in line with U.S. interests.

24. Na 2006, 48, 52.

25. Ramsey 2006, 9; Sawyer 1962, 181.

26. Kane 2006, 8.

27. Ramsey 2006, 10; Sawyer 1962, 160–61, 178–79. This increase in manpower was accompanied by substantial costs. According to a Congressional Research Service report, the Korean War cost the United States $30 billion between 1950 and 1953 (current year dollars). See Daggett 2010, 2.

28. Hastings 1987, 33, 35.

29. The period from June 1950 to spring 1951 is treated as one phase in the war due to the lack of change in South Korea's cost of effort.

30. Reiter 2009, 70.

31. NARA 1949, 12–13.

32. Na 2006, 48–49; Sawyer 1962, 134.

33. Allen 1960, 25, 134, 141.

34. Ramsey 2006, 7.

35. Na 2006, 94.

36. Allen 1960, 117.

37. Ibid., 118; Cumings 2010, 11, 145. Independents and moderates took 130 of the 200 seats available.

38. Schnabel and Watson 1998, 22.

39. Allen 1960, 123–24.

40. Sawyer 1962, 112–13. As early as July 1950, Rhee had written a letter to Truman calling for a "victorious march north," claiming that it would be "utter folly to attempt to

restore the status quo ante, and then to await the enemy's pleasure for further attack when he had time to regroup, retrain, and reequip." Quoted in Cha 2009/10, 173.

41. United States Representative at the United Nations (Austin) to the Secretary of State, January 3, 1951, in U.S. Department of State 1983, doc. 8.

42. Allen 1960, 127, 129–30; Hastings 1987, 90. Public support for Rhee also grew during this period, bolstering his political position. The brutal experience of Communist rule from July through September of 1950 had served to demonstrate to most South Koreans that whatever the deficiencies of the Rhee regime, they were nothing in comparison to Communist tyranny.

43. Sawyer 1962, 167.

44. Hastings 1987, 48–49.

45. Blomstedt 2016, 44.

46. "US Enters the Korean Conflict," n.d.

47. Quoted in Hastings 1987, 58.

48. Quoted in Blomstedt 2016, 44.

49. Hastings 1987, 58.

50. A Department of Defense memo of July 31, 1950, debating the merits of the new strategy, claimed that the benefits of Korean unification would be "incalculable," and that unifying the peninsula would have a "salutary effect upon other areas of the world." Quoted in Reiter 2009, 90. Domestic public opinion was also supportive of the U.S. government's decision to take a bolder stance against the Communist threat. See Hastings 1987, 61; Mueller 1971, 361; Blomstedt 2016, 84.

51. National Security Council 1950.

52. Blomstedt 2016, 84.

53. Sawyer 1962, 167.

54. Reiter 2009, 79; Schnabel and Watson 1998, 149.

55. Malkasian 2001, 23.

56. Cumings 2010, 16; Hastings 1987, 85.

57. Gibby 2012, 143; Sawyer 1962, 137. By November 23, 1950, MacArthur commanded 423,313 ground troops in Korea and 130,000 men in the air and naval forces. Among the ground forces were 223,950 ROK and 178,464 U.S. troops (153,536 army and 24,928 marine corps). See Wainstock 1999, 87.

58. Sawyer 1962, 138. U.S. advisers increased unofficially from 470 in July to 632 in November 1950 and then to 746 in December.

59. Ibid., 148–50, 160.

60. Reiter 2009, 68.

61. "United States Objectives" (1951) 1977.

62. Secretary of State to the Embassy in Korea, February 7, 1951, in U.S. Department of State 1983, doc. 125. Efforts to stabilize military positions along the thirty-eighth parallel should be "accompanied by a thorough program for strengthening of ROK forces to point they [could] replace UN ground forces."

63. See Clodfelter 2002, 711.

64. Schnabel and Watson 1998, 229.

65. Malkasian 2001, 71.

66. Hastings 1987, 205, 315.

67. Blomstedt 2016, 219.

68. Millett 2007, 53.

69. Allen 1960, 133–34.

70. Na 2006, 102–3.

71. Memorandum of Conversation, by the Officer in Charge of Korean Affairs (Emmons), March 22, 1951, in U.S. Department of State 1983, doc. 181.

72. Ibid.

73. Gibby 2004, 177–78; Na 2006, 97. Despite these results and the lack of improvement, Rhee continued to push for additional ROKA divisions and equipment. According to the U.S. ambassador to Korea, John Muccio, "The clamor for arms continues, both directly and indirectly, prior to taking steps toward improving discipline, efficiency, and leadership in the officer and non-commissioned officer corps." See Memorandum by the Ambassador in Korea (Muccio), May 5, 1951, in U.S. Department of State 1983, doc. 277.

74. On seeking to place pressure on Rhee, see Acting Secretary of Defense (Lovett) to the Secretary of State, May 26, 1951, in U.S. Department of State 1983, doc. 301; Secretary of State to the Embassy in Korea, June 29, 1951, in U.S. Department of State 1983, doc. 387.

75. Na 2006, 99.

76. Gibby 2004, 180.

77. Ibid., 173–74; Ambassador in Korea (Muccio) to the Secretary of State, May 6, 1951, in U.S. Department of State 1983, doc. 278.

78. Na 2006, 141–42.

79. President Truman to the President of the Republic of Korea (Rhee), June 5, 1951, in U.S. Department of State 1983, doc. 323.

80. Quoted in Kaufman 1986, 271.

81. Ramsey 2006, 10.

82. HQ Eighth US Army Korea 1952, 8.

83. Sawyer 1962, 180–81, 185.

84. Ramsey 2006, 9.

85. Gibby 2012, 202.

86. Ramsey 2006, 9.

87. Gibby 2004, 288; Steward 2005, 245.

88. Mueller 1971, 361; Hastings 1987, 315; Miyoshi Jager 2013, 267–68.

89. Kaufman 1986, 198.

90. Hastings 1987, 324.

91. Quoted in Memorandum of Conversation, by the Officer in Charge of Korean Affairs (Emmons), June 28, 1951, in U.S. Department of State 1983, doc. 377.

92. Hastings 1987, 322.

93. Lowe 2000, 94. See also Ambassador in Korea (Muccio) to the Secretary of State, July 10, 1951, in U.S. Department of State 1983, doc. 423.

94. Cha 2009/10, 174.

95. Allen 1960, 160.

96. Hermes 1966, 449.

97. Gibby 2012, 257; Miyoshi Jager 2013, 278–79.

98. Kaufman 1986, 185.

99. Deputy Secretary of Defense (Kyes) to the Commander in Chief United Nations Command (Clark), June 29, 1953, in U.S. Department of State 1984, doc. 647.

100. Kaufman 1986, 186. Ellis Briggs told Mark Clark that "our alternatives include trying to bring Rhee into line or, if he is adamant . . . trying to effect his removal. (I am aware from DA940238 and DA940242 that plan "Ever Ready" has been prepared in your headquarters and considered in Washington . . .)" Ambassador in Korea (Briggs) to the Commander in Chief, United Nations Command (Clark), June 20, 1953, in U.S. Department of State 1984, doc. 619.

101. Millett 2007, 84.

102. Quoted in Kaufman 1986, 195. See also Editorial Note, June 18, 1953, in U.S. Department of State 1984, doc. 608.

103. Millett 2007, 92–93; Hastings 1987, 324.

104. Millett 2007, 93.

105. Allen 1960, 168.

106. Cha 2009/10, 176.

107. Memorandum of Conversation, June 28, 1951; Hastings 1987, 322.

108. Editorial Note, June 18, 1953; Millett 2007, 92–93; Hastings 1987, 324.

109. Commander in Chief, United Nations Command (Clark) to the Secretary of Defense (Wilson), July 5, 1953, in U.S. Department of State 1984, doc. 666.

110. Assistant Secretary of State for Far Eastern Affairs (Robertson) to the Department of State, July 7, 1953, in U.S. Department of State 1984, doc. 669.

2

DENMARK, 1940–45

Armed Resistance and Agency Slippage in
Germany's Model Protectorate

Brandon Merrell

> **The Führer needs in Denmark a puppet government which will do
> everything he requires of it. . . . Any resistance, even the slightest,
> must be suppressed by force.**
>
> German diplomat Werner von Grundherr, 1942
>
> **We will be forced to do many things for which people will afterward
> spit at us, if we are to bring Denmark unscathed through this period.**
>
> Danish prime minister Thorvald Stauning, 1940

The German occupation of Denmark illustrates the benefits and challenges of
delegating action to an agent. When the Wehrmacht invaded on April 9, 1940,
Hitler could easily have replaced the Danish leadership with a puppet regime.
Instead, he presented the sitting government with a choice: cabinet members
could retain their titles and influence if they agreed to cooperate with Germany
and to abide by German requests in the years ahead. Although at face value
Hitler's offer seemed generous, it did not stem from benevolence. His decision
was calculated and self-interested, and his motives were threefold. First, Hitler
believed that German and Danish preferences were naturally aligned. He viewed
Denmark as historically Aryan and hoped the Danes would eagerly assume their
rightful place as reliable partners for the Reich. Second, Hitler recognized that a
proxy relationship would enable Germany to avoid the cost of directly adminis-
tering a foreign country. If the incumbent Danish officials were sufficiently compliant, Germany could conserve its own resources and entrust Danish surrogates
to manage the existing bureaucracy. Finally, the führer believed that the image of
a cooperative government in Copenhagen would send a useful signal to domestic and international audiences. Danish citizens would view their government's
cooperation as an indication that they too should contribute to the German war
effort rather than engage in anti-Nazi activity, while other European countries

would observe Denmark's behavior as a model protectorate as evidence that cooperation with Berlin was both painless and profitable.[1]

For the first three years of the occupation, Hitler's plan for indirect control succeeded: Germany issued a series of demands spanning a wide range of policies and the Danish cabinet faithfully executed its orders. Despite this success, Hitler was wrong to assume that Danish preferences were perfectly aligned with his own. Proud of their history of democratic traditions, most Danes viewed Hitler and the German Nazi Party with deep antipathy.[2] Many of the policies that Germany demanded that Denmark institute—such as the imposition of press censorship, restrictions on public assembly, and the passage of anti-Semitic laws—were ones where the preferences of both Danish officials and their constituents were diametrically opposed to those of the Reich. As Prime Minister Thorvald Stauning lamented early in the occupation, Germany ordered the Danish cabinet to do "many things for which people would afterward spit at us."[3]

Rather than attribute Danish cooperation to closely aligned preferences, I argue that Germany succeeded in extracting high effort in large part due to its capacity to coerce. Whenever the Danish government appeared hesitant or resistant, Berlin could force an issue by imposing penalties on Danish leaders and citizens. From 1940 through 1943, the German Foreign Ministry regularly punished or replaced Danish cabinet members whom it suspected of noncompliance. In the most extreme circumstances, Germany threatened to cancel all pretense of negotiation and impose martial law. Faced with the credible threat of regime change at the hands of their occupiers, the Danes were cowed into submission on matters of great importance to Germany. Berlin's success at motivating its agent in Copenhagen illustrates an important facet of indirect control: when principals have large and credible incentive tools at their disposal—such as those that Germany enjoyed early in the war—they can extract useful and productive behavior from their agents.

The initial success, however, was fleeting. Germany eventually encountered challenges that led its relationship with Denmark to collapse. Why was a principal as powerful as Germany unable to permanently extract compliant behavior from a defenseless—albeit high-capacity—proxy? The long-term failure of German-Danish cooperation highlights an important constraint on indirect control: even successful proxy relationships can falter when the agent's costs of effort rise. As the occupation progressed, the Danish cabinet faced mounting political pressure from constituents who opposed the government's role as German lackey. The relationship reached a turning point in August 1943, when thousands of Danish citizens revolted against the government's cooperation with the Reich. Under extreme pressure from its citizens, the Danish cabinet turned a deaf ear to Germany's threats. Unable to efficiently motivate its former agent, Berlin determined that indirect control was no longer viable and instead attempted to administer Denmark directly.

Historical Background

The occupation of Denmark lasted just over five years. It began when Germany launched a surprise invasion on the morning of April 9, 1940. As German troops marched across the Danish border and filled Danish skies, the German ambassador delivered a message to the Danish foreign minister. The memorandum depicted the invasion as a defensive measure designed to protect Denmark from imminent Allied attack. In exchange for Danish cooperation and an immediate cessation of armed resistance, Germany pledged to nominally respect Danish sovereignty, territorial integrity, and neutrality.

The invasion caught the Danish cabinet by surprise. Denmark escaped World War I largely unscathed by maintaining neutrality and even cooperating with Germany economically. Although the Danes received a swath of border territory from Germany as part of the Treaty of Versailles, Germany never signaled any intention to reoccupy the region. Indeed, in 1939 Denmark became the only Scandinavian country to sign a nonaggression pact with the Reich. Danish officials therefore felt confident that even a hostile Nazi regime would exert influence through diplomatic pressure rather than forced occupation.

Because they had made few preparations for war, on the morning of the invasion Danish officials quickly recognized that they had little hope of thwarting German forces. The Danish military was too thinly distributed, insufficiently equipped, and poorly positioned to defend a country that itself provided few geographic barriers to stymie incoming forces. Nor could Denmark turn to external assistance for support. Given the circumstances, King Christian X decided to call off the scattered fighting that his forces were engaged in and to yield, under protest, to German demands.[4] In the process, the king created a platform for negotiations between the two countries in the years ahead.

During the war, German requests of Denmark spanned a wide range of areas, from economic and judicial to military and political. Of all the tasks the Danes were called on to carry out, the most important was the prevention of domestic unrest. Unlike other occupied states, where German troops directly enforced internal security, Denmark was expected to keep its own house in order and to suppress anti-Nazi activity. Discharged from its responsibility for international defense, the Danish Army joined with the police to suppress domestic saboteurs, rebels, and resistance groups.

Early in the war, these disturbances were rare. However, as the occupation progressed, German prescriptions grew increasingly difficult for the Danes to swallow. In late 1942, prospects for German victory dimmed significantly after reversals of fortune on the Eastern Front and in northern Africa. Danish citizens and political officials developed a newfound optimism about their ability to cast off the German occupiers and to placate Allied states by resisting German demands. Internal resistance to Germany increased and ushered in a period of escalating rebel activities and attacks against German personnel, collaborators, and equipment. The policy of formal negotiations reached its conclusion in the summer of 1943. After a violent wave of sabotage and strikes, Germany assumed power, disarmed the Danish military, and imposed martial law under Nazi rule.

With the dissolution of the government in Copenhagen, German officials attempted to monitor Danish civil servants while the Wehrmacht assumed direct authority over the Danish police in hopes of suppressing violence. These efforts were largely ineffective. The Danish underground "liquidated" at least 385 German collaborators in the final two years of the war,[5] and the largest resistance group, Bopa, conducted nearly four hundred attacks against military or industrial targets.[6] In a final attempt to deter violence, Germany fully dissolved the Danish police and began to conduct reciprocal and indiscriminate attacks against Danish citizens. The occupation persisted under direct military rule until the closing stages of the war in Europe.

Theoretical Expectations

The indirect control model offers several predictions in the case of the Danish occupation. Table 2.1 provides a summary, along with a brief account of each country's behavior. As the table demonstrates, one theoretical expectation relates to increases in the agent's cost of effort. Although the Danish government initially faced low political costs for complying with German demands, these costs increased substantially over time. Civilian discontent and antagonism toward Germany rose over the course of the occupation; concessions to German policy that the public initially accepted without question were tolerated resentfully by 1942 and became unthinkable by mid-1943. Similarly, resistance groups expanded in capacity and membership. Maintaining security and suppressing acts of sabotage therefore became increasingly difficult tasks for the government as the occupation progressed.

When an agent's cost of effort increases, a principal must use higher-magnitude incentives to successfully incentivize the proxy. As such, we should see German threats increase in severity and frequency over the course of the relationship.

TABLE 2.1 Theoretical expectations and summary results, Denmark

PERIOD	KEY PARAMETER	THEORETICAL EXPECTATION	OBSERVED ACTION
January 1941– November 1941	Costs of punishment decrease relative to initial occupation period (April–December 1940).	The principal should be more willing to punish/ intervene (H_9).	Germany begins to impose punishment and demands higher effort.
December 1941– December 1942	Danish cost of effort increases.	Disturbances should increase moderately. The principal must use higher-powered incentives (H_7) to extract equivalent effort (H_6).	Denmark resists specific German demands; scattered sabotage attacks occur. Germany temporarily suspends relations, replaces the Danish prime minister, and instructs its officers to rule with an iron fist. Denmark responds to these incentives with renewed effort.
January 1943– August 1943	Danish cost of effort increases further.	Disturbances should increase significantly. The principal should either attempt direct control or should disengage from the situation (H_1).	Denmark openly resists German demands; sabotage attacks escalate dramatically. Germany responds by disbanding the Danish Parliament and imposing martial law.

Furthermore, the model predicts that principals may choose to replace agents in the wake of particularly egregious disturbances. We should therefore observe German attempts to oust Danish officials after significant lapses in security or breaches of compliance—unless Germany believes no suitable replacement agent is available. Finally, the model predicts that if the agent's cost of effort grows too extreme, the principal will terminate the relationship with the proxy and will instead attempt either to ignore the disturbances or to control them directly. Thus, although we should observe German attempts to induce compliant behavior from Denmark in the formative years of the relationship, Germany should eventually abandon the proxy relationship and intervene directly once it concludes that the Danish cabinet—however composed—is no longer reliable.

The model also offers a prediction about the German cost of punishment. The price that Germany paid for imposing punishment on Denmark decreased over time. In the early stages of the war, Germany was deeply concerned about maintaining Denmark's appearance as a "model protectorate." As such, Berlin sought to intervene as little as possible in Danish affairs and was willing to overlook a significant degree of agency slippage. However, as additional European countries aligned against Germany, the pretense of peaceful relations with Denmark became less valuable. Incursions into Danish policy no longer threatened Germany's international reputation, particularly when weighed against the alternative of appearing incapable of maintaining security within an occupied state. According to the theory, as the relative cost of punishment declines, the principal should grow increasingly willing to exercise punishment as a coercive tool. We should therefore observe more frequent and severe threats of punishment from Germany as the relationship progresses.

Disturbances

April 1940–December 1940: Onset of Occupation

Danish leaders initially consented to occupation for several reasons. First, their country was woefully unprepared to resist the invasion via military means. In his New Year's address of January 1, 1940, Prime Minister Thorvald Stauning lamented that his country's geography and small population constrained it from matching the major powers. Minister of Defense Alsing Andersen similarly warned that the government would only attempt to counter violations of neutrality "if there are reasonable expectations of repelling them."[7] On the morning of the invasion, German soldiers deployed to Denmark outnumbered the Danish military roughly three to one. Forced to choose either a futile and costly resistance or a humiliating but tolerable occupation, Danish officials opted for the latter.

The Danes were also encouraged to accept occupation by the favorable terms of the German offer. Hitler was so eager to establish a model protectorate that in exchange for Danish cooperation he offered to formally renounce Germany's claim to Northern Schleswig, a border region that Denmark had acquired under the Treaty of Versailles. Left unspoken was the reciprocal threat: if Denmark failed to accept occupation, Berlin could simply annex the territory. In the process, two hundred thousand Danish citizens would immediately become German residents, subjecting them to the threat of German conscription and repression.[8] Eager to secure the safety of its citizens, the Danish cabinet quickly acquiesced. Temporary sacrifices were acceptable if they staved off permanent sovereignty losses.

Third, Danish leaders assumed the war would be short. If the Allies quickly brokered a new peace with Germany, Berlin was liable to claim all areas of Europe that were under its dominion—particularly those in which Berlin had imposed a new regime. By accepting occupation in exchange for official diplomatic neutrality, Danish politicians could legally retain political control of their own country and, they hoped, ensure that Denmark would remain an independent state when the maps of Europe were redrawn.[9]

Finally, incumbent Danish officials knew that by retaining administrative power they could circumvent or negotiate around particularly brutal Nazi policies.[10] In their letter accepting German occupation, the Danish cabinet members insisted that their country would officially remain an independent and neutral state. Denmark was "occupied," as opposed to "conquered," and the government would act accordingly. The Danish Parliament would continue to debate and adopt Danish laws, Danish police would remain on active duty, and Danish courts would continue to protect the judicial rights of Danish citizens. Moreover, although the cabinet promised to facilitate peaceful cooperation with Berlin, policy changes were ultimately subject to negotiation through the Danish foreign minister. Adoption of the death penalty, the forcible installment of Nazi officials into the Danish cabinet, and the conscription of Danish citizens to fight alongside Germans were unacceptable in the eyes of both politicians and the public. The policy of negotiations was meant to insulate Danish citizens from undue German influence rather than to expedite severe German policies.

In truth, the Danes' emphatic insistence on "negotiation" amounted to little more than "political window-dressing," and the state of neutrality could be overturned at any moment.[11] At this point, however, the fiction of negotiation served German interests by creating an appearance of peaceful cooperation between the two countries. From Berlin's perspective, the Danes could retain the trappings of independence as long as they kneeled to German commands when called on to do so. If Denmark ever forgot which "negotiator" held the upper hand, Germany could simply extract obedience by force.

The first overt sign that Germany was prepared to strong-arm Danish compliance was revealed at the beginning of July, when Germany pressured the Danes to appoint the independent diplomat Erik Scavenius as foreign minister in place of Peter Munch. Scavenius had held the office throughout World War I, during which time he established a reputation as a pragmatist who would sooner accommodate German demands than risk military engagement.[12] Whereas Munch had passively obeyed German requests, Berlin hoped that Scavenius would opt for an activist approach in which he anticipated German desires and acted on them without prompting.[13] Germany's hopes were realized when, upon taking office, Scavenius issued a statement declaring that it was "Denmark's task to find its place in a necessary and mutually active collaboration with the Greater Germany."[14]

For their part, Danish citizens reluctantly acknowledged that resistance was impractical and accepted the government's collaborationist stance. However, the seeds of discontent were sown. The king's quick decision to accept occupation was widely panned by the press, which drew unfavorable comparisons with Norway's prolonged attempt at defense. The lingering public sentiment was that the Danish government ought to have predicted the German invasion and done more to prepare.

Small elements of protest emerged immediately after the invasion. Because Denmark officially maintained neutrality, Germany allowed the Danish Army and Navy to persist, and Danish intelligence officers began to pass valuable information to Britain. Likewise, leaders of the Danish political party Dansk Samling met secretly three days after the invasion. They drafted plans to foster resentment among the Danish population in hopes that this would encourage citizens to take up arms in pursuit of liberation.[15] Over the summer, small groups protested the occupation by hosting community singing events. The first such event occurred on July 4 and involved a modest audience of roughly 1,500 citizens, but participation slowly increased. By September, an estimated 750,000 Danes had attended a patriotic rally, providing an early hint of the level of domestic opposition to Nazism that would emerge in later years.[16]

For now, the Danish cabinet's political calculus was dominated by the penalties that Germany could impose if it suspected overt opposition to its recommendations. To minimize the possibility of such signals, the cabinet directed citizens to eschew behavior that might provoke German displeasure. The administration also created a new office, the State Prosecutor for Special Affairs, which centralized police cooperation with the German military and the Gestapo.[17] The Wehrmacht proposed Thune Jacobsen—a man known for his pro-German attitude—as a suitable candidate for the position, and the Danes quickly agreed.[18] However, even installing the Reich's chosen man as head of the Danish police was not enough to satisfy the occupiers. Germany also demanded that Copenhagen ratchet up the criminal penalties for a wide range of political behaviors, such as expressing anti-German opinions or displaying the flags of countries currently at war with the Reich. The Danish cabinet readily complied.

The second wave of German complaints focused on the underground press, which quickly developed an efficient distribution network. In October 1940, German ambassador Cécil von Renthe-Fink complained that nationalist "whisper-

and-leaflet propaganda" was turning Danish public opinion against Germany.[19] The German press attaché, Gustav Meissner, pressured the Danish Foreign Ministry to either censor or remove journalists who expressed anti-German views. The Danes begrudgingly began to detain and prosecute individuals caught circulating unsanctioned materials, but sentencing remained relatively light.[20]

The final policy concessions that Denmark enacted in mid-1940 were a series of "minor adjustments" that officially curtailed the freedoms of Jewish citizens.[21] Public lectures on Jewish topics were prohibited, Jews lost the right to assemble, and Jewish publications were suspended from print. However, few of these legal adjustments were actually enforced.[22] When the government outlawed attendance at synagogue, the king himself attended in protest. Although such moves appear to signal the Danish government's resistance to German directives, strict cooperation on anti-Semitic issues was never a high priority for Germany. There is little evidence that the Germans were ever motivated to force the issue of Jewish deportation or incarceration. Berlin tolerated breaches of policy in this area to maintain the guise of willing cooperation.

On balance, the concessions that Denmark suffered during 1940 were relatively minor and the Danish cabinet's exertion of effort was quite high. Germany was willing to overlook minor violations in behavior from its Danish agents in order to preserve the outward appearance of a model protectorate. Likewise, the Danish cabinet members viewed the policy changes they were forced to implement as acceptable trade-offs if they were to retain nominal sovereignty or shield their population from direct German rule. As the war intensified, however, the Danish cost of effort gradually increased, triggering the first significant disagreements between Copenhagen and Berlin.

January 1941–November 1941: Initial Interventions

In late 1940 and early 1941, Germany increased pressure on the Danish cabinet to accept Nazi appointments or, at minimum, dismiss members of Parliament who aired anti-German opinions. With the war now in full stride, the value of showcasing a model protectorate had faded significantly. Berlin could therefore impose punishments more cheaply and was increasingly willing to use coercion to ensure that Danish politicians followed protocol. Christmas Møller, the Danish minister of trade, was asked to stand down from his cabinet position after issuing a series of anti-German remarks. Renthe-Fink then informed the Danes that he would suspend bilateral negotiations unless Møller withdrew from Parliament altogether. Other influential politicians were also forced to leave their posts and to withdraw from public life, including Hans Hedtoft-Hansen, who served as prime minister after the war.[23] In July, Germany demanded that the Danes replace Minister of Justice Harald Petersen with Thune Jacobsen, the man the Nazis had previously installed as national police chief. Even Stauning was targeted for removal when the Germans asked their preferred replacement, Scavenius, to spread the idea that the prime minister was too elderly and fatigued to continue running the country. Stauning, however, proved too popular for dismissal. His coalition government rallied behind him when he exclaimed, "Damned if I'm tired! No one is going to believe that."[24]

Additional demands were imposed when Germany attacked the Soviet Union in June 1941. Berlin instructed the Danish police to arrest Communist members of Parliament, along with other prominent Communists located in Denmark. The Danish Constitution outlawed the arrest of sitting MPs, so the police requested and received approval from Stauning before proceeding.[25] Over the next two months, the Danish police conducted 336 arrests.[26] Although 220 of the detainees were soon released, the others were sent to the Horserød prison camp for the duration of the war.[27]

Early 1941 also brought the first German military demands. In February, Berlin asked the Danish Navy to relinquish twelve torpedo boats to German control. The Danish Navy protested strenuously, but the politicians in government feared that failure to make the concession would jeopardize their relationship with Germany.[28] The cabinet's decision to approve the transfer was interpreted icily by the Allies, particularly the British, who considered it a step too far in collaboration with Germany. The move also prompted the first Danish diplomats to break with Copenhagen. Henrik Kauffmann, Danish ambassador to the United States, argued that the transfer of the torpedo boats proved that the Danish government was acting under extreme duress and that he was obliged to forge an independent foreign policy.[29] On the first anniversary of the occupation, Kauffmann authorized the United States to create and utilize Danish military bases in Greenland in order to fight the Axis powers. Although the Danish government quickly charged him with treason, Kauffmann's decision signaled the first clear rejection of the collaborationist policy by a Danish diplomat.

Germany soon moved beyond requisitioning Danish military supplies. In June, the Wehrmacht sought to form a battalion of Danish soldiers who would support German forces on the Eastern Front. The Danish cabinet resisted, but Scavenius argued that the move was essential to retain German favor. In the end, they struck a compromise: the Germans could not conscript Danish citizens, but supporters of Germany were given permission to join the newly created "Frikorps Danmark" (Free Corps Denmark).

Between July and September 1941, 1,600 Danes opted to participate in the group and were outfitted with supplies from Danish military stockpiles.[30] By the end of the war, roughly 13,000 Danish citizens voluntarily joined the German armed services.[31]

The next significant strain on the relationship arrived in October, when an anti-Communist pact signed by Germany and several other European states came up for renewal. At war with the Soviet Union, Finland signaled its willingness to join the treaty on the condition that Denmark also become a member. On November 20, Renthe-Fink commanded that the Danes sign the Anti-Comintern Pact. Scavenius met with the cabinet and spouted the by-now-traditional rationale that it was better to agree quickly to German demands than to prolong the inevitable, suffer penalties in the interim, and risk the dissolution of Danish sovereignty. For the first time, the cabinet stood firmly in opposition. Allowing Germany to bully Denmark into a dramatic change of foreign policy would jeopardize the government's domestic support and intensify Allied disfavor, which had grown ever since the torpedo boats had been turned over to Germany nine months earlier. As deliberations continued, German foreign minister Joachim von Ribbentrop dispatched a message directly from Berlin: if Denmark failed to sign the treaty, the Reich would henceforth consider Denmark a hostile country and German assurances of peaceful negotiation would no longer stand. To lend credibility to the threat, the Wehrmacht placed its German troops in Denmark on high alert, prompting Scavenius to remind his colleagues, "It is an illusion that we have power."[32] With Danish sovereignty at risk, Public Works Minister Gunnar Larsen suggested a compromise whereby Denmark would sign the treaty with an addendum of exemptions.

Scavenius traveled to Berlin to present the new terms. When informed of the Danish proposal, Ribbentrop was furious. He threatened to arrest Scavenius, who nevertheless held his ground. After several rounds of negotiation, they reached a deal: Denmark could attach reservations, but the caveats would be kept secret from the public so as not to diminish the apparent significance of Danish membership.

Denmark's accession to the Anti-Comintern Pact triggered immediate responses on three fronts. The Allies interpreted the move as proof that the Danish government would continue to cooperate with the Axis powers. Where the transfer of the torpedo boats had raised Allied suspicions that the Danes could not be trusted, their signature of the pact confirmed such beliefs. Danish diplomats abroad also reacted unfavorably: nearly one-third of Danish foreign representatives, including Eduard Reventlow, the ambassador in London, followed in Kauffmann's footsteps and severed ties with Copenhagen. Finally, Danish civilians protested the government's latest submission to German demands. Students assembled in Copenhagen, urging the government to embrace "Norwegian conditions" by ending its relationship with Germany. On November 25 and 26, the Danish police arrested 169 protesters.[33]

The negative reaction on all fronts prompted Scavenius to host a series of private meetings with other members of the Danish cabinet to orient their policy going forward. The administration determined that additional sacrifices in three issue areas were off limits. First, Denmark would under no circumstances officially join the Axis powers, regardless of German demands. Second, it would not allow Germans to conscript Danish citizens for the war effort, nor would it allow Danish troops to fight alongside Germany.[34] Finally, the government would not tolerate the deportation of Danish Jews. The political costs of abiding by German demands had substantially increased, and the government responded by outlining new boundaries on its willingness to comply.

December 1941–December 1942: Political Resistance Increases

The police crackdown following the Anti-Comintern Pact protests demonstrated that opponents of the occupation would need to battle both the German occupiers and a coalition government desperate for political survival. The nascent Danish underground switched its priority from hosting patriotic demonstrations to organizing sabotage activities under the radar of the authorities. At the same time, the British Special Operations Executive (SOE) began to contact resistance groups within Denmark. Prime Minister Winston Churchill famously directed the SOE to "set Europe ablaze" by training rebels to conduct terrorist attacks against German troops, supporters, and suppliers.[35] Over time, British assistance would substantially boost the capacity of the resistance.

Nevertheless, although the public had grown disenchanted with occupation and collaboration, the average Dane in 1940 or 1941 did not yet approve of active sabotage. A handful of individuals held opposition demonstrations, slipped sand or sugar into the tanks of vehicles, or secretly circulated anti-German newspapers, but systematic violence was an exception rather than the norm. It would take outside events—the reversal of German fortunes in the East and the entry of the United States into the war—to give the public increased hope that an overthrow of their occupiers was possible.[36] Over the next eighteen months, the string of early German victories faded from memory and Wehrmacht losses in the wider war began to mount. Danish resistance organizations, including Bopa and Holger Danske, convened and conducted their first operations, and attacks against German targets in Denmark significantly increased in frequency. By the end of 1942, acts of resistance surged from a minor nuisance to a steady stream of violence that the Reich could no longer accept.

A downturn in economic conditions also prompted the shift in public sentiment. Despite its need for agricultural and industrial goods, Germany initially sought to minimize its influence on the Danish economy out of concern that major shocks would provoke public unrest.[37] During the early stages of the war, some Danish workers, particularly those involved in agriculture or manufacturing, benefited from soaring exports to Germany.[38] However, as the relationship endured, Berlin garnished a growing share of Danish supplies at below-market rates. Diminished access to goods began to affect Danish citizens seriously in the winter of 1941–42, one of the coldest European winters of the twentieth century.[39] During the year that followed, the number of gasoline vehicles in use plunged by almost 90 percent; commodities such as coffee, soap, and tobacco became scarce luxuries; and the overall purchasing power of the working class declined by approximately 34 percent from its 1939 level.[40] Deteriorating economic conditions—and the belief that they were caused by German exploitation—sparked public frustration with the government's collaborationist stance.

The growth of the illegal press also drove anti-German opinion. In 1940 the underground press comprised two newspapers that together printed only 1,200 total copies. By late 1942, at least forty-nine papers existed, and the number of copies in circulation had swelled to at least three hundred thousand.[41] Despite penalties ranging from imprisonment to execution, illicit publishers continued to advocate for resistance and sabotage. The messages profoundly affected public opinion, and the results were not lost on Danish officials. In January 1942, citizens in Odense petitioned the government to show more resistance to German demands, even if doing so would trigger the imposition of serious penalties. A separate group of 425 Copenhagen-area physicians delivered a letter to the Danish minister of the interior, arguing that "an additional concession to German demands . . . will be tantamount to giving up our national independence."[42]

The shift in public opinion was also evident when the Danish Frikorps members who had volunteered to fight alongside the Wehrmacht returned to Denmark for leave in early September. They anticipated a jubilant propaganda parade but instead were harried by protests and shouts of derision.[43] Altercations between soldiers and civilians continued over the next several weeks; in a single night in Aalborg, eleven people were hospitalized and forty complaints of violence between soldiers and civilians were lodged.[44] The Germans' planned propaganda campaign of uniting the country in support of the Frikorps fighters was a disaster, and there were no further collective visits from the Eastern Front volunteers for the remainder of the war. In combination, German losses in the wider war, the sinking Danish economy, the efforts of the illegal press, and mounting friction between pro-Nazi and pro-Danish factions substantially raised the government's political costs of abiding by German requests.

In May, Vilhelm Buhl replaced Thorvald Stauning as prime minister when the latter succumbed to a brain aneurysm. Under Buhl's watch, acts of sabotage grew more frequent. The first group to engage in premeditated violence was the Churchill Club, a group of schoolchildren in Aalborg who stole weapons and destroyed German rail cars. Although the schoolchildren inflicted relatively little damage, their actions inspired others who followed with more dramatic and costly attacks.

Bopa, a pro-Communist group operating primarily in Copenhagen, carried out thirty-one small bombings against German factories, shops, and transportation depots during July and August.[45] The largest attack, aimed against a shipyard, destroyed two German torpedo boats. Outraged, the Germans informed Buhl that if he failed to suppress acts of sabotage, the Wehrmacht would seize jurisdiction over judicial proceedings, try suspected parties in military courts, and apply the death penalty against perpetrators.[46] Such actions threatened to undermine the fiction of Danish sovereignty permanently, because if Danish civilians were tried as war criminals in foreign courts, the government could no longer credibly claim to use negotiation as a defensive shield for its citizens. Significantly, the German threat of punishment succeeded: to ward off the German threat, Buhl exerted maximum effort to prevent attacks. He publicly condemned acts of sabotage, hired additional Danish guards to protect factories, and asked the police to take all necessary steps to thwart resistance.[47] After the war, former saboteurs complained that the efforts of the Danish police in this period rivaled those of the German security forces that seized control late in the war.[48]

Despite his effort, Buhl was unable to appease Germany entirely. Relations between Copenhagen and Berlin came to a head on September 26, 1942, when King Christian X received a birthday telegram from Hitler. He replied in typical fashion with a brief response: "My very sincere thanks—Christian X."[49] The führer, already annoyed by the spate of attacks that had erupted over the summer, interpreted the note as insultingly abrupt and insufficiently deferential. He placed German troops in Denmark on high alert, dismissed the Danish ambassador in Berlin, recalled his own ambassador from Denmark, and severed diplomatic relations between the two countries. For the next six weeks, Danish leaders worried that Germany was poised for a complete takeover of Denmark.[50]

In November, Ribbentrop resumed contact by calling Scavenius to Berlin for negotiations. Germany demanded that Buhl resign as prime minister and that Scavenius step forward in his place. Furthermore, the new cabinet would henceforth act entirely independently of Parliament, thus ensuring that Germany's chosen agent, Scavenius, would enjoy untrammeled power. After several days of debate, the Danish politicians accepted Scavenius as prime minister, much to the displeasure of the public.[51] Germany also modified its own personnel in Denmark. First, Hitler dismissed Renthe-Fink and selected the SS officer Werner Best as plenipotentiary, instructing him to "rule with an iron hand."[52] In addition,

Hitler appointed Gen. Hermann von Hanneken to command German forces in Denmark.[53]

As 1942 drew to a close, German policy was summarized by Werner von Grundherr of the Scandinavian Foreign Office, who explained, "The Führer needs in Denmark a puppet government which will do everything he requires of it. . . . The head of this government must always be conscious that in the case of a possible withdrawal of German troops he would be hanged on the nearest lamp post. . . . Any resistance, even the slightest, must be suppressed by force. Should it appear that the Danish police force does not suffice or does not act in accordance with our desires, possibly also SS troops will be made available."[54] Those words would prove prophetic in the year to come.

January–August 1943: Collapse of the Relationship

The six months that followed the "Telegram Crisis" were in many respects "the most tranquil and stable period of the occupation."[55] Although Hitler's appointment of Best and Hanneken signaled that Berlin was adopting a firmer stance, Best continued to follow in the pragmatic footsteps of his predecessor. He recognized that diverting German military resources to Denmark would force the Wehrmacht to make sacrifices elsewhere in Europe. On the other hand, continued sabotage and unrest in Denmark threatened to disrupt the supply of important trade goods and strategic supplies. Best therefore hoped that the Danish government, motivated by its recent chastisement, would exert high effort as a compliant and effective agent in controlling public disturbances. From late 1942 through April 1943, the bet paid off. The Scavenius administration, keenly aware that it had only narrowly escaped dismissal by Nazi officials, redoubled its efforts to suppress public unrest. Unfortunately for Germany, the calm did not last.

Over the course of 1943, the tide of the war turned increasingly against the Reich. The Battle of Stalingrad ended with German defeat in late January. At the end of May, Axis forces surrendered in North Africa. The Allied invasion of Italy followed in June, and Mussolini was toppled soon thereafter. As Germany's chances of victory diminished, Danish citizens became increasingly intolerant of their government's concessions to the occupying power. Danes also worried that apparent collaboration with the Nazis would undermine their standing in Allied eyes. Broadcasts from the BBC adopted a threatening tone, warning that the "attitude taken by official Denmark may prove fatal for the future of Denmark in postwar Europe, if the Danish nation does not in time, in an unequivocal manner, make it clear to the free world that it is wholeheartedly on the side of the united nations."[56]

A new wave of sabotage actions were perpetrated in March. Bopa swelled to between fifty and one hundred members operating in the Copenhagen area and increased the frequency and scale of its operations. Tables 2.2 and 2.3 depict the sudden rise in sabotage attacks over time. Whereas in 1942 Bopa members conducted only 59 sabotage operations, the following year they carried out 354 successful attacks in the capital alone.[57] Best noted the increase in bombings in his reports to Berlin, but he continued to back the Danish government, which, he said, was fighting the problem "energetically and successfully."[58] Scavenius, however, worried that the resistance groups were getting the better of the Danish police. He fretted that "the future [of the Danish-German relationship] depends on whether serious sabotage cases occur."[59] General Hanneken's more sobering account paints Denmark as a country on the verge of open rebellion, where "Germans could hardly walk the streets in safety."[60]

Public antipathy to the policy of collaboration was not exclusive to extremists. On March 23, 1943, Denmark became the only country to hold parliamentary elections under German occupation. Danish voters turned out in record numbers, with nearly 90 percent participation, but only 2 percent cast ballots for the Danish Nazi Party. Clashes between casual citizens and German personnel

TABLE 2.2   Danish sabotage attacks, 1940–43

YEAR	NUMBER OF EVENTS
1940	2
1941	12
1942	59
1943	816

Source: Hong 2012, 163.

TABLE 2.3   Danish sabotage attacks, 1943

MONTH	NUMBER OF EVENTS
January	14
February	29
March	60
April	82
May	86
June	47
July	94
August	213

Source: Hong 2012, 163.

or supporters also increased. On July 6, 130 Danish civilians were arrested after a skirmish in which Frikorps soldiers attacked citizens wearing hats resembling the British Royal Air Force roundel.[61] Fights erupted in areas surrounding German garrisons, and antagonism between Danes and German soldiers spread. By August 1943, an illegal poll of the Danish people suggested that 70 percent favored resistance.[62] Danish workers also held workplace strikes to express their discontent with the government's economic and political concessions. Whereas the Danish Employers Association cataloged only 421 firm-strike days in 1940, nearly 29,549 occurred in the first seven months of 1943.[63]

The final wave of political opposition commenced on July 28, when saboteurs damaged a German minelayer in an Odense shipyard. When German troops occupied the yard the following day, workers refused to man their stations.[64] They staged a sit-down strike that was picked up by other businesses throughout Odense over the next several days. By the end of the week, roughly 3,500 Odense workers were protesting in solidarity with the shipyard. Desperate for work to resume, the German troops withdrew. News of the successful strike spread throughout Denmark.

Attempting to discourage additional protests, Ambassador Best directed the Danish cabinet to approve the extradition of all Danish political prisoners who faced sentences exceeding eight years. He reasoned that if incarceration within Denmark was an insufficient threat, Germany could deter civil disobedience by raising the stakes. Unfortunately for Best, the Copenhagen government refused the request, arguing that a new judicial concession would merely inflame public unrest.[65] By this stage, the cabinet recognized that their constituents would tolerate no further cooperation with Germany and that the political cost of effort exceeded the punishment Germany could impose for recalcitrance. Desperate to save face with the Danish people, Scavenius attempted to resign as prime minister so that a more "representative" government could form, but Best rejected the offer and insisted that Berlin's chosen proxy remain in power.[66]

On August 6, saboteurs in Esbjerg set fire to one hundred thousand wooden fish crates, triggering a conflagration that consumed a nearby train station. The fishermen, factory workers, and all public-sector employees—including firefighters and police—stopped work and closed their doors.[67] The German military attempted to impose a curfew, but citizens flooded the streets, where they clashed with troops. In a ham-fisted move, the Germans offered to repeal their curfew if the townspeople returned to work, thereby furthering the perception that protests could succeed in eliciting German concessions.[68]

A second round of strikes soon erupted in Odense, but this time additional German troops were dispatched to control the situation. Between August 16 and 17, a dozen citizens were hospitalized in the city after clashes with the German military. News of the strikes soon reached the führer, including the story of a German officer who was overcome by a Danish mob. The incident outraged Hitler, whose image of a model protectorate now lay in tatters. He ordered that the city be assessed a fine of 1 million kroner, and he dispatched one hundred SS officers to Odense.[69] Nevertheless, the strikes continued until August 23.

Crises also emerged in Aalborg. The shipyard and cement workers went on strike, while German military depots and train locomotives were targeted for sabotage.[70] On August 17, Erik Vangsted, a young bank teller and resistance fighter, was killed by a German patrol. Vangsted's funeral seemed poised to act as a focal point for the venting of Danish grievances against Germany. General Hanneken, unwilling to tolerate further public demonstrations, ordered the family to conduct the funeral early on a Monday morning, with attendance capped at fifty participants. Nonetheless, a crowd broke into the church and held an impromptu service in the afternoon. That evening Hanneken deployed tanks to the city. His soldiers wounded twenty-three Danish citizens, killing two.[71] Another four were killed and fifteen injured the following day when news arrived of a bombing in Copenhagen. A team of saboteurs successfully destroyed the Forum, the capital's largest public hall and a newly converted barracks for two thousand German troops.[72] For Berlin, the bombing was the last straw.

Hitler had harbored doubts about Denmark's value as an agent ever since the Danish government had refused the order to extradite political prisoners. With the destruction of the Forum, the führer lost what little confidence he had left. Without an agent he could trust to follow orders and ensure security, indirect control was impractical and Germany was forced to quell disturbances in Denmark directly. Three days later, Ribbentrop dispatched Best to deliver a deliberately unacceptable ultimatum to the Danish government. He instructed the Danes to forbid assemblies of more than five people, outlaw strikes, institute a nationwide curfew, ban the harassment of Germans or German associates, allow direct German press censorship, create a new system of harsher courts for the prosecution of rioters, and adopt the death penalty for sabotage or resistance activity.[73] On August 28, cabinet members resoundingly rejected the demands and tendered their resignations.

The Germans responded by declaring martial law. They began the task of disbanding Parliament, disrupting civilian communication, deporting prisoners, and disarming the military.[74] The Wehrmacht placed the Danish Army under arrest, seized remaining supplies, and occupied the country's military infrastructure.[75] The Danish Navy successfully scuttled most of its fleet—with a few ships escaping to Sweden—before the Germans could capture the vessels. Germany also took as temporary hostages 250 prominent Danish politicians and cultural leaders, some of whom were held for several months until Germany was satisfied that the country was under control.[76] The proxy relationship between Berlin and Copenhagen was officially over.

September 1943–May 1945: Direct Control

From August 28, 1943, until the end of the war, an official Danish government no longer existed. However, shortly before he was placed under house arrest, King Christian X asked the heads of his government ministries to continue operating their departments. The task of maintaining the machinery of the state was left to civil service officers and individual bureaucrats, each of whom managed his own office under German direction. The administrators could no longer coordinate with each other to negotiate around German policies, but they nevertheless retained some capacity for individual resistance. Even under close German supervision, Danish bureaucrats successfully smuggled millions of kroner out of Danish coffers and into the arms of a resistance movement that enjoyed widespread public support.[77]

From the Danish perspective, the most important result of the break in relations was that it improved Denmark's stature in the eyes of the Allies. The widespread strikes, the sinking of the Danish Navy, the collapse of government negotiations, and the continuation of active resistance sent a clear message that the Danish people were no longer allied with Germany, regardless of what their actions over the previous three years implied. In response, the British increased SOE supply drops to support the resistance movement. Prior to August 1943, shipments from the Allies were a rare gift, but in the final two years of the war, British planes delivered more than a thousand tons of weapons, explosives, and communications equipment to the Danish underground.[78]

With the help of the shipments, the resistance movement expanded even further, creating a state of open warfare with Germany. Bopa carried out nearly four hundred attacks in 1944 and 1945, while resistance elsewhere in the country conducted more than eight thousand acts of sabotage against the Danish railway network. Along with 119 deliberate derailments, at least thirty-one bridges, fifty-eight locomotives, and eighteen water towers were destroyed. Directly suppressing disturbances had become deeply burdensome and resource intensive for the Reich. During the winter of 1944–45, Germany was forced to deploy sentries at intervals of fifty to seventy-five meters along the track, and battalions of Gestapo were dispatched to a country that had previously been monitored by a small contingent of ordinary diplomats.[79] When even these efforts failed, Germany initiated a policy of reciprocal punishments: for each German or Nazi collaborator killed by the resistance movement, the Gestapo retaliated by executing a prominent Dane. In response to the railway attacks, Best authorized the bombing of several crowded passenger trams.[80]

The Nazis made one final attempt to maintain control. After another round of general strikes in late 1944—and rumors that the police would join the Allies in the event of invasion—the Germans disarmed, imprisoned, and deported roughly two thousand Danish police to concentration camps.[81] Thousands of additional police fled underground and in many cases joined with the resistance. In their place, the Gestapo hired volunteers from the Eastern Front who were tasked with forcing the population into submission with retributive attacks. The Hipokorpset, as the group was known, conducted indiscriminate attacks designed to discourage further resistance. They shot random Danes in the street, destroyed occupied buildings, and tortured resistance fighters.[82] Nevertheless, retribution killings of Nazi officials increased. Resistance fighters liquidated 177 suspected Nazis and German sympathizers in the final four months of the occupation.[83]

Germany itself suffered as the war closed. The Gestapo no longer possessed the personnel necessary to maintain order, and even the leadership was in a state of disarray. In January 1945, General Hanneken was court-martialed for corruption. He was replaced by Gen. Georg Lindemann, who oversaw the execution of sixty-five imprisoned resistance fighters between March and April.[84] Lindemann's tenure, however, was short lived, and Denmark was liberated by the British in early May, putting an end to the occupation just over five years after it began.

Alternative Explanations

Why did the Danish relationship with Germany ultimately collapse? I argue that as the political cost of complying with German demands increased, the Danish cabinet grew less responsive to German threats. Eventually, even the prospect of German-imposed regime change paled in comparison to the political penalties that Danish voters and Allied states threatened to impose after the war. The Danish government, concerned about its reputation, changed course and became much more resistant to German coercion. Finding itself without a reliable agent, Germany abandoned its strategy of indirect control and instead chose to administer Denmark itself.

Despite the allure of this explanation, alternative possibilities merit discussion. First, some may assert that the Danish-German relationship was never as cooperative as I contend in this chapter. After all, Germany frequently employed coercive threats, and the magnitude of those threats increased over the course of the relationship. Why would a principal require such instruments if its agent were reasonably compliant? The theory outlined in the introduction provides an important answer to this question. The existence of threats and punishments does not imply that a proxy relationship is unsuccessful. Rather, in a well-functioning proxy relationship the principal should use whichever tools are at its disposal to induce the level of effort it desires from the agent. Coercion is a useful policy tool that we should expect principals to use even in productive and cooperative agency relationships. As evidence of such behavior, note that Germany consistently leveraged the largest possible threats that it could credibly impose. At the beginning of the war, Hitler eagerly sought the appearance of peaceful cooperation. As such, German threats were relatively small and Hitler even offered Denmark territorial rewards to induce cooperation. However, the propaganda value of a model protectorate evaporated as European countries sided against Germany. When the German cost of imposing punishment declined, marginally larger threats became credible. Germany then put these threats to good use by requesting higher levels of effort from its agent.

Another possibility is that the German-Danish relationship was undermined by the continual ratcheting up of German demands. In this view, Germany mismanaged the relationship by expanding the range of tasks that it assigned Denmark. Because the Danes' marginal cost of effort increased with each successive demand, the Danish government eventually lacked the capacity to fulfill German requests even though it was fully motivated to act on them. On its face, this explanation is tempting. German expectations for Denmark no doubt expanded over the course of the relationship. However, the historical record also suggests a swing in Danish preferences independent of the expansion of German demands. Early in the occupation, the Danes agreed to various large sovereignty violations with minimal overt pressure from Germany. In 1941, Copenhagen agreed to transfer its torpedo boats and military equipment to the Wehrmacht before an explicit threat was issued. In 1942, the government accepted Scavenius as prime minister in hopes of repairing its relationship with Germany. However, when widespread strikes signaled overwhelming public opposition to cooperation, the Danish cabinet abandoned all effort to comply with German demands and voluntarily resigned. Although it was surely within the government's power to extradite political criminals to Germany, to order local police and military forces to suppress violence, or to appeal to citizens to return to work, the government refrained from even feigning such efforts. The relationship ended not because German expectations escalated beyond the bounds of what Denmark could achieve or because Germany assigned Denmark new and increasingly costly tasks, but because the appearance of even mild cooperation became politically toxic to the Danish government.

Similarly, it is tempting to conclude that Germany erred by failing to consider how its demands might antagonize the civilian population. In this reading, German threats and demands inspired resentment among Danish citizens, thereby directly eroding public support for collaboration and increasing the Danish government's cost of effort. If this is true, then the rise in the Danish cost of effort was not driven solely by external factors but was instead an unintended consequence of attempting coercion. However, the evidence suggests that the Germans were acutely attuned to the possibility that the concessions they requested might alienate the Danish citizenry. They initially sought to insulate the Danish economy as much as possible and in several cases declined to force issues that the Danish government warned would undermine public support for collaboration. In addition, although Germany might have fostered friendlier relations or built sympathy among Danish citizens by dispersing aid or economic support, the Reich's financial resources were severely constrained. As such, it suffered a forced choice between using its remaining instrument, punishment, or failing to motivate its agent altogether. All told, the swing in Danish public opinion against Germany resulted more from changing external conditions than from a strategic failure on behalf of Germany itself.

Proxy relationships can also end when a principal is no longer sensitive to the costs of disturbances and so has little interest in subsidizing an agent's effort to suppress them. This explanation, however, runs deeply counter to the historical record in the German-Danish case. As German fortunes in the broader war declined, the Reich could scarcely afford to tolerate disruptions in supplies from Denmark, or attacks against personnel located there. Nor did it wish to divert significant resources from other important areas in order to occupy its northern neighbor.[85] If an appropriate and pliable agent existed, Berlin would have strongly preferred to operate indirectly—indeed, the Germans declined Scavenius's offer of resignation in hopes that they could extend his agency at least temporarily. The fact that Germany exerted genuine effort to suppress violence immediately after assuming direct control of Denmark also suggests that it remained sensitive to disturbances. Collectively, these facts suggest that Germany severed its relationship with Denmark not because its desire for an agency relationship had diminished, but rather because it no longer viewed Denmark as a reliable partner.

Finally, the episode presents one curiosity that our theoretical framework does not directly address. The indirect control model assumes that the actors responsible for causing disturbances—in this case, the violent "sabotage" groups within Denmark—are nonstrategic. However, it is also possible that these actors intentionally modulate their efforts in order to influence the principal's behavior. As the introduction explains, a principal can only estimate a proxy's effort by observing the number and intensity of the disturbances that occur. If the level of those disturbances can systematically change due to fluctuations in the belligerent group's behavior rather than because of shifts in the proxy government's level of effort, the principal may face greater difficulty appraising the agent's performance and may therefore be less inclined to pursue indirect control. Indeed, several members of the Danish underground recall that they sought to vary the intensity and appearance of their operations in hopes of spoiling relations between the Danish and German governments. Perhaps the most striking claim was made by the Holger Danske member Jens Lillelund, who reported that his fellow saboteurs "wanted to achieve what we called 'Norwegian conditions,' with positively no cooperation with the Germans. . . . It occurred to us that if we blew [the Copenhagen Forum] up the Germans would be so angry that they would make demands which the government would simply have to reject. . . . In fact, that is just what happened."[86] Although there are good reasons to treat such anecdotes skeptically,[87] future research should investigate how domestic insurgents strategically respond to the existence of proxy relationships and whether such behavior poses additional challenges for principals who attempt indirect control.

The German occupation of Denmark is an ideal case for the indirect control model. The example is especially useful because it avoids three factors that might otherwise complicate the analysis. First, unlike several other cases in this volume, Germany occupied Denmark throughout the entire period under examination. The example therefore allows us to set aside the issue of monitoring: although Nazi officials could never determine precisely what level of effort their Danish proxies exerted, the principal's monitoring capacity was roughly constant over the duration of the relationship. Second, Germany assumed control over an industrialized nation equipped with deeply democratic institutions, a well-functioning police force, and respect for the rule of law. The Reich was therefore never required to invest in capacity building; when Germany ordered Denmark to suppress domestic disturbances and political protests, it could reasonably assume that the Danish cabinet was equipped to execute such tasks. Finally, as an occupying power, Germany could credibly, and at relatively low cost, impose punishment on Denmark. The case therefore allows us to bypass the complex question of whether the principal could more efficiently offer rewards or impose punishments on the agent government.

Within these bounds, the observed behavior closely adheres to the predictions of the theory laid out in the introduction. When the cost of punishing Denmark was high, Germany offered rewards in the form of a territorial concession over Northern Schleswig. As the cost of imposing punishment declined, Germany shifted to threats to extract high effort from its agent. Likewise, when Danish recalcitrance increased, the Germans raised the stakes of noncompliance. They first threatened to dissolve the Danish cabinet when Denmark refused to sign the Anti-Comintern Pact. The following year, they suspended relations during the Telegram Crisis, thereby sending a credible signal that their threats were genuine.

Germany also attempted to replace uncooperative agents with its preferred candidates. It began by naming a state prosecutor and then promoted him to minister of justice. Similarly, the Germans demanded that their political opponents resign from cabinet-level positions and then required those officials to withdraw from Parliament or even from public life entirely. Finally, they appointed Scavenius as foreign minister and then pressured the Danes to accept him as head of government. Once its preferred agent was in control, Berlin was unwilling to suffer his removal and declined to accept Scavenius's resignation in the summer of 1943.

Most important, the case depicts a proxy relationship that succeeded for years, but which nevertheless eventually collapsed when the agent's cost of effort grew excessively high. Early in the relationship, Danish citizens tolerated their government's cooperation with Germany. However, as the occupation endured, the public grew less sympathetic. Eventually the cabinet faced overwhelming domestic opposition to additional concessions. Although Germany promised to dissolve the government or imprison Danish cabinet members if disturbances continued, even these extreme threats fell on deaf ears: the political price that Denmark faced for complying with German demands exceeded any costs that the Reich could credibly impose. Without a reliable agent at its disposal, Germany recognized that the costs of indirect control exceeded the potential benefits. It therefore chose to terminate its relationship with Danish proxies and to instead shoulder the full burden of governing Denmark directly.

NOTES

1. The German Foreign Ministry had an additional interest in pursuing indirect control. Because most European states either severed diplomatic ties with Germany or fell under German military control, Denmark was one of the few countries with which the ministry could directly interact. Moreover, the policy of "negotiation" created a unique opportunity for the ministry to exercise authority. German foreign minister Joachim von Ribbentrop therefore hoped to delay the establishment of a military protectorate for as long as possible (Dethlefsen 1996, 33).

2. Thomas 1976.

3. Quoted in Yahil 1969, 33.

4. Haestrup 1976.

5. Maier 2007.

6. Thomas 1976.

7. Quoted in Dethlefsen 1996, 29.

8. Thomas 1976.

9. Dethlefsen 1996, 32.

10. Collaboration also created opportunities for political entrepreneurs. Subservience to Germany provided politicians with a useful scapegoat for unpopular policies and also

eliminated potential opponents. Few members of the parliamentary majority protested when, in the summer of 1941, Germany ordered the arrest of the few Communist representatives who acted as the political opposition in the assembly (Hollander 2016, 50–52).

11. Mazower 2009, 104.

12. Scavenius notably allowed the Germans to mine the Danish narrows in the prelude to World War I (Lambert 2010, 58). Once the conflict was underway he opposed defense buildups that he feared would be perceived as anti-German (Clemmesen 2010, 178).

13. Thomas 1976.

14. Quoted in Hong 2012, 37–38. Scavenius later claimed the message was an attempt to establish goodwill with Berlin and to forestall additional demands, but it permanently altered the opinion of Danish citizens, who henceforth viewed Scavenius as the personification of German collaboration (Haestrup 1976).

15. Thomas 1976.

16. Dethlefsen 1996, 35.

17. Hong 2012.

18. Hollander 2006.

19. Hong 2012, 47.

20. An exception occurred when Vilhelm la Cour was caught circulating deeply anti-German lectures. La Cour was initially sentenced to eighty days in prison, but the Danish Supreme Court increased the sentence to eight months at Berlin's insistence, then kept la Cour under surveillance after release to prevent him from further provoking the Nazis.

21. Abrahamsen 1987, 9.

22. Jews continued to attend religious services and to print religious fliers without significant fear of prosecution until the Germans disbanded the Danish government in September 1943.

23. Haestrup 1976.

24. Quoted in Hong 2012, 69.

25. Yahil (1969, 46) argues that the Danes arrested many of the Communists in order to prevent their capture and deportation by the German military. However, others note that Communist MPs were the legislative opponents of the governing Danish coalition. As such, the arrest of the Communists—carried out with remarkable alacrity—may have served the political interests of the Danish cabinet (see, for example, Hollander 2013).

26. Hollander 2006.

27. Hong 2012.

28. Haestrup 1976.

29. Hong 2012.

30. Ibid.

31. These numbers increased late in the war as German sympathizers joined the Wehrmacht to flee the country and evade liquidation by Danish resistance groups (Christensen, Poulsen, and Smith 1997, 65).

32. Quoted in Hong 2012, 83.

33. Hong 2012.

34. Personnel were still allowed to resign voluntarily from the Danish military to join Frikorps Danmark.

35. Quoted in Jespersen 2002, 38.

36. Thomas 1976.

37. Giltner 2001. At the start of the occupation, German general Leonhard Kaupisch warned that Germany might wind up with "a few million useless and unhappy foreigners to feed" if it was not careful (quoted in Hong 2012, 40).

38. Mazower 2009, 277.

39. Lejenäs 1989.

40. Hong 2012. Nevertheless, conditions in Denmark remained comfortable relative to those in other occupied or war-afflicted states (Mazower 2009).

41. Thomas 1976.

42. Hong 2012, 113.

43. Hollander 2016, 55.

44. Hong 2012.

45. Thomas 1976.

46. Hong 2012.

47. Thomas 1976.

48. Hong 2012.

49. Thomas 1976.

50. Haestrup 1976.

51. The cabinet did manage to prevent the installation of several Danish Nazis to ministerial positions (Haestrup 1976).

52. Hollander 2016, 55.

53. Thomas 1976.

54. Quoted in Paulsson 1995, 444.

55. Dethlefsen 1990, 204.

56. Quoted in Hollander 2016, 56. The British underlined their threat with air strikes against Danish industrial targets. The bombings—particularly one targeted at the Burmeister and Wain shipyard—inspired a surge in Danish support for the resistance movement as Danish citizens realized that sabotage attacks were less likely to result in collateral damage than aerial bombardments (Thomas 1976).

57. Thomas 1976.

58. Quoted in Hollander 2016, 51.

59. Quoted in Hong 2012, 155.

60. Quoted in Paulsson 1995, 446.

61. Hong 2012.

62. Thomas 1976.

63. Hong 2012, 173.

64. Thomas 1976.

65. Hong 2012.

66. Ibid.

67. Thomas 1976.

68. Hong 2012.

69. Thomas 1976.

70. Hong 2012.

71. Ibid.

72. Thomas 1976.

73. Haestrup 1976; Hong 2012.

74. Thomas 1976.

75. Maier 2007.

76. Hong 2012.

77. Thomas 1976.

78. Ibid.

79. Thomas 1976; Hollander 2006, 131.

80. Paulsson 1995.

81. Ibid.

82. Maier 2007.

83. Hong 2012.

84. Ibid.

85. Until late 1943, Germany consistently sought to minimize the resources it was forced to allocate in Denmark. Whereas German administration of Norway required roughly three thousand personnel, the monitoring of Denmark was accomplished by a force of fewer than two hundred Germans (Hollander 2016, 49). The ratios of German officials to local administrators were similarly skewed, at 1:43,000 in Denmark and 1:3,700 in Norway (Mazower 2009, 238).

86. Quoted in Thomas 1976, 193–94.

87. These recollections may simply depict post hoc strategizing or self-aggrandizement by individual saboteurs. There is little supporting evidence that resistance groups deliberately eschewed or delayed especially dramatic operations in order to influence the German-Danish relationship. Appearances suggest that saboteurs consistently sought to conduct the highest-magnitude attacks that they could feasibly accomplish. To the extent that resistance fighters sometimes temporarily avoided dramatic operations, they did so primarily because they lacked resources or because such attacks were considered high risk for the persons involved.

3

COLOMBIA, 1990–2010

Cooperation in the War on Drugs

Abigail Vaughn

The U.S. "War on Drugs" in Colombia demonstrates the benefits of pursuing indirect control rather than direct action. Using a combination of rewards, punishments, and capacity improvements in Colombia, the United States managed to slightly suppress cocaine production and reduce Colombian instability to lower levels than would have been feasible in the absence of a proxy relationship. However, the effort to reduce cocaine production and narcotics trafficking also required significant U.S. investments. Colombia is today the fifth-largest recipient of American military aid, and the United States has delivered tens of billions of dollars to the country over the past two decades.[1] How can a series of tremendously expensive policies that produced few obvious successes nevertheless represent efficient and desirable action on behalf of the United States?

To answer this question, this chapter examines U.S. efforts to reduce cocaine production and establish regional security in Colombia across four Colombian presidencies: those of César Gaviria (1990–94), Ernesto Samper (1994–98), Andrés Pastrana (1998–2002), and Álvaro Uribe (2002–10). I leverage variation in the degree of each president's interest alignment with the United States to observe how optimal agency contracts change with the agent's cost of effort.[2] The results support the predictions of the indirect control model. When the interests of Colombia and the United States were closely aligned, the United States either sought to build Colombian capacity or offered an informal contract of rewards and punishments conditional on the level of observed disturbances. Likewise, when the two states' interests diverged, the United States sought to further induce Colombian cooperation by using more powerful incentives. Most important, by

adjusting its coercive tools to reflect each Colombian president's level of interest alignment, the United States was able to better achieve its objectives relative
to what it might have accomplished through the alternative strategies of direct
control or disengagement.

Background

American interest in the narcotics trade ignited in 1971 when President Richard Nixon declared a war on drugs to address rising rates of heroin use. By the
mid-1980s, attention had shifted to a new threat: cocaine.[3] Wrapped in the
broader narrative of the culture war, national news media fueled Americans'
interest in the fight against narcotics. *Time* magazine cover artwork featured
martini glasses overflowing with white powder under taglines such as "the bloody
business of cocaine wars" and dire warnings about "crack kids."[4] According to a
1988 poll conducted by CBS News and the *New York Times*, 48 percent of Americans viewed drugs as the principal foreign policy challenge facing the United
States.[5] Sensitive to domestic interest in the issue, politicians were desperate to
avoid appearing weak or even flexible on drug policy.[6] The U.S. Congress quickly
imposed draconian sentences for drug-related crimes. President Ronald Reagan
similarly signaled his commitment to the war on drugs with National Security
Directive 221, which labeled drug trafficking a threat to national security and
sought to eliminate the supply of cocaine that entered the country.[7]

The war on drugs became increasingly international under President George
H. W. Bush. Whereas previous counternarcotics policies focused primarily on
interdiction at U.S. ports, as early as his 1988 campaign Bush argued that "the
cheapest way to eradicate narcotics is to destroy them at their source."[8] After
assuming office, Bush marshaled resources against the international suppliers
of cocaine. In late 1989, the National Defense Authorization Act empowered the
Pentagon to engage in counternarcotics operations for the first time.[9] In September of that year, the president also unveiled his "Andean Strategy," a five-year,
$2.1 billion package of military, economic, law-enforcement, and U.S. Drug
Enforcement Administration (DEA) assistance directed toward the three largest
producers of cocaine: Bolivia, Peru, and Colombia.[10]

At the beginning of the 1990s, Colombia served primarily as a processing
and smuggling hub for Peruvian and Bolivian cocaine. However, production
in the country soon escalated. Although the United States faced difficulty measuring the precise amount of cocaine that each country produced, government
officials were able to estimate the metric tonnage of production using data on
hectares of land under cultivation, coca leaf yields, and the coca-leaf-to-cocaine

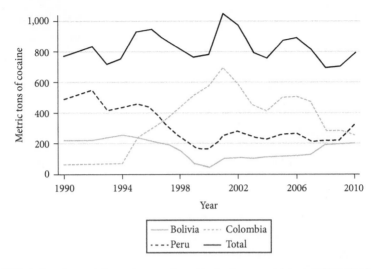

FIGURE 3.1. Potential cocaine produced in Andean countries, 1990–2010. Potential cocaine production is estimated by multiplying the hectares of coca cultivation with the average kilogram-per-hectare coca leaf yield figure and coca-leaf-to-cocaine transformation ratios. Data from U.S. Department of State, various years; UNODC 2007, 2010, 2013

transformation process.[11] Figure 3.1 shows the potential cocaine production of each Andean country between 1990 and 2010.[12]

Three distinct factors precipitated the substantial increase in Colombian coca cultivation during this time period. First, smugglers faced rising transit costs for the importation of coca into Colombia for processing. The U.S. air bridge denial program, a component of Bush's Andean Strategy, put pressure on aerial smugglers.[13] Unable to bring sufficient Peruvian coca into Colombia for processing, the cartels instead made Putumayo, a state in Colombia's southern region, the new epicenter of coca cultivation.[14]

Around the same time, several prominent cartel kingpins and officers were captured or killed. The resulting changes in leadership spurred the creation of loosely organized "baby" cartels that splintered from their predecessors. Without the coordination provided by the kingpins and their established relationships with foreign coca suppliers, the new cartels sought to vertically integrate their operations within Colombia, a move that exacerbated demand for domestic coca cultivation. Although the new cartels were less powerful than the organizations they replaced, the fragmentation of existing networks created new challenges for counternarcotics officers, who struggled to acquire targeting information on cartel leaders. Violence also increased as rival groups competed to fill the power vacuum and to obtain larger shares of the narcotics market.[15]

The final change that triggered a rise in Colombian cocaine production in the 1990s was increased collaboration between armed groups and drug traffickers. While multiple insurgent groups emerged following the Colombian civil war in the 1950s, many were quickly eliminated as the national government consolidated power.[16] Two exceptions were the guerrilla group Fuerzas Armada Revoluionarios de Colombia (FARC) and, to a lesser extent, the Ejécito de Liberación (ELN), which persisted and expanded their jurisdictions.[17] FARC initially taxed marijuana and cocaine traffickers, but in the 1990s it began to charge coca producers a tax in exchange for protection from government interference.[18] Because most coca cultivation occurred in areas that historically had been FARC strongholds, as coca production expanded so too did FARC's tax revenue. By the end of the 1990s, FARC resources had grown so much that the group was able to quadruple its forces and gain additional territory for coca production.[19] As a result, by 1997 Colombia had surpassed Bolivia and Peru as the primary supplier of the world's cocaine.[20]

In addition to the rise in coca cultivation, another major change in Colombia bears mention. Throughout the 1990s, conflict mounted between insurgents and paramilitary groups, and eventually the level of violence threatened to undermine the stability of the Colombian state. Paramilitaries originally emerged in opposition to FARC, the ELN, and violence perpetrated by the Medellín cartel.[21] However, by the mid-1990s, an estimated 70 percent of paramilitary finances were related to the drug trade.[22] The largest and most well-known paramilitary was the Autodefensas Unidas de Colombia (AUC), which by 2002 had established thirty-two blocks across the country.[23] As paramilitaries and insurgent groups grew and competed for power, they wreaked havoc on each other and on the government of Colombia in two ways. First, ongoing violence directly threatened the security of the state. Second, the presence of armed groups protecting coca growers greatly increased the cost to Colombia of suppressing cocaine production.

Finally, while cocaine production remained a concern for the United States, the rise in violence also drew U.S. attention to the threat of instability. Figure 3.2 illustrates how threats to Colombian security, measured by the number of kidnappings, selective killings, and massacres, varied over time. In 1999, following a dramatic rise in Colombian violence over the preceding half decade, the United States placed FARC, the ELN, and the AUC on its list of foreign terrorist organizations. U.S. concern about insurgent groups further increased after 9/11 as policymakers in Washington came to terms with the destabilizing abilities of violent groups. Collectively, the changes in cartel organization, cocaine production, and armed groups resulted in greater U.S. policy attention to both coca cultivation and the security apparatus of Colombia over the time period covered in this chapter.

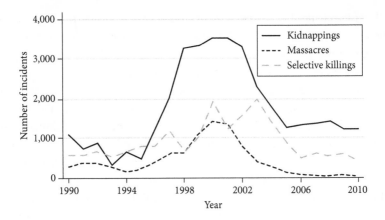

FIGURE 3.2.   Threats to Colombian security, 1990–2010. Data from Centro Nacional de Memoria Histórica, Bases de datos ¡Basta Ya! ¡Basta Ya! Colombia: Memorias De Guerra y Dignidad, http://www.centrodememoriahistorica.gov.co/micrositios/informeGeneral/basesDatos.html

The Principal-Proxy Relationship

To achieve its counternarcotics objectives, the United States contracted with the Colombian president to suppress coca-related activity. As the longest-running democracy in South America, Colombia was a natural ally to the United States.[24] The Colombian president was also uniquely situated to eliminate cocaine production: he controlled the police and military and could impose legal reforms that reinforced direct suppression efforts. Finally, Colombia's intimate knowledge of the terrain and local population made it more efficient for the United States to engage a proxy, rather than attempt to combat the narcotics trade unilaterally.

While the rationale for the United States' preference for a proxy relationship is clear, why would Colombia participate? As Arlene Tickner argues, "For the Colombian government, the interest was born out of a need to combat an insurgency."[25] Colombian politicians feared that continued violence from guerrillas and cartels could permanently undermine the state's legitimacy. Whereas the narcotics trade was initially tolerable—indeed, some Colombian officials actually supported cocaine production on the belief that the associated revenue would strengthen the country's faltering economy—insurgent violence posed a genuine threat to the government's survival. As narco-traffickers and insurgents forged new ties and violence levels spiked, the interests of Colombia and the United States rapidly converged.

We can estimate the effectiveness of the U.S.-Colombian proxy relationship based on the extent to which Colombia complied with U.S. demands. Two counternarcotics metrics are particularly important. The first relates to Colombian attempts to suppress coca cultivation via manual removal and aerial eradication. Figure 3.3 tracks both these measures over time.

The second metric focuses on Colombia's effort to remove processed cocaine and traffickers from circulation. The United States monitored cocaine seized through interdiction, the number of processing labs destroyed, and the strength of Colombian law enforcement at arresting traffickers, enforcing sentences, and complying with U.S. extradition requests. Figure 3.4 shows the annual metric tons of cocaine that were seized, relative to coca production.[26]

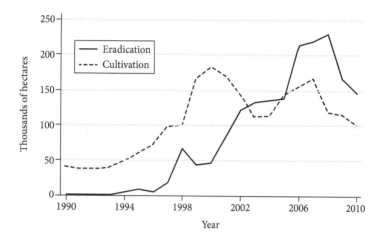

FIGURE 3.3.   Colombian coca eradication and cultivation, 1990–2010. Data from U.S. Department of State, various years; UNODC 2007, 2010, 2013

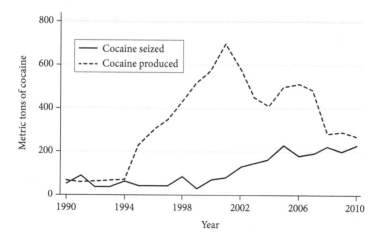

FIGURE 3.4.   Colombian cocaine production and seizure, 1990–2010. Data from U.S. Department of State, various years; UNODC 2007, 2010, 2013

The United States, in a situation distinct from many of the other case studies in this volume, enjoyed relatively high visibility into Colombian efforts. The DEA and Department of State's physical presence in Colombia permitted the United States to monitor Colombia's antidrug efforts with high accuracy. American monitoring capability peaked under Plan Colombia, a large U.S.-led counternarcotics initiative and foreign aid package, when additional U.S. personnel were stationed in Colombia and the United States exerted increased control over counternarcotics operations. Despite this monitoring capability, the case still involved uncertainty for the principal because the United States was unable to observe the cost of effort that each Colombian president faced when pursuing U.S. objectives. Moreover, several Colombian presidents had incentives to exaggerate these costs so that U.S. policymakers would demand less effort than they would if they assumed Colombia could control disturbances with relative ease.

Colombia's costs of effort took two forms. The first was the direct cost that the government paid to suppress disturbances and fund counternarcotics forces. The second was the political cost that each Colombian administration faced for pursuing policies that conflicted with the desires of its selectorate or that would provoke the ire of the drug cartels, increasing the incidence of violence targeting Colombian citizens. Despite a series of political reforms in the 1980s and 1990s, corruption persisted, and drug cartels were often able to coerce politicians through bribes or violent threats. Citizens also pressured Colombian presidents through traditional political avenues, and would protest against the incumbent government when cartels or armed insurgent groups engaged in civilian-directed violence in response to government policies. Finally, civilians whose livelihood suffered as a result of aerial fumigation also directed protests at Colombian presidents. The extent and type of effort cost that each Colombian president faced played a significant role in determining the degree of counternarcotics policy alignment between the United States and Colombia.

U.S. policymakers relied on a variety of tools to induce Colombian cooperation when they believed interest alignment was low. The United States could reward Colombia by providing economic assistance or diplomatic awards when Colombia demonstrated sufficient effort. Economic aid could also be reallocated in a manner that would benefit Colombian leaders. Economic Support Funds (ESF) were often used for infrastructure and development projects. International Military Education and Training (IMET) funds were similarly used as rewards because they paid for professional military education and training on U.S. weapons systems. Colombian leaders sometimes dispensed resources as patronage by offering their friends and political allies free trips to the United States.[27] Other forms of military aid, however, were primarily designed to build

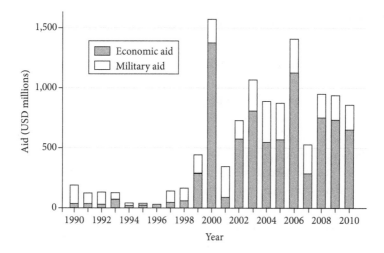

FIGURE 3.5.   U.S. aid to Colombia, 1990–2010. Data from USAID, U.S. Overseas Loans and Grants: Obligations and Loan Authorizations July 1, 1945–September 30, 2014

Colombian capacity, enhance Colombian security, and provide the resources necessary to professionalize the Colombian military. Figure 3.5 shows the proportion of U.S. military and economic assistance given to Colombia each year from 1990 to 2010.

However, most nonmilitary aid to Colombia required annual certification and could be suspended if the United States decided that Colombia was no longer fully cooperative.[28] The certification process provided the United States with a straightforward means of imposing punishment. Threats to suspend aid were also credible given the intense domestic pressure that American presidents faced to crack down on drug-producing countries. If decertification occurred, the United States would impose mandatory sanctions as well as a series of discretionary penalties. Mandatory sanctions included the termination of most forms of foreign assistance and bilateral loans, as well as a U.S. vote against loan requests in multilateral development banks.[29] Discretionary punishments included the loss of trade preference status, the suspension of sugar quotas, tariff penalties, and the curtailment of transportation arrangements.[30] These penalties created further economic hardships for Colombian leaders and, when imposed, delivered a clear signal that the United States sought to impose costs on Colombia's president. Diplomatic rewards and punishments were essentially costless for the United States to impose, but were highly visible and could engender either international pride or embarrassment.

Theoretical Expectations

This case examines four distinct periods of U.S.-Colombian relations, which coincide with Colombian presidential terms. A key source of variation between periods is the degree of interest alignment between the principal and agent and, thus, the agent's cost of effort. Applying the model's logic, at the commencement of each presidential term, the United States estimated Colombia's interest alignment and then offered Colombia a schedule of incentives and punishments that the United States promised to fulfill, contingent on Colombian effort.[31] The United States enforced these terms until it either obtained new information about the agent—in which case the United States could alter the terms—or a new Colombian president was elected.

The model makes several predictions that are relevant to this case. First, when the United States—the principal—believes the Colombian agent has closely aligned interests, it should seek to build capacity in order to reduce the agent's costs of effort. For example, Presidents Pastrana and Uribe both held preferences that were closely aligned with those of the United States; however, both presidents also faced difficulty suppressing disturbances due to very direct high costs of effort. The theory predicts that the United States should attempt to help Colombia build capacity during these periods (H_{12}). On the other hand, Presidents Gaviria and Samper held preferences that diverged substantially from those of the United States. The indirect control model predicts that no capacity building should be evident during these terms.

Second, the model predicts that when new Colombian presidents face higher costs of effort than the leaders they replace, the United States must either accept lower effort from the new agent or use higher-powered incentives to extract the same level of effort (H_7). When the United States uses higher-powered incentives, the Colombian president should be more likely to exert effort to suppress the disturbance (H_6). While the incentives used may be either punishments or rewards, the incentives must be sufficiently large to motivate the agent. The Colombian costs of effort increased gradually throughout the Gaviria, Samper, Pastrana, and early Uribe administrations, before declining slightly in the latter half of Uribe's term. The indirect control model therefore makes two empirical predictions: either the United States should accept lower levels of effort from each successive Colombian administration, or, alternatively, the United States should threaten larger punishments and offer more generous rewards to each new Colombian president to achieve the same level of effort as the predecessor.

Third, the coercive mechanism depends on the observed level of disturbance within a period. When the United States observes high disturbances relative to its expectations, it should be more likely to punish the agent, but when the United States observes low disturbances, it should be more likely to reward the agent

TABLE 3.1 Theoretical expectations and summary results, Colombia

PERIOD (AUGUST)	KEY PARAMETER(S)	THEORETICAL EXPECTATION	OBSERVED ACTION
1990–94	Partial interest alignment; increasing agent's cost of effort; low level of disturbance.	Principal should use low-level rewards after observing zero or small disturbances (H_2).	Principal used low-level rewards and punishments after observing small disturbances.
1994–98	Diverging interest alignment; increasing agent's cost of effort; increasing level of disturbance.	Principal should punish after observing high levels of disturbance (H_3). Principal should use high-powered incentives to account for diverging interest alignment (H_7). Agent should be more likely to exert effort when high-powered incentives are used (H_6).	Principal used more frequent and larger punishments in response to high levels of disturbance. The agent exerted greater effort to suppress the disturbance in response to the higher-powered incentives used.
1998–2002	Increasing interest alignment; increasing agent's cost of effort; increasing level of disturbance.	Principal should punish after observing high levels of disturbance (H_3). Principal should be more likely to engage in direct control and build capacity to reduce agent's cost of effort (H_{12}).	Principal did not engage in direct control or threaten punishments after observing high levels of disturbance because interests were sufficiently aligned. Principal built capacity under Plan Colombia.
2002–10	High interest alignment; decreasing agent's cost of effort; decreasing level of disturbance.	Principal should build capacity (H_{12}) and reward the agent for decreased levels of disturbance (H_3).	Principal rewarded the agent after observing decreased levels of disturbance and the principal continued to build capacity under Plan Colombia.

(H_2, H_3). In the context of this chapter, the United States should be more likely to punish when it concludes that Colombia has failed to exert sufficient effort given U.S. expectations. This is especially evident during Samper's term. Table 3.1 summarizes the expected U.S. incentives for each period given estimated levels of the relevant variables.

Colombia, 1990–2010

Period 1: President César Gaviria (1990–94)

When César Gaviria assumed office in August of 1990, cartel violence was already rising dramatically. From 1989 to 1990, cartels and insurgent groups planted forty car bombs that left more than five hundred civilians dead.[32] An estimated 350 judicial workers, along with hundreds of other officials, reporters, and even presidential candidates, had been murdered by the Medellín cartel in retaliation for antidrug policies such as the extradition of suspected narcotics smugglers.[33] All told, from 1984 to 1989 approximately thirty-one thousand deaths were attributed to drug traffickers.[34] The violence reached its zenith when the presidential favorite Luis Galán was assassinated by drug cartels for appearing friendly with the United States.[35] Given the circumstances, Gaviria staked his 1989 presidential bid on a promise to reduce cartel violence. He campaigned as a hard-line antidrug candidate and made democratic and judicial reform a high priority for his administration.[36]

Before Gaviria assumed office, President George H. W. Bush initiated the Andean Strategy, which provided aid and identified broad policy objectives for the region. While the plan primarily targeted Peru's coca production, it also required Colombia to increase military operations, strengthen its laws against drug traffickers, dismantle drug organizations, arrest key narcotics personnel, and minimize corruption. Judicial reform ranked as a particularly important U.S. objective for Colombia.[37] The United States therefore initially interpreted Gaviria's policy interests as being close to its own, with the notable exception of Gaviria's opposition to extradition, which he assumed would incite rather than reduce violence. A U.S. General Accounting Office (GAO) report stated that "Colombia [was] the most dedicated of the Andean countries to reducing the production and shipment of cocaine."[38]

The United States further assumed that Gaviria's direct cost of effort was also low. After all, members of the Colombian public were clamoring for a security apparatus that would curb the rising violence.[39] This perception, however, does not paint a full picture. Gaviria faced more moderate costs in two respects. First, cartel violence increased substantially in opposition to U.S. political demands. The losses of life and equipment that Colombian security forces incurred made it more difficult for them to conduct antidrug operations. Second, Gaviria faced political opposition to the United States' controversial fumigation policy. Locals resented aerial eradication, which damaged farmers' crops in areas near coca cultivation and destroyed a major source of income for agricultural communities.[40]

Despite the moderate cost of effort that he faced, Gaviria met U.S. demands to reduce the total supply of cocaine. Total Colombian coca cultivation remained relatively low and even decreased in 1991 and 1992. Cocaine seizures—another noisy signal of production—likewise increased from fifty-three to eighty-six metric tons in the first two years of his term, but decreased thereafter (see figure 3.4). Finally, Gaviria made significant progress in destroying processing laboratories, closing 269 in 1990 and 401 in 1993.

Colombian effort in the realm of judicial reform also matched U.S. expectations. In July of 1991, the Colombian Assembly ratified a new constitution that established an independent judiciary and created the Court of Public Order, which provided additional safeguards to protect judges from cartel violence. From January 1991 to September 1992, the Court of Public Order convicted 70 percent of the eight hundred individuals tried for drug- and terrorism-related crimes, whereas under the previous court system the conviction rate was only 12 percent.[41] Shortly afterward, the United States rewarded Colombia with a six-year, $36 million grant based on the Colombian government's demonstrated commitment to reform.[42]

Finally, Gaviria achieved significant public success in combating Pablo Escobar and the Medellín cartel. Although in 1992 Escobar escaped from prison, much to Gaviria's embarrassment and the consternation of the United States, Gaviria responded by forming the Bloque de Búsqueda, a group tasked with locating Escobar. A March 1993 DEA report suggests that the United States was encouraged by Gaviria's effort and that the Colombian police had disrupted many of the Medellín cartel's activities.[43] Finally, in December 1993 the Bloque succeeded in capturing and killing Escobar, providing Gaviria with another visible success.

Despite curbing the reach of cartel money in the judiciary and combating the Medellín cartel, Gaviria's costs of effort inhibited him from wholly fulfilling U.S. demands in other areas. Bending to Congressional pressure, Gaviria began by reducing drug-related sentences by a third and pledging to prevent the extradition of drug traffickers who turned themselves in and confessed to at least one crime.[44] The extradition pledge was heavily favored by the public, who believed that it would decrease cartel influence while still preserving Colombian sovereignty. Public opinion also motivated Gaviria to cooperate with the Colombian Congress on a constitutional amendment that banned the extradition of Colombian citizens. By 1993, the United States was also increasingly concerned that Gaviria was deliberately treating the Cali cartel with a lighter touch than he had used to suppress the Medellín cartel.[45] One reason for the suspicion was that Gaviria had relied on Cali for information regarding Medellín cartel operations.[46] To allay U.S. concerns, the Colombian police conducted a large operation against the Cali cartel in late 1993 that resulted in the seizure of more than $54 million in bank accounts.[47] As a result, the United States concluded that Colombian effort was sufficiently high and that the Gaviria administration had demonstrated its commitment to counternarcotics.[48]

The model outlined in the introduction predicts that if the principal observes small and infrequent disturbances, it should be more likely to reward the agent. During Gaviria's term, the rate of coca cultivation remained low and the amount of pure cocaine produced varied only slightly. The model predicts that U.S. assistance, particularly economic aid, should therefore have increased as a reward for sufficient effort by Gaviria. Such rewards are directly observable in several instances, such as the $36 million grant that followed Gaviria's judicial reforms.[49] The proportion of economic aid also increased during the period, including ESF and IMET funds that Colombian politicians could use to dispense political favors. Most striking, perhaps, was the significant increase in economic assistance in 1993 in the wake of Escobar's death. Thus, although Gaviria's moderate level of effort caused him to reject U.S. demands in some areas, his general success in quelling cocaine production, fighting the Medellín cartel, and enacting judicial reform led the United States to offer moderate rewards in hopes of inducing continued effort from his administration.

Period 2: President Ernesto Samper (1994–98)

U.S. policy goals remained consistent when Ernesto Samper assumed the Colombian presidency. As before, the United States maintained that Colombia should strengthen sentencing for drug traffickers, stem the flow of cocaine, and eliminate corruption within the Colombian government. The United States paid particular attention to the last of these issues, with U.S. ambassador Myles Frechette even commenting that "corruption in Colombia is the greatest single impediment to a successful counternarcotics effort."[50]

Although U.S. interests remained consistent between the Gaviria and Samper administrations, the same cannot be said for those of the two Colombian presidents. While Samper's true policy preferences remain ambiguous, it was widely believed—and reported in the U.S. press—that Samper was receiving Cali cartel money.[51] Samper's cartel ties compromised his will to effectively combat the drug trade and increased the price he paid for complying with U.S. policies.[52] In addition, Samper faced steep direct costs of pursuing counternarcotics policies in the form of widespread cartel violence, which increased during his tenure.[53] Samper therefore needed to balance the threat of possible punishment for failure to achieve U.S. goals with the threat of cartel retaliation if he hewed too closely to U.S. demands.[54]

As coca growers moved into Colombia from Peru and Bolivia, aerial eradication increasingly became the preferred U.S. counternarcotics strategy. The policy was massively unpopular with Colombians, who took to the streets to voice their discontent, further increasing Samper's political cost for compliance.[55] The model predicts that with Samper's heightened costs of effort, the United States would be forced to use higher-magnitude rewards or punishments to induce sufficient effort. In addition, we should expect to observe punishments when disturbances grow especially large during a given period. The following narrative provides evidence that supports these expectations.

Utilizing the same metrics as described earlier, it appears that on some issues Samper exerted moderate effort. For example, during Samper's tenure a greater number of cocaine labs were destroyed than under Gaviria. The amount of coca that was eradicated also increased in 1995, dropped slightly in 1996, and then rebounded significantly in 1997 and 1998 (see figure 3.3). On other issues, however, Samper's performance was mixed: arrests declined during Samper's term, as did the amount of cocaine seized through interdiction until 1998. The dramatic spikes in coca cultivation and cocaine production are the most worrying signals of Samper's willingness to exert effort. Closer analysis of the U.S.-Colombian relationship further reveals that what little effort Samper did contribute was motivated primarily by a series of very large punishments and limited rewards.

Because of Samper's links to the cartels, the United States significantly decreased the amount of assistance it promised to Colombia, from $117.5 million in 1993 to only $34.7 million in 1994.[56] Fearing further reductions, Samper pushed for stricter sentencing laws to assuage U.S. beliefs that he was too soft on drugs.[57] In December 1994, Samper launched Operation Splendor, a controversial fumigation effort in the South. In response to Samper's compliance with U.S. aerial eradication demands, thousands of farmers who earned their livelihoods from coca production protested in the streets and bombed forty thousand barrels of oil coming from Ecuador.[58]

The United States rewarded Colombia for its effort in 1995 by certifying that Colombia could receive additional counternarcotics assistance. Nevertheless, U.S. officials continued to worry that Samper's personal ties to the cartels would discourage him from exerting full effort. Consequently, Colombia was only certified with a national interest waiver, and its promised assistance remained around $32 million.[59] Despite the certification, President Bill Clinton stated that Colombia was not cooperating fully in the drug war and that the political will of the Colombian government to act forcefully against the cartels remained a major concern.[60] As a result, the United States offered only small and infrequent rewards, preferring instead to induce effort by threatening punishment.

The Department of State made these threats explicit by demanding that Colombia achieve four objectives by June 1995 in order to avoid decertification the following year. First, the United States ordered Colombia to meet several aerial eradication targets. In this respect, Colombia exceeded expectations.[61] Second, it required Samper to arrest at least one senior member of the Cali cartel. Once again, Colombia succeeded.[62] Results on the third directive were more mixed. Colombia passed Law 190 in response to U.S. demands for money-laundering legislation. However, the United States viewed the legislation as weak and worried that Colombia would neither implement nor enforce the law.[63] Finally, the United States demanded that Colombia pass tougher sentencing laws for those involved in the narcotics trade. In this respect, Colombia failed entirely. Top Cali cartel leaders received light sentences and several previously captured leaders continued to run their operations from jail.[64] Furthermore, when Samper's campaign treasurer and defense minister were arrested for accepting bribes from the Cali cartel, he attempted to decriminalize that behavior and halted an investigation into his administration.[65] While the threat of punishment induced some compliance from Samper's government, the weak money-laundering legislation and the failure to crack down on the cartels indicated that the United States required even larger punishments if it was to induce higher levels of Colombian cooperation.

In March 1996, the U.S. enforced its threat by declining to certify Colombian compliance with antidrug efforts and suspending most U.S. assistance to Colombia. Citing corruption as a primary concern, U.S. congressman Jesse Helms stated that "no government can be completely committed to obliterating the drug cartels, drug corruption, and drug-related violence, nor effective in the achievement of these goals, if its senior officials owe fealty to drug kingpins."[66]

In response to the punishment, Samper proposed and eventually passed an antinarcotics reform package that included stronger asset forfeiture laws.[67] Samper also appeared to exert effort by publicly advocating for a constitutional amendment that would permit extradition, a salient U.S. objective.[68] However, when U.S. Attorney General Janet Reno demanded that Colombia extradite four Cali cartel leaders in June 1996, Samper reneged on his commitments and ignored the request.[69] Scarcely a month later, the U.S. Senate Foreign Relations Committee heard testimony that Samper had accepted Cali cartel money as payment for his refusal to extradite.[70] Once again, the United States responded with punishment by revoking Samper's visa, a move that embarrassed Samper and apparently chastened him into launching Operation Condor, a new series of aerial spraying operations and cocaine seizures.[71] Although Samper once again faced domestic backlash when thirty thousand farmers protested the aerial eradication program, he permitted U.S. instructor pilots to participate in the program beginning in late October.[72]

Due to Samper's mixed effort in 1996, the United States once again decertified Colombia in 1997. The Department of State justified the decision by explaining that Colombia not only lacked adequate political will but also suffered from rampant corruption and an underfunded judicial system.[73] The United States specified five goals for Colombia to meet if it was to prevent similar decertification in 1998. First, the Colombian government needed to introduce a new, U.S.-preferred herbicide for aerial eradication. In June of 1997, the Colombian government approved this change.[74] Second, the United States ordered Samper to actually implement the extradition amendment that he had advocated and extradite the four Cali kingpins that the United States had requested the previous year. In November, the Colombian Congress partially complied by passing the constitutional amendment to allow extradition but declining to apply it retroactively, a move that protected the Cali leaders.

The United States' third request of 1997 was that Samper implement his laws on asset forfeiture, money laundering, and sentencing. Samper was also ordered to accept a U.S. maritime agreement that would improve interdiction of cocaine by increasing the number of ships that counternarcotics agents could inspect. On February 19, the Colombian Congress passed Samper's antinarcotics reform package, which strengthened penalties for money laundering and moderately increased sentencing. While actual prosecutions remained scarce, Colombian banks strengthened their oversight of unusual deposits. The following day, the Colombian government accepted the maritime agreement as ordered. Procedures that would allow seizure of drug traffickers' assets, however, remained problematic. In forty cases investigated by the Colombian National Police, only one resulted in a final asset seizure.[75]

Fourth, the United States demanded that Colombia investigate and try corrupt officials. In August, a series of prominent politicians were sentenced for illicit enrichment, including the former president of the Chamber of Representatives, the mayor of Cali, Samper's campaign manager, his former attorney general, and several members of Congress. Fifth and finally, the United States demanded that Colombia tighten prison security to prevent captured drug traffickers from managing their operations from behind bars. In April, the Colombian National Police assumed control of the maximum-security wings of Colombia's major prisons. While this was considered an improvement, the United States continued to desire additional action.[76]

As figure 3.6 illustrates, estimated coca cultivation increased substantially over Samper's term. As per the predictions of the theory, the United States utilized large punishments such as decertification to coerce Samper into exerting additional effort. The evidence from 1996 and 1997 suggests that although Samper was hesitant to cooperate, the credible application of these punishments motivated the Colombian president to comply with U.S. demands. Although estimated coca growth and cocaine production continued to rise, Samper did meet many of the specific goals that the United States required of him. The fact that

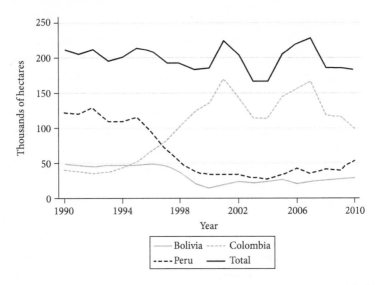

FIGURE 3.6. Estimated coca leaf cultivation in Andean countries, 1990–2010. Data from U.S. Department of State, various years; UNODC 2007, 2010, 2013

Samper exhibited positive effort despite the political costs he faced at home indicates that the incentives at least pushed him in the right direction. Absent the threat of decertification, it is unlikely that Samper would have fulfilled the United States' requests, particularly given his close links to the cartels and his desire to avoid public wrath. One possible explanation for the continued rise in disturbances is that Colombia lacked the capacity to fully quell cocaine production, but Samper's interests diverged sufficiently that the United States was unwilling to help him build additional capacity. That concern would change with the arrival of Pastrana.

Period 3: President Andrés Pastrana (1998–2002)

When Andrés Pastrana assumed the presidency in 1998, coca cultivation had doubled and cocaine production had quintupled since 1994.[77] Colombia had become the world's largest coca grower, replacing Bolivia and Peru.[78] Internal security had eroded: homicides, massacres, and kidnappings from various armed groups continued unabated. Escalating violence was an alarming sign that the Colombian state was deteriorating.[79] Fearful of the government's inability to provide security, more than seven hundred thousand Colombians fled the country between 1995 and 2000.[80] By 1998, it was clear that shifts in the nature of the disturbances—namely, the intersection of growing conflict between baby cartels and the heightened involvement of insurgents in narcotics—had greatly impeded the Colombian president's ability to suppress narcotics activity.

Resolving guerrilla violence became the central issue of the 1998 Colombian election. Pastrana pledged to initiate peace talks with the rebels, reform the judicial system, and secure a negotiated settlement that could end the conflict.[81] Pastrana's interest in stemming corruption and in creating an effective judicial system aligned well with U.S. objectives, which included the implementation of asset-forfeiture and money-laundering laws; extensions that would make extradition retroactive; expanded eradication efforts in the South, particularly Putumayo; crackdowns on corruption; and the recapture of Colombian territory from guerrillas and paramilitary groups. Finally, the United States emphasized expanding aerial eradication methods. Whereas President Samper had been barred from visiting the United States, the newly elected Pastrana was invited for talks due to apparent interest alignment. Moreover, despite rising cocaine production, Colombia was certified in 1998 by a national interest waiver, a move that signaled U.S. willingness to provide assistance if the new administration proved cooperative.[82]

Relative to previous periods, Pastrana's direct costs of effort rose significantly, while his political costs remained moderate. Direct suppression costs were driven by four factors. First, Colombia's resource base contracted, limiting its ability to finance counternarcotics operations. The economy took a sharp downturn, with only 0.5 percent growth in 1998 and a 4 percent contraction in 1999—problems that were magnified by a freeze in international credit markets.[83] Unemployment likewise ballooned to 18.2 percent in 1999.[84] Second, the cost of eradication increased as insurgent and paramilitary groups, now involved in narcotics, imposed greater physical costs on government forces. During this time, FARC and ELN forces swelled to more than eighteen thousand fighters who controlled 14 percent of Colombia's 1,070 municipalities, and were active in two-thirds of the country.[85] The GAO reported that two-thirds of FARC members and one-third of ELN units financed their activities with the drug trade.[86] FARC controlled most of the coca-growing territory in Putumayo, and frequently planted land mines and improvised explosive devices (IEDs) in coca fields, making manual eradication all but impossible.[87] They fired on planes sent to fumigate coca fields, increasing the difficulty of aerial eradication as well. As FARC's power and control grew, so did the cost of antidrug operations. Pastrana's costs also rose as baby cartels proliferated and competed for power. Disaggregation from largely hierarchical cartel organizations to more diffuse groups increased the difficulty the government faced in acquiring useful information about high-level cartel officials. Finally, changes in cocaine production also raised new challenges, as stronger strains of coca leaf facilitated an increase in production, the advent of "black cocaine" impeded detection by drug-sniffing dogs,[88] and coca farmers adapted to eradication efforts by spraying molasses over their plants to protect them from herbicides.[89]

While Pastrana still faced a political backlash related to aerial eradication, these costs were moderated by enhanced public support for ending guerrilla and cartel violence. In October 1999, more than one million Colombians marched in nationwide protests against FARC.[90] Even in Putumayo, the state that benefited the most from coca growth and the presence of FARC, Governor Jorge Devia was elected with the campaign slogan "Putumayo without Coca."[91]

Shortly after assuming office, Pastrana announced an antidrug strategy called "An Integrated Policy on Drugs for Peace," fulfilling a U.S. objective that the previous administration had failed to accomplish. The plan included implementation of alternative crop development, increased eradication and interdiction efforts, and legislative and institutional reforms to combat drug-trafficking organizations. Pastrana emphasized alternative development programs such as crop substitution in hopes of attenuating the domestic backlash from increased fumigation. Because the plan paralleled many American policy objectives, the United States authorized $2.6 billion in assistance over a three-year period.[92] However, the U.S. preferred aerial fumigation to crop substitution, and as a result, most of the aid was delivered to the Colombian National Police for eradication operations. The fact that crop substitution was included in the package at all was likely a reward to Pastrana designed to encourage continued effort.

By the end of 1998, Colombia had seized record amounts of cocaine and achieved its best eradication year yet, resulting in full certification for 1999. However, the United States became increasingly concerned that a new demilitarized zone that emerged from Pastrana's peace talks with FARC and the ELN would negatively affect counternarcotics efforts.[93] After FARC members murdered three U.S. activists who were visiting Colombia to support the Uwa indigenous people, reports from the Department of State identified guerrillas and paramilitaries as the most immediate impediments to U.S. interests.[94] The Department of State eventually encouraged Pastrana to step back from the peace talks, and in June 1999, the United States pressured Colombia to expand eradication into FARC's southern strongholds.[95]

Pastrana initially worried about the cost of the new eradication efforts, given his government's resource constraints, FARC's increased power, and the economic impact on farmers who lacked alternative development options. Nevertheless, in October 1999 the Colombian government announced its desire to enact a $7.5 billion policy known as Plan Colombia, which aimed to attract international funding in order to reduce cultivation, processing, and distribution of narcotics by 50 percent over six years.[96] The plan centered on five key strategies: advancing peace talks, improving the economy, combating narcotics with eradication in the South, reforming the judicial system, and supporting democratization and social development.[97] The following month, as a signal of Pastrana's genuine intentions toward eradication, the government extradited a Colombian citizen for the first time in nine years.[98] The United States again rewarded Colombia for good behavior by fully certifying Colombia's cooperation against drug trafficking. The certification stated that, "Colombian drug efforts ... demonstrate the true commitment of the Pastrana administration to cooperate fully with the United States in the illegal trafficking of drugs."[99] Both ESF and IMET aid continued to increase.

By the start of 2000, Colombia produced 75 percent of the world's cocaine. Its estimated coca cultivation also continued to rise despite increased effort from Pastrana. Nevertheless, the announcement of Plan Colombia convinced U.S. officials that Pastrana's interests were closely aligned with their own. At the same time, they recognized that Pastrana could not manage the direct costs of suppressing cocaine production. GAO reports from the time period frequently cite Colombia's lack of capacity as an impediment to achieving eradication objectives. As armed groups joined with cartels, the United States concluded that it would need to help Colombia address these security threats as a first step toward achieving its counternarcotics goals.[100] As a result, in July 2000 the United States agreed to provide $860 million to Colombia for the 2000–2001 fiscal year in addition to the $330 million that was already promised, thereby doubling overall assistance from 1999 levels.[101] The United States directed most of the assistance to training and equipping Colombian military personnel, who were necessary to provide security for the police-directed eradication push in Putumayo. The plan also included antiterrorism assistance to train Colombian units, and increased the number of U.S. personnel on the ground. However, this number was capped to appease U.S. congressional concerns[102]

Although disturbances under Pastrana increased at a similar rate as under Samper, U.S. responses differed markedly. Because Pastrana's interests were more closely aligned with those of the United States, American officials began to invest in capacity rather than threaten punishments. The near-perfect convergence between the two actors was reflected in the revised Plan Colombia, which became fully operational in 2001. Both coca cultivation and cocaine production reached their highest levels ever in 2001, but declined once Plan Colombia's capacity building began to translate into results. Threats to Colombian security followed a similar trend by declining in 2001 after a peak in 2000.[103]

The theory makes two predictions relevant to this period. First, when the agent's cost of effort increases—as Pastrana's did relative to the preceding administrations—the principal should be more likely to engage in direct control.

However, in this case the United States realized that the agent's interests were aligned with its own and that capacity building therefore remained preferable to direct action. While U.S. support for Plan Colombia entailed an increase in U.S. training and personnel on the ground, most assistance was allocated to the Colombian military and police, which remained under Pastrana's control.

This also explains why the United States declined to punish Colombia despite observing the largest disturbances to date. Coca cultivation and cocaine production rose in all years apart from 2002. It appears, however, that the United States recognized Pastrana as a closely aligned proxy who shared U.S. interests but was unable to suppress disturbances due to a lack of capacity. U.S. assistance to Plan Colombia closely aligns with this prediction: punishments were unnecessary because Pastrana's motivation was already high. Moreover, the United States preferred to send economic and military assistance to Pastrana rather than either disengage or attempt to eradicate cocaine production directly.

Period 4: President Álvaro Uribe (2002–10)

Colombia's next president, Álvaro Uribe, campaigned as a hard-liner who promised to restore security and stability throughout Colombia. This was not simply bluster—Uribe's father was murdered by FARC in a botched kidnapping attempt, and as a politician Uribe himself was a consistent and vocal opponent of guerrilla groups.[104] He became the embodiment of burgeoning anticartel sentiment among the Colombian public, and his 2002 election came with a mandate to dismantle insurgent groups and impair cocaine producers. So strongly was Uribe associated with these efforts that on the day he was sworn into office a series of protest bombings killed nineteen people and injured sixty others only blocks away from the inauguration site.[105] Rather than intimidate Uribe, the event merely reaffirmed his desire to demolish FARC.

President George W. Bush considered Uribe a perfect match. Both presidents regarded security threats as a top priority and believed that military action was the most effective means to achieve stability. In the wake of 9/11, the U.S. security establishment was also sensitive to the threat of terrorism and organized violence, and State Department reports from the time period pinpoint the international drug problem as the single largest source of illegal revenue for violent insurgents.[106] While the United States was still concerned with its original counternarcotics goals of drug interdiction and crop eradication, Colombian security threats were now important even independent of their effect on narcotics production. As a result, Uribe enjoyed an ideal confluence of circumstances and interests: he faced low political costs from a Colombian public that had grown weary of violence,[107] and he also benefited from obvious interest alignment with the United States, which encouraged Washington policymakers to offer assistance. Over time, the capacity improvements Uribe received lowered his direct costs of effort and enabled him to accomplish his goals.

One change that highlighted the shift in U.S. priorities was the relaxation of aid restrictions in Plan Colombia so that assistance could be used to combat insurgents directly.[108] Uribe's new "Plan Patriota" used U.S. aid to further professionalize the Colombian Army and launch offensives in the demilitarized FARC zone. Uribe also devoted resources to strengthening police presence, and in 2004 he achieved the goal of significantly improving police capabilities in all 1,098 Colombian municipalities.[109] The security investments produced record results. Uribe's administration averaged 57,247 arrests per year, compared to 13,278 under Pastrana. Likewise, while only 129 labs were destroyed in 2002, this figure increased to 4,869 in 2010. Cocaine seizures, eradication efforts, and extraditions also peaked under the Uribe administration.

Uribe also made significant progress toward dismantling illegally armed groups. In 2003 he negotiated a peace deal with the AUC to demobilize its 20,000 fighters over the next several years. By 2004, more than 4,600 AUC militants had demobilized.[110] In addition, FARC membership dropped by half, from around twenty thousand fighters in 2002 to between eight thousand and ten thousand in 2009.[111] Plan Patriota's offensives led to the capture of many FARC members and the assassination of several of its leaders, including Raul Reyes, Alfonso Cano, and Mono Jojoy.[112] Finally, Uribe implemented antiterrorism laws that allowed the police greater surveillance powers and facilitated arrests.[113] Colombia's security and stability improvements enabled the country to attract foreign investment, which helped the Colombian economy grow. This created a positive feedback loop in which Colombia could redirect additional resources toward security. From 2000 to 2009, Uribe tripled his defense budget, which allowed Colombia to assume primary responsibility for restoring the state's security apparatus.[114]

For most of his presidency, Uribe's interests were almost perfectly aligned with those of the United States.[115] Two scandals, however, indicate potential divergence. First, in early 2006, the "parapolitics" scandal revealed that top politicians in Uribe's administration had inappropriate ties to the AUC. The extent to which Uribe was involved remains ambiguous, but he spearheaded the investigation and removed several politicians from power. The second scandal, "False Positives," occurred in 2008 when Colombian security forces killed civilians and dressed them as guerrilla fighters to inflate casualty rates. Despite the scandals, Uribe enjoyed high favorability ratings throughout his presidency and is considered one of the most popular Colombian presidents. Uribe left office in 2010 with approval ratings above 70 percent.[116] The scandals did not seem to bother the United States, which in January 2009 awarded Uribe its Presidential Medal of Freedom.

Overall, the Uribe period closely reflects two significant predictions of the indirect control model. First, when agents are closely aligned with principals, they can expect to receive assistance in the form of capacity improvements. Thus, when the United States identified Uribe as a closely aligned agent, it offered significant military assistance. Even during Uribe's second term, aid levels remained high compared to earlier periods. Although Uribe continued to face high direct costs of suppressing disturbances, U.S. support for military professionalization significantly reduced these costs and allowed Colombia to expand the breadth of its operations.

The second prediction relates to the probability of rewards conditional on performance. When disturbances are sufficiently low, principals should be more likely to reward their agents. Coca cultivation and cocaine production decreased during Uribe's administration from their 2001 levels, and though they rose slightly in 2005, they then continued their descent from 2007 to 2010, never again reaching pre-Uribe levels. Likewise, threats to Colombian security showed a marked decline until they leveled off in 2006; they then continued to decline throughout Uribe's second term. For his efforts, Uribe was rewarded with capacity-building assistance from the United States, the Presidential Medal of Freedom, and reprieve when the United States decided not to penalize him for his political scandals. There were no observable punishments during either of Uribe's terms. The smaller rewards and the lack of any punishments suggest that with a nearly perfectly aligned agent, the United States did not need to utilize many incentives to motivate the agent to expend sufficient effort.

Alternative Explanations

Throughout this chapter I argue that the U.S.-Colombian relationship is an example of successful indirect control. Using a combination of punishments, rewards, and capacity building, the United States encouraged Colombia to exert significant effort at managing both domestic instability and the narcotics trade. However, despite the apparent success, the case presents several curiosities that require additional consideration.

First, were U.S. coercion and incentives actually necessary to motivate Colombia, or would the various Colombian presidents have exerted effort even in the absence of U.S. influence? With the exception of Uribe, Colombian presidents faced real and significant domestic backlash against counternarcotics policies. Until the mid-1990s, there was also some civilian support for the drug trade. Many Colombians believed that on balance the cocaine trade helped the economy despite the increase in cartel violence. As a result, in the absence of U.S.

incentives it is unlikely that Colombia's presidents would have vigorously pursued aerial eradication or other counternarcotics initiatives even if the leaders personally opposed cocaine production.

Another important question is whether the United States should have attempted to build Colombian capacity earlier. After all, capacity building would have lowered the costs that Colombian leaders faced when combating the narcotics trade. However, the fact that several Colombian presidents lacked independent motivation to pursue counternarcotics policies helps to explain the United States' decision. State Department and DEA reports consistently highlight the ubiquity of corruption as a main impediment to counternarcotics operations. Of particular concern was the Colombian National Police, which was widely thought to have close links to the cartels. As the indirect control model illustrates, the United States was unlikely to expend resources on capacity improvements if it feared that corrupt Colombian officials would divert those funds to alternative ends.

When the United States chose to initiate capacity building, was it motivated by an alignment of interests, or were there other forces in play? For example, some may argue that U.S. domestic preferences shifted in favor of capacity-building strategies and that this prompted the launch of Plan Colombia. There are credible reasons to doubt this alternative explanation. While U.S. policymakers negotiated the details of Plan Colombia, it was abundantly clear that they were under pressure from domestic interests to avoid a deep and lengthy engagement.[117] The United States therefore placed significant constraints on the number of personnel and aircraft that it would provide Colombia, as well as on the uses to which these resources could be applied. If U.S. domestic pressure was a driving force behind capacity building, such limitations would not have occurred. For further evidence that increased interest alignment facilitated capacity building, consider changes in the proportion of U.S. aid in Plan Colombia that was delivered directly to the Colombian president for improvements in the Colombian military or police. Under Gaviria and Samper, military and police aid were relatively limited and closely monitored by the United States. Under Pastrana and Uribe, however, the United States both increased the supply of such funding and also allowed Colombia substantially greater discretion over how the aid should be used.

Another factor that complicates this analysis is whether the provision and withdrawal of assistance to Colombia was attributable to variation in Colombian effort or, alternatively, resulted from coordination failures among U.S. agencies involved in Colombia. It is clear from U.S. government statements regarding the 1996 and 1997 decertifications that assessments of Colombian effort played a significant role in the decision to provide or withdraw aid. While those documents reveal some coordination difficulties at the start of Plan Colombia, these were generally resolved within a year or two following implementation. Incentives appeared to work as expected and were necessary to produce the high levels of effort observed during that period.

Overall, the patterns of historical behavior between the United States and Colombia closely match the theoretical predictions of the indirect control model. Both Gaviria and Uribe appeared to make progress in controlling disturbances and so received substantial rewards for their effort. Samper, on the other hand, held conflicting interests with the United States and faced stiff penalties when he failed to control disturbances. However, the United States still induced effort by Samper, at least partially, through the credible use of high-powered incentives. Finally, when the United States believed Colombian interests were highly aligned with its own, it invested in capacity to reduce Colombia's future costs of effort, as evidenced by the assistance that it provided Pastrana and Uribe under Plan Colombia.

What insights about the effectiveness of capacity building can be gleaned from this case? Among policymakers, Plan Colombia has been highly praised. In 2016, Secretary of State John Kerry claimed that "it had helped transform a nation on the verge of collapse into a strong institutional democracy with historically low levels of violence."[118] Other policymakers have advocated applying the strategy elsewhere. Robert Kaplan, a senior fellow at the Center for a New American Security, stated, "Colombia is what Iraq should eventually look like, in our best dreams."[119] Is Colombia a model for proxy drug wars?[120] The evidence from this chapter suggests two conclusions. First, capacity building should be applied only when the United States identifies a reliable agent whose interests are closely aligned with its own. Second, principals should be aware that their agents may exert significant effort toward particular objectives while largely ignoring others. So principals should prioritize the elements that they most strongly wish to have the proxy state carry out.

The fact that principals often make a series of differing demands for their agents is usefully illustrated by the continued evolution of Plan Colombia. Under President Barack Obama, for example, Plan Colombia was designed for the dual purpose of counterinsurgency and counternarcotics. The United States largely achieved its security aims with limited investment of military force.[121] On November 24, 2016, Colombian president Juan Santos signed a peace deal with FARC, after five decades of fighting.[122] The deal required that FARC fully dissolve, and marked an incredible success for both the Santos administration and Plan Colombia's objectives. On the counternarcotics front, however, Plan Colombia has been less successful. Although coca cultivation declined during Uribe's term, it has gradually increased since 2014. According to a recent RAND report, "Strategic cooperation and large amounts of U.S. aid failed to stem the production of narcotics. Nearly two-thirds of global cocaine continues to be produced in Colombia."[123]

Perhaps rising coca production is simply no longer a salient issue for the United States. After all, over the time period covered by this chapter, U.S. cocaine consumption decreased by 30 percent.[124] However, if the United States is not currently satisfied with Colombian counternarcotics efforts, then U.S. policymakers should clarify the terms they set. Separating counternarcotics and counterinsurgency into two separate policies—as opposed to combining them within a single package—may allow the United States to more directly motivate Colombian effort in each issue area by using a more closely tailored combination of rewards, punishments, and capacity-building initiatives than was applied in the past.

NOTES

1. Shifter 2012, 3.
2. See the introduction to this volume.
3. An estimated 5.7 million Americans used cocaine in 1985 (U.S. ONDCP 1999).
4. Tate 2015, 35.
5. Tokatlian 1994.
6. Ibid.
7. Tate 2015, 36.
8. Andreas et al. 1991, 108.
9. Tate 2015.
10. U.S. Congressional Budget Office 1994.
11. See UNODC 2010.
12. Because Colombia played a prominent role in narcotics trafficking as well as cultivation, the United States also evaluated the Colombian government's effort to eliminate cocaine production based on the amount of cocaine the country seized and the incarceration rate of traffickers. Throughout the chapter, I also reference these measures when considering Colombia's observable level of effort.
13. Mejia 2016.
14. Tate 2015.
15. Beginning in the 1980s, violence in Colombia was increasingly linked with the narcotics industry. More than thirty-one thousand deaths in Colombia from 1984 to 1989 are attributed to drug trafficking alone. See U.S. GAO 1992.
16. Commonly referred to as La Violencia, the ten-year civil war estimates casualties between two hundred thousand and three hundred thousand. See Simons 2004.
17. FARC operated in 175 municipalities in 1985, but by 1995 had expanded to 622 municipalities—almost half of Colombia's total. FARC had 10,500 fighters with 105 fronts in 1994, up from 7,700 fighters and 80 fronts in 1991 (Steele 2017, 96).
18. FARC charged a per-gram surcharge on coca paste produced by small farmers.
19. Tate 2015.
20. The following year, three-quarters of the world's cocaine was grown in Colombia (U.S. Department of State, Bureau of International Narcotics and Law Enforcement Affairs 1999).
21. Los Pepes, a violent vigilante group opposed to Pablo Escobar, emerged as a counter to the Medellín cartel. Armed self-defense forces were legalized under Gaviria and supported through Samper's "Convivir" program. However, the groups' tendency to use

high levels of indiscriminate violence led to the Constitutional Court's 1997 prohibition on the receipt of weapons. See Tate 2015.

22. U.S. GAO 1999.

23. Tate 2015.

24. All Colombian presidents in this study had received some of their postsecondary education in the United States, as was typical for the Colombian political elite.

25. Quoted in Whitelaw 2008, 3.

26. Once the armed groups and cartels converged, the United States also evaluated the strength of Colombia's security apparatus, measured as the extent of police presence and the rate of insurgent demobilization.

27. Elite training in the United States was considered a reward. Officers routinely received trips to Walt Disney World. See Tate 2015.

28. The narcotics certification process was established in 1986 by the Foreign Assistance Act and was replaced by the Foreign Relations Authorization Act (FRAA) in 2002. Similar to certification, the FRAA mandated that the president publish a "Majors list" identifying all major illicit drug-producing and drug-transit countries and determine whether countries have "failed demonstrably" to make substantial efforts to adhere to international counternarcotics agreements. See "'Majors List' Presidential Determination," n.d.

29. Mandatory decertification sanctions applied against Colombia in 1996 and 1997 included restrictions on sales and financing under the Arms Export Control Act, nonfood assistance under Public Law 480, financing by the U.S. Export-Import Bank, and most other foreign assistance. Disaster and humanitarian aid were not subject to restrictions. See U.S. GAO 1998.

30. Ibid.

31. The Colombian president begins his term in August and serves for four years. Until 2005, presidents only served one term. Reelection was forbidden.

32. Lee and Clawson 1998.

33. A Colombian survey showed that at least 25 percent of judges reported that they or their families had been threatened. See U.S. GAO 1992, 1.

34. Stokes 2005.

35. Crandall 2002.

36. U.S. GAO 1992.

37. U.S. GAO 1991a.

38. Ibid., 15.

39. The extent to which Colombians blamed Gaviria for increased violence is murky for two reasons. First, Colombia has a long history of violence and Gaviria's term was not distinct from recent prior periods of violence. Second, Colombia has multiple groups engaging in violence, many for political aims. The public may have been uncertain about which group was directly responsible for the unrest.

40. Sharpe 1988.

41. U.S. GAO 1992, 4.

42. Ibid., 2.

43. Menzel 1997.

44. Crandall 2002. Pablo Escobar famously turned himself in along with other top Medellín members, although U.S. intelligence suggests that he was able to operate the cartel from behind bars (U.S. GAO 1993).

45. Crandall 2002.

46. Ibid.

47. Ibid.

48. Ibid.

49. While total assistance decreased between 1990 and 1991 (see figure 3.5), this was likely reallocation rather than punishment; $100 million in previously committed Andean Strategy funds were redirected to higher-priority foreign policy objectives, one of which may have been the Gulf War (Tate 2015).

50. Quoted in GAO 1995a, 9.

51. Crandall 2002.

52. U.S. Department of State, Bureau of International Narcotics and Law Enforcement Affairs 1997.

53. See figure 3.2.

54. On November 4, 1996, a van loaded with 360 pounds of explosives was placed in front of an industrial plant owned by a senator who publicly favored a repeal of the extradition ban. The van was widely believed to have been planted by the cartels (Crandall 2002).

55. In November 1994, a mass protest was staged in response to fumigation. The next month another protest paralyzed public life in three municipalities. Antifumigation protests also occurred in 1996 and lasted for more than three months. See Tate 2015.

56. U.S. GAO 1995b, 2. The decrease in economic assistance can be interpreted as consistent with the predictions of the model in two ways. First, the United States was reducing capacity building to an agent whose interests were no longer closely aligned with its own. Second, the United States was punishing Samper for allowing disturbances to occur in the form of corruption within his administration.

57. Crandall 2002.

58. "Standing Guard" 1995.

59. U.S. GAO 1995b.

60. U.S. Department of State, Bureau of International Narcotics and Law Enforcement Affairs 1996.

61. Ibid.

62. A GAO report in August 1995 remarked that the arrest of several senior Cali members was a positive sign but that more effort was desired (U.S. GAO 1995a).

63. U.S. Department of State, Bureau of International Narcotics and Law Enforcement Affairs 1996.

64. Ibid.

65. Crandall 2002.

66. Quoted in Crandall 2002, 119.

67. In December 1996 the Colombian Congress enacted a bill making asset forfeiture retroactive, although this continued to face constitutional challenges.

68. U.S. Department of State, Bureau of International Narcotics and Law Enforcement Affairs 1997.

69. Crandall 2002. See also U.S. Department of State, Bureau of International Narcotics and Law Enforcement Affairs 1997.

70. Crandall 2002.

71. Ibid.

72. "Coca Clashes" 1996; U.S. Department of State 1997. The program still fell short of U.S. goals, in part because the Colombian government delayed testing a more effective herbicide.

73. U.S. Department of State, Bureau of International Narcotics and Law Enforcement Affairs 1998.

74. Ibid.

75. Ibid.

76. Ibid.

77. See figures 3.4 and 3.6.

78. U.S. GAO 2000.

79. Tate 2015.

80. Shifter 2012, 4.

81. Tate 2015; U.S. Department of State, Bureau of International Narcotics and Law Enforcement Affairs 1999.

82. Because Pastrana was elected in August of 1998, the United States based its certification decision for the 1998 calendar year on its assumed interest alignment with Pastrana rather than on Samper's performance (U.S. Department of State, Bureau of International Narcotics and Law Enforcement Affairs 1998).

83. World Bank, World Development Indicators, accessed May 25, 2018, https://data.worldbank.org/indicator/NY.GDP.MKTP.CD?locations=CO&view=chart. See also Tate 2015.

84. Sales 2013, 2.

85. Tate 2015.

86. U.S. GAO 1999.

87. Mejia 2016.

88. Black cocaine is cocaine mixed with zinc or other pigments and dyes. The mix absorbs odors and turns the substance black, evading typical detection efforts (U.S. GAO 1999).

89. Mejia 2016.

90. The march was called "No Más" (Shifter 2012).

91. Tate 2015.

92. U.S. GAO 1999.

93. Ibid. The zone was roughly the size of Switzerland and allowed insurgents to operate with impunity. Nevertheless, the United States was willing to tolerate the plan as long as it did not interfere with coca eradication (Tate 2015; Crandall 2002).

94. Tate 2015; U.S. Department of State, Bureau of International Narcotics and Law Enforcement Affairs 2000.

95. U.S. GAO 2002.

96. U.S. GAO 2000, 1.

97. The Colombian judicial system was still very weak. Less than 3 percent of all cases, including drug-related cases, were prosecuted (U.S. GAO 1999, 15).

98. U.S. Department of State, Bureau of International Narcotics and Law Enforcement Affairs 2000.

99. "Certification Decisions: Individual Statements of Explanation," March 1, 2000, in U.S. Department of State, Bureau of International Narcotics and Law Enforcement Affairs 2000.

100. Tate 2015.

101. U.S. GAO 2000, 1.

102. Prevost et al. 2014.

103. See figure 3.2.

104. Uribe even left his own Liberal Party after it supported Pastrana's 1991 peace talks with FARC (Sales 2013).

105. McDermott 2010.

106. U.S. Department of State, Bureau of International Narcotics and Law Enforcement Affairs 2002. FARC, the ELN, and the AUC had been placed on the Bureau of Counterterrorism's Foreign Terrorist Organizations list in 1999.

107. Even criticism of aerial eradication diminished over time as the United States shifted toward manual eradication and the country grew more secure.

108. Shifter 2012.

109. U.S. Department of State, Bureau of International Narcotics and Law Enforcement Affairs 2005, 128.

110. Ibid.

111. Shifter 2012.

112. Steele 2017.

113. McDermott 2010.

114. Shifter 2012, 4.

115. When the restriction on Colombian presidents' running for a second term was removed in 2005, Uribe became the first president to be reelected. See Simons 2004.

116. Isacson 2010.

117. Prevost et al. 2014.

118. Kerry 2016.

119. Quoted in Tate 2015, 221.

120. Over the last ten years, Mexico has experienced a staggering rise in cartels and drug-related violence.

121. In 2004, only eight hundred U.S. military personnel and six hundred private contractors were in Colombia (Shifter 2012, 5).

122. Negotiations began in 2012 with full support from President Obama (Casey 2016).

123. Quoted in Tate 2015, 222.

124. Almost 40 percent of Colombian cocaine is now directed toward European markets (UNODC 2013).

4

LEBANON AND GAZA, 1975–2017

Israel's Extremes of Interest Alignment

Matthew J. Nanes

Israel's disengagement from Gaza in 2005 presented the Israeli government with a challenge: How could it prevent Gaza from serving as a launching pad for terrorist attacks without maintaining a permanent military presence in the territory? The challenge of preventing attacks from a neighboring territory while minimizing direct military involvement was a familiar one. Since Israel's independence, but especially since 1975, Palestinian nationalist groups had used southern Lebanon as a base of operations, forcing Israel to find ways to degrade the capabilities of these groups without taking actions that could inflame tensions with its Arab neighbors. This chapter argues that in both southern Lebanon and Gaza, Israel attempted to meet these challenges by indirect control; that is, by managing local proxies tasked with combating the threat of violence on its behalf. While in both cases Israel pursued the same end goal of preventing attacks, dramatic differences in Israel's interest alignment with its proxies called for different strategies of proxy management, consistent with the agency model described in the introduction. In Lebanon, Israel held interests closely aligned with those of the South Lebanon Army (SLA), allowing Israel to focus primarily on building capacity for its proxy. In contrast, the highly divergent interests of Israel and Hamas necessitated the use of high-powered incentives, including punishments in response to attacks emanating from Gaza, to incentivize cooperation. Specifically, Israel responded to violence originating from Gaza with the use of force against Hamas even when Hamas was not the perpetrator.

In Lebanon, Israel first attempted to induce the government in Beirut to rein in the actions of the Palestinian Liberation Organization (PLO). However, it eventually recognized that Beirut was unable to take the necessary actions to prevent disturbances. In the mid-1970s, as Lebanon fractured into civil war, Israel focused its efforts on keeping the PLO away from the Israel-Lebanon border. To do so, it turned to the SLA, a militia led by former Lebanese military officers. A division of labor in which the SLA defended a buffer zone along the border while Israeli forces carried out periodic counterattacks against Palestinian fighters eased the burden on the Israel Defense Forces (IDF) and reduced the risks to Israeli soldiers. The SLA shared Israel's interest in keeping PLO and Hezbollah fighters out of southern Lebanon, although the militia's leaders occasionally clashed with their Israeli handlers on how best to achieve this goal. Thus, Israel focused primarily on bolstering the capacity of the SLA to defend its swath of territory by providing military equipment and logistical support. Israel and the SLA maintained a close principal-agent relationship until 2000, when Israel severed the partnership by suddenly withdrawing its troops from the buffer zone, leading to the collapse of the SLA. The end of Israel's relationship with the SLA, and a corresponding return to attempts to incentivize Beirut to rein in Hezbollah (which had fully displaced the PLO), reflected an evolving security threat that could no longer be contained by a militia whose influence was limited to southern Lebanon.

In Gaza, Israel withdrew its military forces and dismantled civilian settlements in 2005, expecting that the Palestinian Authority, led by the Fatah party, would govern the territory. However, Hamas's takeover of power in Gaza in 2006 turned Israel's strategy on its head. From 2007 through 2017, Israel managed a proxy relationship with an agent whose long-term objectives were nearly diametrically opposed to its own.[1] While Israel sought to prevent attacks, Hamas preferred to see the Israeli state destroyed. Israel's response to attacks—high-intensity punishment of Hamas regardless of whether Hamas perpetrated the attack in question—illustrates proxy management by indirect control under the most extreme preference divergence we see in this volume. This response differentiates indirect control from a standard model of deterrence.[2]

Theoretical Expectations

The two subcases differ significantly in the agent's cost of effort, specifically those costs generated by interest divergence between Israel and its agent. Whereas in Lebanon, Israel and the SLA shared a preference for keeping the PLO, and later Hezbollah, away from the border, in Gaza Israel was stuck with an agent with dramatically divergent preferences. While Israel and Hamas may both benefit from the suppression of other militant groups operating within Gaza, Hamas faces considerable pressure from the Palestinian population and the Arab world more broadly to resist Israel. This difference in the two agents' costs of effort suggests that Israel should employ different management strategies in southern Lebanon and in Gaza. In particular, the SLA's closely aligned interests imply that Israel should focus primarily on capacity building. In contrast, Israel should respond to attacks from Gaza by punishing Hamas in an effort to induce Hamas to exert greater effort toward preventing attacks. Critically, these responses should be directed against Hamas even when a different group is responsible for the initial attack, as the principal holds its agent accountable for all disturbances that originate in its territory.

In addition to the differences in interest alignment between the two subcases, Israel's behavior in managing its proxies also varied over time depending on the apparent effort those proxies exerted. As the introduction to this volume explains, the principal does not observe the proxy's effort directly; as such, Israel assumed that effort was relatively lower when disturbances occurred. Israel responded by using conditional rewards and punishments depending on periods of unusually low or high levels of violence, respectively. Finally, because Israel's proxy in Lebanon, the SLA, suffered from limited capacity, Israel also responded to periods of intense disturbances with increased use of direct action. Table 4.1 summarizes

TABLE 4.1 Theoretical expectations and summary results, Lebanon

SUBCASE (PERIOD)	KEY PARAMETER	THEORETICAL EXPECTATION	OBSERVED ACTION
Southern Lebanon/SLA (1975–82)	Increased disturbance intensity as Lebanese government control of the South erodes.	Principal should become more likely to engage in indirect control, including incentives (H_{11}) and capacity building if interests aligned (H_{12}). Agent complies (H_6).	Israel provides SLA with weapons, ammunition, logistical support, political support. Israel takes lead role in offensive operations, allowing SLA to maintain its defensive position. SLA exerts effort.
Lebanon (1982–85)	Increased disturbance intensity from PLO and Hezbollah outside SLA zone.	Principal should become more likely to engage in indirect control, including incentives (H_{11}) and capacity building if interests aligned (H_{12}).	Israel engages in direct action versus PLO and Hezbollah (outside of SLA zone). Israel attempts to create proxy relationship with Gemayel government in Beirut, but fails with Gemayel assassination. No capacity building. Proxy relationship with SLA continues.

SUBCASE (PERIOD)	KEY PARAMETER	THEORETICAL EXPECTATION	OBSERVED ACTION
Lebanon/SLA (1985–2000)	Increased disturbance intensity from Hezbollah within and outside SLA zone.	Principal should become more likely to engage in indirect control, including incentives (H_{11}) and capacity building if interests aligned (H_{12}). Agent complies (H_6).	Israel provides SLA with weapons, ammunition, logistical support, political support. Israel takes lead role in offensive operations, allowing SLA to maintain its defensive position. SLA exerts effort. Israel uses deterrence against Hezbollah.
Lebanon/SLA (2000–2006)	Increased disturbance cost from Hezbollah within and outside SLA zone, including rocket threat from beyond SLA zone.	Principal should become more likely to engage in indirect control, including incentives (H_{11}) and capacity building if interests aligned (H_{12}). Or, agent becomes redundant and case moves out of scope.	Israel abandons SLA. Replaces agency relationship with deterrence versus Hezbollah, and new attempt to incentivize Lebanese government using conditional punishments for Hezbollah-perpetrated disturbances.
Gaza/Hamas (2007–17)	Low preference alignment (relative to Lebanon/ SLA).	Principal should use punishments in Gaza rather than capacity building in southern Lebanon (H_{12}). Principal should use high-powered rewards and punishments in Gaza (H_7). Proxy is more likely to respond with effort the more higher-powered are the incentives (H_6).	Israel uses high-powered punishments in Gaza; no capacity building. Israel uses capacity building and rewards in southern Lebanon, but no punishments. Despite preference misalignment, Hamas often exerts effort to suppress disturbances, including its own.

the predictions derived from the differences in interest alignment between Israel and its two agents, as well as changes over time in observed disturbance intensity.

The destructive nature of punishments suggests that they may serve a dual purpose when the agent itself poses a threat to the principal, as in the case of Hamas launching rockets at Israel. As outlined in the introduction, the primary purpose of a punishment is to impose costs on the agent for failing to prevent disturbances perpetrated by other actors. At the same time, however, punishments tend to reduce the agent's capacity for future action—for example, by destroying infrastructure or imposing crippling sanctions. Thus, in a case such as Gaza in which the agent poses a security threat to the principal, destructive punishments have a secondary benefit of directly harming the agent's capacity to attack the principal. In contrast, when the agent is not a direct threat to the principal, as in the case of the SLA, destructive punishments are costly for the principal because they reduce the agent's capacity to exert future effort toward preventing disturbances perpetrated by other groups. Thus, we should see the use of extensive punishments against Hamas but not the SLA, not only because the SLA's preferences are closely aligned with Israel's but also because Hamas, but not the SLA, poses a direct threat to Israel's security.

Southern Lebanon, 1975–2006

Israel has an unusual relationship with its neighbor to the north. The Lebanese Army has not posed a significant threat since Israel won its war of independence in 1948. Although Lebanon has never officially been at peace or had diplomatic relations with Israel, it did not join the neighboring Arab countries in fighting Israel in 1956, 1967, or 1973, and there was little indication that its government had any desire to inflame tensions with Israel during the period of this study. Yet Israel has faced a significant security threat from Lebanon over the past half century: the threat of terrorist attacks through incursions, rockets, mortars, and attacks on Israeli interests abroad carried out by irregular forces using Lebanese territory as a base. Thousands of Palestinian refugees living in Lebanon remained committed to continuing the fight against Israel long after governments and armies signed armistice agreements. This pool of potential recruits, along with the central government's lack of control over much of its territory, made Lebanon an attractive base for Palestinian nationalist groups. The primary agitator in Lebanon until the 1980s was the PLO, the umbrella organization for a number of anti-Israel resistance groups. The PLO was headquartered in Lebanon until it was driven from the country by an Israeli invasion in 1982. Just as the PLO was uprooted, a new threat emerged in the form of Hezbollah, a Shia-dominated political party and militia backed by the Iranian government. Like the PLO before it, Hezbollah sought to use southern Lebanon as a base for launching attacks against Israel in the name of Palestinian nationalism.

The nature of the threat from Lebanon during this period, as well as Israel's early attempts at shifting responsibility for preventing attacks to a local proxy, is evident in the journalist Robert Fisk's account:

> From 1968, the PLO sent raiding parties into Israel from southern Lebanon and the Israelis responded by launching their own revenge raids, often against Lebanese villages. The motive was simple and comparatively cost-free: if the Lebanese villagers allowed armed Palestinians to take shelter among their homes, then they would be made to pay for it in blood. The only way to avoid Israeli attack was to eject the Palestinians from their villages. This, of course, the Lebanese could not do. The national army was too weak—both militarily and politically—to remove the Palestinians.[3]

Terrorism originating from Lebanon took on heightened importance in the early 1970s due to a series of high-profile attacks. On May 30, 1972, the Popular Front for the Liberation of Palestine (a subgroup of the PLO) carried out an attack on Israel's main international airport.[4] Three attackers trained by the PLO in Baalbek, Lebanon, arrived at the airport on a commercial flight from Europe. Once inside, they opened fire on civilians and security forces, killing twenty-six and injuring eighty. A few months later, the Palestinian group Black September killed eleven members of the Israeli Olympic team in Munich. The Black September attack was also orchestrated by the PLO from its base in Lebanon. These and other attacks on Israelis by irregular forces organized in Lebanon are the disturbances considered in this chapter.

Israeli Interests and Agent Selection

Israel's primary goal in Lebanon was to prevent attacks from Palestinian nationalist groups such as the PLO and from Hezbollah. Israeli policymakers sought to accomplish this goal without taking direct military action on Lebanese soil by supporting the efforts of groups that it believed held preferences compatible with its own. As early as 1957, Lebanese military officers stationed in the South and perceived as friendly to Israel, or at least unfriendly to anti-Israel factions, periodically received a carful of weapons from the IDF.[5] These actions—supplying local forces rather than deploying Israeli troops—illustrate the use of indirect control. This choice was likely influenced at least in part by Israel's fear of spreading its forces too thin by committing troops to Lebanon, and consequently leaving its borders with Jordan, Syria, and Egypt exposed. Furthermore, Lebanese fighters operating on their home soil held informational and operational advantages, allowing them to operate more efficiently than an invading force of Israeli troops. Local fighters are more familiar with the topography, can navigate villages and areas populated by civilians more confidently, and have access to better networks for gathering intelligence. Finally, Israeli policymakers knew that large-scale incursions into Lebanon would have meant sending large numbers of Israeli troops into harm's way, almost certainly leading to a politically unpalatable number of casualties. This ability to use indirect control to avoid such casualties while also drawing on the local expertise of Lebanese militias meant that while Israel was certainly capable of deploying its own troops into Lebanon (and indeed did exactly that numerous times during the period of interest), it had good reason to attempt to engage in indirect control where feasible. Thus, two questions emerged. First, which group should play the role of proxy? Second, how could Israel incentivize its proxy to take the desired actions in the face of difficulties in monitoring proxy effort in preventing attacks?

Israel first attempted to convince the Lebanese government to rein in the actions of the PLO. It did so with limited success. A law passed by Beirut in 1968 prohibited armed groups from infiltrating Israel from Lebanese territory, but it was halfheartedly enforced at best.[6] The prohibition was also contradicted by the 1969 Cairo Agreement between PLO chairman Yasser Arafat and the Lebanese Army, which permitted any Palestinian in Lebanon "to participate in the Palestinian revolution."[7] Israel attempted to increase the costs of noncooperation by using military force as a punishment. In December 1968, in response to Beirut's silence in the face of a growing number of border incursions, Israeli forces blew up thirteen planes belonging to a Lebanese airline parked at the airport in Beirut. The attack, understood by all to be retaliation for the Lebanese government's tolerance of PLO activities, focused public attention on the PLO's operations in Lebanon, leading to demonstrations both against the PLO and in support of it.[8]

A year later, on the night of December 31, Lebanese soldiers were ordered not to interfere as armed PLO members crossed the Israeli border from the town of Kila and kidnapped a watchman from the Israeli settlement of Metula. In response, Israeli soldiers captured the customs building in Kila and took prisoner the Lebanese soldiers barracked within, then blew up the building. It is revealing that the prisoners they took were not members of the PLO, but Lebanese soldiers who had nothing to do with the attack. The situation was resolved when the Lebanese Army reprimanded and replaced the sector commander, and soldiers in the South were given new orders to stop further PLO operations.[9]

Nevertheless, the general perception held by the Israelis was that Beirut was unable to impede the actions of the PLO, particularly in the region along the Israeli border. According to Beate Hamizrachi, the Lebanese Army's focus on the areas around Beirut, and its lack of attention to the South, "gave the people of Lebanon the impression that there was an unwritten gentleman's agreement between the Lebanese Army and the IDF, according to which Israel was responsible for policing the south while the army was active further back."[10] The problem for Israel, of course, was that it preferred not to be directly responsible for policing its neighbor's territory. By the time the Lebanese civil war began in 1975 as a result of long-simmering tensions throughout the country, the government had virtually no control over southern Lebanon and Israel was forced to find a different proxy.[11]

The South Lebanon Army

Israel began working more closely with militia groups operating in the South following the start of the civil war in 1975. One officer, Maj. Saad Haddad, formed a particularly close relationship with Israel. Haddad and his troops defected from the Lebanese Army in April 1979, and declared the territory that they held in southern Lebanon to be "Independent Free Lebanon." Haddad's troops first went by the name "Free Lebanon Army," which was later changed to "South Lebanon Army" around 1980. The SLA comprised six infantry battalions, along with heavy artillery and several dozen armored tanks. For all intents and purposes, the SLA was not a guerrilla force but a full-fledged army—but one without a civilian command structure at the top.

The goal of Haddad and his army was to control southern Lebanon, both militarily and politically. As Lebanon descended into civil war in 1975, the country was carved up into fiefdoms controlled by militias such as the SLA. The SLA never seemed seriously inclined to try to capture territory in other parts of the country but rather focused on maintaining control over its eleven-mile-wide strip of land along the Israeli border. There were benefits to being the only armed group in town, primarily safety and security for locals who were threatened by the militias of other religious groups, as well as the customs and tax revenues that come with territorial control. The sectarian nature of Lebanon's civil war made Haddad particularly wary of armed Muslim groups such as the PLO. According to Beate Hamizrachi, "Haddad's strong and consistent objection to the Palestinians was the result of his distrust of Moslems in general and of his conviction that the military presence of the Palestinians in Lebanon posed a threat to his country's existence, or at least to the 'status quo' that had kept it functioning for so long."[12] Israel, of course, cared little about Haddad's ability to extract revenue from the territory or to consolidate his fiefdom into a sustainable political entity, but was happy to support the SLA in keeping the PLO, and later Hezbollah, away from its border. Thus, while Israel and the SLA were motivated by different long-term goals, they had a shared interest in degrading the capabilities of the PLO and

Hezbollah in southern Lebanon. Israel benefited from a reduced threat of attack, and the SLA benefited from being the most powerful armed group in the region. The close relationship between principal and agent was immediately apparent to observers, including Robert Fisk, who noted, "When you visited Haddad's little realm with its Israeli-made roads, its Israeli beer for sale in the shops, its Israeli food and Israeli-registered cars and Hebrew road-signs, its Israeli-armed militiamen, and its complement of Israeli soldiers, it was occasionally possible to believe that this was Israel rather than Lebanon."[13]

The SLA's primary cost of effort came from the physical costs of military engagement. Skirmishes between SLA and PLO or Hezbollah fighters were frequently "fair" fights, with each side incurring significant casualties. Thus, the SLA favored a defensive policy in which it secured control over the border area but refrained from provoking Palestinian groups unnecessarily. At first an additional cost was incurred by publicly allying with Israel. Fighting in Lebanon as an independent militia was one thing, particularly in the context of the civil war, but allying with Israel made the group pariahs in the eyes of the entire Arab world. Once the relationship was known, however, public support from Israel became a boon as it reinforced the notion that an attack on the SLA risked a response not just from Haddad's militia but also from Israel's powerful military forces. For this reason, further displays of cooperation that occurred once the relationship between the SLA and Israel became widely known in the late 1970s can be thought of as rewards that bolstered the SLA leadership's standing in the eyes of the South Lebanese population and served as a deterrent against aggression by other militias.

Most civilians in South Lebanon supported the SLA's pro-Israel stance. These civilians relied on Israel's "Good Fence policy" not only for economic and medical assistance but also for their physical safety. The policy allowed Lebanese civilians to work in northern Israel, and for supplies to pass from Israel into Lebanon. "Accustomed to the Lebanese system of give-and-take," writes Beate Hamizrachi, "they accepted Israel's demands for a local security shield in the south in return for Israel's protection of their villages and their land. If the price for the benefits of the open gates was cooperation with Israel, most Lebanese and Israelis in the border region were ready to pay the price."[14]

Interest Alignment

Israel and the SLA held closely aligned interests on the issue of keeping Palestinian nationalist fighters out of southern Israel, but those interests diverged on the question of how best to allocate resources to achieve this goal. Specifically, the SLA wanted Israel to contribute more troops and equipment to the fight, and for

SLA fighters to be used only to defend territory in the security belt and not to pursue PLO and Hezbollah fighters deeper into Lebanon.

From one operation to another, Israel and the SLA disagreed on whose troops and resources should be placed at risk. Haddad frequently pushed Israel for more and better weapons, as well as IDF ground and air support to reduce his forces' exposure. Israel wanted to commit as few of its own troops as possible to Lebanon, and for the SLA to aggressively pursue PLO and Hezbollah fighters throughout the region. Finally, the SLA's actions were limited by its relatively low capacity. It simply did not possess a sufficient number of fighters to mount a significant offensive against entrenched Hezbollah positions, and it relied heavily on Israel for supplies, ammunition, updated weaponry, and even uniforms to clothe its soldiers.

In general, we should expect to see more frequent and more intense punishments when the agent's cost of effort is higher, and more rewards when the agent's cost of effort is lower.[15] Since the principal cannot observe the agent's cost of effort directly, in practice we should observe more punishments when there are more disturbances, and more rewards when there are fewer disturbances. The closely aligned interests between Israel and the SLA on major issues suggest a strategy based around capacity building and rewards so as to avoid degrading the SLA's capacity even further with damaging punishments. That is, punishments that impose costs on an agent through destruction—for example, by bombing the agent's military forces or weapons caches—not only punish inadequate past effort but also degrade the agent's ability to engage in future effort. Israel's and the SLA's closely aligned interests imply that a lack of capacity, not a lack of effort, was to blame for increases in disturbances. Therefore we should primarily expect to observe Israel providing the SLA with rewards when the SLA engages in anti-Palestinian fighting, and to withhold those rewards when Israel is forced to do the fighting itself.

1975–82: Capacity Building and Rewards

Israel's attempts to recruit local proxies in Lebanon went into high gear with the start of the Lebanese civil war in 1975. Between 1975 and 1977, the Israeli government invested $150 million in building up Maronite forces, including the future SLA.[16] Israeli colonel Benjamin "Fuad" Ben-Eliezer became the main point of coordination between the IDF and Lebanese militias in the summer of 1976. Ben-Eliezer was responsible on multiple occasions for persuading Haddad to take action against the PLO or for providing advice on how to respond to PLO aggressions.[17] According to Beate Hamizrachi, cooperation between Israel and Lebanese militias was so close that training exercises "usually ended with the participants raising both the Israeli and Lebanese flags."[18] Israeli activities in Lebanon were strictly covert during the early years, and Defense Minister Shimon Peres resisted the provision of any support that could be traced back to Israel.[19] It was not until August 1977 that Prime Minister Menachem Begin officially revealed to journalists that Israel was providing military assistance to Lebanese Christians.

Israel's strategy during this period focused on providing rewards as incentives. In addition to the Good Fence policy mentioned above, in which consumer goods were imported from Israel into the security belt, Israel frequently provided the SLA with weapons and ammunition. Fisk recounts his personal observation in 1976 of Israeli soldiers along the Lebanese border passing arms to members of the Phalange, one of several militias operating in the South and one that was vehemently opposed to PLO influence.[20] A notable reward occurred in September 1977 when Defense Minister Ezer Weizman presented Haddad and another SLA officer with the Exemplary Conduct Medal, the first time the IDF had ever awarded medals to foreign officers. Weizman reaffirmed the link between Israel and the SLA during the ceremony, saying, "We promise you that if the situation [in southern Lebanon] deteriorates once more, we shall intervene in even greater force. . . . We shall return to fight shoulder-to-shoulder with you."[21] The presentation of these awards, an unprecedented step that publicly committed Israel to cooperation with the SLA, was a clear reward for the SLA's role in freeing Israel from the burden of maintaining a permanent military force in Lebanon.

Despite the alliance, disturbances did occur throughout this period. The PLO carried out a particularly violent attack on March 11, 1978. Thirteen Palestinian fighters left Lebanon by boat, intending to attack a hotel in Tel Aviv, but the attackers ended up landing forty miles north of their intended target. They hijacked a bus full of tourists and drove south, firing at passing cars and eventually taking over a second bus. By the time the police halted the attack, thirty-eight civilians were dead and seventy-one were wounded. Israel responded on March 15 by launching Operation Litani, an Israeli military incursion into Lebanon to attack PLO bases. The weeklong operation represents a brief period of direct action by Israel, bypassing its fledgling proxy militias in the South and largely ignoring the Lebanese government in Beirut. Twenty-five thousand Israeli troops advanced as far north as the Litani River. Both sides agreed to a cease-fire on March 28, and Israeli troops withdrew in the following weeks. As they left, the territory was handed over to Haddad and to various smaller militias to form a security belt along the Israel-Lebanon border. Robert Fisk notes that "although actually under Israeli military orders, [the security belt's] nominal masters were the Christian militiamen who had been fighting the Palestinians and leftists for the previous four years, a murderous collection of Phalangist gunmen, renegade soldiers from the national army, and local thugs."[22]

Operation Litani was not a punishment, as it did not target SLA positions or interests. In fact, the IDF's invasion solidified the SLA as the most powerful group in the region. By clearing out PLO positions and driving these fighters back from the border, Israel changed the SLA's status from one of a handful of militias operating in the South to *the* armed actor in the area. In this sense, Israel responded to the disturbances not by punishing its agent but by bolstering the agent's capacity, presumably because it recognized that limited capacity, not misaligned preferences, was to blame for the security failure. Rather, Operation Litani was a period of direct action in which Israeli forces eliminated threats that the SLA was unable, but not unwilling, to eliminate for it.

The SLA continued to have limited success at stopping cross-border incursions. In April 1979, fighters from a PLO subgroup, the Popular Front for the Liberation of Palestine (PFLP), infiltrated the northern city of Nahariya, killing five Israelis. Shortly afterward, PLO members detonated a bomb during a holiday celebration in Tiberias, killing two and wounding thirty-six. During this period, barrages of rocket and artillery fire targeting northern Israel's population centers were common.[23] Between July 1981 and June 1982, the Israeli government recorded 270 PLO attacks against Israel, as well as 20 attacks on Israeli interests abroad.[24] Finally, on June 3, 1982, an assassination attempt was made against Israel's ambassador in London, allegedly by a PLO faction led by Abu Nidal.

1982–85: Direct Control and the Emergence of Hezbollah

By June 1982, Israeli leadership decided that the frequency and magnitude of PLO attacks from Lebanon was unacceptable. Once again, Israel's response suggests that it did not believe the problem was a lack of effort by the SLA, but rather that the SLA's territorial control was limited, and that the militia was unable to defend against attacks originating deep within Lebanon. On June 6, Israel invaded Lebanon, beginning a distinct period of direct control. The war is well detailed elsewhere.[25] In addition to driving out the PLO, Israel hoped to install a pro-Israel government in Beirut.[26] In other words, while Israel continued to foster a relationship with the SLA in the South, it aspired to more. Even as Haddad's forces were largely cooperative in joining Israeli efforts against Palestinian militias, there was a recognition that the small regional militia could not prevent disturbances from being planned and launched from the rest of Lebanon. For that, Israel would have needed a capable government in Beirut to cooperate on security issues. According to Minister of Defense Ariel Sharon, "Israel's objective is to see to it that Lebanon becomes an independent state that will live with us in peace and be an integral part of the free world, as well as to solve the problem of the Syrian presence in that country."[27] The 1982–85 war marked a clearly defined period of Israeli direct action forced by the capacity limitations of the SLA.

In the end, Israel was unable to find the proxy it sought in Beirut. Bashir Gemayel's Phalangists, Israel's favored recipient of control in Beirut following the war, proved unwilling to take orders from Israel. The root of the problem of Phalange cooperation with Israel was the Phalange's concern that it would be unable to keep control of Lebanon if the Lebanese people saw it as Israel's lackey. Gemayel, the Lebanese president-elect in 1982, told the Israelis, "I'm not afraid [of cooperation]. But in that case you will find me at the head of a small Christian state within a divided Lebanon under constant threat from its neighbors."[28] At a meeting with Gemayel shortly after his election, Israeli prime minister Menachem Begin demanded a formal peace treaty between Lebanon and Israel. Gemayel declined, suggesting he could not enter into such an agreement without national consensus. The relationship between Tel Aviv and Beirut soured after the meeting. According to Robert Fisk, "Bashir Gemayel's relations with the Israelis were at best cautious, at worst permeated with deepest suspicion. Many times he had said that every square kilometer of Lebanon should be free of foreign domination and now he made it clear that this included the Israelis."[29] Any remaining Israeli hopes of a cooperative government in Beirut were dashed in September 1982 when Habib Shartouni, a member of the Syrian Social Nationalist Party, assassinated Bashir Gemayel. The Lebanese elected Bashir's brother Amin Gemayel, an ally of Syrian president Hafez al-Assad, to replace him as president. In an ironic twist, Amin bowed to Syrian pressure to resist Israel's presence, meaning that Syria succeeded in installing its own proxy where Israel had failed. Thus, when the war ended in 1985, Israel had failed in its goal of installing a proxy in Beirut.

The war did succeed in uprooting the PLO leadership from Lebanon. With the removal of the PLO, Hezbollah emerged as the new primary threat to Israel from Lebanon. Made up primarily of Lebanese Shia, and trained and funded by the Iranian Revolutionary Guard, Hezbollah sought to repel Israel from Lebanon and ultimately to destroy the Israeli state. In southern Lebanon, Hezbollah picked up where the PLO had left off, engaging in guerrilla warfare against IDF forces on both sides of the border and periodically launching short- and medium-range rockets into Israel, including toward areas populated by civilians.

1986–2000: Capacity Building, Direct Action, and a Division of Labor

The 1982 war bolstered the SLA's position. After withdrawing from most of Lebanon, Israel maintained a military presence of about a thousand troops in the southern portion of the country. These troops, along with 2,500 to 5,000 SLA fighters, created a security belt along the Israeli border. The IDF and the SLA settled on a division of labor in which the SLA played defense while the IDF played offense. This arrangement freed Israel from having to maintain a much larger standing force in Lebanon, allowing the IDF to bring in troops temporarily as needed for larger operations. In turn, the creation of the security zone in South Lebanon enabled the SLA to consolidate its power and govern unopposed. Israel's military support for the SLA changed the status of the group from a militia to a de facto government, providing it with all the benefits implied by this status, such as levying taxes and imposing policies. Every direct military action by the IDF that degraded other militias, including Hezbollah, strengthened the SLA's hold on the South. Thus, Israeli operations against Hezbollah were not just independent actions against a threat; they also increased the SLA's relative capacity.

The SLA did much of the IDF's "dirty work" during this period, including running the al-Khiam prison near Marjayoun. Hundreds of Lebanese were held in al-Khiam without trial, often under inhumane conditions.[30] Israeli officers passed questions to the SLA guards to be asked on their behalf. SLA fighters also manned the most dangerous positions in the security belt, which likely contributed to the two-to-one ratio of SLA to Israeli casualties. SLA soldiers were sometimes referred to as the "sand bags of Israel" because they were positioned to absorb the brunt of any assault on the IDF's position.[31] Israel's insistence that SLA fighters be used for the most dangerous assignments constituted a major source of disagreement between the principal and its agent. The standard response was to provide additional equipment and supplies, including uniforms, ammunition, and vehicles, as a reward for cooperation.[32] The rewards appear to have been successful in making the SLA leadership feel secure. During an interview in 1993, Antoine Lahhad, the leader of the SLA at the time, was asked what would happen if the Israelis withdrew from the security zone. He replied that such a betrayal simply would not happen. "There is an agreement between Israel and the SLA," he said, "that they [the Israelis] will not withdraw from here before the establishment of peace and a solution has been found for the SLA and the people of the area."[33]

Disturbances continued during this period. In March 1987, two PFLP fighters infiltrated Israel's northern border near Kiryat Shmona by flying gliders from southern Lebanon. One was quickly apprehended, but the other killed six Israeli soldiers and wounded several others before being killed. Skirmishes between Israeli and Hezbollah forces within the security belt were also common during this period, resulting in casualties on both sides. For instance, in February 1992 Hezbollah infiltrated an IDF camp and killed three soldiers. Israel responded by blowing up a convoy carrying the Hezbollah leader Abbas al-Musawi two days later. All the while, SLA fighters manned the front lines of the security zone, easing the burden on IDF troops and bearing the brunt of any attempted ground assault into the buffer area.

Israel launched a handful of retaliatory raids into Lebanon during this period. These raids should be seen as interludes of direct action rather than punishments against the SLA, as they avoided imposing any sort of costs on the SLA. After Hezbollah rockets killed five IDF soldiers in early July 1993, Israel launched Operation Accountability, which involved strikes against Hezbollah-controlled areas using artillery and aircraft.[34] Civilian infrastructure such as bridges and power stations was also destroyed in Hezbollah-controlled areas. In April 1996, Hezbollah guerrillas fired rockets into Israel, and Israel once again responded with air strikes and shelling of Hezbollah territory in Beirut and the Bekka Valley. Israel does not appear to have believed that the "disturbances"—that is, the increases in rocket attacks—were the result of the SLA exerting insufficient effort. Rather, Israel held out hope that it could incentivize the Lebanese government to exert greater effort toward stopping Hezbollah. According to one analyst, "Both operations unleashed massive destruction in South Lebanon in order to pressure the Syrian-backed Lebanese government to halt Hezbollah's attacks on northern Galilee. . . . Israeli strategists believed that Lebanese officialdom's shaky solidarity with [Hezbollah] could be exploited if the cost of the allegiance was made unacceptable through massive retaliation."[35]

2000–2006: Abandonment

Israeli casualties along the border escalated throughout the 1990s, and public support for the IDF's presence in Lebanon waned.[36] Ehud Barak's Labor Party won the 1999 elections, and in May of the following year Israel withdrew its troops from the security belt suddenly and with no warning to the SLA.[37] Without Israeli support, SLA fighters were suddenly vulnerable to Hezbollah. According to one former militia member, "We could hardly stand on our own two feet with all the support of Israel that we had. So how could we stand on our own in the face of the resistance which had threatened to kill us?"[38] Many fighters fled to Israel; others surrendered to the Lebanese authorities. Their weapons, including at least two tanks and several armored vehicles, were captured by Hezbollah.[39] In the town of Marjayoun, the former headquarters of the IDF in Lebanon, a statute of the SLA founder Saad Haddad was dragged through the streets.

The obvious explanation for Israel's sudden abandonment of the SLA is that Israel no longer believed that a proxy relationship in Lebanon made sense, yet the events of the next few years suggest a more nuanced interpretation. In July 2006, Israel once again sent troops into Lebanon in pursuit of Hezbollah after an Israeli patrol along the border was ambushed.[40] Notably, Israeli forces targeted not only Hezbollah fighters but also infrastructure belonging to the Lebanese government.[41] Israel's frustration with Beirut's lack of effort was clearly evident in the statements of its political leaders. Israeli foreign minister Tzipi Livni commented on the Lebanese government's refusal to take any sort of military action against Hezbollah: "In a way," she said, "Israel is doing the Lebanese government's job for it."[42] Dan Gillerman, the Israeli ambassador to the United States, "remarked that the Lebanese government had brought its current crisis upon itself by having failed to honor a long-standing Security Council resolution requiring it to assert control over southern Lebanon and to disarm Hezbollah."[43] Israeli chief of staff Dan Halutz called for a response against "Hezbollah and the Lebanese government. Both of them."[44] Aware of Beirut's resistance to getting involved in the conflict, Halutz said, "We have to put out all the lights in Lebanon. We can shut off their electricity for a year, damage at a cost of billions."[45] Livni told reporters that the goal of the war was "to promote a process that will bring about a long-term and fundamental change in the political reality," and that Israel's use of force against Lebanon would make it easier for Beirut to justify the prevention of future Hezbollah attacks.[46] Israeli forces seemed to select their targets using a similar logic, focusing not only on Hezbollah areas but also on those controlled by the Lebanese government. Israel bombed the Beirut airport and several civilian power plants.[47]

Clearly, Israel had not rejected the proxy strategy in Lebanon as a whole. It still attempted to incentivize a new proxy—the Lebanese government—by punishing it following Hezbollah-caused disturbances. Yet Israel abandoned the SLA as a proxy despite never indicating that the SLA was exerting insufficient effort. Why? The most likely possibility is the changing nature of the threat to Israel. When Israel first engaged with militias in southern Lebanon as proxies in the 1970s, the primary threat was cross-border raids, which Israel believed could be reduced by maintaining a proxy presence along the border. Over time, the range of rockets available to Hezbollah increased dramatically. By 2000, the buffer zone controlled by the SLA was no longer deep enough to prevent Hezbollah rockets from reaching populated areas. Combined with the political and military costs of propping up the SLA by maintaining an IDF presence in Lebanon, it was simply no longer worthwhile for Israel to maintain the relationship. In contrast, it was still beneficial to attempt to induce Beirut to rein in Hezbollah, as Beirut's influence extended far beyond the reach of the SLA.

Gaza, 2007–14

Israel's actions in Lebanon between 1975 and 2000 provide a precedent for the use of local proxies to implement indirect control. Perhaps it is not surprising that Israel would employ a similar strategy in Gaza. On ideological grounds, the use of Hamas as a proxy represents a difficult test of the logic of incentivized agency due to the extreme divergence in preferences between it and Israel on seemingly existential issues. The second half of this chapter suggests that despite these differences, a narrow area of alignment in short-term interests between the two parties led Israel to use conditional punishments and rewards to incentivize cooperation on security issues.

Israel disengaged from Gaza in 2005, dismantling civilian settlements and withdrawing its military forces. It was once again faced with the challenge of how to prevent a neighboring territory from being used as a base for terrorist operations without maintaining a permanent military presence. Israel was particularly concerned with two types of attacks. First, Israel needed to prevent suicide bombings or other incursions into Israel by fighters intending to harm soldiers or civilians. Despite a physical barrier separating Gaza from Israel, tunnels and other breaches made it impossible to prevent incursions entirely. Second, as with Hezbollah's strategies in southern Lebanon, Palestinian nationalist groups in Gaza increasingly fired mortars and rockets into Israel as a form of resistance. These attacks started as crude short-range projectiles fired in the general direction of nearby towns and the city of Sderot, but the range and accuracy of rockets available to Gazans improved steadily. In 2006, only 3 percent of Israelis lived within range of rockets from Gaza. By 2009, the number had grown to 14 percent, and by 2014 most major population centers were in range, including Tel Aviv, Haifa, and Jerusalem.[48] Thus, Israel's primary security goal was the prevention of Gaza-originated attacks against Israeli civilians, and especially the suppression of rocket fire.

Several militant groups operate within Gaza and pose a threat to Israeli security. Palestinian Islamic Jihad (PIJ), the Army of Islam, the Popular Resistance Committee (PRC), and the Sheikh Omar Brigades have all been responsible for employing violence against Israeli civilians. However, the most active group since 2006 has been Hamas, the Palestinian nationalist and Islamist organization responsible for dozens of terrorist incursions into Israel and thousands of rockets launched toward populated areas. In addition to the crude short-range rockets available to most armed factions within Gaza, Hamas also controls an arsenal of longer-range rockets capable of targeting large cities throughout Israel.

As it did in southern Lebanon, Israel turned to the cultivation of a proxy as a strategy for reducing the frequency of attacks from Gaza. Israel's relationship with the Palestinian Authority, dominated by the Fatah party, was quite effective (see chapter 7). Israel hoped to extend this relationship in Gaza after disengagement, providing Israel with a state-like actor that could develop a monopoly on the use of force within the territory and provide accountability in the event of disturbances. However, the rival party Hamas unexpectedly won a majority in the Palestinian Authority's legislative elections in January 2006. When the incumbent Fatah-led government refused to hand over power, Hamas took control of Gaza by force, leaving Israel with a potential proxy that was itself the source of significant disturbances.

Hamas as a Proxy

The primary challenge in using Hamas as a proxy is that the group's preferences diverge wildly from those of Israel. During the period in question, Hamas's goals as an organization included the establishment of an Islamic state in Palestine and the destruction of Israel—goals incompatible with those of the Israeli government.[49] Indeed, Hamas officials have publicly encouraged violence against Israel on numerous occasions, including one instance in 2006 in which Interior Minister Said Sayyam announced that he would not order the arrest of anyone accused of carrying out attacks against Israel.[50] A speech by Hamas chairman Khaled Meshaal in Gaza in 2014 reaffirmed Hamas's commitment to armed struggle against Israel and its rejection of a Jewish state in Palestine. Yet it is possible that such statements and speeches are political posturing, and that there remain areas of possible cooperation between Israel and Hamas. Indeed, Hamas's leaders, including Meshaal, have argued that the clause in the group's 1988 charter that calls for the destruction of Israel is outdated and no longer represents the true goals of the organization, and that Hamas is willing to negotiate with Israel peacefully under the right circumstances.[51] Hamas released a document in 2017 that rolled back many of the most objectionable (from the Israeli perspective) parts of its original charter. In particular, the 2017 document accepts the creation of a Palestinian state along the 1967 borders, specifies that the conflict with Israel is a political rather than a religious one, and distances the group from the Muslim Brotherhood.[52] In other words, despite earlier public statements to the contrary, Hamas's preferences may not be strictly incompatible with Israel's.

While there is no doubt that Israel and Hamas remain widely divided on many issues, there are key areas of agreement, particularly with regard to the activities of other armed groups in Gaza. Israel would benefit from the existence of an effective government in Gaza, one with a monopoly on the use of force. Eliminating Gaza's other militant groups, or at least driving them so far underground as to make them irrelevant, would provide Israel with a single negotiating partner. The presence of numerous splinter groups makes it difficult for any agreement to satisfy everyone, and the absence of a group with a monopoly on the use of violence allows those who oppose peace to continue fighting regardless of negotiated agreements. Andrew Kydd and Barbara Walter describe five strategies of terrorism, two of which—outbidding and spoiling—are relevant when the potential terrorist actor is competing with other groups for the support of a domestic audience.[53] Outbidding is the use of violence to demonstrate to the domestic audience that the group in question is best suited to represent them. For example, the PIJ might launch rockets into Israel after a Hamas rocket attack to signal to Palestinians that it too has the capacity for armed resistance. Spoiling refers to the use of violence by a third party to disrupt an agreement between two sides in order to demonstrate that one of the parties to the agreement is not powerful enough to maintain it. In Gaza, the PIJ has engaged in spoiling by launching rockets into Israel during cease-fires negotiated between Israel and Hamas in an attempt to undermine the agreement. By reducing the power of competing groups in Gaza, Israel can remove certain types of incentives for terrorism. Finally, political domination by a single group would provide Israel's military forces with a clear list of targets to retaliate against in the event of an attack, making threats of deterrence more credible and efforts to suppress attackers more effective.

The key to the Israel-Hamas principal-agent relationship is that Hamas would also benefit from being the only armed game in town. In addition to the standard ways in which governments benefit from controlling territory, which of course apply here, the elimination of other Palestinian militias in Gaza would free Hamas to dictate the terms of any interactions with Israel. As mentioned above, cease-fires between Israel and Hamas are frequently "spoiled" by third-party attacks, embarrassing Hamas by demonstrating its lack of control and eliminating its ability to use cease-fires as bargaining chips. Hamas's efforts to consolidate its position have brought it into conflict with other groups committed to resistance against Israel despite overlapping ideology and goals. According to Jonathan Schanzer, "Hamas even found itself in conflict with the PIJ. Although the two groups typically were aligned, tensions were reported immediately after the coup. Part of the problem was that Hamas insisted that it was the only faction allowed to carry weapons in Gaza."[54] Thus, Israel and Hamas share common ground in their desire to degrade the capabilities of other armed groups in Gaza.

This narrow area of shared interests forms the basis for a limited principal-agent relationship between Israel and Hamas. Hamas does not serve as an agent voluntarily; rather, the relationship is one of induced cooperation. Hamas's long-term goal of removing Israel and creating a Palestinian state that it governs cannot be achieved without first achieving certain short-term goals in which its interests overlap with those of Israel. Israel's objective as a principal, then, is to incentivize Hamas to exert greater effort than it otherwise would in those narrow areas of short-term agreement.

Despite the overwhelmingly hostile tone of relations between Israel and Hamas, we do observe periodic glimpses of cooperation. For example, neither the Israeli government nor Hamas's leadership were willing to publicly deny rumors in June 2015 that negotiations regarding a truce were taking place. According to one analyst at the time, "The picture that emerges [from these negotiations] . . . is nevertheless one of a convergence of interests between Israel and Hamas."[55] Hamas, the argument goes, would benefit from a truce because it would marginalize rival Fatah by making it irrelevant in Gaza. Israel would benefit from the consolidation of Hamas's position in Gaza because it would drive a wedge between the political leaderships in Gaza and the West Bank, pushing a unified Palestinian state further out of reach.[56]

Hamas incurs considerable costs from cooperating with Israel. These costs flow from the appearance that Hamas is not dedicated to resistance against Israel and the establishment of a Palestinian state. Gazans who believe that Hamas might jeopardize or negotiate away Palestinian land in return for political cooperation with Israel may withdraw their support from the group. The rivalry between Fatah and Hamas remains intense, and any sign of weakness by Hamas risks undermining its political position.

Given the lack of other potential agents, Israel was left with only three options following Hamas's takeover in Gaza. First, it could destroy Hamas entirely, leaving a power vacuum in Gaza that would be filled either by an Israeli reoccupation or by some other group. Second, it could allow Hamas to remain in power but make no attempt to manage it as an agent against other groups. Third, it could attempt to engage Hamas in a proxy relationship and induce the group to suppress threats to Israel's security. Israel selected the last strategy, the management of Hamas as an agent, by using punishments to induce cooperation on key issues.

This conceptualization of the Israel-Hamas relationship views Hamas as a unitary actor. Alternatively, we might view Hamas's political and military wings as distinct actors. The two wings of the organization have different leadership and operate in different locations. The military wing frequently carries out attacks without the prior knowledge of Hamas's political leadership. Speaking about the 2014 kidnapping of three Israeli civilians in the West Bank, a high-ranking Hamas official stated, "Hamas truly does not know who stands behind the operation, because there is a separation of duties between the military and political branches of the movement. The politicians instruct the military to find a solution to the prisoner dossier, and the men on the ground have the freedom to choose the time, place, and operational details."[57] In this typology, Hamas's political wing serves as Israel's begrudging proxy agent, while its military wing is another source of disturbances, alongside the PIJ and other militias, which Israel wishes to suppress.

2007–15: Frequent Disturbances Followed by Large Punishments

Periods of violence between Gaza and Israel occurred at regular intervals following Hamas's takeover of Gaza in June 2007.[58] If Israel was indeed managing Hamas as a proxy, we should expect to see two patterns in this violence. First, significant increases in the frequency or magnitude of attacks from Gaza into Israel should be followed by an increase in the frequency or magnitude of Israeli military operations in Gaza. The logic of the proxy relationship suggests that Israel should use punishments against Hamas when Hamas does not exert effort toward preventing attacks. Given that Israel cannot observe Hamas's level of effort directly, it must surmise that effort is low when more attacks occur. Thus, we should generally observe a pattern in which Israeli punishments become more frequent and more intense following the occurrence of rocket attacks.

A second expectation distinguishes between punishments in a proxy relationship and tit-for-tat deterrence. This distinction is relevant in this unusual case in which the proxy itself is a source of disturbances. Because Hamas is directly responsible for a large proportion of rocket attacks, we cannot simply assume that Israeli military responses are intended to incentivize Hamas to exert effort against other groups. They may be intended to prevent Hamas from launching rockets in the future, or to deter Hamas from doing so by demonstrating that doing so is costly. A pattern in which Israel responds to Hamas rocket attacks by using force against Hamas would be consistent not just with a proxy management strategy but also with a strategy of deterrence. To determine whether Israel is engaging in proxy management rather than deterrence, we must observe not only the timing of an Israeli response but also the target of the response. The main indication of a proxy management strategy is the targeting of Israeli punishments toward Hamas even when attacks were not carried out by Hamas. Evidence that Israel responds to rocket attacks by using military force targeted at Hamas regardless of the perpetrators' affiliation would suggest that Israel is attempting to provide Hamas with incentives to suppress third-party attacks.

Patterns of Disturbances and Punishments

While sporadic exchanges of violence have marred the eleven years since Israel's disengagement from Gaza, a clear pattern emerges in which spikes in disturbances are followed by intense Israeli military action. A major increase in violence occurred in early 2008. On February 27 of that year, militants launched forty rockets from Gaza into Israel. Israeli forces quickly responded by destroying the launch sites. In addition, Israeli missiles targeted the Palestinian Interior Ministry and a police station controlled by Hamas.[59] Two days later, Israel initiated Operation

Hot Winter, a weeklong ground and air offensive that left 112 Palestinians dead. During the operation, Israeli forces attacked both military and political assets belonging to Hamas, aiming simultaneously to impress on Hamas's leadership the importance of preventing attacks from other groups and to degrade Hamas's capacity to attack Israel in the future. The conflict ended with a cease-fire in June.

Violence spiked again several months later. From the beginning of November through the first half of December 2008, more than two hundred rockets were fired from Gaza into Israel.[60] Israel responded by launching air strikes on December 27, followed by a ground invasion on January 3, 2009. During Operation Cast Lead, Israeli forces struck Hamas military bases, training areas, and weapons caches, as well as civilian infrastructure including houses, schools, and mosques. The BBC reported that Israel's goal was to "stop the firing of rockets into Israel" and to "destroy or reduce Hamas as a fighting force and to capture its stocks of weapons to help achieve this."[61] By the time Israeli forces withdrew from Gaza on January 21, more than 1,300 Palestinians had been killed,[62] making this one of the bloodiest surges in hostilities between Israel and Hamas during the period of study.

Not all instances of Israel-Gaza violence fit the pattern of Israeli punishments in response to disturbances. Violence flared twice in 2012; both occurrences were precipitated by targeted strikes by Israel against leaders of Palestinian organizations in Gaza. On March 9, an Israeli air strike killed Zhair al-Qaisi, the secretary general of the PRC. On November 14, Hamas military wing chief Ahmed Jabari was killed. In each case, Israel's targeted killing was followed by an escalation of hostilities between Israeli and Hamas forces. In March, Operation Returning Echo led to 23 Palestinian deaths, while October's Operation Pillar of Defense caused the deaths of four Israelis and approximately 167 Palestinians.[63] Unlike the other instances of increased conflict intensity, however, these were precipitated not by rocket fire from Gaza but by Israel's move to neutralize a target.

The last major increase in hostilities during this period occurred in the summer of 2014. The conflict began on June 12 when two attackers kidnapped and killed three Israeli teenagers in the West Bank.[64] Israel responded by raiding Hamas targets in the West Bank almost immediately. Over the next two and a half weeks, Israeli forces arrested hundreds of Hamas affiliates in the West Bank.[65] As the raids intensified, Hamas factions and other groups, including the PIJ, launched dozens of rockets from Gaza into Israel. On July 2, Hamas reportedly tried and failed to convince the PIJ and other militant groups to refrain from launching rockets into Israel in an effort to avoid further escalation.[66] As rockets continued to target the Israeli civilian population, Israeli aircraft attacked Hamas targets throughout Gaza. On July 17, Israeli ground forces joined the fight. Intense fighting continued for more than two weeks. Israel withdrew most of its troops from Gaza on August 3, but air strikes by Israel and rocket fire by

Hamas continued. Finally, on August 26, the two sides agreed to a cease-fire. All told, approximately 2,200 Gazans were killed in the fighting.[67]

Israeli violence against Gaza is usually, but not always, precipitated by earlier Gaza-originated violence against Israeli civilians. This pattern is consistent with a strategy of proxy management in which the principal responds to an increase in disturbances by punishing the agent with violence. In the absence of clear information on whether Hamas, the agent, is exerting effort toward preventing attacks against Israel, Israel operates under the assumption that disturbances are more likely to occur when its agent is exerting lower levels of effort, and therefore responds to disturbances by using violence against Hamas.

Targets of Israeli Punishments

The timing of Israeli military actions in response to rocket attacks is only half of the story. The second characteristic of an attempt at proxy management, and the characteristic necessary to distinguish proxy management from other strategies such as deterrence, is whether Israel targets Hamas even when an attack was perpetrated by a different group. If Israel is indeed attempting to incentivize Hamas to rein in the actions of other militant groups, we should observe Israel using force against Hamas even when Hamas did not initiate the attack.

Indeed, Israel's standard policy is that Hamas should be held responsible for all rocket attacks originating in Gaza. Following a rocket attack in March 2016 and an Israeli military response against Hamas, Israeli defense minister Moshe Yaalon said that Israel had intentionally struck back against Hamas-controlled areas even though the rockets had been launched by "rogue militant groups." He added, "We will not tolerate the disruption of calm and the daily life of the residents who live around the Gaza Strip . . . which is why we reacted strongly against Hamas assets and we will act even more harshly if these attempts continue."[68] Incidents in which Israel responded to a disturbance caused by a third party by attacking Hamas are common. After a group calling itself the Sheikh Omar Brigades launched two rockets into southern Israel in June 2015, Israel responded not by attacking the perpetrators but by bombing fields used by Hamas fighters.[69] A similar scenario occurred in September of the same year, when Israel responded to rockets launched by the Sheikh Omar Brigades with air strikes against what a reporter described as a "Hamas site" in northern Gaza.[70] The IDF spokesman's office issued a statement explaining the IDF's choice of target, saying that "the terrorist group Hamas is the sovereign, and it carries the responsibility" for the attack.[71] Events were repeated just a few weeks later when, following a rocket attack on Ashdod, Israeli jets attacked four targets in Gaza. At least two of the targets belonged to Hamas. The rocket had originated far from the locations targeted by the IDF, and the Sheikh Omar Brigades once again claimed credit for the attack, but an IDF spokesman, Lt. Col. Peter Lerner, said, "Hamas is responsible and will be held accountable for *every* attack emanating from the Gaza Strip."[72] Israel's efforts to induce Hamas to suppress rocket fire appear to be effective at least some of the time; Hamas responded to a barrage of rockets launched at Israel in May 2015 by arresting several PIJ militants it claimed were responsible for the attack.

We observe several instances of Israeli direct action in Gaza in conjunction with punishments against Hamas. On August 18, 2011, militants carried out a coordinated attack on civilian and military targets in southern Israel outside the city of Eilat. According to Israel, the attackers belonged to the PRC.[73] Israel responded with air strikes against PRC targets in Gaza. The strikes killed six, among them PRC chief Kamal an-Nairab.[74] In addition to this direct action against the PRC, Israeli forces also targeted Hamas security installations in Rafah.[75] Al Jazeera reported that an IDF spokeswoman, Avital Leibovich, "told Al Jazeera that Israeli forces were targeting 'not only specific terror organizations in Gaza, but rather anyone who has some influence . . . with terror,' including groups of people it suspects of launching rocket attacks."[76]

An Effective Strategy for Israel?

The evidence presented in this chapter indicates that Israel used indirect control in both southern Lebanon and Gaza with the goal of reducing the frequency of attacks from groups operating in the two locations. Israel used a combination of punishments and rewards conditional on the frequency of disturbances, along with unconditional capacity building, to manage proxies in both cases. Differences in interest alignment necessitated different strategies. In Lebanon, where Israel's proxy held interests compatible with its own, Israel focused primarily on capacity building, alongside instances of rewards following particularly noteworthy periods of cooperation. In Gaza, circumstances forced Israel to manage an agent with highly divergent interests. It did so by using high-powered incentives in the form of punishments conditional on the occurrence of disturbances. These punishments usually took the form of air strikes against Hamas targets, but periodically included very costly and destructive incursions by ground troops. Given that Hamas itself was the source of a significant security threat, these punishments served two purposes. First, by being conditional on attacks by third parties, they imposed costs on Hamas for allowing other groups to attack Israel from Gaza. Second, by destroying Hamas's infrastructure, they reduced Hamas's capacity for engaging in direct attacks against Israel.

At first glance, these attempts at managing proxies appear to have had limited success. Israel was successful at pushing the PLO out of Lebanon, but only via direct action. Furthermore, the PLO's departure from Lebanon was followed almost immediately by the rise of a new threat: Hezbollah. The SLA allowed Israel to maintain a security belt along its border using fewer troops than it otherwise would have needed, but the presence of the security belt was only somewhat effective in preventing Hezbollah incursions into Israel. Ultimately another costly direct action in 2006 was necessary to reduce the threat from Hezbollah. Yet Israel's proxy strategy in Lebanon must be evaluated with appropriate expectations. Israeli policymakers held no illusion that the SLA was capable of eliminating the threat of attack from Palestinian nationalist groups in Lebanon. Rather, the SLA played the role of "sandbags" in the security zone to keep IDF soldiers out of harm's way and allow them to be deployed as needed. In this respect, the SLA was quite successful. Israel was able to maintain a large security belt with only about a thousand troops, and its casualty rate was significantly lower than that of the SLA. Whether the security belt itself was a successful policy is a separate question.

Why did Israel abandon the SLA and allow it to collapse in 2000? It may be that Israel decided that the costs of capacity building necessary for the SLA to remain viable were too high, particularly since these costs involved keeping IDF troops in Lebanon and in harm's way. Another possibility is that the new administration in Jerusalem simply held a different evaluation of the effectiveness of the security belt and placed a priority on the withdrawal of all Israeli troops from Lebanon. A third possible explanation is that the threat from Hezbollah had evolved to make the security belt ineffective. The range of rockets in Hezbollah's arsenal increased to the point that they could reach Israeli population centers from deep inside Lebanese territory. This increased range made the maintenance of a proxy in southern Lebanon ineffective, as the disturbances were originating from beyond the SLA's territory. Each of these explanations is consistent with the model. Either the expected benefits of indirect control decreased due to a change in the nature of the way policymakers perceived the threat, the expected costs of proxy management increased due to increasing difficulty in helping the SLA address a changing threat, or some combination of both occurred.

In Gaza, apparent attempts to manage Hamas as an agent appear to have failed to stem the threat of rocket attacks and incursions, and Israel engaged in several large-scale ground assaults into Gaza. These frequent periods of direct control have been costly to Israel in terms of military resources and loss of life, and perhaps even more costly in terms of its reputation abroad.[77] The large numbers of civilian casualties caused by these operations harm Israel's global standing in a way that makes it less secure. Should we consider the proxy relationship with Hamas to be an effective arrangement? If not, why does Israel continue to engage in such a strategy?

Principal-agent relationships are two-sided. The evidence presented in this chapter suggests that Israel has attempted to manage Hamas as an agent, but it says little about Hamas's willingness to cooperate with Israel. The regular, high-intensity Israeli military operations leading to significant loss of life in Gaza are the result of a proxy relationship under vastly divergent preferences. The gap in interests between Israel and Hamas is so wide that very large punishments are needed to impose costs sufficient to induce Hamas to alter its behavior. To evaluate whether the proxy relationship is successful, we must consider what the level of violence would look like in its absence. In the case of Gaza, Israel's alternatives include destroying Hamas and implementing direct control, allowing Hamas to continue to govern Gaza without attempting to incentivize it to prevent attacks by other groups, or attempting to replace Hamas with another agent. It is difficult to imagine that any of these alternatives would result in a better outcome for either Israel or Hamas.

NOTES

1. The relationship was ongoing at the time of this writing.
2. Schelling 1966.
3. Fisk 1990, 74.
4. Hamizrachi 1988, 36.
5. Hamizrachi 1988, 19.
6. Hamizrachi 1988.
7. Fisk 1990, 74.
8. Hamizrachi 1988, 28; Fisk 1990, 75.
9. Hamizrachi 1988, 34.
10. Ibid., 37.
11. For accounts of how the Lebanese government's control over its southern territory waned leading up to the civil war, see Friedman 1995; Fisk 1990; and Schiff and Ya'ari 1985.
12. Hamizrachi 1988, 184.
13. Fisk 1990, 137.
14. Hamizrachi 1988, 185.
15. Padró i Miquel and Yared 2012.
16. Sahliyeh 1986, 4–5.
17. Hamizrachi 1988, 87.
18. Ibid., 66.
19. Hamizrachi 1988.
20. Fisk 1990, 106.
21. Hamizrachi 1988, 153.
22. Fisk 1990, 136–37.
23. "Terrorist Attacks in Israel" 2011.
24. Becker 1984, 275.
25. Friedman 1995, Schiff and Ya'ari 1985, and Fisk 1990 provide excellent accounts.
26. Schiff and Ya'ari 1985, 42.
27. Quoted in Schiff and Ya'ari 1985, 42.
28. Ibid, 200.
29. Fisk 1990, 340.

30. "Bitter Retreat" 2000.
31. Trendle 2010.
32. Hamizrachi 1988.
33. Quoted in Trendle 2010.
34. Harik 2004.
35. Ibid., 112–14.
36. Trendle 2010.
37. Harel and Issacharoff 2008.
38. "New Dawn" 2010.
39. "Bitter Retreat" 2000.
40. See Myre and Erlanger 2006 on the details of the ambush.
41. Cordesman with Sullivan and Sullivan 2007.
42. Lambeth 2011, 45.
43. Ibid., 177–78.
44. Ibid., 23.
45. Quoted in Harel and Issacharoff 2008, 78.
46. Inbar 2007.
47. Cordesman with Sullivan and Sullivan 2007; Harel and Issacharoff 2008.
48. Getmansky and Zeitzoff 2014, 591.
49. Hamas 1988.
50. Schanzer 2008, 136.
51. Falk 2012.
52. "Hamas Accepts Palestinian State" 2017.
53. Kydd and Walter 2006. The five strategies are attrition, spoiling, intimidation, out-bidding, and provocation. Both spoiling and outbidding can be neutralized when there is only one group opposing the state.
54. Schanzer 2008, 187.
55. Savir 2015.
56. Ibid.
57. Quoted in Abu Amer 2014.
58. Nanes 2017.
59. "Airstrike Hits Gaza" 2008.
60. Sofer 2008.
61. "Q&A: Gaza Conflict" 2009.
62. B'Tselem, n.d.
63. Al-Mughrabi 2012; B'Tselem 2013.
64. Rudoren and Kershner 2014; "Mashal" 2014.
65. Zitun 2014a.
66. Al-Ghoul 2014; Hodgkins 2014.
67. United Nations Human Rights Committee 2015.
68. Al-Mughrabi 2016. Also see Al Waheidi 2016.
69. "Rockets Fired from Gaza" 2015.
70. Shuttleworth 2015.
71. Ibid.
72. *Times of Israel* 2015.
73. Pollard 2011.
74. Ibid.
75. "Israel Launches Strikes" 2011.
76. Ibid.
77. Nanes 2017.

5

EL SALVADOR, 1979–92

Revisiting Success

Ryan T. Baker

Beginning in 1979, the United States provided military equipment, training, and economic assistance to the Salvadoran government to help it defeat an insurgency aligned with the Soviet Union. The intervention lasted more than a decade, and was the most expensive U.S. military intervention between the Vietnam and the Persian Gulf Wars.[1]

This case is especially important given its role in ongoing U.S. defense policy debates. The dispiriting outcome and immense cost of U.S.-led interventions in Iraq and Afghanistan have led policymakers to search for more efficient ways to deal with threats that emanate from troubled states. An influential school of thought has formed around the idea that "small footprint" interventions in places like El Salvador—those that rely on a small number of U.S. personnel to provide training and advice over long periods of time, coupled with infusions of U.S. equipment and economic assistance—have been both comparatively cheap and relatively successful.[2] Indeed, at first glance it appears that the United States achieved a kind of resolution in El Salvador that it has not yet achieved in either Iraq or Afghanistan, despite investments in money and personnel two orders of magnitude larger.[3] The Salvadoran model is consequently invoked regularly in policy debates, and is highlighted in both the 2006 and 2014 versions of the U.S. military's field manual on counterinsurgency as an example of a low-cost intervention with a clear, positive outcome.[4]

A closer look at the conflict reveals a different logic at work, however—one that more closely follows the principal-agent theory developed in the introduction. Although U.S. assistance may have prevented the collapse of the Salvadoran regime and modestly improved its military and economic institutions, it did not end the insurgency. Rather, after some initial gains by the Salvadoran government, the conflict entered a protracted stalemate that lasted until shifting incentives and exogenous events created the space for a political settlement. In the interim, key factions within the regime strongly resisted reforms such as professionalizing the military and modernizing the economy, which would have reduced the political appeal of the insurgency and made the Salvadoran government a more effective counterinsurgent.

At stake was the balance of political power within El Salvador. Although the Salvadoran government wanted to defeat the insurgency, it was deeply opposed to U.S.-backed reforms that would loosen its grip on power. The United States, for its part, had limited leverage throughout most of the conflict and used incentives inconsistently, leaving a gap between U.S. and Salvadoran interests that stalled the effort against the insurgency.[5]

The El Salvador case underlines how difficult it is for principals to use indirect control successfully when there is significant preference misalignment and the agent faces high costs of effort, a combination that generates misaligned interests. The model presented in the introduction implies that indirect control will be less effective in these settings and that principals should avoid them in favor of either direct control or walking away. The United States chose indirect control in El Salvador anyway and, as the model predicts, struggled to incentivize the Salvadoran regime to exert effort.

More generally, this is a case where the model predicts the agent's behavior well but the principal often deviates from optimal behavior. The United States used incentives inconsistently, barely monitored its Salvadoran agent, and chose indirect control when conditions made it unlikely to succeed. Given the principal's suboptimal choices, however, the agent behaved largely as the model prescribes: it pursued its own interests as far as it could without shutting off the flow of assistance from the United States, though when the principal attached conditions to its assistance El Salvador usually responded as expected.

Background

In 1979, the military had been in control of El Salvador for almost half a century. It came to power in a coup in 1931 and entrenched itself while suppressing a massive popular uprising a few weeks later.[6] During its rule, the military served primarily to protect the interests of a small number of very wealthy families in exchange for social privileges and an outsized share of the economic rents. This coalition of "oligarchs and officers" protected their position through a combination of political exclusion and violent repression, which over time created unrest and dis-affection among the general population.[7] This resentment deepened in the decade preceding the civil war, as economic inequality worsened and the regime manipu-lated the results of national elections in 1972 and 1977.[8] At the same time, the rise of liberation theology in local Catholic churches inspired many Salvadorans to organize against the government (some violently, but many not). The regime responded to the rising unrest by becoming increasingly repressive, using security forces and paramilitary "death squads" to assassinate those perceived as disloyal.[9] Events finally spiraled out of control in 1979 when the military president was deposed and the country slid rapidly into civil war.[10]

The principal in this case is the U.S. government, which became concerned about El Salvador's stability in the late 1970s during the Carter administration. In 1979, a Marxist insurgency in neighboring Nicaragua toppled the U.S.-aligned dictatorship of Anastasio Somoza Debayle, and the United States wanted to pre-vent a similar outcome in El Salvador. The United States feared the Soviet Union would use Nicaragua and El Salvador to subvert U.S. interests in Central America and tie down American resources in its own "backyard." The U.S. government was therefore focused on defeating the insurgency and dismantling its sources of influence within Salvadoran society.[11]

The agent is the government of El Salvador beginning in 1979, when the coun-try's military president was deposed in a bloodless coup by midlevel military officers. The junta that took power sought to reform the regime and prevent the country from descending into civil war, but it was stymied by conservative elements within the military and the wealthy elite.[12] The result was a series of nominal leadership transitions, escalating violence against opposition groups, and, ultimately, civil war. The Salvadoran government's primary goal during the conflict was to maintain its control over Salvadoran society.[13]

El Salvador received a range of assistance from the United States during the conflict. Its military received training from both a cadre of U.S. personnel in El Salvador and from U.S.-run schools overseas.[14] It also received significant quan-tities of military equipment, including, among other things, helicopters, light aircraft, artillery pieces, armored personnel carriers, small arms, and ammu-nition.[15] The U.S. Central Intelligence Agency (CIA) provided covert support to help interdict insurgent supply lines and increase domestic support for the regime in Salvadoran elections, and the U.S. government sent billions of dollars in economic aid over the course of the war. All told, El Salvador received more than $6 billion in assistance from the United States (in current dollars) between 1979 and 1992—an amount that at times accounted for more than 50 percent of El Salvador's annual budget.[16] Figure 5.1 summarizes USAID Overseas Loans and Grants ("Greenbook") data for El Salvador during this period.

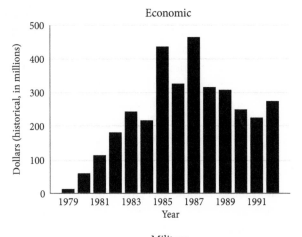

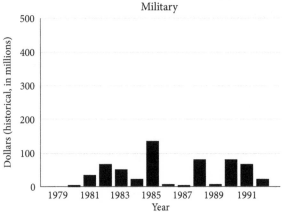

FIGURE 5.1. U.S. assistance to El Salvador, 1979–92. Data from U.S. Agency for International Development, U.S. Overseas Loans and Grants: Obligations and Loan Authorizations, July 1, 1945–September 30, 2014

This assistance was a combination of noncontingent capacity building and contingent rewards, with the proportion of each changing over time. The precise mix is sometimes difficult to disentangle empirically, for reasons discussed in the introduction, but noncontingent capacity building was almost certainly highest during the stalemate from 1985 to 1989, while contingent rewards (incentives) were likely highest in the early 1990s.

The disturbance in this case is defined as the strength of leftist insurgency in El Salvador.[17] The Farabundo Martí National Liberation Front (FMLN), as the insurgency was known, was a coalition of five preexisting resistance organizations that came together in late 1980 with the help of Cuban intermediaries. It was the military component of a larger opposition movement composed of a variety of popular organizations, and sought to overthrow and replace the ruling regime in El Salvador.[18] Throughout the conflict, the FMLN received weapons, ammunition, and other material support from third parties, especially Cuba and Nicaragua.[19]

Theoretical Predictions

The cost of proxy effort was generally high in El Salvador. The Salvadoran Armed Forces (ESAF) began the conflict as an ill-provisioned and poorly trained garrison force that clearly lacked the capacity to defeat the FMLN. The ESAF became larger and somewhat more capable over time as a result of U.S. assistance, but it never became broadly proficient in the kind of counterinsurgency operations necessary to finally defeat the FMLN. The Salvadoran government thus faced significant direct costs associated with fully suppressing the disturbance.

The indirect costs were also high (except for a brief period early in the conflict, an important fact I return to later). To make it easier to defeat the insurgency, the United States pressed for institutional and economic reforms that would make the FMLN less appealing politically and make the ESAF more effective on the battlefield. These included land reform, democratic elections, professionalizing the military, and a variety of other initiatives.[20] These reforms, however, would fundamentally alter the balance of political power within El Salvador and effectively destroy the ruling oligarchy that had dominated the country for generations.[21] So although the U.S. and Salvadoran governments both wanted to defeat the FMLN, they differed sharply on the relative importance of related issues. In particular, the United States sought the ultimate defeat of the insurgency and the grievances that helped generate it—at the expense of the regime's social and economic privileges if necessary. The Salvadoran regime, by contrast, was willing to live with a simmering insurgency if defeating it required reforms that would risk deposing the oligarchy. These divergent interests proved largely irreconcilable and, together with the direct costs the ESAF faced, imply that the Salvadoran regime's overall cost of effort was high throughout most of the conflict.

The indirect and political costs were imposed primarily by hard-liners among the economic elite, the military, and their supporters in the Salvadoran public. These groups either controlled or heavily influenced large parts of El Salvador's security apparatus, legislature, and judiciary, and were willing to use violence and intimidation to enforce their will. They had the revered archbishop Óscar Romero assassinated, for example, and successfully co-opted the junta of junior officers that led the coup of 1979. They of course also worked hard to undermine moderate members of the government and their supporters for years thereafter.[22] These groups retained much of their influence even after the adoption of a more democratic constitution in 1982 and the election of a comparatively moderate president in 1984.

U.S. assistance during the war was weighted more toward noncontingent capacity building than contingent rewards.[23] Although there were conditions built into U.S. aid from the beginning—and they played an important role in the trajectory of the conflict—they were often rescinded when the threat from the FMLN became too great. The Reagan administration fought hard to keep as few conditions on U.S. assistance as possible, arguing to a skeptical U.S. Congress that conditions undermined rather than reinforced U.S. interests in the conflict. A series of compromises between the Reagan administration and Congress early in the war produced a flow of assistance that mixed noncontingent capacity building with contingent rewards, but from about 1985 to 1989 this gave way to an almost exclusive focus on noncontingent capacity building. The balance then shifted back toward incentive contracts when the Bush administration took office in early 1989.[24]

The scale of monitoring in El Salvador was consistently low. One of the compromises Congress was able to extract from the Reagan administration was a cap on the number of advisers the U.S. military could have in El Salvador. As a result, the U.S. mission never had more than about 150 advisers on the ground, none of whom were allowed to accompany Salvadoran troops on combat operations.[25] This made it very difficult for the United States to know how hard its agent was working against the disturbance or to know which rewards or punishments would be most likely to create high levels of effort. This problem became more pronounced over time as the Salvadoran military grew from about ten thousand to fifty-six thousand personnel between 1979 and 1987.[26] The international press corps helped fill some of the monitoring gap, but it was too small, and it focused only on a subset of the issues of potential concern to the United States.

The size of the disturbance was large enough that direct U.S. action against the FMLN was a credible threat, as the many comparisons between El Salvador and the early days of the Vietnam War attest.[27] In that sense this case clearly meets the scope condition described in the introduction. Although the United States ultimately avoided sending ground troops into combat (and the U.S.

government often downplayed the idea), many Americans believed it would intervene if an FMLN victory became imminent.[28] After all, President Reagan repeatedly argued that an FMLN victory would give the Soviet Union a new base of operations on America's doorstep, forcing the United States to pull resources away from Europe, the Middle East, and other important theaters for territorial defense.[29] "El Salvador," he explained, "is nearer to Texas than Texas is to Massachusetts. Central America is simply too close, and the strategic stakes are too high, for us to ignore the danger of governments seizing power there with ideological and military ties to the Soviet Union."[30] Reagan also demonstrated a willingness to intervene directly elsewhere—especially in Grenada and Lebanon—and believed that a lack of resolve was a major reason the United States had failed in Vietnam. It is therefore unsurprising that both the American public and the FMLN believed that direct U.S. intervention was a real possibility. A Gallup poll conducted in September 1983 found that two-thirds of the American population thought it was at least fairly likely that, as with Vietnam, the United States would become more deeply involved in El Salvador over time, and the FMLN's 1981 "final offensive" was in part timed to take control of the country before Reagan took office and could push the United States deeper into the conflict.[31]

The cost of the disturbance stayed roughly constant for the first decade of the conflict, but fell significantly after the end of the Cold War. As the Soviet Union receded, the United States became less worried about its influence in Central America and more open to a negotiated settlement on terms the FMLN could accept. In this situation, the model leads us to expect that the United States would face strong incentives to disengage from the conflict.

Taken together, these predictions imply that the United States should have struggled to defeat the insurgency using indirect control through its Salvadoran agent (H_1), and that most noncontingent capacity-building assistance would essentially be wasted (H_6). Given the regime's high cost of effort, the model prescribes large incentives and extensive monitoring to induce El Salvador to prioritize U.S. preferences over its own (H_7)—except for very early in the conflict, when the threat of overthrow was especially high and the cost of effort was comparatively low. However, the United States never had more than about 150 advisers on the ground, and while it frequently attached conditions to its aid, incentives were applied inconsistently and were often modest compared to the full cost of effort. There is thus little reason to expect El Salvador to exert significant effort against the FMLN of the type the United States preferred (H_6). Table 5.1 summarizes the model's most important predictions and how well the El Salvador case conforms to them.

TABLE 5.1   Theoretical expectations and summary results, El Salvador

PERIOD	KEY PARAMETER(S)	THEORETICAL EXPECTATION	OBSERVED ACTION
1979–85	Preference misalignment low initially, but increases steadily throughout this period	Principal should steadily increase the power of incentives it offers the agent (H_7); in absence of incentives, proxy is noncompliant (H_6)	United States uses fewer incentives as misalignment increases; Salvadoran behavior diverges from U.S. preferences
1985–89	Preference misalignment plateaus at high level around 1985	Principal should increase the power of incentives or resort to direct control (H_7); in absence of incentives, proxy is noncompliant (H_6)	United States uses very few incentives; conflict enters prolonged stalemate
1989–92	Size and cost of the disturbance decreases with the end of the Cold War	Principal becomes more likely to withdraw from the conflict; when incentivized, proxy is compliant (H_6)	United States pushes to negotiate end to conflict; use of incentives increases; Salvadoran behavior converges with U.S. preferences

El Salvador, 1979–92

This section reviews the three distinct phases of the war and traces key changes in the model parameters over time.[32] It argues that very early in the conflict, when the strength of the insurgency peaked and the threat of overthrow was greatest, U.S. and Salvadoran preferences briefly converged and the cost of proxy effort was comparatively low. Aided by the consistent use of incentives, U.S. assistance worked more or less as intended early in this period: ESAF proficiency improved, death squad activity declined, and the Salvadoran government implemented some nontrivial democratic reforms.[33]

As U.S. assistance steadied the regime and the threat of overthrow declined, however, U.S.-backed reforms became the more immediate threat to the regime's hold on power, and the cost of effort steadily increased. Because the United States stopped using incentives around 1984, interest divergence was large enough by 1985 to stall progress against the insurgency entirely, and the conflict entered a stalemate that lasted until the end of the Cold War.

After the Soviet Union collapsed and the Sandinistas were voted out of power in Nicaragua, the conflict entered a new phase in which the cost of the disturbance to the United States decreased and the cost of the conflict to the insurgents increased—that is, the United States became less concerned about Communist expansion in Central America, and external support for the FMLN (including from Nicaragua and Cuba, the FMLN's most important external benefactors) shrank.[34] This structure of costs and benefits, combined with war weariness, a new economic reality in El Salvador, and a renewed emphasis on the use of incentives by the United States, helped produce a political settlement in 1992. Table 5.2 provides a timeline of some of the conflict's key events.

TABLE 5.2   Timeline of key events, El Salvador

October 1979	Romero regime overthrown in a coup; replaced by a reform-minded junta
January 1980	First junta collapses; replaced by another, more conservative one
February 1980	Carter administration threat to remove aid prevents right-wing coup
March 1980	Second junta collapses; replaced by a third junta
November 1980	FMLN formally established (unites five preexisting groups)
December 1980	Carter administration suspends all assistance to El Salvador
December 1980	Third junta collapses; replaced by a fourth (led by Duarte)
January 1981	FMLN launches "final offensive"
January 1981	Assistance to El Salvador reinstated
January 1981	Reagan administration assumes office
April 1982	United States uses conditions to prevent D'Aubuisson from becoming president
April 1982	Constituent Assembly elected; Magaña elected president of the assembly
December 1983	U.S. vice president George H. W. Bush visits; urges the ESAF to reform or lose aid
May 1984	Duarte elected president of El Salvador
June 1985	FMLN formally switches to guerrilla tactics
January 1989	George H. W. Bush administration assumes office
February 1989	U.S. vice president Dan Quayle visits; urges the ESAF to reform or lose aid
March 1989	Alfredo Cristiani elected president of El Salvador (assumes office in June)
June 1989	Quayle visits again; urges the ESAF to reform or lose aid
October 1990	U.S. Congress votes to withhold half of all assistance to El Salvador
January 1992	Conflict ends with Chapultepec Accords

Sources: Drawn from Gettleman et al. 1986, 53–64; Manwaring and Prisk 1988, xlix–liii; Moroni Bracamonte and Spencer 1995, 23; LeoGrande 1998, 574–75; Ladwig 2016, table 1.

Crisis: 1979–85

When the conflict began, the Salvadoran military was a small, unprofessional force of ten thousand men ill prepared for a fight with the FMLN. Its soldiers were poorly equipped and spent more time in garrison than in training.[35] When U.S. brigadier general Frederick Woerner led a team of military advisers to assess the state of the ESAF early in the conflict, he concluded that it was incapable of defeating the FMLN in its current state.[36]

The ESAF's deficiencies became obvious in early 1981 when the FMLN launched a massive operation modeled on the successful 1979 "final offensive" in Nicaragua. Although the El Salvador version was ultimately unsuccessful, it was an impressive demonstration of strength for such a young organization—the FMLN successfully occupied eighty-two municipalities and seized large swaths of Salvadoran territory.[37] This began a series of large engagements and raids in which the FMLN proved to be as capable as the ESAF, and sometimes more so. The FMLN destroyed more than half of the Salvadoran Air Force in a raid in 1982, for example, and in 1983 it launched a sophisticated attack on an ESAF brigade headquarters at El Paraíso. The latter involved months of surveillance, a well-planned feint, coordinated indirect fire, an effective signal plan, and some three hundred fighters. The FMLN even successfully ambushed the ESAF reinforcements rushing to the scene. More than one hundred ESAF soldiers were killed in the raid, and the FMLN captured a significant amount of equipment before destroying much of the base.[38]

Faced with such an acute threat, the Salvadoran regime became increasingly willing to accept significant U.S. assistance—and U.S. interference—to address it. This was a major shift from a few years earlier, when the (precoup) regime of Gen. Carlos Humberto Romero had suspended all U.S. military assistance and condemned U.S. interference in Salvadoran affairs.[39] The United States became more pliant too, as the fear of "another Nicaragua" was strong enough to overcome the Carter administration's deep concerns about the Salvadoran government's atrocious human rights record.[40]

The result was an influx of U.S. resources into El Salvador, but they came with some important strings attached. No sooner had the Carter administration announced that it would assist the new junta than it began to pressure influential Salvadorans to reduce human rights abuses, and quietly made it clear that the United States would withdraw its assistance if hard-liners intervened to overthrow the new government.[41] The threat apparently worked, as the promise of future aid forestalled a coup by hard-liners in February 1980.[42] In 1982, the United States threatened to withhold military assistance if the newly formed Constituent Assembly elected the popular but repressive hard-liner Roberto D'Aubuisson as the interim president of El Salvador. This worked too, as the assembly reluctantly elected a more moderate candidate.[43] In 1983, U.S. vice president George H. W. Bush traveled to El Salvador and threatened to withdraw U.S. assistance unless the regime removed certain officers from the security forces and curtailed death squad activity, after which state-sponsored violence declined and several implicated officers were exiled or involuntarily retired.[44] In 1984 and 1985, the U.S. Agency for International Development also successfully required the Salvadoran government to devalue its currency and adopt some austerity measures in order to secure economic assistance.[45]

The incentive program did not always work this cleanly, however. In December 1980, the United States suspended aid entirely after four American churchwomen were brutally raped and murdered by government security forces, but it backtracked almost immediately in the face of the rising threat from the FMLN (economic aid was restored a week later, and military aid was restored the following month, after the FMLN launched its final offensive). The Carter administration tried to condition future aid on the investigation of those responsible for the murders, but this requirement was rescinded by the Reagan administration when it took office a month later.[46] These events suggest that assistance during this period was oriented as much toward noncontingent capacity building as toward incentives (or, at the very least, that there was some basic amount of assistance the United States was unwilling to make contingent).

Yet the combination of incentives and interest alignment during this period led to a brief spurt of reform in the early 1980s, including nationalizing the banking system and establishing a program to redistribute land ownership.[47] The military improved too, notwithstanding some early setbacks. By the end of 1983, more than half of the ESAF officer corps had been trained by the United States (almost all outside of El Salvador so as to undermine unhelpful local traditions), and death squad activity declined significantly.[48] By the end of 1984, the ESAF had grown to more than forty thousand men and was successfully repelling FMLN attacks on its positions, and by the end of 1985, the Salvadoran Air Force was using its U.S. training and equipment to devastate FMLN formations in the field.[49] This improvement came despite the fact that the FMLN was growing stronger until about 1983.[50]

As the government regained its footing and the threat from the FMLN gradually became less acute, however, conservative elements within the government and the military regained influence and actively worked to undo many of these changes. The clearest example is the steady erosion of the initial land reforms. The program was deeply unpopular among the Salvadoran elite and was resisted to some extent from the beginning, but after 1982, it was systematically undermined by conservatives working through the National Assembly. As a result, the second phase of the plan was never implemented, and the proportion of Salvadorans who benefited from the reforms actually declined over time.[51] The military also became much less receptive to U.S. advice. Whereas early in the conflict it had understood and accepted the need for major reform in order to survive, it became increasingly intransigent over time.[52] When the United States imposed conditions on its assistance, it could still coerce at least partial compliance (as was the case with some economic austerity measures in 1984–85), but resistance was increasing.

Stalemate: 1985–89

By 1985, the conflict was stalemated. This was widely acknowledged at the time, including by four prominent U.S. colonels (authors of the "Colonels' Report") and a Salvadoran colonel who would go on to become the country's defense minister.[53] The faltering progress is especially notable because it occurred despite the massive increase in the size of the ESAF, the declining fortunes of the FMLN, and the ESAF's superior equipment, training, and resources.[54]

The increased use of U.S.-supplied airpower by the Salvadorans made it much more difficult for the FMLN to operate in large formations, forcing it to adopt more guerrilla-style tactics beginning around 1985. The shift away from direct confrontations with the ESAF and toward infrastructural and economic targets (not to mention the FLMN's adoption of forced recruitment around the same time) alienated many Salvadorans from the FMLN cause, while the killing of four off-duty U.S. marines at a local restaurant and the kidnapping of Duarte's daughter in 1985 dampened pro-FMLN sentiment abroad. As a result, by 1986 the FMLN was down to about half its original size and could no longer take and hold territory from the ESAF.[55]

Yet the ESAF made scant progress against its weakened enemy. This was partly due to the inability of U.S. advisers to convince the ESAF to adopt counterinsurgency techniques to counter the FMLN's new tactics (the ESAF continued to rely on massed firepower and resisted U.S. efforts to modify its approach).[56] However, the larger problem was that the United States removed nearly all incentives from its assistance during this period. Duarte's election in 1984 was heralded as a major victory for the U.S. effort, and the attention of Congress shifted from El Salvador almost entirely.[57] This gave the Reagan administration a free hand to provide capacity-building assistance without any strings, something it had long sought.[58] As a result, the only real condition on U.S. assistance during this period was a $5 million annual withholding (about 1 percent of all assistance, on average) tied to the prosecution of those responsible for the 1981 murder of two Americans working in El Salvador.[59] This had little if any effect, and there were no other meaningful conditions until after the Bush administration took office in early 1989.

Progress was stalled along the other lines of effort as well. The "Special Investigative Unit" that President Duarte set up in 1984 under U.S. pressure to investigate the most salient political murders (many of them likely committed by the ESAF, which the handful of U.S. advisers in the country could not monitor closely) lasted barely a year and achieved little. The conservative-dominated legislature also staunchly resisted judicial reform and continued to undermine the 1980 land reform package.[60] In fact, there were no major reforms implemented during this period, and those that had been implemented earlier were steadily eroded.

El Salvador therefore made less progress toward U.S. goals—both against the FMLN and against the country's malformed political institutions—during this period than any other. The government and the ESAF gestured toward reform to secure U.S. aid, but conservatives had regained enough influence that the cost of effort was again very high, so the status quo nearly always prevailed.[61] Now that the FMLN was no longer capable of directly overthrowing the government (and the United States was no longer attaching meaningful conditions to its assistance), those in power were much less willing to oppose entrenched interests and risk their privileged positions to secure the final defeat of the insurgency. An indefinite stalemate was preferable to fundamental reform that might diminish their influence.

Resolution: 1989–92

Events beginning in 1989 finally broke the stalemate and created space for a political settlement. One was the reintroduction of conditionality. Right after George H. W. Bush was inaugurated as U.S. president in 1989, he sent Vice President Dan Quayle to El Salvador to emphasize the importance of prodemocratic reform and to threaten to withhold assistance if the Salvadorans did not prosecute those responsible for a 1988 massacre.[62] Then in 1991, Congress withheld half of all military assistance and threatened to withhold the rest unless the Salvadorans negotiated with the FMLN, abstained from violence against civilians, and resolved the case of the 1989 murder of six Jesuit priests by the ESAF.[63]

Another important change was that, unlike early in the conflict when the United States used incentives to coerce the Salvadoran regime to defeat the insurgency outright, the United States now used them to coerce the Salvadoran regime to end the conflict through political negotiation. The collapse of the Soviet Union in the early 1990s lowered the stakes for the United States and therefore significantly reduced the cost of the disturbance.[64] The Soviet Union never provided much support to the FMLN directly (despite frequent U.S. claims to the contrary), but the threat of Soviet influence in El Salvador is what had drawn the United States into El Salvador in the first place. Soviet collapse thus made U.S. indirect control less desirable and gave the United States reason to actively support a negotiated settlement.

The Salvadoran regime's preferences were somewhat different, of course. The ESAF strongly opposed a settlement, and the Duarte government rejected the first serious proposal from the FMLN in 1989. Duarte's successor, Alfredo Cristiani, was elected after promising to negotiate with the FMLN, but his government did not do so in good faith at first.[65]

Two factors helped spur negotiations: renewed conditions on U.S. aid (discussed earlier) and a major FMLN offensive in late 1989. The three-week-long offensive was concentrated in the cities and was the most successful FMLN operation in many years. The rebels captured a sizable chunk of the wealthy suburbs, including a hotel occupied by the secretary general of the Organization of American States and a handful of U.S. Special Forces (a standoff ensued until mediators brokered a local truce and the FMLN retreated).[66]

The offensive revealed, in a rather damaging fashion, just how little progress the ESAF had made since 1985. U.S. advisers on the ground lamented the ESAF's lack of skill and discipline during the fight, and the commanding general of U.S. Southern Command openly conceded that he did not think the ESAF capable of defeating the FMLN. The ESAF was more effective than it had been during the 1981 offensive—it was eventually able to dislodge the FMLN from its positions—but it did so by embracing the kind of gratuitous brutality that U.S. advisers had spent a decade trying to expunge from ESAF culture. The ESAF thus revealed that it was neither capable of defeating the insurgency nor willing to adjust its tactics and institutional habits in order to do so.[67]

Ironically, the ESAF's poor showing actually reduced the regime's political costs associated with negotiating with the FMLN. A new urban elite was on the rise in El Salvador, one whose businesses required stability and security to be successful. The 1989 offensive demonstrated the ESAF's inability to provide that stability and persuaded the new elite that they would be better off with a negotiated settlement that ended the war.[68]

The operation pushed the FMLN toward a settlement too. The offensive failed to topple the government, and the FMLN was eventually forced to withdraw (at least in part because its attack did not spark the wider insurrection the FMLN believed it would). This failure was a major blow, and it left the insurgency without a clear path forward just as its international allies in Nicaragua and the Soviet Union were on the decline (the Sandinistas were voted out of power in 1990). As a result, the FMLN became progressively more open to a negotiated settlement after 1989—though it remained a substantial military threat in the short term and continued to harass the ESAF and the Salvadoran government until the end of hostilities in 1992.[69]

This unusual combination of events—the collapse of the Soviet Union, which lowered the stakes for the United States; new conditions on U.S. aid, which encouraged the Salvadorans to negotiate; the fall of one of the FMLN's major patrons in Nicaragua; and the 1989 offensive that was just successful enough to reduce the agent's political costs of negotiation—shifted U.S., Salvadoran, and FMLN interests enough that a negotiated settlement became possible. UN-brokered talks began in earnest in early 1990. The 1992 agreement that ultimately ended the war committed the Salvadoran government to significant reforms: reducing the size of the ESAF, and amnesty for many FMLN fighters. It also committed the FMLN to disarmament and integration into the democratic political process. The agreement was a significant achievement, but the alignment of interests that made it possible was created by events largely exogenous to the U.S.-Salvadoran relationship.[70]

Objections and Alternative Explanations

In the U.S. defense community, the most prominent alternative to the interpretation presented here is the view that American aid and advice were largely responsible for ending the conflict in El Salvador. Proponents argue that U.S. military trainers gradually coaxed their Salvadoran counterparts into creating a significantly more professional military, and that U.S. economic and political support enabled the Salvadoran regime to make steady progress against the FMLN until it could enter negotiations on favorable terms and end the conflict.[71] In this view, the small size of the intervention was critical for success as it allowed the United States to (1) rely almost exclusively on elite units with the right combination of regional expertise, military knowledge, and diplomatic skill; (2) leave these units "in country" long enough to gain the trust of their Salvadoran counterparts without bankrupting the American taxpayer; and (3) avoid the moral hazard associated with larger interventions, where the agent has an incentive to shirk because the principal is heavily engaged and thus more likely to step in and fight the insurgency itself when things get out of hand.[72]

This explanation is a form of the noncontingent capacity-building argument discussed in the introduction, and thus has very different policy implications than the agency model discussed here. Instead of relying on monitoring and conditionality to incentivize agents to work toward U.S. goals, this approach urges small, relatively cheap interventions focused on building rapport and patient persuasion.

If this "small footprint" account is accurate, however, the influence and capability of the FMLN should have gradually declined over the course of the conflict, and the capacity of the Salvadoran government and military should have gradually increased. There should also be a clear connection between relative capability and the outcome of the conflict.

That is not what we observe.[73] Rather, the conflict had been stalemated for years when exogenous events set off a chain of events leading to a peace settlement.[74] The Salvadoran government ceased to make meaningful progress against the insurgency after about 1985, and a major FMLN offensive in 1989 convinced many that the government was simply not capable of defeating the FMLN. It is true that the FMLN became somewhat weaker toward the end of the war, but it remained a match for the Salvadoran regime until the end. When the process leading to the settlement began in 1990, the CIA noted that the FMLN still posed "serious problems for the government" and continued to operate "relatively freely in the capital."[75]

Moreover, it is difficult to square the provisions of the peace agreement with this narrative. Among other things, the Salvadoran government agreed to cut the size of its military and security apparatus, strip the armed forces of their police powers, strengthen electoral safeguards, establish a professional judiciary, and offer amnesty to the vast majority of FMLN fighters. The FMLN was not forced to dissolve, but rather transformed into a legal political party, and its willingness to abide by the terms of the peace agreement was essential for ending the conflict. This "negotiated revolution," as one author put it, is hard to explain if the Salvadoran government were in a position of real strength at the end of the war.[76]

In many ways, this case turns on why the conflict became stalemated around 1985. This chapter argues that increasing interest divergence, combined with the removal of conditions on U.S. assistance, stalled further progress toward U.S. goals. Others have suggested that a major reason the conflict stalled in 1985 was that the FMLN switched to guerrilla tactics, which successfully countered the ESAF's conventional military approach.[77] While there was indeed some mismatch between the ESAF's methods and the nature of the problem it faced, the shift to guerrilla tactics around 1985 cannot account for the stalled effort in the nonmilitary dimensions of the conflict. Recall that judicial reform also stagnated after the regime felt safe, and that after 1985 there were no major reforms passed until well into the Bush administration (when conditionality returned). One might counter that the lack of military progress created the political impetus to oppose reform, but opposition to reform became strong well before the conflict was stuck in a grinding stalemate. While the ESAF was making nontrivial gains against the FMLN in 1984, conservatives were working hard to undermine the

1980 land reform package and the ESAF was actively resisting U.S. efforts to hold members of death squads accountable.[78]

A deeper objection to the chapter's account derives from the principal-agent framework itself, and in particular from the unitary actor assumption as applied in this case. Preference alignment plays a central role in the explanation, but, of course, the principal and the agent were composed of multiple competing factions, each with competing interests of its own. Throughout much of the conflict, there was significant infighting within the ESAF between those who were open to reform and those who were not. The original coup was led by a reformist faction but thwarted by a conservative one. At various times, similar factions existed within the government (Duarte versus D'Aubuisson) and among the economic elite (the landed oligarchs versus the urban elite).[79] Moreover, the balance between these various factions shifted over time, most notably the alignment between the landed oligarchs and the conservative leadership of the military. In the United States, clashes between the Reagan administration and Congress account for the otherwise strange decision to suddenly cease attaching conditions to U.S. assistance from 1984 to 1989. The impetus for conditionality came almost entirely from Congress, and when Congress lost interest in the conflict after the Salvadoran elections of 1984, the Reagan administration was able to secure aid free of conditions. The transition to the Bush administration led to the reintroduction of conditionality in 1989.

One way to deal with the multiplicity of actors and interests would be to define the agent simply and narrowly as the "chief of government," as several cases in this volume do. The problem with this approach in the Salvadoran case is that the leader of the country never had anything approaching full control over the institutions the United States sought to reform. Portions of the military, in particular, wielded so much influence in El Salvador that the United States occasionally dealt with its leadership directly rather than with the president of the country.

Another approach is to define the agent broadly to encompass all the actors the principal sought to influence directly and then assess net behavior, as this chapter does. In making this simplification, this chapter aligns itself with a long tradition of work that abstracts rich historical detail in favor of theoretical precision and parsimony. This approach is not without cost, but it can be worthwhile. To know whether it is in this case requires an assessment of how helpful the theory is for understanding patterns and making predictions—that is, whether the simpler theory is useful. In this case, a principal-agent framework provides a compelling interpretation of the Salvadoran conflict that, among other things, can account for variation in outcomes over time, and provides a plausible explanation for why the United States was less than fully successful. This account is not definitive, of course—there is only so much to be inferred from a single case—but the fact that the framework is also useful in the wide variety of other cases discussed in this volume strongly suggests that principal-agent theory has something to offer here as well, and that this parsimonious approach is at least defensible.[80]

The success of the model in this case is partial. It captures the agent's behavior well—the Salvadorans responded to incentives as expected and maximized their own interests as far as information asymmetry would allow—but captures that of the principal less well. In theory, principals should offer indirect contracts to proxies with relatively aligned interests, and when they do, use monitoring to identify slack and condition assistance efficiently. Noncontingent capacity building should be reserved for proxies with very aligned interests. Yet in El Salvador, the political cost of fulfilling U.S. objectives was nearly always high, the extent of monitoring was nearly always low, and the use of conditionality was inconsistent over time. As a result, this case highlights how suboptimal policy choices by the principal can degrade the efficiency of indirect control. There was enough interest alignment and conditionality that the Salvadorans were persuaded to take some steps toward U.S. goals, but not enough to overcome the cost of the effort required to fundamentally reform the government and defeat the insurgency. The resulting agency slack was then magnified by the uneven use of incentives and a lack of monitoring by the principal.

Despite the flawed execution, however, the United States made some progress in El Salvador, especially early on. It successfully prevented the FMLN from overthrowing the Salvadoran government, coerced it into adopting some (partial but) important reforms, helped reduce (but not eliminate) human rights abuses, and improved the professionalism and competence of the ESAF. As a result, the Salvadoran government in 1992 was significantly more democratic and inclusive than it was in 1979. These achievements were modest and incomplete, but real nonetheless.

NOTES

1. Crandall 2016, 1.

2. See, for example, Malkasian and Weston 2012, 114; Hammes 2012, 51; Reynolds 2014, 64. For other summaries of this debate, see Biddle, Macdonald, and Baker 2018; Crandall 2016, 2–4.

3. The United States spent about $6 billion (in current dollars) on the El Salvador campaign (Schwarz 1991, 2). On the cost of the Iraq and Afghanistan conflicts, see Belasco 2014. The Salvadoran conflict is often coded as either an incumbent victory or an outcome favoring the incumbent (see, e.g., Boot 2013; Paul, Clarke, and Grill 2010, 37), but some prominent scholars think the outcome was less decisive—Lyall and Wilson (2009) code it as a draw and the Correlates of War project (version 4.0) codes it as a compromise.

4. See Department of the Army 2006, para. 6–5; Department of the Army 2014, para. 11–3.

5. For complementary accounts of the conflict, see U.S. GAO 1991b, 2; Schwarz 1991, v–xiv; LeoGrande 1998, 583–84; Peceny and Stanley 2010, 68–70; Ucko 2013, 669–70; and especially Ladwig 2016, 2017. For more on agency slack in international politics, see Hawkins et al. 2006b, 8.

6. The uprising was led by a young Communist named Augustín Farabundo Martí Rodríguez, who would become the namesake of the Farabundo Martí National Liberation Front. For overviews of Salvadoran politics leading up to the civil war, see LeoGrande and Robbins 1980, 1084–93; Stanley 1996, 41–132; Wood 2003, 20–26; Crandall 2016, 15–75, 90–101.

7. "Oligarchs and officers" is borrowed from LeoGrande and Robbins 1980. See also Wood 2003, 24–25.

8. Wood 2003, 23–24; Crandall 2016, 23–24, 57.

9. Crandall 2016, 56–57, 95–99, 112–13; LeoGrande 1998, 38–40.

10. Dunkerley 1982, 132–35, 162–63; Stanley 1996, 133–217; Wood 2003, 26–27; Greentree 2008, 78–80.

11. Reagan 1983.

12. See Stanley 1996, 133–77; Greentree 2008, 78–79. Leftist groups that believed they could compel more radical reform through violence also created problems for the junta. See Crandall 2016, 126–28.

13. For brief overviews of this period, see LeoGrande 1998, 40–43; Crandall 2016, 122–31. On Salvadoran interests during the conflict, see Schwarz 1991, 61. This chapter uses "government" and "regime" interchangeably when referring to El Salvador. Also, because the form of the Salvadoran government varied between 1979 and 1992 (from a military presidency to a series of juntas to an interim government to an elected presidency), and because the military retained so much power that U.S. emissaries sometimes dealt with it directly rather than with the country's elected leadership, this chapter defines the agent broadly as "the government of El Salvador." This is not to deny that there were important differences between and within the groups that compose the agent, but to assert that the net behavior of the regime can still be identified and usefully evaluated using agency theory. See this chapter's penultimate section for more on this point.

14. Bailey 2004; Crandall 2016, 352–54.

15. Bacevich et al. 1988, 29; Peceny and Stanley 2010, 79; Crandall 2016, 364. See also SIPRI's Arms Transfer Database, available at https://www.sipri.org/databases/armstransfers.

16. Bacevich et al. 1988, 5; Crandall 2016, 217, 318, 329, 357.

17. To be more precise, the disturbance was the degree of Soviet influence in El Salvador. However, since the United States acted as if Soviet influence were identical with the size and strength of the insurgency (except for a brief period near the end of the conflict), the insurgency is the proximate disturbance and the appropriate focus of this case.

18. Manwaring and Prisk 1988, 79–88; Oñate 2011; Crandall 2016, 65–75.

19. U.S. CIA 1990, 7–11; Moroni Bracamonte and Spencer 1995, 175–86; LeoGrande 1998, 68–69; Crandall 2016, 167–75.

20. For an overview and critique, see Schwarz 1991, 6–56.

21. Bacevich et al. 1988, 24–27; Schwarz 1991, 59–62. The internal balance of power is a common concern of weakly institutionalized states; see, for example, North, Wallis, and Weingast 2009, 18–21; Talmadge 2015, 18–23.

22. See, e.g., Schwarz 1991, 59–60; LeoGrande 1998, 46–47; Greentree 2008, 79; Crandall 2016, 136, 157–58, 188–92.

23. This is suboptimal behavior, given the high cost of effort.

24. See Ladwig 2016, esp. table 1.

25. Some, however, flouted the rules and went anyway. See Bailey 2004, 24–25.

26. The monitoring problem was explicitly acknowledged in the 1984 "Kissinger Report" (Crandall 2016, 301; National Bipartisan Commission on Central America 1984). See also Bailey 2004, 24–25; U.S. GAO 1990, 5. On the growth of the ESAF over time, see Bacevich et al. 1988, 5.

27. See, for example, Herring 1986; Crandall 2016, 232–38.

28. For example, see Crandall 2016, 234. Some members of the Reagan administration also occasionally argued for various kinds of direct action. See Crandall 2016, 202, 214–16, 282–83. For an example of Reagan downplaying the idea of deep involvement, see Clines 1981.

29. The Carter administration also thought the outcome in El Salvador was vital to U.S. national security. See Arnson 1993, 40–41; Crandall 2016, 132–39.

30. Reagan 1983. For more on how the Reagan administration viewed the threat, see Kirkpatrick 1979; Reagan 1981; Crandall 2016, 202.

31. On the timing of the final offensive and the FMLN's assessment of Reagan's intentions, see Manwaring and Prisk 1988, 106–9; Arnson 1993, 50–51; LeoGrande 1998, 68; Crandall 2016, 176–77.

32. The phases mark key changes in the nature and size of the disturbance. For similar periodizations of the conflict, see Moroni Bracamonte and Spencer 1995, 37–39; Peceny and Stanley 2010, 69–70.

33. On the decline of death squad activity, see Wood 2003, fig. 1.3.

34. LeoGrande 1998, 572–73; Crandall 2016, 487; U.S. CIA 1990, iii–iv (although see also Moroni Bracamonte and Spencer 1995, 182).

35. See, e.g., Bacevich et al. 1988, 24; Woerner 1981, 142–46.

36. On the size of the ESAF, see Bacevich et al. 1988, 5; Woerner 1981, 67. On the content of the Woerner report, see Taubman 1983; LeoGrande 1998, 137–38 and notes. Note that most of the criticism of the ESAF in the Woerner report remains redacted.

37. Manwaring and Prisk 1988, chap. 5; Crandall 2016, 176–77.

38. Bacevich et al. 1988, 5–6; Peceny and Stanley 2010, 75–76; Crandall 2016, 347–48, 366. Elements of the FMLN received training from the Cuban military during the conflict; see Moroni Bracamonte and Spencer 1995, 73–76; Crandall 2016, 347.

39. Romero's decision was a response to new U.S. conditions that required more accountability on human rights issues (LeoGrande 1998, 38; Crandall 2016, 109).

40. The coup also simplified the politics of providing assistance, since the juntas were at least nominally reform oriented and lacked Romero's brutal past. See Crandall 2016, 111–13, 132–33.

41. Crandall 2016, 135–36, 139. After 1975, U.S. law prohibited assistance to countries engaged in gross violations of human rights unless the aid would directly benefit those afflicted, or the president determined that the assistance was vital to U.S. national security. See Crandall 2016, 103.

42. LeoGrande 1998, 44. Hard-liners (including Roberto D'Aubuisson) planned another coup a few months later, after differences within the State Department prevented the United States from following through on its promise. The plot was discovered before it could succeed. See also Crandall 2016, 136.

43. Crandall 2016, 269–70. This was only a partial victory, since D'Aubuisson ended up as the head of the National Assembly, where he worked to dismantle U.S.-backed political reforms.

44. Bacevich et al. 1988, 25; U.S. GAO 1991b, 27; Wood 2003, fig. 1.3; Crandall 2016, 293–99. U.S. assistance was also probably contingent on José Napoleón Duarte's winning the 1984 presidential election (he did, with U.S. help), since the U.S. Congress would be unlikely to provide direct assistance to a D'Aubuisson government. See Crandall 2016, 317–18.

45. Ladwig 2016, 132.

46. Gettleman et al. 1986, 57; Crandall 2016, 181. The requirement to investigate the murders of the churchwomen was reinstated via legislation in 1983 that withheld 30 percent of military aid until the Salvadoran courts reached a verdict in the case. This led to a conviction in May 1984. See U.S. GAO 1991b, 27.

47. See Manwaring and Prisk 1988, 169–76; Crandall 2016, 149–51; Ladwig 2016, 112, table 1.

48. The *tanda* system was one such local tradition; it fused each graduating class of the ESAF military academy into a tight-knit group that prized loyalty—first to their tanda, then to the army, and then to their country. See Crandall 2016, 60–64, 353. On the decline in death squad activity, see Crandall 2016, 295–96; Ladwig 2016, 129.

49. Bacevich et al. 1988, 5–6, 24–33; Moroni Bracamonte and Spencer 1995, 22; Crandall 2016, 364.

50. U.S. CIA 1990, iii; Moroni Bracamonte and Spencer 1995, 5; Crandall 2016, 366.

51. Crandall 2016, 149–57 (esp. 156). See also Chavez 1983; Schwarz 1991, 44–49 (esp. 48); Ladwig 2016, 131–32.

52. Compare the openness of the ESAF to reform (Manwaring and Prisk 1988, 209–21) to their later resistance (U.S. CIA 1984; U.S. Department of State 1990; Schwarz 1991, 17–43; Ladwig 2016, 132–33). It is also revealing that the junta leader and future president José Napoleón Duarte actively resisted greater U.S. involvement in El Salvador early in 1981, but then requested more U.S. equipment and support just weeks later after the FMLN again appeared to be gaining strength. See Dunkerley 1982, 184; Crandall 2016, 217–18.

53. The "Colonels' Report" is another name for Bacevich et al. 1988. See also Schwarz 1991, 3n10, 4; Crandall 2016, 410. Scholars also widely characterize this period as stalemated; see Schwarz 1991, 3; Peceny and Stanley 2010, 79–82; Ucko 2013, 675; Ladwig 2016, 131.

54. The force ratio increased from roughly one to one in 1979 to more than eight to one in 1987. See Bacevich et al. 1988, 5; Peceny and Stanley 2010, 79.

55. For estimates of the FMLN's size over time, see U.S. CIA 1990, iii; U.S. GAO 1991b, 14; Moroni Bracamonte and Spencer 1995, 5; Crandall 2016, 70, 366; Ladwig 2016, 133. On the shift in FMLN strategy, see Moroni Bracamonte and Spencer 1995, 23–30; Montgomery 1995, 197–98; Peceny and Stanley 2010, 75, 80; Crandall 2016, 366–70. Note that although the size of the disturbance had significantly declined, it remained a military concern for both the United States and the Salvadoran government throughout the period. See U.S. Director of Central Intelligence 1989, iv; U.S. CIA 1990, iv; U.S. GAO 1991b, 14.

56. Peceny and Stanley 2010, 80; Ladwig 2016, 132–33.

57. Arnson 1993, 162–63. It is also relevant that Duarte—who was very popular among U.S. policymakers—took the position that conditions undermined his authority and hampered his ability to implement reforms; see Crandall 2016, 385–86. Note that Duarte's popularity among U.S. leaders is a major reason why replacement was never seriously considered during the war. The United States did not think there was someone better who could replace him (Arnson 1993, 67).

58. Arnson 1993, chap. 3, 152–63.

59. U.S. GAO 1991b, 9, 27; Ladwig 2016, 131.

60. Schwarz 1991, 59–60; LeoGrande 1998, 564–65; Crandall 2016, 407–8; Ladwig 2016, 131–32. Note that some of the gains from land reform were never entirely reversed.

61. Schwarz 1991, 59–62.

62. Crandall 2016, 420, 428–29.

63. President Bush used an escape clause to reinstate the aid some time later. See LeoGrande 1998, 574–75. See also Crandall 2016, 450–51; Ladwig 2016, 135–38. The massacre of the Jesuit priests sparked widespread outrage in the United States.

64. See LeoGrande 1998, 572–73; Peceny and Stanley 2010, 70; Ucko 2013, 676; Crandall 2016, 417. Recall also that the disturbance in this case was ultimately the degree of Soviet influence in El Salvador, which of course declined when the Soviet Union collapsed.

65. Cristiani supported negotiations with the FMLN, but at first was not willing to concede anything unless the FMLN effectively surrendered (the FMLN did not always negotiate in good faith either). This changed after the 1989 attack and the imposition of U.S. conditions. See, e.g., Montgomery 1995, 213–14; LeoGrande 1998, 568.

66. For brief overviews of the offensive and its effects, see LeoGrande 1998, 568–72; Crandall 2016, 431–41.

67. On the ESAF's limited progress, see U.S. GAO 1991b, 4; Schwarz 1991, 18; Crandall 2016, 437–39; Ladwig 2016, 132–33. On the brutal tactics used by the ESAF during the offensive, see Stanley 1996, 248–49; LeoGrande 1998, 569–71; and Crandall 2016, 442–44; although see also Ladwig 2016, 134. The FMLN had recently acquired man-portable anti-aircraft missiles, which further complicated matters. See U.S. CIA 1991; Crandall 2016, 453–60.

68. LeoGrande 1998, 572–73; Peceny and Stanley 2010, 83–84; Crandall 2016, 438.

69. U.S. CIA 1990, iv; Karl 1992, 151; LeoGrande 1998, 572–73; Wood 2003, 29; Ucko 2013, 676; Crandall 2016, 487.

70. The reintroduction of incentives by the Bush administration after 1989 certainly helped matters, but those incentives were not sufficient to end the conflict by themselves—similar conditions earlier in the conflict produced only limited compliance.

71. For variations of this argument, see Hennelly 1993; Malkasian and Weston 2012; Hammes 2012; Reynolds 2014.

72. The acronym "KISSSS" was sometimes used to describe the U.S. approach: "Keep it simple, sustainable, small, and Salvadoran." See Montgomery 1995, 148; Crandall 2016, 352.

73. Although not discussed in detail here, there is also evidence that the small footprint did not solve the moral hazard problem (see Schwarz 1991, 61–62; Crandall 2016, 110–11) and that the United States did not send its most capable soldiers to El Salvador (see Bacevich et al. 1988, 16–18; Crandall 2016, 356).

74. For a more complete discussion of the factors leading to the end of the conflict, see, for example, Ucko 2013, 675–81; Peceny and Stanley 2010, 82–85.

75. U.S. CIA 1990, iv. See also Wood 2003, 29.

76. Karl 1992. See also Crandall 2016, 472–74; and the Peace Accords Matrix, Kroc Institute for International Peace Studies, University of Notre Dame, which tracks peace agreements and their implementation (Chapultepec Peace Agreement, accessed May 27, 2018, https://peaceaccords.nd.edu/accord/chapultepec-peace-agreement).

77. See, for example, Bacevich et al. 1988, 29–30; Peceny and Stanley 2010, 79–81; Ladwig 2016, 132–33.

78. Schwarz 1991, 45–49 (esp. 47); U.S. CIA 1984.

79. See, for example, Stanley 1996, 233–42.

80. For other applications of principal-agent theory to the U.S. intervention in El Salvador, see Ladwig 2016, 2017; Biddle, Macdonald, and Baker 2018.

6

PAKISTAN, 2001–11

Washington's Small Stick

Clara H. Suong

Speak softly and carry a big stick; you will go far.
Theodore Roosevelt, 1901

U.S.-Pakistan cooperation in counterterrorism efforts from 2001 to 2011 high-lights the success and failure in translating U.S. influence into effective indirect control of high-cost agents in proxy wars. After the 9/11 attacks, the U.S. government and the Pakistani military leadership made an implicit contract regarding Pakistan's cooperation in counterterrorism efforts. However, the growing divergence in interests between principal and proxy, as well as the rising cost of effort, induced the proxy to shirk and the principal to resort to direct action. The resurgence of the Afghan Taliban after 2004 and the U.S. policy shift to deter them exacerbated the conflict of interests between the United States and Pakistan. Growing domestic opposition within Pakistan to its cooperation with the United States also increased Pakistan's cost of effort, leading to shirking by Pakistan. Consequently, the United States shifted to direct action using drone attacks.

The Pakistani case also highlights the importance of the scope conditions for effective control of proxies specified in the introduction to this volume. Puzzlingly, we see little punishment of the Pakistani military leadership by the United States despite its lack of effort. Instead, the United States continued to reward Pakistan with aid and diplomatic concessions. This behavior by the United States toward Pakistan illustrates some constraints on the principal. At times, the principal cannot use negative inducements in proxy wars not only because monitoring of the proxy is imperfect but also because punishment of the proxy is risky. For the United States, conditioning punishment on the level of Pakistani effort was difficult because the punishment, even when weak, could backfire and degrade the capability of both the agent and the principal to control disturbances. In fact, conditioning and suspending U.S. aid to Pakistan in 2009 and 2011 contributed to the deterioration of the principal-proxy relationship: Pakistan shut down ground supply lines to Afghanistan in 2011. The shutdown imposed large strategic and economic costs on the U.S. government and forced it to eventually back down.

Theoretical Expectations

This chapter analyzes interactions between the principal, the United States, and its proxy, the Pakistani military leadership, in counterterrorism cooperation from 2001 to 2011. During this period, the disturbance to the United States was violence against U.S. citizens and forces in Afghanistan by al-Qaeda and Taliban militants and their affiliates, beginning with the 9/11 attacks. Many of the militants had been covertly supported by the Pakistani military, in particular the Inter-Services Intelligence (ISI), the main intelligence branch of the Pakistani military, and had fled into Pakistan when the U.S. campaign in Afghanistan started. Throughout this period, the disturbance was considered extremely costly to the United States, causing the deaths of many U.S. troops and citizens. The Pakistani military leadership was not as concerned about the disturbance as the United States was, yet it possessed a comparative advantage in suppressing the disturbance due to its proximity to and knowledge about the militants.

To deter violence by the extremists, the United States could either take direct action against them by conducting military operations in Pakistan or pursue indirect control by delegating to a proxy, the Pakistani military leadership, to suppress them. Specifically, the United States was left with two choices: conducting covert operations in Pakistani territory (direct action) or taking no direct action in Pakistan and fully delegating to the Pakistani military leadership (indirect control). The extremely high potential cost to the United States of overt military action in Pakistan ruled it out as an available and feasible option; only covert military operations were potentially feasible.[1]

However, direct intervention against the militants with ties to Pakistan, even when covert, was not expected to be cheap for the United States. Expanding direct action to Pakistan was politically burdensome to a United States preoccupied with fighting wars within Afghanistan and Iraq, wars that were growing unpopular among the American public. Direct intervention, even in the form of covert operations, was also not welcomed by Pakistan, adding to the U.S. cost of direct action.

Due to the high cost of direct intervention, indirect control was preferable for the United States in theory. Accordingly, immediately after the 9/11 attacks, the

United States established an implicit contract with the Pakistani military leadership to deter al-Qaeda and Taliban militants in Pakistan.[2] The Pakistani military was expected to halt its financial and military support for al-Qaeda and the Taliban; provide the United States with military, intelligence, and logistical support; and conduct counterterrorism operations against the militants.

However, the Pakistani military leadership was a high-cost agent throughout this period. Cooperation with the United States was highly unpopular among the military's rank and file, political allies and foes, and the Pakistani public, due to previous U.S. foreign policies and Pakistan's domestic politics.[3]

Moreover, the increasing divergence in interests of the U.S. government and the Pakistani military leadership regarding the threat from the Afghan Taliban added to the latter's cost of effort, increasing the leadership's shirking behavior and making indirect control increasingly inefficient for the United States from 2004 onward. Prior to the Taliban's resurgence in 2004, the United States and the Pakistani military leadership had largely shared interests, prioritizing the proxy's role in suppressing al-Qaeda in Pakistan. After 2004, however, the United States prioritized countering the Taliban threat, whereas Pakistan did not. For Pakistan, suppressing the Afghan Taliban was perceived as extremely costly; it implied reversing Pakistan's thirty-year policy of using the same militants as their own proxies, which would have resulted in Pakistan's loss of influence in Afghanistan. Moreover, the U.S. government's monitoring of the Pakistani military leadership's efforts was imperfect and delayed, impeding effective indirect control.

The high cost of the Pakistani military leadership eventually led the U.S. government to employ other means of controlling the disturbance: direct control through drone strikes. This is congruent with the theory's prediction that the high cost of the agent leads to the principal's direct control or inaction (H_1).

However, the theoretical prediction about the proxy and the principal with misaligned preferences diverges from the observational outcome. In theory, the United States was likely to motivate the Pakistani military leadership with high-powered incentives, such as large rewards and costly punishments, and Pakistan was likely to comply when the interests of the two parties misaligned after 2004 (H_6). While the United States attempted to incentivize Pakistan with costly punishments, it could not fully implement its strategy of conditioning and withholding aid. In response, the Pakistani military did not comply after its preferences began to move away from those of the United States in 2004.

The divergence between the prediction and the realized outcome stems from the two scope conditions for the theory: private information about the proxy's efforts, and the proxy's subordination. It was difficult for the United States to monitor Pakistan's "positive" efforts to counter the militants because it had a small footprint in Pakistan. It was also difficult to assess Pakistan's "negative" efforts in supporting the militants because those efforts were covert. It was not until 2007 that the United States concluded that Pakistan was shirking.

Another reason for the divergence between the prediction and the actual outcome is the lack of the proxy's subordination. The Pakistani military leadership was not a proxy subordinate to the U.S. government, but a peer-like ally. Pakistan had powerful leverage over the United States through its monopoly on cheap supply lines to Afghanistan. Thus, the United States was constrained by the high cost of imposing negative inducements on the Pakistani military leadership, including punishment or replacement of the incumbent leadership. Punishing Pakistan by stopping or conditioning aid was risky for the United States, as this could have resulted in Pakistan's retaliatory closure of the supply lines.

In sum, agency theory predicts that the United States is likely to use indirect control before 2004 but direct action after 2004, due to the increase in Pakistan's cost of effort and the divergence in interests between the two countries. The theory also predicts that the United States is likely to provide the Pakistani military leadership with large rewards and costly punishments when engaged in indirect control. Furthermore, the comparison between the theory's predictions and observational outcomes shows that the Pakistani military leadership is an example of a high-cost and peer-like proxy that nearly violates the theory's scope condition about the proxy's subordination, as shown in table 6.1.

TABLE 6.1   Theoretical expectations and summary results, Pakistan

PERIOD	KEY PARAMETER(S)	THEORETICAL EXPECTATION	OBSERVED ACTION
2001–4	Disturbances are high. Interests between proxy and principal are aligned.	Principal will use indirect control.	Principal engages in indirect control.
2004–7	Proxy's cost of effort increases. Interests of proxy and principal are misaligned.	Principal will use direct action (H_1) and/ or high-powered incentives (H_6). Proxy will comply.	Principal engages in direct action (drone strikes) and provides large rewards. Proxy does not comply.
2007–11	Proxy's cost of effort remains high. Interests of proxy and principal are misaligned.	Principal will use direct action (H_1) and/ or high-powered incentives (H_6). Proxy will comply.	Principal engages in direct action (drone strikes), provides large rewards, and attempts to impose costly punishments. Proxy does not comply.

Pakistan, 2001–11

2001–4: Establishment of the Proxy Relationship and Outward Cooperation by Pakistan

The U.S.-Pakistan relationship had been rocky prior to the 9/11 attacks. In the 1980s, Pakistan was considered an important ally because of its geographical proximity to Afghanistan. Pakistan became a key transit country through which the United States supplied arms to the Afghan resistance after the Soviet invasion and occupation. Consequently, Pakistan received a substantial amount of military aid from the United States.

In the 1990s, however, Pakistan's nuclear activities and the Soviet withdrawal from Afghanistan prompted U.S. disengagement from the region. The United States stopped providing Pakistan with significant military aid around 1991. By 2001, the United States had imposed trade sanctions on Pakistan, including one for its nuclear test in 1998. Preoccupied by regions other than South Asia, the United States considered Pakistan a troublesome ally at best. Figure 6.1 illustrates historical trends in U.S. aid to Pakistan, which reflect U.S. disengagement from Pakistan from 1991 to 2001.

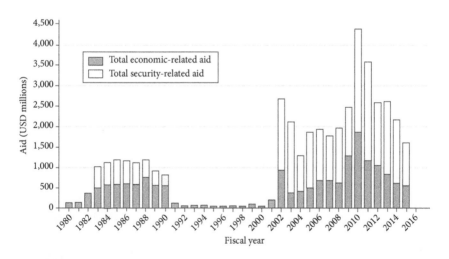

FIGURE 6.1.   U.S. aid to Pakistan, 1980–2015. Data from Birdsall, Elhai, and Kinder 2011; Epstein and Kronstadt 2011, 2013; "Sixty Years of U.S. Aid to Pakistan" 2011. Data on aid for FY 1980–2010 is from Birdsall, Elhai, and Kinder 2011, and is in 2009 constant U.S. dollars. Data on aid for FY 2011–2015 is from Epstein and Kronstadt 2011, 2013 and is not in constant U.S. dollars

The turbulent relationship was exacerbated by Pakistan's hawkish, security-driven, and ideology-driven military regimes and the power they wielded. In Pakistan, democracy has long been overshadowed by the military, which perceives itself as the protector of Pakistan's security and its Muslim identity.[4] Military regimes have ruled Pakistan longer than civilian regimes, which were noted for their inefficiency and for being overly influenced by the military.[5] The Pakistani Army in particular has long dominated the country's foreign and military policy, either by forcing its preferences on the civilian government or through the civilian government's fear of a coup.[6]

The 9/11 attacks dramatically changed the stagnant relationship between a wary United States and its troublesome ally into a major principal-agent relationship. Immediately after the attacks, the administration of President George W. Bush realized that getting Pakistan to cooperate was vital in fighting terrorism and tracking down al-Qaeda and its affiliates. The administration swiftly established an agreement with the Pakistani military leadership, headed by Gen. Pervez Musharraf, Pakistan's chief of army staff from October 1998 to November 2007 and its president from June 2001 to August 2008.

The implicit contract was accompanied by an explicit threat by the United States against the Pakistani military leader. On September 12, 2001, Secretary of State Colin Powell called Musharraf and told him, "You are either with us or against us," which Musharraf interpreted as "a blatant ultimatum."[7] The arrangement also included a list of explicit demands by the principal of the proxy. On September 13, 2001, Wendy Chamberlin, the U.S. ambassador to Pakistan, presented a list of those demands, which included (1) stopping al-Qaeda operatives at the Pakistani border and preventing the supply of all weapons and logistical support to Osama bin Laden; (2) immediately providing the United States with intelligence on terrorists, as well as immigration and internal security information; (3) cutting off all fuel supplies to the Taliban and preventing its recruiting activities from within Pakistan; (4) breaking off diplomatic relations with the Taliban government in Afghanistan, and assisting in the destruction of bin Laden and his network; (5) providing access to Pakistani airspace to conduct military and intelligence operations; and (6) providing territorial access, including naval ports, air bases, and strategic locations in the border regions.[8]

Facing the Bush administration's firm post-9/11 stance, Musharraf initially seemed eager to curry favor with the Americans. Responding to pressure by the administration, Musharraf publicly pledged to cooperate with the United States. In televised speeches on September 19, 2001, and January 12, 2002, Musharraf condemned the 9/11 attacks and stated that Pakistan would help the United States with its counterterrorism campaign against bin Laden, al-Qaeda, and the Afghan Taliban with intelligence and information, access to Pakistani airspace, and general logistical support. Capitalizing on the elites' concerns about Pakistan falling behind India in the geopolitical competition, he justified Pakistani cooperation by emphasizing that India had offered access to all of its military facilities and full logistical support in order to enter into an alliance with the United States and get Pakistan designated a terrorist state.[9] U.S. officials generally accepted Musharraf's public commitment as legitimate; after the televised speech on January 12, 2002, Chamberlin reported to Powell that "Musharraf had delivered everything the Americans had on their wish list," according to the author Ahmed Rashid.[10]

Consistent with Musharraf's promise to the United States, the Pakistani military launched major campaigns against militants in the Federally Administered Tribal Areas (FATA), participating in the U.S.-led Operation Enduring Freedom from 2001 to 2002 and conducting Operation Al Mizan from 2002 to 2006.[11] In Operation Enduring Freedom, the Pakistani military supported U.S. forces in capturing or killing members of the Afghan Taliban and al-Qaeda. Units from Pakistan's regular army, the Special Services Group, the Frontier Corps, and the ISI were deployed to the border regions to target al-Qaeda and Taliban members.[12] In Operation Al Mizan, the Pakistani military launched a campaign to target non-Pakistani fighters in the FATA. Approximately seventy thousand to eighty thousand troops were deployed to the FATA and conducted around fifty operations against the extremists.[13]

The Pakistani military also arrested several high-profile al-Qaeda militants during this period. For instance, Pakistani authorities arrested Ibn al-Sheikh al-Libi, who ran an al-Qaeda training camp in Afghanistan, and turned him over to the U.S. government in November 2001.[14] On March 28, 2002, Abu Zubaydah, al-Qaeda's head of military operations, was arrested near Lahore. On March 1, 2003, in Rawalpindi, Pakistani forces captured Khalid Sheikh Mohammed, al-Qaeda's third in line and the mastermind of the 9/11 attacks.[15]

Musharraf's efforts were generously rewarded by the United States. The establishment of the proxy relationship in the aftermath of the 9/11 attacks was followed by a spike in U.S. assistance to Pakistan. The package included financial assistance of nearly $2 billion per year, reimbursements, and military and economic aid (see figure 6.1). In particular, the Coalition Support Funds program allowed Pakistan to be reimbursed by the United States for its expenditures in the "global war on terror."[16] In September 2001 the United States also obliged the Pakistani request for forgiveness of its $3 billion debt.[17]

Moreover, the Bush administration rewarded the Pakistani military regime by lifting nuclear- and coup-related trade and financial sanctions. On October 27, 2001, President Bush signed into law a bill to exempt Pakistan from sanctions under the condition that the president determines that aid to Pakistan "facilitates the transition to democratic rule in Pakistan" and "is important to United

States efforts to respond to, deter, or prevent acts of international terrorism."[18] By 2004, Pakistan had established itself as a key non-NATO ally of the United States. In the Department of State's *Country Reports on Terrorism 2004*, Pakistan was referred to as "one of the United States' most important partners in the war on terrorism."[19]

However, the Pakistani military's role in the fight against terrorism was limited. The Musharraf regime's domestic alliance with the Muttahida Majlis Amal (United Action Front), a loose coalition of six Islamist parties, may have constrained it from pursuing militants too aggressively.[20] Despite its inception as an anti-Musharraf coalition, the United Action Front made a deal with Musharraf after the 2002 national elections, which enabled Musharraf to win a vote of confidence and guaranteed his presidency through 2007. Historically, the Pakistani military has maintained a political alliance with Islamist parties ("the military-mullah alliance"); Musharraf had no intention of breaking that alliance.[21]

The United States was also less ambitious in its requests of Pakistan. The Bush administration allowed Pakistani forces to prioritize attacks on al-Qaeda and anti-Musharraf insurgents, the shared interest of the two countries.[22] According to Karl Eikenberry, former U.S. ambassador to Afghanistan, "Until at least 2005, the Bush administration simply did not prioritize the Taliban's Quetta sanctuary in its discussions with Pakistani officials. Al-Qaeda dominated U.S. attention. Pakistanis saw this as a green light to keep doing what they were doing with the Taliban."[23]

The Pakistani military's unwillingness to control the border regions allowed the Afghan Taliban to relocate to Pakistan, sowing the seeds of future resurgence. By early 2002, the majority of hard-core Afghan Taliban and al-Qaeda leaders had fled Afghanistan and sought refuge in the autonomous FATA, Khyber Pakhtunkhwa (KP), and Baluchistan.[24] For instance, Mullah Mohammed Omar, the leader of the Afghan Taliban, settled in Quetta, Pakistan, in late 2002 and began reorganizing his fighters in Afghanistan, allegedly under the protection of the ISI and the extremist political party Jamiat Ulema-e-Islam, which controlled the provincial government.[25] Other members of the Taliban and al-Qaeda also moved war supplies to Pakistan, raised funds for military campaigns from Pakistan, and managed training camps in Pakistan.

The period from 2001 to 2004 represents a quid pro quo principal-proxy relationship between the United States and Pakistan. The Bush administration made explicit demands of the Pakistani military leadership for its cooperation in counterterrorism operations. In return, Pakistan was generously rewarded with aid and diplomatic concessions. That relationship was enabled by the aligned interests of the two countries, both of which implicitly prioritized the threat from al-Qaeda over that from the Afghan Taliban.

2004–7: A Rude Awakening, and Transition to Direct Action by the United States

Disturbances grew more frequent and costly to the United States from 2004 to 2007. After the initial retreat from Afghanistan, by 2004 the Afghan Taliban had regrouped and strengthened in Pakistan. In 2003, the Afghan Taliban began its military campaign in eastern Afghanistan and ended up controlling Zabul Province. The Taliban's resurgence intensified in 2004, with control of four provinces in southern Afghanistan. By 2007, the Taliban's sphere of influence included not only regions in southern and eastern Afghanistan but also Ghazni Province in central Afghanistan.[26]

Yet suppressing the Afghan Taliban would have undermined Pakistan's development of "strategic depth" in Afghanistan.[27] Even before the inception of the Taliban regime, the Pakistani military had been an important supporter of the group, providing it with financial, military, and intelligence support in its takeover of Afghanistan in the 1990s.[28] The Pakistani military leadership's amicable relationship with the Afghan Taliban and its extremist affiliates had enhanced Pakistani influence over the neighboring country.[29] Countering the threat from the Afghan Taliban meant Pakistan's loss of that influence.

Moreover, the Musharraf regime faced increasing domestic costs of effort, due to the growing opposition to its policy of cooperating with the United States and India. In particular, the regime's continued cooperation with the United States caused internal opposition within the military. Due to the rank-and-file Pakistani forces' strong identification and shared ethnicity with the militants, many of them left their extremist Pashtun brothers unscathed and arrested only Arab militants. They also tended to arrest militants in cities but turned a blind eye in rural regions, including in the FATA and Baluchistan.[30]

Musharraf's cooperation with India also drew heavy criticism. Wary of India's growing influence in Afghan affairs and its cooperation with the United States, Musharraf urged the United States to help resolve the Kashmir dispute with India. In return, the United States and India demanded that Pakistan stop supporting militants fighting the Indian military in Kashmir. Subsequently, Musharraf ordered the military, and the ISI in particular, to stop pushing militants into Kashmir. However, this enraged the military and the public in Punjab Province, where there was strong support for operations by India- and Kashmir-oriented militants, and drew criticism from the political opposition, which called for reciprocation by India.[31] Musharraf's policy of favoring India over the militants contributed to his growing unpopularity and coincided with the Pakistan-based terrorist group Lashkar-e-Taiba's bombing attacks in Mumbai in July 2006, which killed more than two hundred.[32]

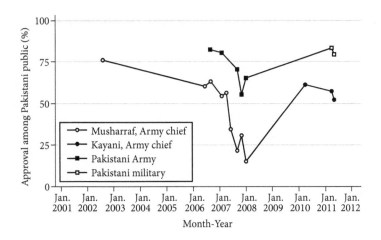

FIGURE 6.2. Popularity of the Pakistani military leadership, 2001–12. Data from Wike 2007; Pew Research Center 2011, 2012; International Republic Institute 2008

Musharraf's balancing act of catering to both domestic political interests and U.S. demands began to take its toll after 2004.[33] Domestically, his regime became increasingly unpopular; public approval of Musharraf plunged from 60 percent in June 2006 to 30 percent in November 2007 (see figure 6.2).[34]

With Musharraf's popularity in free fall, the reformist Pakistan People's Party (PPP) on the rise, and the end of his presidential term approaching, Musharraf was preoccupied by domestic political turmoil. His dismissal of Chief Justice Iftikhar Muhammad Chaudhry in March 2007 provoked street protests by lawyers, supported by the opposition and civil society groups. Feeling vulnerable, he began negotiations with former prime minister Benazir Bhutto over her return to Pakistan. After he passed the controversial National Reconciliation Ordinance to allow Bhutto to return, Musharraf was reelected president for another term, assisted by Bhutto's PPP's abstention from voting. Yet this was the beginning of the end, and he eventually stepped down as military leader in November 2007 and as president in 2008.

Domestically beleaguered, the Musharraf regime shirked from deterring the Afghan Taliban and Taliban-affiliated groups in Pakistan from 2004 to 2007. Instead it was preoccupied with controlling domestic disturbances that posed a threat to the *Pakistani* regime but not to the United States. The regime concentrated on making political deals with anti-Pakistan militants in the FATA and KP regions, such as the Shakai Agreement in April 2004, the Srarogha Peace Agreement in February 2005, the Waziristan Accord in September 2006, and the Swat Agreement in May 2008.[35]

However, U.S. officials were still willing to publicly give Musharraf the benefit of the doubt, attributing the lack of effort to his subordinates or to the difficulties of the task. For instance, on October 1, 2003, Deputy Secretary of State Richard Armitage said, "I personally believe that President Musharraf is genuine when he assists [the U.S. government] in the tribal areas . . . but I don't think that affection for working with [the U.S. government] extends up and down the rank and file of the Pakistani security community."[36] Michael Hayden, director of the Central Intelligence Agency (CIA), praised Pakistan in January 2008, saying that the United States has "not had a better partner in the war on terrorism than the Pakistanis," and attributing the deteriorating situation to the inherent difficulties and complexities in fighting extremism.[37]

Accordingly, the United States continued to reward Pakistan by providing aid despite the regime's delinquency. One analyst characterized the package as follows:

> Senior administration officials considered the package more like a reward for wartime services Pakistan had already rendered than as a point of leverage for new negotiations. The administration chose to focus on what Pakistan had provided—from high-level arrests of al-Qaeda operatives to logistical support for the U.S. invasion of Afghanistan—and not on what Pakistan had failed to do, like taking a decisive stance against the Taliban fighters who fled from Afghan battlefields.[38]

The United States also rewarded Pakistan diplomatically. In March 2006, President Bush made the first presidential visit to Pakistan in six years. During the visit, Bush and Musharraf acknowledged the U.S.-Pakistan "strategic partnership" and called for a "strategic dialogue" and "significant expansion of bilateral economic ties."[39] Bush also publicly praised Musharraf for his efforts in hunting down al-Qaeda operatives in Pakistan and for his long-term commitment to democracy.[40]

Additionally, the United States came to the defense of the Pakistani military against political attacks by the opposition. When Benazir Bhutto, a major political rival of Musharraf's, was assassinated on December 27, 2007, in Rawalpindi, many Pakistanis accused the military of being behind the assassination.[41] The United States publicly endorsed the Pakistani government's claim. Hayden, in a media interview in January 2008, blamed members of al-Qaeda and allies of Baitullah Mehsud, leader of the Pakistani Taliban, for the assassination, consistent with the Musharraf regime's assertion.[42]

Yet behind closed doors, U.S. views of Pakistan were slowly changing, as the United States began to prioritize the threat of the Afghan Taliban. By 2007, the Bush administration realized that the Taliban had regrouped in Pakistan and formed a violent insurgency in Afghanistan with other groups.[43] The administration also began to note the selective nature of the Pakistani military's counterterrorism efforts: while Pakistan cooperated with the United States in deterring al-Qaeda, it had continued to support Afghanistan-oriented militants, such as the Taliban and the Haqqani network.[44] The more important fighting the Taliban insurgents became, the further apart the Bush administration and Pakistani military leaders grew.

Instead of imposing any punishment on Musharraf for noncompliance, however, the United States turned to direct action—launching drone strikes.[45] In 2004, the CIA started carrying out targeted killings by armed drones in Pakistan. On June 18, 2004, Nek Mohammed, a former Pakistani ally of the Taliban, was killed in a drone attack in South Waziristan. On May 14, 2005, another successful drone attack occurred in North Waziristan, killing Haitham al Yemeni, a high-ranking al-Qaeda weapons expert.[46] On December 3, 2005, Abu Hamza Rabia, a member of al-Qaeda, and four followers were killed by a drone strike in North Waziristan. Neither government acknowledged that drones launched these strikes, nor admitted U.S. involvement in the killings.[47]

While these attacks did not elicit any immediate public reaction, a later strike on January 13, 2006, resulted in civilian deaths, and protests broke out. That attack aimed to kill Ayman al-Zawahiri, al-Qaeda's second-in-command, but it missed, killing eighteen civilians, including five women and five children. Following the burial of the victims, approximately eight thousand Pashtuns marched in protest, and anti-American sentiment spread across the country.[48] On October 30, 2006, the CIA launched an attack on a madrassa in Chenagai in the Bajaur Tribal Agency, targeting Mullah Liaqatullah, a pro-al-Qaeda and pro-Taliban militant. The strike killed about eighty of his followers, believed to be in military training at the madrassa. Despite the Pakistani government's reassurance that those killed were in "no way innocent students," thousands of locals marched in protest, chanting anti-American and anti-Musharraf slogans.[49]

2007–11: The Vicious Circle of Attempted Punishments and Strong Retaliations

From 2007 to 2011, extremist violence in Afghanistan continued after militants settled in safe havens in Pakistan, resulting in increased fatalities among U.S. forces (see figure 6.3). Pakistan's failure to deter the Afghan Taliban became increasingly costly as the Afghanistan war grew increasingly unpopular among the U.S. public. This put pressure on the Bush administration and the new Obama administration to control the violence in Afghanistan more effectively.

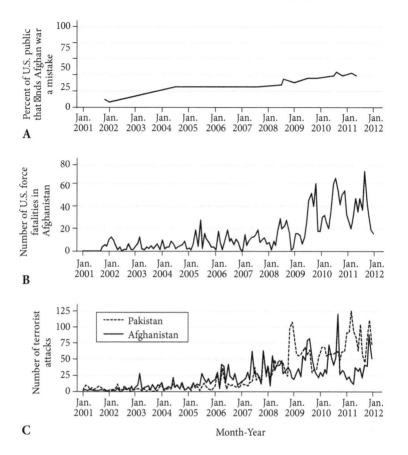

FIGURE 6.3. U.S. domestic pressure and disturbances to the United States and Pakistan, 2001–12. Data for A from Gallup quoted in Newport 2014; "ABC News/Washington Post Poll" 2012; "Chicago Council on Global Affairs Poll" 2014; "In the Fight against Islamic Extremists" 2015a, 2015b. Data for B from Operation Enduring Freedom, iCasualities.org, http://icasualties.org/ OEF/index.aspx, accessed August 25, 2016. Data for C from Global Terrorism Database, National Consortium for the Study of Terrorism and Responses to Terrorism, University of Maryland, https://www.start.umd.edu/gtd/, accessed August 15, 2016

To stabilize Afghanistan and to bring about the eventual drawdown in the war, the Obama government launched several policy initiatives, including the massive counterinsurgency (COIN) campaign against the Taliban in Afghanistan. Modeled on the 2006–7 success in Iraq, the COIN campaign included a "surge" in the number of troops deployed to Afghanistan.[50]

The Obama administration determined that a further lack of Pakistani action against Afghan insurgent safe havens would endanger the COIN strategy in Afghanistan.[51] In fact, the administration increasingly began to view Pakistan as a bigger problem than Afghanistan: the former harbored militant groups, failed to secure the border between the two countries, suffered from ineffective governance, and possessed nuclear weapons.[52]

The importance of dealing with Pakistan's noncompliance also coincided with the fall of Musharraf in 2007, which ushered in Ashfaq Parvez Kayani as the new chief of army staff. It also brought into power a civilian government under Asif Ali Zardari, the late Benazir Bhutto's husband, who was elected president in September 2008. Yet the U.S. government saw Kayani, not the civilian government, as its proxy in counterterrorism efforts.[53] A former director of the ISI and confidant of Musharraf, Kayani led the Pakistani Army from November 2007 to November 2013.

To induce the cooperation of the new military leadership, the Obama administration continued to reward Pakistan with aid and launched new cooperative initiatives, such as border coordination meetings; combined trilateral planning between Americans, Pakistanis, and Afghans; and coordinated operations on either side of the Pakistan-Afghanistan border.[54] However, Pakistan remained unwilling to take action against the Afghan Taliban.

Four categories of Islamist militant groups with ties to Pakistan were active in the area during this post-Musharraf period: (1) Pakistan-oriented militants who targeted the Pakistani military and government, such as the Tehrik-i-Taliban Pakistan (the Pakistani Taliban); (2) globally oriented militants, including al-Qaeda and its Uzbek affiliates, operating out of the FATA and in Karachi; (3) Afghanistan-oriented militants, including the Afghan Taliban insurgency led by Mullah Omar and operating from Quetta in Baluchistan Province and Karachi, the Haqqani network led by Jalaluddin and Sirajuddin Haqqani in the North Waziristan and Kurram Tribal Agencies of the FATA, and the Hizb-I-Islami operating from the Bajaur Tribal Agency; and (4) India- and Kashmir-oriented militants, including the Lashkar-e-Taiba, Jaish-e-Mohammed, and Harakat-ul-Mujahadeen, based in Punjab Province and the Pakistani part of Kashmir.[55]

Fundamentally, the United States and the Pakistani military leadership had diverging interests and priorities in dealing with these groups. Both opposed Pakistan-oriented militants, particularly the Pakistani Taliban, who carried out attacks mostly on Pakistani soil and were a threat to the Pakistani government.[56] Both parties also opposed the anti-American, globally oriented militants, such as al-Qaeda, but these were a significantly lower priority for Pakistan as most of those militants' attacks took place in Afghanistan (see table 6.2).

TABLE 6.2 Number and location of terrorist attacks by major extremist groups, 2001–11

	NUMBER OF ATTACKS 2001–11	
PERPETRATOR	AFGHANISTAN	PAKISTAN
Pakistani Taliban (Tehrik-i-Taliban Pakistan)	4	545
Al-Qaeda	31	21
Afghan Taliban	1,626	41
Haqqani network	39	1
Hizb-I-Islami	30	0

Source: Global Terrorism Database, National Consortium for the Study of Terrorism and Responses to Terrorism, University of Maryland, accessed August 15, 2016, https://www.start.umd.edu/gtd/.

The divergent interests of the United States and Pakistan were most evident in the case of Afghanistan-oriented groups, such as the Afghan Taliban, the Haqqani network, and the Hizb-I-Islami. Pakistani leaders saw the U.S. presence in Afghanistan as temporary and viewed the Hamid Karzai regime skeptically.[57] To them, sustaining the relationship with Afghanistan-oriented militants was crucial to maintaining Pakistan's influence over Afghanistan in the long run.[58] In particular, the ISI was instrumental in organizing Pakistani support of Afghanistan-oriented groups under the cover of plausible deniability. Reportedly, the "S" Directorate of the ISI was responsible for Pakistan's covert proxy operations, which included programs for the Afghan Taliban.[59] Headquartered in Rawalpindi, the "S" Directorate employed retired officers from the Pakistani Army and Special Forces, who worked as the handlers of the Taliban, coordinated Pakistani support for Taliban offensives, and provided fuel, ammunition, and logistical support.[60]

In contrast to the United States' focus on the Afghan Taliban after 2004, the Pakistani military's emphasis was on antiregime militants. Many of Pakistan's former protégés began targeting the Pakistani military and government to protest its partnership with the United States.[61] In 2007, these militants eventually united as the Pakistani Taliban, led by Baitullah Mehsud.[62] The group began to attack Pakistani government officials and installations, as well as civilians.[63] In response, the Pakistani military struck back with counterterrorism operations by the Pakistani military, paramilitary, and police forces, which resulted in a significant increase in the number of nonstate combatants killed, injured, and arrested (see figure 6.4a).

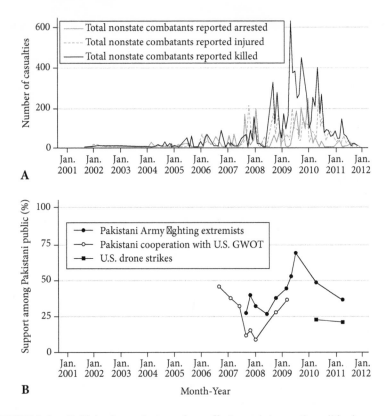

FIGURE 6.4. Pakistani counterterrorism efforts and domestic political pressure, 2001–12. Data for A from Bueno de Mesquita et al. 2013, 2015. Data for B from International Republic Institute 2008; Pew Research Center 2011, chap. 2; 2012, chaps. 1, 5

The Pakistani military's belated counterterrorism efforts were a response to a domestic political calculus rather than to incentives by the United States. Counterterrorism operations against anti-Pakistan militants were strongly supported by the Pakistani public. Yet throughout this period, the public remained skeptical of the Pakistani military's cooperation with the United States and critical of U.S. drone strikes (see figure 6.4b).

Initially it was not easy for the United States to monitor Pakistani efforts to deter militants, due to its small footprint in Pakistan. Monitoring the connection or lack thereof between the ISI and the Taliban was difficult, as the ISI's role in supporting the Taliban was, according to Carlotta Gall, "designed to be deniable." It was not until 2007 that the CIA began to monitor the links between the ISI and the Taliban.[64]

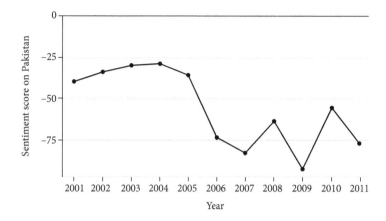

FIGURE 6.5. U.S. assessment of Pakistan's counterterrorism efforts, 2001–11. Data from U.S. Department of State reports to Congress *Patterns of Global Terrorism* (2001–2003) and *Country Reports on Terrorism* (2004–2010)

However, the United States was able to indirectly monitor Pakistani forces' lack of effort by inferring it from the level of disturbances, as predicted by the theory in the introduction. Figure 6.5 reports the U.S. State Department assessment of Pakistan's counterterrorism efforts between 2001 and 2011.[65] The tone of the reports' sections on Pakistani efforts was less negative from 2001 to 2005, but scores dropped significantly in the 2006 report (published in 2007) and remained low afterward, reflecting growing U.S. frustration with Pakistan's efforts.

Consistent with the 2006 drop in assessed Pakistani counterterrorism efforts, the United States began to question the effectiveness of aid to Pakistan in 2007 and 2008.[66] To incentivize Pakistan's military leadership, the United States attempted to punish it by conditioning aid. The punishments resulted in a strong backlash from Pakistan, forcing the United States to back down.

For instance, the Enhanced Partnership with Pakistan Act backfired, jeopardizing the fragile relationship between the two countries. The act, passed by Congress in October 2009, tripled nonmilitary aid to Pakistan for a five-year period but came with strings attached, specifying additional conditions for military aid. The law required the secretary of state to certify that the Pakistani government had "demonstrated a sustained commitment to and [was] making significant efforts towards combating terrorist groups" and that the Pakistani military was "not materially and substantially subverting the political and judicial processes of Pakistan."[67] The secretary of state was also obligated to submit routine reports to Congress on the Pakistani civilian government's control of the military.[68]

Pakistani military leaders considered the act intrusive and were especially upset about the requirement for reports on civilian control over the military.[69] U.S. policymakers in the executive branch had been wary of the legislation from the beginning, concerned that such measures of Pakistan's counterterrorism performance might "impede the effectiveness of [U.S.] assistance or play to the 'trust deficit' that plagues [the] bilateral relationship and promotes distrust among the Pakistani people," according to Richard Holbrooke, U.S. special representative for Afghanistan and Pakistan.[70] Consequently, a blanket certification for Pakistan was issued by Secretary of State Hillary Clinton in March 2011, followed by the Obama administration's waiver of the certification requirements up to 2015.[71]

Due to the growing divergence in interests and the ineffectiveness of inducements, the United States increasingly relied on direct action against the extremist threat. In July 2008, the Bush administration launched Special Forces raids against Afghan Taliban camps in the FATA without prior consent from the Pakistani military.[72] The Obama administration subsequently increased the frequency of drone strikes in the FATA, launching 38 strikes in 2008, 54 in 2009, 128 in 2010, and 75 in 2011.[73]

The tension between the principal and the proxy exploded with the discovery of, and subsequent attack on, Osama bin Laden. The dramatic event demonstrated the Pakistani military's inability or unwillingness to track down America's most-wanted terrorist and the Obama administration's willingness to take direct action. On May 2, 2011, U.S. Navy SEALs successfully conducted a night raid to kill bin Laden in Abbottabad, home of the prestigious Pakistan Military Academy. U.S. officials suspected that the Pakistani military, the ISI, or some of its members knew about bin Laden yet hid the information from the United States.[74] Subsequently, the Obama administration announced in July 2011 that it was withholding $800 million in military aid as Congress debated whether to decrease or condition aid to Pakistan.[75]

Direct action by the United States against al-Qaeda or the Afghan Taliban, by publicly encroaching on Pakistani territory, had been anathema to the Pakistani military leadership. Accordingly, the operation against bin Laden resulted in political embarrassment for the regime: the military leadership was heavily criticized for lacking the capability or willingness to prevent the violation of sovereignty by the United States.[76]

Still, direct intervention by the United States was limited, in that it usually involved covert operations. The Pakistani military leadership's tacit approval, if any, of such tactics was never publicized for fear of backlash by the already anti-American Pakistani opposition and public. Plans to expand direct action were often not implemented for the same reason. In 2009, President Obama considered conducting drone strikes beyond the FATA, including in Baluchistan

Province, where senior members of the Afghan Taliban were believed to live. According to Daniel Markey, the plan was eventually dropped due to the fear of a backlash, as "most of Pakistan . . . perceived a difference between the remote 'tribal areas' where strikes had so far taken place and the 'settled areas' where new strikes were being contemplated."[77]

Fundamentally, the United States was prevented from imposing substantial punishment on Pakistan due to its reliance on Pakistan for cheap and convenient access to Afghanistan. Pakistan offered the most cost-effective route for providing war supplies to U.S. and NATO forces in Afghanistan. The forces had two main ways into landlocked Afghanistan: air, road, and rail routes via the Northern Distribution Network through multiple former Soviet republics, including Russia, Azerbaijan, Georgia, Armenia, Kazakhstan, and Uzbekistan; or land or air routes via the Southern Distribution Network through Pakistan.[78]

The Pakistani ground routes (Ground Lines of Communications) were shorter, more direct, and cheaper than any other option. On the Pakistani land routes, according to C. Christine Fair and Sarah Watson, "goods were offloaded at the Karachi port and then transferred onto thousands of privately owned local transport trucks for the trip into Afghanistan, either through the pass at Chaman (in Baluchistan) or through Torkham (in Khyber Pakhtunkhwa)."[79] In contrast, the northern ground routes, while cheaper than the air routes, required long trips by land and cooperation from multiple countries, including Russia. The northern routes used Latvia, Estonia, or Lithuania on the Baltic Sea or Georgia on the Black Sea as initial landing spots.[80] On the Baltic route, supplies were transported by truck and train through Russia, Kazakhstan, and Uzbekistan before reaching Afghanistan.[81] On the Georgian route, they were carried through Georgia, Azerbaijan, and, after a trip across the Caspian Sea, Kazakhstan and Uzbekistan before reaching Afghanistan.[82] Due to the costs of the northern routes, 90 percent of nonmilitary supplies to U.S. forces in Afghanistan arrived via the Pakistani routes, according to a 2009 estimate.[83] Moreover, the U.S. military's 2009–10 surge in Afghanistan required a substantial increase in the logistic need to transport troops in and out.

Pakistani ground supply lines' importance to the United States was demonstrated when the Pakistani government closed them in November 2011. The closure was allegedly prompted by a friendly-fire incident on November 26, 2011, in which twenty-four Pakistani soldiers were killed by U.S. and NATO air strikes on two Pakistani military checkpoints at Salala. Investigations by the United States and NATO concluded that their forces did not knowingly attack the checkpoints. The United States expressed its "deepest condolences" but did not apologize.[84] Rejecting the findings, the Pakistani Parliament ordered the closure of the supply routes and declared that they would be opened only after the United States apologized for the attack.[85]

The United States and NATO were not without options. Beginning in 2009, U.S. and NATO military forces began to diversify their portfolio of transit routes, shifting supplies from the Pakistani routes to the northern routes. By 2011, the U.S. military had shifted as much as 40 percent of its overall logistics supply to the Northern Distribution Network. By mid-2010, more than half of NATO's total supplies had been rerouted to that network as well.[86] However, only "nonlethal" supplies were allowed on the Northern Distribution Network, in accordance with agreements with the Central Asian transit countries.[87]

Avoiding the supply routes through Pakistan ended up being very expensive. By January 2012, rerouting supplies to alternative routes was "costing [the United States] $104 million a month, a huge increase over the pre-closure monthly cost of $17 million," according to an ABC News Radio report.[88] The impending drawdown of forces in Afghanistan aggravated the situation, driving up U.S. and NATO logistics needs by as much as 200–300 percent.[89]

After lengthy negotiations, during which Pakistan demanded that the United States pay transit fees (reportedly $5,000 per truck), Pakistan reopened the supply routes in July 2012 after Secretary of State Clinton issued a formal apology for the Salala attack. The United States also agreed to continue its reimbursements to Pakistan as part of the Coalition Support Funds program, which had been halted with the closure of the supply lines.[90]

The period between 2007 and 2011 was marked by growing interest divergence between the United States and the Pakistani military leadership, by U.S. attempts to punish Pakistan, and by Pakistani retaliation. The United States wanted Pakistan to deter Afghan Taliban leaders based in the Pakistani border regions, but Pakistan was, as Daniel Markey puts it, "unwilling to sever ties with" the Afghan Taliban and its affiliates.[91] Yet the U.S. effort to rein in the Pakistani military leaders by conditioning and suspending aid was rendered ineffective by their strong opposition, forcing the United States to rely on unilateral action. Moreover, retaliation against the United States by Pakistan proved costly: when Pakistan closed the supply lines to Afghanistan in 2011, U.S. and NATO forces had to use more expensive routes to Afghanistan. This period revealed the constraints on the United States' ability to punish Pakistan, due to Pakistani leverage.

The principal-proxy relationship between the United States and the Pakistani military leadership in counterterrorism efforts from 2001 to 2011 exemplifies the difficulty of a principal incentivizing a proxy that has a high cost of effort. Faced with violence by militants with ties to Pakistan, the United States engaged in indirect control, designating the Pakistani military leadership as its proxy. The Pakistani military initially exerted some effort in suppressing the militants, earning them financial and political rewards from the United States. However, as the major relocation of the Taliban to Pakistani tribal areas and domestic opposition in Pakistan made cooperation with the United States costly, the regime shirked in its efforts as a proxy. As the theory predicts, the United States transitioned from indirect to direct action against disturbances, launching drone attacks to target militants in Pakistan.

The case also highlights a constraint on the principal in utilizing an ally as a proxy, captured by the scope conditions specified in the theory in the introduction. The United States was unable to use rewards and punishments with its proxy effectively, due to its reliance on Pakistan for access to Afghanistan, which increased with U.S. force size in Afghanistan. Pakistan possessed increasing leverage over the United States, and a willingness to use it. The United States was unable to impose punishment on the Pakistani military leadership; when it attempted to do so, Pakistan promptly retaliated by closing down the supply routes to Afghanistan.

An alternative explanation for the lack of punishment by the United States is that the Pakistani military leadership was willing to deter the Taliban insurgents but was simply incapable of doing so. It is possible that the Pakistani military had some limitations in controlling militants in the border regions, given the porous borders and weak governance in the region.[92]

However, most scholars and analysts attribute the Pakistani military's lack of effort more to its unwillingness to suppress the militants, driven by its ambition to use them as proxies against Afghanistan and India, than to its inability to deter them.[93] Experts have noted the military's extremely high capacity, in both professionalism and cohesiveness.[94] Furthermore, from 2007 to 2011 the Pakistani military showed that it had the military capacity to suppress anti-Pakistan militants in the short run when it had the political will to do so.

Some may also attribute the lack of punishment by the United States to the ignorance of U.S. officials. This may have been true in the early stage of the proxy relationship when, according to Carlotta Gall, "American officials failed to recognize the huge investment in time, money, and military effort that Pakistan had put into the Taliban from 1994 to 2001."[95] In fact, the theory captures this inherent difficulty for the principal in monitoring the proxy's level of effort and the proxy's informational advantage over the principal with regard to its own cost of effort. For the United States, monitoring was especially difficult since Pakistan's "negative" effort—supporting militants—was largely covert and designed to be plausibly deniable by its leadership. Yet ignorance alone does not explain the lack of punishment. Even after the United States recognized the Pakistani military's duplicity, it refrained from applying punishment. A more plausible explanation is that the United States was constrained from punishing Pakistan because of the high cost of doing so.

Pakistan's possession of nuclear weapons is another possible explanation for the lack of U.S. punishment against the Pakistani military leadership during this period. It is true that the United States was somewhat concerned about a collapse of the Pakistani regime and the consequential possibility of "loose nukes" ending up in the hands of terrorists, as evidenced by policy discussions among Obama administration officials.[96] However, it is unlikely that a fear of Pakistani regime collapse explains the lack of punishment. This alternative explanation requires that punishment in the form of a decrease or halt of U.S. aid to Pakistan in and of itself would have resulted in the collapse of the regime. However, it is far-fetched to say that decreasing, conditioning, or cutting U.S. aid to Pakistan alone would have driven the regime out of power. Even if it did, it should have been the Pakistani military regime, not the U.S. government, that was more concerned about its own political survival; after all, a collapse could have resulted in the leader's exile, as in the case of Musharraf, or imprisonment, as in the case of Nawaz Sharif. Thus, it is the Pakistani military leadership that would have been more motivated to prevent this from happening, making it highly unlikely that the possibility of regime collapse could be used as leverage by the Pakistani military leadership over the United States.

Moreover, it was not only the United States but also the Pakistani military leadership that wanted the latter to have firm control of its nuclear weapons. Pakistan had been proactive in increasing the security of its nuclear arsenal.[97] The Pakistani military leadership had strengthened export control rules, enhanced personnel security, and participated in international nuclear security cooperation programs since the 2004 revelations of a procurement network led by A. Q. Khan.[98] The ability of the Pakistani military to control and secure Pakistan's nuclear weapons was publicly reaffirmed by U.S. officials, including Chairman of the Joint Chiefs of Staff Adm. Michael Mullen in 2008, U.S. ambassador to Pakistan Richard Olson in 2015, and Defense Intelligence Agency director Vincent Stewart in 2016.[99] A former administration official wrote in an email to the Congressional Research Service in September 2014 that "the likelihood [of] terrorists obtaining nuclear weapons or nuclear material from Pakistani facilities is currently very low because of the extraordinary measures the Pakistan government and military have taken over the last decade. . . . Pakistani nuclear materials do not pose the concerns that they once did."[100]

The U.S.-Pakistan dynamics from 2001 to 2011 discussed in this chapter continue to affect the relationship between the two countries. To the United States, Pakistan remains a difficult and unreliable proxy, a circumstance that has forced the United States to take direct action against disturbances. Under the Obama administration, direct U.S. action against the Taliban and its affiliates continued in the form of drone strikes. The number of U.S. strikes significantly decreased after debates about their legitimacy emerged and intensified following a 2015 operation that accidentally killed American and Italian hostages in Pakistan. Yet drone strikes in Pakistan remain central to U.S. policy toward Afghanistan and Pakistan and, more broadly, the U.S. fight against terrorism, as demonstrated by the successful attack on Mullah Akhtar Muhammad Mansour, the leader of the Afghan Taliban, in May 2016.

Recent events also highlight Pakistan's intransigence and its reluctance to be a reliable U.S. proxy. In January 2018, the Department of State announced that the administration of Donald J. Trump was "suspending security assistance" to Pakistan, estimated to be at least $900 million, "until the Pakistani Government takes decisive action against groups, including the Afghan Taliban and the Haqqani Network."[101] While the move was applauded by some lawmakers who were frustrated by Pakistan's "double game," there remain concerns about Pakistan's possible retaliation against the United States by shutting down its ground and air supply routes to Afghanistan.[102] It remains to be seen whether and for how long the United States can sustain its hard-line stance against Pakistan and whether this will result in any change in Pakistan's behavior.

NOTES

1. Actions by the principal and the proxy often exist on a spectrum and differ by case, so operationalization of the theory requires a careful consideration of the model in the context of each case. The model of Padró i Miquel and Yared (2012) assumes that direct control is feasible for the principal. The model in the introduction differs, assuming only that (more limited) direct action is a feasible alternative if indirect control is ineffective.

2. Musharraf 2006, 20; Shah 2014, 189.

3. Markey 2013, 72–104.

4. Fair 2014a, 201.

5. In Pakistan's history, civilian governments have often been cut short by coups, notably by Gen. Ayub Khan in 1958, Gen. Zia-ul-Haq in 1977, and Gen. Pervez Musharraf in 1999. Only from 1988 to 1999 were civilian governments voted into power, rendering the military less visible on the political scene but still powerful in the background. During this period, Benazir Bhutto, leader of the Pakistan People's Party, and Nawaz Sharif, leader of the Pakistan Muslim League-Nawaz, each served as prime minister.

6. Fair 2014a, 23, 30.

7. Musharraf 2006, 20; Shah 2014, 189.

8. Musharraf 2006, 20; Shah 2014, 189. Musharraf states in his autobiography that he refused to give blanket permission for territorial access for military operations, but instead granted limited access to two military bases only for logistics (Musharraf 2006, 20).

9. Rashid 2008; Ahmed 2013.

10. Rashid 2008, 146.

11. Fair and Jones 2009, 165–73.

12. Ibid.

13. Ibid.

14. Al-Libi was the first source of detailed information about the terrorists who carried out the 9/11 attacks (Rashid 2008, 224).

15. Ibid., 224–25.

16. This program was later criticized for being too favorable to Pakistan, with little oversight (Fair and Watson 2015, 3).

17. Rashid 2008, 31.

18. Shah 2014, 356.

19. U.S. Department of State 2004, 74.

20. Jalal 2014.

21. Rashid 2008, 149.

22. Fair and Jones 2009, 168; Markey 2013, 23.

23. Quoted in Markey 2013, 127.

24. Rashid 2008; Markey 2013, 115; Gall 2014.

25. Rashid 2008, 242. In July 2015, the Taliban announced the death of Mullah Mohammed Omar and his succession by Mullah Akhtar Mohammad Mansour. Mullah Mansour was killed by U.S. drone strikes in May 2016.

26. Rashid 2008.

27. Fair 2014a.

28. Gall 2014.

29. Ibid.

30. Rashid 2008; Fair and Jones 2009.

31. Markey 2013.

32. Fair 2014b, 268.

33. Gall 2014, 88.

34. Wike 2007.

35. Fair and Jones 2009, 170; Khattak 2012, 11–13; Shah 2014, 357.

36. Quoted in Rashid 2008, 229.

37. Warrick 2008.

38. Markey 2013, 113.

39. Kronstadt 2006, 1.

40. President Bush's visit to Pakistan was overshadowed by his earlier stop in India, where he announced an agreement on civilian nuclear cooperation between the United States and India (Kronstadt 2006).

41. Gall 2014, 180.

42. Warrick 2008.

43. Fair and Watson 2015, 3.

44. Markey 2013, 162.

45. It is estimated that the CIA carried out a single attack in 2004, three in 2005, two in 2006, and five in 2007, according to the Bureau of Investigative Journalism (Ross and Serle 2014). Data on drone attacks and casualties have also been collected by the New America Foundation (Johnston and Sarbahi 2016).

46. Williams 2010, 875–76.

47. Ibid.

48. Ibid.

49. Ibid.

50. Obama 2009.

51. Dale 2012, 15.

52. Sanger 2012, 20; Markey 2013.

53. Fair and Watson 2015, 3; Sanger 2012, 6.

54. Dale 2012, 15.

55. Shapiro and Fair 2010, 85–88. Immediately after the 9/11 attacks, Musharraf told Wendy Chamberlin, the U.S. ambassador to Pakistan, that while Pakistan would assist in capturing al-Qaeda operatives who fled to Pakistan, India- and Kashmir-oriented groups would not be targeted in Pakistani counterterrorism efforts (Riedel 2012, 66; Gall 2014, 62).

56. However, there is anecdotal evidence that the Pakistani Taliban was, according to Carlotta Gall (2014, 180), sometimes "another proxy force that the ISI tolerated and used for its own purposes, for leverage against Afghanistan or India, to keep some kind of order over the thousands of militants in the tribal areas, and even to use against its own people."

57. Markey 2013; Gall 2014.

58. Fair 2014a, 133–35.

59. Gall 2014, 159.

60. Ibid.

61. See figure 6.3 for the rise in the number of terrorist attacks in Pakistan.

62. Fair 2012, 107. Baitullah Mehsud was killed by a drone attack in August 2009.

63. Ibid.

64. Gall 2014, 159.

65. Sentiment scores assess the positive or negative valence of documents. The sentiment analysis here was done via a dictionary method, using a predetermined list of English words rated for valence with integer values between −5 and +5. The lower the score, the more negative words the document contains. The analysis used the AFINN dictionary (Nielsen 2011).

66. Fair and Jones 2009, 162.

67. Quoted in Markey 2013, 141.

68. Markey 2013.

69. Ibid., 142.

70. Holbrooke 2009, 10.

71. Epstein and Kronstadt 2013, 13.

72. Markey 2013, 155.

73. Ross and Serle 2014. In July 2016, the Office of the Director of National Intelligence released counts of combatant and noncombatant deaths from "counterterrorism airstrikes," most of which are considered to be drone strikes. The government estimated that 473 strikes had been conducted "against terrorist targets outside areas of active hostilities"—namely, in Pakistan, Libya, Somalia, and Yemen—resulting in 2,372–581 combatant deaths and 64–116 noncombatant deaths, according to Savage and Shane 2016.

74. Gall 2014, 249.

75. Kronstadt 2013, 4; 2015, 13–14.

76. Rollins 2011, 11–13.

77. Markey 2013, 159.

78. Anwar 2013.

79. Fair and Watson 2015, 2.

80. Baldauf 2011; Anwar 2013.

81. Baldauf 2011; Anwar 2013.

82. Baldauf 2011; Anwar 2013.

83. Baldauf 2011.

84. Masood and Schmitt 2011; CNN Wire Staff 2012.

85. Gregory 2012.

86. Baldauf 2011; Kronstadt 2012.

87. Quoted in Kronstadt 2012, 33.

88. "Afghanistan War" 2012; Muñoz 2012.

89. Baldauf 2011.

90. CNN Wire Staff 2012; Muñoz 2012.

91. Markey 2013, 163.

92. Ibid.

93. Ibid.; Fair 2014a; Gall 2014.

94. Markey 2013, 47; Shah 2014.

95. Gall 2014, 54.

96. Sanger 2012, 58–61.
97. Markey 2013, 27; Kerr and Nikitin 2016, 25–27.
98. Kerr and Nikitin 2016, 25–27.
99. Ibid., 17–18.
100. Quoted in Kerr and Nikitin 2016, 18.
101. U.S. Department of State 2018; Reuters 2018.
102. Fair 2018; Reuters 2018.

NOT DARK YET

The Israel-PA Principal-Agent Relationship,
1993–2017

Alexei S. Abrahams

This chapter analyzes the security relationship between Israel, in partnership with the United States, and the Palestinian Authority (PA) on the West Bank during the period 1993–2017. From the perspective of Israel's leadership, Palestinian militants were a security problem that generated disturbances in the form of attacks on Israeli civilian and military targets. Israel had historically adopted a strategy of direct control (1967–93), employing the Israel Defense Forces (IDF) and Shin Bet intelligence service to suppress militant activity. The events of the First Intifada (1987–91), however, convinced several Israeli leaders and a majority of Israel's electorate that direct control was no longer efficient. Especially under the Rabin-Peres administration, Israel actively began to seek a political agreement with the Palestine Liberation Organization (PLO), at that time the champion of armed struggle against Israel. Such an agreement promised to benefit Israel in diplomatic and economic theaters that went well beyond security, but achieving greater security was a nonnegotiable bottom line for Israel. A series of secret talks culminated in the September 1993 signing of the Oslo Accords, wherein it was agreed that the PLO would establish an administrative apparatus, the PA, in the Palestinian Territories. The PA was envisioned to become the government of the Palestinians, who were intended eventually to achieve limited self-rule approaching sovereignty over some significant portion of the territories.

Israel, however, as the stronger party by far, could withhold the reward of this so-called two-state solution or impose other sanctions if the PA failed to suppress disturbances. In this sense, through the lens of the model laid out in the introduction, the PA can be thought of as an agent incentivized by an Israeli principal to achieve security objectives. Given the PLO's and Israel's history of mutual antagonism prior to 1993, the word "agent" is used here exclusively in the technical sense defined in the introduction, and in defiance of its colloquial usage, that is, as an interest-aligned implementer of the principal's wishes. Simply, we think of the PA as an entity that often does not share Israel's security objectives yet can be manipulated to perform tasks on behalf of Israel under the threat of punishment or the promise of rewards. The goal of this chapter is to review the dynamics of this Israel-PA security relationship from 1993 through the present, assessing the degree to which the actors' behavior has conformed with the predictions of the model.

The chapter's main finding is that against great odds this unlikely partnership generated periods of stability and minimal Israeli casualties, especially in the late 1990s under Yasser Arafat, and under the Abbas/Fayyad administration (2007–13). Consistent with the model's predictions, those periods of relative alignment in political interests between Israel and the PA produced high effort by the agent, security capacity building funded by the United States with Israeli approval, and low levels of violence against Israel, which were rewarded with foreign aid and territorial concessions to the PA. These episodes of successful cooperation are remarkable considering that the relationship was fraught from early on by ultimately unbridgeable divisions inside both Israeli and Palestinian polities. Although the PLO was initially recognized as the legitimate representative of the Palestinian people, the Islamic Resistance Movement (Hamas) would soon emerge as an increasingly popular and capable contender. This may have influenced the Fatah/PLO-dominated PA to abandon security cooperation with Israel and return to armed struggle (2000–2004). It certainly had everything to do with its disastrous loss of Gaza in June 2007, persistent political disunity and dysfunction, and the suspension of democratic elections in both the national legislative and executive branches since 2006. Meanwhile, although the Rabin-Peres administration was elected in 1992 with a mandate to achieve peace, over time a growing number of Israelis have come to oppose the process. This led indirectly to Rabin's assassination in November 1995, and later to repeated victories for right-wing Israeli governments under Ariel Sharon and Benjamin Netanyahu. It is also the likeliest explanation for why PA prime minister Salam Fayyad was allowed to fail politically in 2013. Israel's steady rightward march ultimately precludes territorial concessions and, in so doing, is guaranteed to erode either the PA's security relationship with Israel or the PA's legitimacy among its own constituents, in the near future.

Historical Background

After its stunning Six-Day War victory in June 1967, the State of Israel found itself in control not only of the Egyptian Sinai and Syria's Golan Heights, but also of the territories of the West Bank and Gaza, with their one million Palestinian residents. Yitzhak Rabin, then commander-in-chief of the IDF, advocated that these territories be ceded to the Palestinians in exchange for peace. Indeed, under this "land for peace" logic, Israel would return the Sinai to Egypt in 1979, obtaining a lasting peace. It was a logic that appealed both to the Israeli Left and to pragmatic, security-minded figures on the Right. From the start, however, a critical mass of Israelis favored retaining the territories, in no small part because their capture was viewed as a fulfillment of holy destiny, a reclamation of the land promised to Moses and the Israelites in ancient times.[1] Thus began a military occupation that is now well into its fiftieth year, and a civilian movement to settle the territories that has grown relentlessly, now numbering 350,000 (excluding East Jerusalem). The appeal of the "land for peace" logic would glow brighter at times, but right from the beginning there was an internal fracture in Israeli thinking that would later constrain and ultimately undermine Israel's capacity to deliver on its end of the security bargain with the PA.

From 1967 to 1993, Israel administered the territories directly without a Palestinian intermediary. Capture by Israel generated some immediate benefits to Palestinians, who suddenly could access the Israeli labor market. Many Palestinians abandoned agrarian living and began to commute to Israel to fill relatively lucrative low-skill construction and agriculture jobs.[2] These short-term benefits to military occupation, along with the vigilance of the Israeli army and Shin Bet, helped keep violence against Israelis to a minimum. After the Israeli economy's post-1973 slowdown, however, declining employment opportunities for Palestinians, coupled with sustained expansion of Israeli civilian settlements inside the West Bank, slowly escalated tensions until they exploded in December 1987.[3] For the next four years, Israel suffered elevated levels of violence and disruption (see figure 7.1) that, according to Daniel Kurtzer and his coauthors, "shattered the myth that Israel's occupation of the West Bank and Gaza could continue indefinitely at little cost."[4]

The Rabin-Peres administration was subsequently elected in 1992 with a mandate to reach a peace agreement, and as Kurtzer and his coauthors note, "Rabin believed that the cost of holding on to the West Bank and Gaza had become too high for Israel."[5] Official negotiations between Israeli and Palestinian representatives had already commenced in 1991 during Israeli prime minister Yitzhak Shamir's tenure, but Rabin authorized parallel, secret talks with the PLO in Oslo,

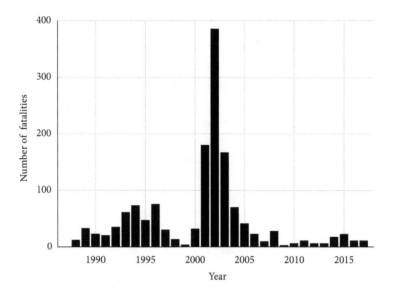

FIGURE 7.1.   Israeli fatalities in Israel and the West Bank, 1988–2017. Data from B'TSelem, https://www.btselem.org/statistics

Norway. Since its founding in 1964, the PLO, led by its iconic and charismatic chief, Yasser Arafat, had been dedicated to violent struggle against Israel, and it was responsible for many Israeli deaths over the years. For these reasons both the Israelis and the Americans were initially reluctant to engage the PLO in talks openly and directly.[6] Nevertheless, the UN and the international community recognized the PLO as the primary and legitimate political representative of the Palestinian people, and many argued that a peace agreement could not realistically be reached without its participation.

The PLO was by this time weakened by several external factors, including the loss of funding from the Gulf states following its support for Saddam Hussein's invasion of Kuwait, and the loss of its Soviet benefactor with the Cold War's end. Israel's desire for an agent to whom it could delegate security responsibilities therefore came as something of a lifeline, and it is alleged that Arafat's personal desire to retain a dominant role in the proceedings went a long way toward softening PLO negotiating positions in Oslo.[7] The PLO agreed to accept Israel's right to exist and to forswear armed resistance. In return, it was granted permission to enter the Palestinian Territories and establish an administrative apparatus or protogovernment, the PA. According to the plan, continued negotiations would then define the borders, diplomatic features, and other "final status" issues of a new Palestinian state. Progress toward statehood, however, would effectively be contingent on the PA ensuring Israel's safety from militant attacks. "Israel and the

PLO," Kurtzer and his coauthors observe, "understood early on each other's bottom line: Palestinians needed to know that autonomy would lead to a state; Israel needed to be assured of security; and thus . . . Palestinians were led to believe that they could get a state if Israel's security needs were met."[8] The agreement—the Oslo Accords—was ratified by Arafat and Rabin in September 1993. Nine months later, Arafat triumphantly entered Jericho with his security forces, and the civil and security institutions of the PA began to take shape.[9]

On the Palestinian side, Oslo had many opponents. The rejectionist Left inside the PLO thought that too much had been conceded; indeed, the agreement undercut the contemporaneous Madrid talks.[10] There were fears, soon to be fulfilled, among leaders within the territories that the PLO returnees (al-'a'ideen) would dominate the PA. But Oslo's most aggressive opponent was the grassroots-based Islamic political movement, Hamas. Hamas derived its strength from decades of Islamic civil society organizing in the refugee camps of Gaza and the West Bank. Inspired by the Muslim Brotherhood in Egypt, these activists focused on nonviolent social welfare provision, instilment of Islamic values, and community organizing.[11] In the 1970s and 1980s their work was encouraged by Israel, which saw them as a nonthreatening foil to the PLO, drawing Palestinians' loyalty away from armed resistance. In the 1980s, however, the civil organizations developed militant wings. Hamas was founded in December of 1987, just days after the First Intifada's spontaneous beginning. Throughout 1988, Israel and Hamas continued to communicate with each other over the possibility of negotiating a two-state solution, but by mid-1989, ties were severed.[12] Perhaps due to the strong loyalty networks from which it sprang, Hamas immediately proved to be a deadly enemy of Israel.[13] By 1992, it was also clashing violently with PLO-aligned forces.[14]

Theoretical Expectations

Throughout the period 1993–2017, the basic features of the West Bank context satisfy the scope conditions of the model. First, at the outset the principal (Israel) faced disturbances large enough to merit attention or response. Figure 7.1 indicates an escalation in violence in the lead-up to the Oslo Accords (1987–92). Indeed, Palestinian militants killed 118 Israelis, and Israeli security forces were unable to suppress militants or quell protests despite killing 693 Palestinians. As noted in the previous section, Rabin and the Israeli electorate agreed that the security situation was unacceptable and could no longer efficiently be handled by direct control.

Second, the model requires asymmetric power relations between principal and agent from the outset of the relationship. Asymmetric military power was obviously the case by 1993. The Israeli army had defeated neighboring Arab armies in 1967, staved off invasion in 1973, and flushed the PLO out of Lebanon in the early 1980s. The PLO could only reenter the territories in 1993 with Israel's permission. With continued control over the West Bank's borders, Israel can deny the PA access to tanks, fighter jets, and weapons of mass destruction, all of which the Israelis possess. The power relations were therefore decidedly asymmetric at the outset, and they have remained so.

A third condition is that Israel should have delegated security responsibility to the PA only if it believed that the PA had an advantage in suppressing disturbances. It is clear from several sources that suppressing disturbances in the West Bank most often boils down to using informants to gather information on plots, then foiling those plots before they can be hatched.[15] Israeli security has a distinct disadvantage in this regard: apart from the obvious linguistic and cultural gaps that raise immediate difficulties, Israel is viewed by Palestinians as an illegal military occupier of the West Bank. To convince a Palestinian to betray his or her own community to Israel is not an easy thing, and indeed many exposed informants have been executed and their families shamed.[16]

A further condition is that Israel should not have been able to perfectly monitor the PA's suppression effort. Intelligence gathering of the nature described above is notoriously secretive, so it is safe to assume that the agent's efforts to suppress disturbances go at least partially undetected by the principal.[17] Indeed, in an example of *negative* effort demonstrative of the agent's capacity to conceal, Arafat secretly funded and directed attacks against Israel for at least a year before documents confirming these activities were captured by the Israeli army.[18]

Finally, it is required that the PA should have had sufficient capacity to reduce disturbances at some cost to itself. As we will discuss in detail later, the PA began its tenure in the West Bank with distinct tactical advantages over other militias. Israeli-U.S. capacity-building initiatives would later widen this tactical gap in the late 1990s, and again under the Abbas/Fayyad administrations (2005–13). The PA did not retain a tactical advantage, however, during the Second Intifada (2000–2004), when its capacity was destroyed by Israel.

Whenever the scope conditions are satisfied, we expect to see several different causal relationships between variables. We focus on the agent's marginal cost of effort as the most important explanatory variable. Consistent with the other chapters in this volume, the marginal cost of effort is defined as the gap that the PA leadership had to bridge between the demands of its constituency and the demands of the Israeli principal. To the degree to which militant operations against Israel were looked on sympathetically by Palestinians as acts of resistance, the PA's efforts to suppress such operations cost them political legitimacy. The "key parameter(s)" column of table 7.1 tracks changes in this cost of effort ("misalignment") for each of five time periods.

TABLE 7.1   Theoretical expectations and summary results, Palestinian Authority

PERIOD	KEY PARAMETER(S)	THEORETICAL EXPECTATION	OBSERVED ACTION
1993–2000	Interest alignment starts high, but declines as support for peace process erodes among both Israelis and Palestinians.	Agent exerts moderate effort; principal incentivizes with rewards (H_2, H_6), builds capacity (H_{12}).	Israeli casualties increase in 1993, then decline sharply from 1997 through 1999. Israel makes territorial concessions, while permitting capacity building.
2000–2004	Complete interest misalignment.	Agent shirks; principal punishes, replaces, and takes direct control (H_3, H_5).	PA funds attacks against Israel. Israel destroys PA infrastructure, reoccupies West Bank, and pressures Arafat out of power.
2005–7	PA and Israeli interests align on combatting Hamas.	Agent complies; principal builds capacity, rewards (H_2, H_{12}).	PA/Fatah accepts funding and training to confront Hamas.
2007–13	Alignment high, but principal's cost of rewarding rises.	Agent complies, but receives fewer rewards than it expected, and greater punishment/replacement (H_8).	Fayyad and PA crack down on Hamas. Attacks on Israel decline to an all-time low, and aid to PA reaches an all-time high. Israel neither cedes territory nor grants sovereignty, and funding lags for Fayyad's reforms. Fayyad is undermined.
2013–17	Agent interest alignment declines as its legitimacy erodes.	Agent effort declines, increasing disturbances. Principal adopts higher-powered incentives (H_6).	Attacks on Israelis increase somewhat, but the PA remains largely compliant while stifling popular dissent. Israel threatens to reduce aid to PA if attacks escalate.

The "theoretical expectation" column articulates the model's predictions for Israel's behavior. Whenever the PA's cost of effort increased, we expect that Israel took direct action (H_1). Whenever disturbances were small, we expect that Israel rewarded the PA or built its capacity (H_2). Whenever disturbances were large, we expect that Israel punished the PA, destroyed its capacity, or replaced its leadership (H_3, H_5). Whenever there was greater interest misalignment, but not so much as to provoke direct control, we expect that Israel adopted higher-powered incentives (H_6). As the costs of rewards increased, we expect that Israel leaned on its other policy levers, punishing or replacing PA leadership (H_8). Finally, whenever the PA's interests were not too misaligned, we expect that Israel facilitated capacity building (H_{12}).

The Oslo Era (September 1993–September 2000)

As Arafat and the PA set to work, they found the Palestinian polity very divided over Oslo. Attitudes ranged from tentative optimism among the broader Palestinian public, to an identity crisis within the ranks of PA security forces, to pessimism among some secular elites and supporters of the Islamist opposition. At the time of Oslo's signing in September 1993, a Jerusalem Media and Communications Center (JMCC) poll estimated that 69 percent of Palestinians endorsed the agreement, with 60 percent believing that it "constitute[d] a realistic step that may lead [them] toward statehood."[19] A 2011 JMCC report shows how the Palestinian public's sympathy for militant operations against Israel trended over time. Although data are unavailable before 1997, it is clear that for all the data available prior to September 2000, Palestinian public support for operations was at least as low as at any other time during 1993–2017.[20]

If, however, a majority of Palestinians were initially unenthusiastic about militant operations against Israel, it was another thing entirely to confront militants, arrest or kill them, or otherwise foil their plots. Responsibility for those difficult tasks fell to PA security forces, most of whom had been militants themselves. Indeed, the PLO's Palestine Liberation Army (PLA) contributed twelve thousand troops to the PA's security branches, including the majority of troops in the National Security Forces (NSF), the PA's "unofficial army."[21] PLA troops were veterans of conflict in Lebanon and Jordan, and had been loyal to Arafat and the PLO for decades. Ostensibly, PA security was well situated to confront militants. NSF troops received three months of basic training and were armed with AK-47s. In addition to these forces, Arafat could draw on the support of the territories' homegrown Fatah militia, the Tanzim, which had an estimated thirty thousand to fifty thousand members. In summary, according to Hillel Frisch, "However potent the Islamist challenge to PA control over the areas it had jurisdiction, the PA security forces clearly had the upper hand."[22]

But whether they had the stomach for actually arresting and shooting fellow Palestinians on behalf of Israel was another question. There was evidently some scope for this, as PLO-aligned forces had already been clashing violently with Hamas forces in 1992.[23] Arafat recognized, however, that popular support only extended so far. For example, he did not insist on a monopoly of violence, permitting local militias and, most important, the brigades of Hamas and Islamic Jihad to remain armed.[24] Moreover, although Arafat "gave up the use of force by agreement," as Daniel Kurtzer and his coauthors observe, he "also recognized that the limited existence of some militant groups kept the pressure on the Israelis and that shutting them all down would be costly at home and could reduce the leverage as the big issues were negotiated."[25] In short, Arafat suspected that Israel would renege on the security agreement if it came to perceive itself as completely safe from harm. A certain frequency and intensity of attacks, low but nonzero, was judged useful to prevent Israel from reneging. Being overly compliant with Israel's security demands therefore not only was seen as politically jeopardizing but also risked undermining a key scope condition of the principal-agent relationship: disturbances needed to be sufficiently large to merit Israeli attention.

These internal tensions presented Arafat with a moderate cost of effort relative to later time periods. The model accordingly predicts that Arafat's effort should have been similarly moderate, thus permitting a moderate degree of violence against Israel relative to later periods. Indeed, events unfolded largely as the model would predict. Figure 7.1 indicates an average of 65 Israeli fatalities per year during the 1994–96 period, the first three years of the PA's existence. While this is fully three times the annual average of 21 during the First Intifada, Israeli fatalities would later average 145 per year during the Second Intifada.

Moreover, as figure 7.1 indicates, fatalities declined dramatically in the final years of the Oslo era (1997–2000). In the words of Ami Ayalon, then the head of Shin Bet, this had mostly to do with "cooperation between [Israel] and the [PA]. I met with all the top Palestinian security officials, all of them, once a month, to coordinate intelligence."[26] Such coordination did not reflect convergent preferences. The relationship, Ayalon said, remained coldly transactional, and both sides were keenly aware of it: "They always told me, 'We're not your agents. We don't put Hamas members in prison for your sake. We only do it because our people believe that, at the end of the day, we'll have a state beside Israel. When we no longer believe that, forget about us.'"[27] Security coordination was meanwhile enhanced by American capacity-building initiatives, according to the authors Beverley Milton-Edwards and Stephen Farrell: "The CIA . . . moved into an important oversight and training support role in the developing security relationship between the PA and Israel."[28] Although subsequent PA effort was not fully observable, they note, intermediate consequences were apparent:

> Thousands of Palestinian security forces were deployed in the move against Hamas. Over 2,000 leaders, members, activists and supporters were arrested and thrown into Palestinian jails and so-called detention centres. Hundreds of mosques, where Hamas had reigned supreme, were placed under the direct authority of the PA. Many institutions in

Hamas's network of social, welfare, political, educational, research and medical institutions were raided and closed down.[29]

Consistent with the model, Israel responded to these developments by taking publicly observable steps to reward Arafat, withdrawing the Israeli army from Area A of the West Bank. Area A roughly included Palestinian cities, towns, and villages, and the built-up areas surrounding them, so withdrawals would have been noticed by the Palestinian public. Withdrawals continued even under Netanyahu's Likud administration, following the Wye River Memorandum: "Israel agreed to pull back from an additional 13 percent of the West Bank and to release 750 Palestinian security prisoners," note Kurtzer and his coauthors. "The PA agreed to combat terrorist organizations, arrest those involved in terrorism, and collect all illegal weapons and explosives."[30] Judging by documented withdrawals, these rewards were politically beneficial to Arafat, and were interpreted as evidence that the territories were slowly but surely being "liberated."[31]

Territorial concessions were also politically costly to the Israeli leadership, however. Although Israelis elected the Rabin-Peres administration in 1992 on a mandate to negotiate peace with the Palestinians, opponents of the Oslo process held increasingly large and vitriolic rallies over 1993–95. This dark period would see several spectacular acts of violence, including the Abraham Mosque massacre of thirty-nine Palestinian worshippers by an Israeli settler, and the assassination of Prime Minister Rabin himself in November 1995 at the hands of an ultra-Orthodox college student after a peace rally in Tel Aviv. Although Prime Minister Peres would carry the peace process forward in Rabin's stead for six more months, he was narrowly defeated by Netanyahu in May 1995, signaling the mainstreaming of political views that rejected the peace process.

As PA security cooperation improved in the latter 1990s, Israeli leadership was therefore under pressure from the Clinton administration (as guarantors of the contract) to deliver on territorial concessions and freeze settlement growth. Yet Netanyahu was also under immense pressure from his right-wing constituency to do the opposite. When he agreed to cede Hebron to the PA, according to Kurtzer and his coauthors, "Palestinians cheered the withdrawal, but Jewish settlers felt betrayed."[32] The Wye River deal would subsequently cost Netanyahu his right-wing coalition and the January 1999 elections.[33]

The Second Intifada (September 2000–December 2004)

Despite the positive Israel-PA security cooperation that emerged in the latter years of Oslo, negotiations on final status agreements for a two-state solution ultimately stalled. Since the signing of the accords in 1993, the Israeli civilian settler population of the West Bank grew apace, increasing by 74 percent, from 110,000 to 191,000. Along with the physical expansion of settlements, write Kurtzer and his coauthors, this had the effect of "undermining confidence among Palestinians about Israel's ultimate intentions."[34] Meanwhile, they add, Palestinian militant attacks had the effect of "engendering among many Israelis the belief that Palestinian territorial demands were not confined to the West Bank and Gaza."[35] As succinctly phrased by Ayalon, "[Israelis] wanted security and got more terrorism. [Palestinians] wanted a state and got more settlements."[36] A JMCC poll conducted in December 1999 found that just 34.7 percent of Palestinians believed the Oslo process would lead to a peace agreement.[37] By mid-2000, it was clear that political costs to the agent were on the rise as Palestinians' patience for the peace process wore thin. The ensuing failure of the Camp David talks in the summer of 2000 was the last straw. Although the Clinton administration would successfully portray the failure as owing to Arafat's intransigence over negotiating positions, Kurtzer and his coauthors offer a more nuanced account. Violence erupted spontaneously in early autumn but was quickly seized on by Arafat, who "came to believe that it could serve as an instrument of pressure on the Israelis."[38] In what followed, Arafat exerted negative effort, redirecting PA funding and resources to equip militants and plan and execute militant operations against Israelis. He authorized the formation of Fatah's al-Aqsa Martyrs' Brigades, a militant wing that proceeded to carry out numerous suicide and conventional attacks against Israeli targets.

There is strong evidence that, consistent with the model, Arafat's abandonment of the security relationship with Israel was provoked by his constituency's shifting demands. While the rejectionist attitude of Hamas and Islamic Jihad toward Oslo had not gained much popular traction in the early 1990s, Palestinians turned to it with renewed interest as the peace process stagnated. JMCC poll data show how support for violent operations trended rapidly upward during this time.[39] Sensing the popular shift, Arafat sought to modify Fatah's image by launching militant attacks of its own and drawing Israeli fire. Thus the al-Aqsa Martyrs' choice of a religious name, as well as other unmistakably religious aspects of their suicide-attack rituals, were all part of a marketing strategy by Arafat and the PA leadership to soften the contrasts between the PA/Fatah and their increasingly popular Islamist opposition.[40]

Low effort predicts high disturbances, and indeed figure 7.1 clearly indicates that disturbance levels during the Second Intifada were higher than at any other time during 1993–2017. An average of 166.4 Israelis were killed each year during 2000–2004 in the West Bank, nearly four times the 1993–2015 average of 45.9. The majority of these were due to suicide attacks conducted by Hamas, Islamic Jihad, and al-Aqsa Martyrs operatives crossing over from the West Bank to Israel.

This era included the deadliest year on record (2001), during which 385 Israelis were killed.

Consistent with the model's predictions, the Israeli army responded by reasserting direct control. Having withdrawn from built-up Palestinian areas in the West Bank (Area A) during the Oslo era, the army reoccupied all areas of the West Bank starting in March 2002 as part of Operation Defensive Shield. A five-hundred-kilometer separation barrier was erected, purportedly to thwart suicide-bombing operations, and hundreds of fixed and temporary checkpoints were deployed along the West Bank's internal road network in order to intercept militants.

As the model predicts, the principal not only chose direct control but also inflicted punishment and even capacity destruction on the agent. PA security infrastructure was destroyed, and some personnel were killed or arrested. Some observers draw a direct causal link from disturbances to punishments, as Hillel Frisch does when he notes that "Israel's first major attack on the PA infrastructure occurred on 20 November [2000], in retaliation for a missile attack at a bus near the settlement of Kfar Darom in Gaza."[41] Unintentionally by the principal, but suiting Arafat's objectives, such punishments may have been politically beneficial to the PA: being targeted, it could appear to be in solidarity with the Palestinian public, less the agent and more the fellow victim.[42]

Finally, Israel moved to isolate Arafat as its agent. In January 2002, Israel intercepted a PA-owned vessel near the Suez Canal. The vessel was allegedly bound for Gaza and its cargo hold was full of heavy weaponry. After the incident, Sharon felt he had conclusive proof of Arafat's complicity in militant operations, and ordered the army to surround Arafat's compound in Ramallah. The Bush administration mediated the standoff over several months as the army destroyed more and more of the compound while stopping short of arresting or killing Arafat himself.[43]

In March 2003 Israel succeeded in formally replacing Arafat. He resigned under pressure from the U.S., ceding power to his protégé, Mahmoud Abbas, who was widely viewed as a moderate within the PLO. This formal conferral of power did not resolve the matter, however; it was only after Arafat's untimely death in November 2004 that the way was paved for the United States and Israel to engage new PA leaders and reactivate the security relationship.

Transition (January 2005–June 2007)

By the end of 2004, the economic catastrophe of the Second Intifada had prompted many Palestinians to question the efficacy of continued violence against Israel, lowering the effort cost of suppressing militant violence. A Palestinian Center for Policy and Survey Research (PCPSR) poll conducted in September in the Palestinian Territories found that 83 percent supported a "mutual cessation of hostilities."[44] By March 2005, a PCPSR poll found that just 29 percent of Palestinian adults in the territories supported suicide bombings, and 84 percent supported a return to the negotiating table.[45] JMCC polling likewise found that by 2005 the public's appetite for armed resistance had declined to pre–Second Intifada levels.[46]Among the difficulties facing Palestinians, unemployment and poverty were identified as the most salient (41 percent). With interest divergence reduced between the Palestinian public and Israel, Abbas won a resounding victory in the presidential election of January 2005; he was vaulted into office with a 62 percent mandate to negotiate a cease-fire and reestablish security control of the West Bank.

With his constituency weary of armed resistance and desiring a return to normalcy, the time was ripe for Abbas to repair the Israel-PA security relationship. He set about restoring a monopoly of violence and reining in non-PA militias: "[Abbas's military strategy's] basic parameters," writes Hillel Frisch, "called for the weakening of the two major militias, Hamas' Izz al-Din al-Qassam battalions and Fatah's [al-Aqsa Martyrs]. If necessary this would be accomplished through internecine fighting, paralleled by the continuous strengthening of the forces loyal to Abbas, particularly the NSF."[47] Indeed, resuscitating PA security was a priority, since it had "borne the brunt of Israeli attacks during the height of [the uprising]." As the PA minister of the interior observed in July 2005, the security services "were in shambles and unprepared to wage a battle against the security chaos and anarchy they inherited"[48] Indeed, even the PA's police presence was minimal, and many neighborhoods had devolved into clan rule.[49]

The United States appointed Lt. Gen. William Ward to head the United States Security Coordination (USSC) effort to assist with reforming, retraining, and professionalizing PA security. In mid-2005, he found the forces in considerable disarray, divided up into ill-equipped and unmotivated "fiefdoms," according to Frisch. "Their communication systems [were] destroyed," Frisch notes, "and . . . only a third [of the personnel] showed up on any given working day. The forces lacked radios, vehicles, standardized uniforms, realizable weapons, and suffered from a shortage of ammunition."[50]

Although Abbas's political mandate for restoring order and normalcy indicated that agent effort cost was low, we see a medium level of forty Israeli fatalities in the year 2005, perhaps due to the agent's low capacity. Fatalities declined over 2005–7, averaging just 15.5 over 2006–7, nearly identical to the quiet 1997–99 years. This decline is likely due to increased effort, the success of U.S. capacity-building efforts, and coordination with the IDF.

Indeed, in view of the political mayhem that was to ensue, it is remarkable that there was such progress in PA security reform. Although supportive of Ward's project, the Bush administration made the fateful decision to insist on PA legislative elections. Hamas had boycotted the presidential elections, but it indicated its intention to compete for legislative seats. According to Secretary of State Condoleezza Rice, Abbas felt that "no election that excluded Hamas would be legitimate . . . and he even seemed to have a sense that it could help to start to either moderate Hamas' behavior or expose them as not capable of moderation."[51] The Bush administration insisted that elections go forward. Figure 7.2 indicates a spike in U.S. aid to the PA during 2005 as the administration sought to use development assistance to bolster Fatah's political campaign against its political rivals, mainly Hamas.

By all accounts, then, it came as a complete surprise when Hamas's "Change and Reform Party" dramatically upset Fatah in the January 2006 legislative elections, winning 56 percent of the seats and the right to choose a prime minister (Ismail Haniyeh). While in a de jure sense this implied that a Hamas-run PA might now take over as Israel's security agent, the reality was that Israel and the United States never seriously considered engaging Hamas in this role. They did immediately demand that Hamas renounce violence, acknowledge Israel's right

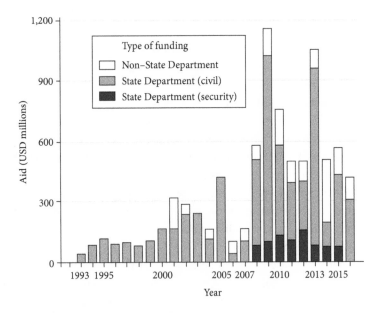

FIGURE 7.2. U.S. aid obligations to the Palestinians, 1993–2016. U.S. Agency for International Development, Foreign Aid Explorer: The Official Record of U.S. Foreign Aid, https://explorer.usaid.gov/data.html#tab-data-download

to exist, and agree to honor all preexisting PA agreements, but in reality, according to Daniel Kurtzer and his coauthors, "the idea of giving a Hamas government an opportunity to change . . . was never given serious consideration."[52] Meanwhile, Abbas retained the loyalty of much of the civil service and all of the PA security services, which were dominated by Fatah loyalists. As such, the agent during this time period is best understood as the de facto PA under Abbas.

The Palestinians' vote for a majority Hamas legislature in January 2006 might at first glance appear to have been a vote in favor of violence. It was not, however. Rather, Palestinians were frustrated by the corruption and extravagance of the ruling party, Fatah, which had failed to make any tangible progress toward reform during 2005. Hamas, building on decades of grassroots social-welfare provision, could credibly position itself as the Change and Reform Party, promising to clean up PA inefficiency and corruption.[53] Hamas was also able to frame Sharon's unilateral withdrawal from Gaza in August 2005 as evidence that its hard-line approach to Israel yielded results that Fatah's peace process could not.[54] In the January elections, then, many Palestinians voted for Hamas candidates to protest against Fatah, not anticipating that the aggregate consequence would be to vote in a majority Hamas government and trigger international sanctions, a brief civil war, and a lasting estrangement between Gaza and the West Bank.

With the disturbance elected to be a government, Israel and the U.S. moved quickly to disempower it, and to increase the capacity of its Fatah/Abbas agent. The campaign began with the Israeli army's arrests of sixty-eight of the seventy-four elected Hamas legislators, followed by sweeping international sanctions and the freezing of funds to the PA. Israel, which is obligated under the Paris Protocol to collect taxes from Palestinian laborers in Israel and transfer these so-called clearance revenues to the PA on a monthly basis, refused to hand over $60 million owed. Clearance revenue transfers would not resume until Hamas's complete ejection from the PA in June 2007. The relatively high level of aid in 2005 was consistent with U.S. efforts to bolster Abbas and create a favorable climate for Fatah ahead of the January 2006 legislative elections (see figure 7.2). By contrast, aid to the PA plummeted in 2006.

Meanwhile, the United States began to fund the arming and training of Fatah security forces to prepare them to overthrow the Hamas PA. Although funding for this effort is not recorded in the data reported in figure 7.2, Secretary of State Rice and Deputy National Security Adviser Elliott Abrams requested $86 million from Congress to train and equip Fatah security forces in the Gaza Strip under PA security chief Muhammad Dahlan, supervised by Lt. Gen. Keith Dayton.[55] According to a report by the International Crisis Group, "Dahlan, with the help of the government of Israel, was bringing in weapons, ammunition, vehicles . . . through Israeli crossings. . . . Dahlan, it was alleged, was also encouraged to form his own Special Force . . . preparing them through intensive training for a showdown."[56] When Fatah and Hamas appeared to heal the rift between them by forming a Saudi-brokered unity government in February 2007, Secretary Rice was, *Vanity Fair* reported, "apoplectic" over this apparent reversal of proxy effort. The Bush administration continued to pressure Fatah to confront Hamas militarily.[57] In March 2007, a document detailing U.S. capacity-building efforts was leaked to the Jordanian newspaper *Al-Majd.* According to *Vanity Fair,* the document, entitled "Plan B," also "called for Abbas to 'collapse the government' if Hamas refused to alter its attitude toward Israel."[58] Preempting any such maneuvers, Hamas moved forcibly to take control of the Gaza Strip in June, routing Fatah security forces (see chapter 4 for details).

Fayyadism (June 2007–13)

The loss of Gaza to Hamas led to greater interest alignment between Israel and the PA, which moved swiftly to eviscerate Hamas in the West Bank. The crackdown commenced with almost eighty arrests of Hamas affiliates on June 14, the day after Hamas completed its takeover of Gaza. On June 15, Abbas dissolved the Fatah-Hamas unity government and installed former PA finance minister Salam Fayyad as prime minister. Enjoying political support for a return to normalcy and stability, the PA faced a low domestic cost of effort and indeed proceeded to exert a high degree of effort, arresting upward of two thousand alleged Hamas affiliates in the West Bank.

Fatah also attacked Hamas's social welfare infrastructure, shuttering more than a hundred charities believed to be affiliated with the Islamic movement. These included an orphanage for girls in Hebron, schools for the handicapped in Qalqiliya, and a shopping mall in Nablus. In some cases, the organizations would be permanently shuttered, and certain materials (school buses, sewing machines) were confiscated. In other cases, Hamas-affiliated management was replaced with management friendly to Fatah.[59] The PA also purged its civil service of Hamas affiliates and outlawed Hamas as a political party.[60] Consistent with the model's prediction of high effort, Israeli fatalities during 2007–13 (9.9 per year) reached some of the lowest levels observed throughout 1993–2017 (see figure 7.1).

The PA was not at full strength when it initiated its crackdown, and it took more than a year to reestablish a monopoly of violence over the West Bank. Though the campaign against Hamas began on June 14, 2007, arrests of Hamas affiliates continued through at least August 2008. Although the northern governorates of Jenin and Nablus were targeted early on, the more unruly governorate of Hebron was judged at first to be beyond the PA's capacity to control. As capacity building proceeded, and at Fayyad's insistence, the PA eventually reasserted control over the Hebron governorate in late 2008.[61]

The 2007–13 period saw unprecedented levels of aid from the United States to support the PA in its newfound vigilance. The West Bank, it was decided, would be held up as an example to Palestinians of the benefits of choosing a cooperative leadership, in contrast to the blockaded "Hamastan" of Gaza: "The U.S. and Western aid spigot," write Kurtzer and his coauthors, "was quickly turned back on in an effort to bolster Abbas and Fayyad."[62] U.S. aid obligations were higher in every year from 2008 (the first full year of Fatah-PA rule) onward than they had ever been in any single year previously (see figure 7.2). Indeed, U.S. aid to the PA exceeded $1 billion in 2009. A major source of this funding was the U.S. Department of State. Starting in 2008, the department funneled aid to the PA through the Bureau of International Narcotics and Law Enforcement to build security capacity (colored black in figure 7.2). This bureau funded the mission of Lieutenant General Dayton and the USSC to equip and train battalions of carefully vetted Palestinian recruits to make them the PA's most trusted elite security personnel. Although the PA was not permitted to form an army, these eight-thousand-plus gendarmes would form the backbone of PA security and be relied on to suppress disturbances and act as a deterrent to Hamas.[63] In a 2009 speech, Dayton extolled their performance in the campaign against Hamas: "Senior IDF commanders ask me frequently, 'How many more of these new Palestinians can you generate, and how quickly, because they are our way to leave the West Bank.'" He went on to recount several stories of IDF leadership gradually trusting PA security more and delegating larger areas of operation to them, including parts of Area B.[64]

Along with building the capacity of security forces, the PA spent nonsecurity aid on the reformation of PA civil institutions as part of an ambitious plan by Prime Minister Fayyad. The plan, dubbed "Fayyadism," was to improve the quality of PA governance so much that the international community would have no choice but to acknowledge that Palestinians were ready to govern themselves independently, forcing Israel to return to negotiations. In fact, in September 2009 Fayyad publicly announced a two-year deadline for such recognition,[65] stating his belief that "the reality of [a Palestinian] state [would] impose itself on the world."[66] Echoing Fayyad, senior PA officials viewed "good governance as the highest form of resistance."[67]

No such recognition, however, was extended by Israel and its allies. Moreover, when aid did not keep pace with the reforms budget, PA debt increased dramatically, quickly exceeding $2.5 billion. Subsequent disillusionment with the peace process and austerity measures generated a powerful political backlash that forced Fayyad's resignation in June 2013.

The principal's behavior here may seem puzzling. Interest alignment on suppressing disturbances was at an all-time high, agent effort was high, disturbances were low, and the agent's civil reforms appeared to be laying the groundwork for a peaceful future. Why would the principal allow the agent to fail? An explanation consistent with the model is that rewards gradually became more politically costly for the principal to dispense. Fayyad's state-building objectives dovetailed with the principal's interests insofar as they directly suppressed militant activity, and insofar as they undermined sources of militancy by closing what Ashraf Ghani and Clare Lockhart (2009) call the "sovereignty gap." But insofar as Fayyad's reforms hastened the two-state solution timetable, they put the principal, especially the Israeli army, in an awkward situation. "In terms of assigning responsibilities to the Palestinians and increasing their operational area," remarked one IDF brigadier general, "I think we are close to the ceiling of the security cooperation, at least if there is no political process to accompany it."[68] The PA's diligence in suppressing disturbances meant that the Israeli army could withdraw from the West Bank, confidently ceding responsibility to the PA. Palestinians would have viewed Israeli withdrawal as evidence of "liberation," so the PA stood to benefit politically. The PA repeatedly called for such withdrawal,[69] and the Israeli army largely favored it.[70] Politically, however, withdrawal had become very costly. The Israeli electorate's enthusiasm for ceding territory had been declining since at least the early 1990s, and according to Hillel Frisch, "By the [Second Intifada's end], successful Israeli counter-terrorism had considerably reduced the costs of staving off Palestinian independence."[71]

An unintended consequence of the PA's security efforts during 2007–13 was to cement the Israeli public's perception that the decades-old trade-off of "land for peace" was not necessary. In Gaza, land had been ceded via Sharon's unilateral withdrawal in 2005, but rocket attacks had subsequently increased. In the West Bank, meanwhile, no land had been ceded; on the contrary, settlement growth had continued unabated. Yet peace (in the limited sense of low disturbances) seemed to have been achieved. Coupled with the Israeli electorate's rightward drift, the climate for granting territorial concessions had therefore soured. There was now a low "ceiling" to what the army was permitted to cede, effectively capping rewards despite unprecedented compliance by the agent. Lack of concessions undermined the legitimacy of Fayyad's policies in the eyes of his constituents, who viewed the concessions as having profited only Israel, not the Palestinians. With the rising awkwardness of Israel's position, funding for Fayyad's reforms from Israel's allies fell short, leading directly to PA fiscal debt, austerity measures, popular backlash, and Fayyad's ejection.

The Post-Fayyad Era (2013–17)

Since Fayyad's departure, the political costs of PA compliance with Israel have been on the rise, owing to Palestinian frustration with economic stagnation and the lack of progress toward a political resolution of the conflict. As in the 1990s, this frustration has partly translated into support for Hamas, with a March 2016 poll suggesting that if presidential elections were held, Hamas's Ismail Haniyeh would win, 52 percent to Abbas's 41 percent.[72] An October 2017 PCPSR poll reached similar results (Haniyeh 50 percent, Abbas 42 percent).[73]

Hamas's persistent popularity means that the PA cannot hold elections without either risking a repeat of January 2006 or delegitimizing itself by forbidding Hamas candidates to compete. Accordingly, no legislative elections have been held, and Abbas has continued to extend his tenure. This devolution into authoritarianism has been accompanied by a tightening grip on sources of dissent in news and social media, and an overall sense that the PA prioritizes the interests of Israel and the United States over those of its Palestinian constituency. Already by fall 2015, a PCPSR poll found that more than half of Palestinians favored the dissolution of the PA altogether.[74] Two years later, the PCPSR found that 46 percent of West Bank Palestinians view the PA as a "burden," 60 percent wish Abbas would resign, and an "overwhelming majority" fear for the future of civil liberties under the PA.[75]

With the PA cost of effort trending upward, the model predicts declining effort to suppress militancy and rising Israeli fatalities. Strictly speaking, this prediction is borne out by the data: across 2013–17, Israeli fatalities averaged 19.9 per year in Israel and the West Bank, twice the 9.9 average of the Fayyad era. In figure 7.1, however, note that 19.9 is still low relative to earlier periods. Moreover, the average falls to 13.3 if we exclude 2014, which was a year of greater overall unrest given the major conflagration in Gaza. The so-called "Knife Intifada" that began in late 2015 and carried on through much of 2016, though it generated much press coverage, in reality consisted of a series of spontaneous, disorganized assaults, and led to rather few Israeli casualties. In April 2016, a purported member of Hamas carried out the first suicide bus bombing attack since 2005 in Jerusalem, causing no fatalities but some significant injuries. Later, in June, two Palestinian militants killed four Israeli civilians at a café in Tel Aviv. A year later, in July 2017, Palestinian militants killed two Israeli police officers near the Al-Aqsa Mosque, generating a series of countermeasures and volatile protests in Jerusalem. Yet these isolated incidents serve mostly to accentuate the pervading absence of any organized, sustained militant campaign against Israel. The relative stability of this period, despite widespread political frustration among West Bank

Palestinians, suggests that PA security continues to exert high effort, working vigilantly behind the scenes to suppress militancy.

The PA's puzzling compliance does not appear to reflect a shift in Israeli behavior. Israel has not responded to the increase in disturbances with capacity-building initiatives, since PA security capacity remains high after the training and arms it received during 2007–13. Facing decreasing returns from capacity building, Israel has instead threatened to adopt higher-powered incentives. For example, a January 2016 *Wall Street Journal* editorial by Israel's deputy minister of foreign affairs, Tzipi Hotolevy, advised the United States to cease funding the PA as punishment for its perceived complicity in violence against Israel.[76] Following the June 2016 death of an American citizen in a Palestinian knife attack in Tel Aviv, the U.S. Congress did indeed take steps toward jeopardizing aid flows to the PA, echoing Hotolevy's advice.[77] By 2017's end, however, the U.S. did not appear to be scaling back aid. Given the PA's high level of effort, this initiative will most likely persist as an unrealized threat.

The PA's cooperativeness during the post-Fayyad era, despite its constituency's growing dissatisfaction and in the absence of any notable changes to the rewards schedule, suggests a general decoupling of the PA's interests from those of the Palestinian people, and increased effectiveness in co-option and repression of dissenters. Israel will likely continue to succeed in incentivizing the PA to sustain security cooperation, until such time as Palestinians regain leverage over their own leadership. In this regard, it remains to be seen whether recent reconciliatory gestures between Fatah and Hamas will translate into further consolidation of power in the hands of the PA, or greater accountability to its constituents.[78]

Alternative Explanations

This chapter argues that changes in actors' behaviors, and ultimately changes in Israeli fatalities, were induced mostly by changes in Palestinians' political tolerance for security cooperation between the PA and Israel (i.e., suppressive effort) and by changes in Israel's willingness to make concessions on statehood. The behavior of Hamas, Islamic Jihad, and various militant groups is taken as constant or at least exogenous. Alternatively, Barbara Walter and Andrew Kydd put forward an argument that Hamas and Islamic Jihad acted strategically during 1993–96 as "spoilers," intensifying violence against Israel in a deliberate attempt to undermine trust between Israel and the PA, discrediting the Rabin-Peres administration, and bolstering Netanyahu's right-wing Likud Party.[79] Indeed, a series of suicide bombings organized by Hamas in the spring of 1996 eroded popular support for Shimon Peres's pro-peace platform in the months leading up to national elections, allowing the Likud Party to eke out a narrow victory in May.[80] Pursuing this logic, the subsequent decline in Israeli fatalities in 1997–99 can be explained quite simply: Hamas stopped attacking Israelis, satisfied that it had achieved its goal of bringing to power a hard-line Israeli administration. Later in 2005, when debating whether or not to allow Hamas to participate in the legislative elections, Abbas would argue, "If you don't let them into the process, they're going to be a spoiler," suggesting that the PA leadership shared this interpretation of events.[81]

There are, however, several reasons to dispute this narrative. First, in an example illustrative of a more general lesson, the string of Hamas suicide attacks in early 1996 was actually in retaliation for Israel's high-profile targeted killing of the Hamas operative Yahya Ayyash in January. Peres himself ordered the assassination, breaking a cease-fire with Hamas that had persisted for more than six months. Second, in the opinion of then Shin Bet director Ami Ayalon, the post-election decline in Israeli fatalities was primarily thanks to enhanced security cooperation with the PA. Third, the election of Netanyahu and the Likud, while clearly unhelpful, did not torpedo the peace process. Not only did security cooperation and capacity building increase, but Israel delivered on territorial concessions under the Wye River Memorandum, and returned to the negotiating table at Camp David in 2000 under Ehud Barak. If Hamas were a spoiler, it should have maintained an aggressive posture during 1997–99 in order to undermine these positive steps.

As for the decline in Israeli fatalities after the Second Intifada, it is sometimes argued that the Israeli separation wall, not enhanced PA security cooperation, was the cause. In reality, however, the wall is quite porous. Although construction was initiated in 2002, sections of the wall remain incomplete even fifteen years later. Indeed, sources within the Israeli defense establishment claimed as recently as 2014 that there are on the order of six thousand illegal crossings per month, with as many as eighty thousand West Bank Palestinians dwelling illegally inside Israel.[82] Moreover, many Israeli settlements lie deep inside the West Bank, beyond the protection of the wall. Just east of the Palestinian town of Al-Bireh, Palestinian traffic regularly passes to within one hundred to two hundred meters of the Israeli settlement of Beit El, unchecked by Israeli security and within full view of houses and backyards. In the Old City of Hebron, some Israeli settlements are built *on top* of Palestinian residences, and can be approached to within ten to twenty meters without one's ever passing through an Israeli checkpoint.

While these "omitted variables" explanations do not hold up to scrutiny, our narrative is assailed by at least one potential concern of endogeneity. Amaney Jamal draws on in-depth survey evidence from Jordan, Kuwait, and several other Arab countries to argue that Arab citizens are aware that their leaders are clients of external patrons, and that these citizens understand the dangers of disappointing the patron.[83] As such, they are more reluctant to overthrow or vote against their authoritarian leaders if they anticipate that the patron will respond with sanctions or forcible regime change. Consider how the election of a majority Hamas legislature in January 2006 provoked Israel and the United States to impose crushing sanctions throughout 2006 and the first half of 2007, and to instigate a civil war between Fatah and Hamas. Palestinians learned from this experience, Jamal argues, and subsequently expressed support for the Abbas/Fayyad PA so as not to provoke any further wrath from Israel or the United States. "That Palestinians are willing to accept the authoritarian abuses linked to Fayyad's 'reforms,'" she writes, "is witnessed in his growing approval ratings . . . but they are less about outright support for the authoritarian [PA] . . . and more a means to get on with life in accordance to the preferences of the United States and Israel."[84] That there may have been an underlying current of resentment toward Fayyad all along is supported by grassroots-level interviews by Alaa Tartir.[85] Jamal's argument also helps explain why the PA's suspension of democratic elections since at least 2009 has not provoked a greater backlash.

Without wishing to detract at all from her argument's ingenuity and region-wide breadth, there are nevertheless some reasons to contest Jamal's narrative with respect to the Abbas/Fayyad administration. First, JMCC polls (cited earlier) strongly indicate that, in the wake of the Second Intifada, Palestinians were eager for the PA to reassert a police presence and restore rule of law. The Abbas/Fayyad administration delivered on this demand, so its popularity had a more first-order explanation. Second, if Jamal's argument is the overriding logic of PA legitimacy, then the post-Fayyad Abbas administration ought to have been as popular as ever among Palestinians. Instead, poll data indicated that Palestinians were deeply frustrated with the PA and advocated its dissolution.[86]

This chapter analyzes the security relationship between Israel and the PA from 1993 to 2017 through the lens of the volume's principal-agent model. Despite both its Israeli and Palestinian detractors, the relationship delivered periods of remarkable calm, especially in the years 1997–99 and 2007–13. I divide the timeline into five periods, and find in each of them that the model's predictions are borne out by the data. The principal responded appropriately to agent effort with rewards and capacity building, while assuming direct control and destroying agent capacity during 2000–2004 when agent effort was low (negative). The only apparent inconsistency in the principal's behavior was in the matter of undermining Fayyad: despite enjoying very high levels of cooperation under Fayyad (2007–13), Israel and the United States undermined his efforts by falling short in financial aid and offering no progress in territorial concessions, thus enabling his ouster by political rivals. This apparent inconsistency, however, reflects the principal's rising cost of rewarding the PA, as the Israeli electorate's long-term rightward political trend constrained the leadership from making concessions.

Meanwhile, the PA's cooperation with Israel during 2007–17 despite Israel's failure to grant concessions or engage meaningfully in negotiations reflects an internal schism in Palestinian politics. Since at least January 2006, security cooperation with Israel has been seized on by the Fatah PA as a vehicle by which to monopolize political power and forcibly marginalize Hamas as a political opponent. The security relationship thus persists mostly due to its private value to the Fatah PA itself, while contravening the political preferences of the Palestinian public, which largely favors reunification with Hamas and even supports dissolving the PA altogether. The relationship's future depends on the degree to which the Fatah PA can regain political legitimacy or intensify its grip on power by other means. If this interpretation is correct, then, combining this analysis with that of chapter 4 on Gaza, Israel has achieved an uneasy interest alignment over threat suppression with each of the dominant political entities in the Palestinian Territories, Fatah and Hamas, despite an underlying misalignment with the Palestinian public over autonomy and statehood.

NOTES

1. Ephron 2015.
2. Hilal 1977.
3. Milton-Edwards and Farrell 2010.
4. Kurtzer et al. 2012, 8.
5. Ibid., 34.
6. Ibid.
7. Ibid.; Khalidi 2013.
8. Kurtzer et al. 2012, 49.
9. Frisch 2010.
10. Khalidi 2013.
11. Milton-Edwards and Farrell 2010.
12. Ibid.
13. Berman 2009.
14. Frisch 2010.
15. International Crisis Group 2010; Moreh 2012.
16. Schirman 2014.
17. International Crisis Group 2010; Moreh 2012.
18. Frisch 2010. The agent who is also a source of disturbance is familiar from the analysis of Hamas, in chapter 4.
19. JMCC 1993.
20. JMCC 2011, 10.
21. Frisch 2010.
22. Ibid., 85.
23. Frisch 2010.
24. See esp. Frisch 2010, 83; International Crisis Group 2010.
25. Kurtzer et al. 2012, 116.

26. Quoted in Moreh 2012.
27. Ibid.
28. Milton-Edwards and Farrell 2010, 222.
29. Ibid., 219.
30. Kurtzer et al. 2012, 114.
31. See, for example, Frisch 2010, 75–76.
32. Kurtzer et al. 2012, 114.
33. Ibid.
34. Ibid., 54.
35. Ibid.
36. Quoted in Moreh 2012.
37. JMCC 1999.
38. Kurtzer et al. 2012, 148.
39. JMCC 2011, 10.
40. Frisch 2010, 113.
41. Ibid., 102.
42. Frisch 2010.
43. Ibid.
44. PCPSR 2004.
45. PCPSR 2005.
46. JMCC 2011, 10.
47. Frisch 2010, 140.
48. Quoted in Frisch 2010, 146.
49. International Crisis Group 2010.
50. Frisch 2010, 147.
51. Quoted in Kurtzer et al. 2012, 198.
52. Ibid., 202.
53. Milton-Edwards and Farrell 2010.
54. Kurtzer et al. 2012.
55. Rose 2008.
56. International Crisis Group 2010.
57. Rose 2008.
58. Ibid.
59. Roy 2013.
60. International Crisis Group 2010.
61. Ibid.
62. Kurtzer et al. 2012, 218.
63. Thrall 2010; International Crisis Group 2010.
64. Dayton 2009, 8.
65. Danin 2011.
66. Quoted in Thrall 2010.
67. Quoted in International Crisis Group 2010.
68. Quoted in International Crisis Group 2010.
69. Ibid.
70. They still do; see Ravid and Levinson 2016.
71. Ephron 2015; Frisch 2010, 116.
72. Weitz and Khouri 2016.
73. PCPSR 2017.
74. Shikaki 2015.
75. PCPSR 2017.
76. Hotolevy 2016.

77. Taylor Force Act, H.R. 1164, 115th Cong. (2017), https://www.congress.gov/bill/115th-congress/house-bill/1164.

78. El Kurd 2017.

79. Kydd and Walter 2002.

80. Ephron 2015.

81. Kurtzer et al. 2012, 199.

82. Zitun 2014b.

83. Jamal 2012.

84. Ibid., loc. 5098 of 7289.

85. Tartir 2015.

86. PCPSR 2017.

8

YEMEN, 2001–11
Building on Unstable Ground

Ben Brewer

After September 11, 2001, George W. Bush's administration tasked U.S. security and foreign policy apparatuses with conducting a "global war on terror." Part of their approach involved securing some of the world's ungoverned and semi-ungoverned spaces, which were foci for transnational criminal organizations, including terrorist networks. Yemen was one of these places.[1] This chapter investigates the evolving principal-agent relationship between the United States and Yemen from 2001 to 2011.

For the purposes of the model, we view the Bush administration as the principal and Yemen's president, Ali Abdullah Saleh, as the agent. They initially shared an interest in stabilizing a country suffering violent changes in leadership. Prior to Saleh's taking control of the northern part of the country in 1978, the Yemen Arab Republic (North Yemen) had cycled through five heads of state: two had been assassinated, two had been deposed, and one had voluntarily left office fearing he would soon be killed. Northern instability was matched in the southern half of the country, which Saleh would take charge of, where, during roughly the same two-decade period, the People's Democratic Republic of Yemen (South Yemen) had seen five different rulers, two of whom were deposed and one assassinated. When he took power in the North, Saleh, for his part, was so concerned that he might be killed that he immediately arranged for his fellow tribesman Ali Mohsen to assume control if a successful assassination took place.[2]

Despite strong shared interests in creating a robust state in Yemen, ideological differences ultimately encumbered cooperation between the United States and Yemen. The Bush administration, acting on the belief that effective states were democratic and built on formal-legal notions of legitimacy, would in the course of time push Yemen to develop its governance institutions along Western-approved lines—promoting democracy and reducing corruption. Although modern political institutions were not new to Yemen, the political landscape had been shaped by thick patronage networks and tight relations among competing, often tribal, groups. Bringing true institutional change to Yemen threatened the nation's most powerful political actors, who had made their livelihoods in this personalist environment. They therefore had strong incentives to resist structural change, incentives felt most acutely in the highest echelons of the Yemeni government, including by Saleh. Both the United States and Saleh wanted Yemen to be well governed; they had very different beliefs as to what this entailed.

This case displays the issues that arise as a principal's and agent's interests diverge. In the first period under investigation, the Bush administration's desires were aligned with Saleh's. The administration was most interested in weeding out terrorists who were scattered across Yemen, and Saleh was happy to comply. In the second period, interests diverged as the Bush administration, viewing the immediate Yemeni terrorist threat as having been addressed, began to pressure Saleh to make political reforms. Saleh, seeing this move as an unexpected and undesirable reworking of their contract, only complied after being punished.

The model posits that an increase in the agent's cost of effort in one period makes reducing disturbances more difficult in the next. This is the case in Yemen, where we see significant downstream effects resulting from the Bush administration's shifting of the goalposts. Saleh became less trusting of the U.S. government. He did far less to advance the U.S. "war on terror." He even undid some of his own past work, freeing captured terrorists who were being prosecuted.

In the final period under examination, we see what happens when an agent's capacity (ability to address disturbances) diminishes. In this period, Saleh turned his attention to domestic opponents. The newly inaugurated Obama administration worked to salvage Saleh's government, which had enmeshed itself in extremely costly domestic fights. Applying a capacity theory of state building, the Obama administration bolstered Saleh's capacity so he could both stabilize Yemen and suppress disturbances. These attempts were ultimately insufficient, and the disturbances had to be dealt with directly (that is, the principal took direct action).

Background

Before delving into the details of the case, it is worth noting a few things that make Yemen a unique actor and agent. For several decades Yemen has been debilitated by a multilayered crisis that stems from three sources. Forming the bedrock of this grim stack are structural issues—persistent shortages of food, water, and oil—that have left Yemen one of the poorest countries in the Middle East. The second and third layers of the crisis ravaging Yemen are political. There are threats of secession from the South and, starting in the early 2000s, threats of rebellion from the Houthis in the North. More generally, Yemen's civil society has been peppered with extremist fighters coming back from Afghanistan, homegrown terrorists, and tribal groups, many of whom play important and often contentious roles in local and national politics.

At the local and national levels, most influential actors in Yemen have ties to at least one tribe. These relations serve as the foundation on which subsequent connections are built. This is the case for President Saleh (part of the Sanhan tribe, allied with the Hasid Federation), for the Houthis (who draw support from the Bakil Federation), and for homegrown terrorists who hide among different tribes in the eastern expanses of Yemen (particularly in the Marib, often under the control of tribes connected to the Madhaj Confederation). Only the southerners lack a strong tribal network as a basis of support.

In Yemen, tribes are mostly regional and highly factional. Tribal politics is local politics. Tribes regularly settle local disputes and can have their own systems of justice. The most influential tribal groups in Yemen are the Hashid, Bakil, and Madhaj tribal confederations. These confederations are large and powerful enough that they can, and do, regularly intermingle with the state apparatus. The state, when "run properly," tries to play tribes off each other, while tribes tend to try to enmesh themselves in the state apparatus to secure patronage and positions of power (for example, key military and parliamentary positions). During his reign, Saleh was quite adept at this game, which he compared to "dancing on the heads of snakes."[3]

Two of these tribal confederations (Hashid and Bakil) are located in the North, and the remaining one (Madhaj) is located in the center. This is critical, as it means that tribal power is concentrated outside the South, which, among other things, makes it much more onerous for a southerner to run a united Yemen. This is one of the reasons why Saleh's replacement, Abdrabbuh Mansur Hadi (a southerner), has had far more difficulty maintaining control of Yemen than Saleh did.

Tribal relations are often the constituent parts of which other relationships are built; however, they are by no means unique in their ability to foster strong allegiances in Yemen. The Houthis, and to a certain extent homegrown terrorists (almost all of whom are part of al-Qaeda and its affiliate groups), have done an exceptional job of drawing passionate supporters to their transtribal movements. Conscious of tribal conflict across Yemen, these groups have worked to remain "atribal" as they gather like-minded individuals to their respective causes.

Southern Yemenis are quite distinct from the groups discussed thus far. Unlike in the North, where tribal politics has played an interminable role in national politics, in the South of Yemen an ideologically oriented, party-based state has existed for decades. South Yemen is currently quite hostile toward the North; its residents feel they were wronged during the national post–civil war merger and during the years that followed, when the government in Sana'a refused to pay southern pensions and failed to invest in developing the South.[4]

Theoretical Expectations

The formal model we use throughout this volume can speak to several components of the U.S.-Yemeni principal-agent relationship. First, one of the model's main postulates is that the cost of the disturbance must be sufficiently high for the principal to view expending resources on retaining and monitoring an agent as expedient (H_{11}). This component is central to the first period in the Yemeni case (2001–5), as the Bush administration's view of terrorism in Yemen as threatening changed over time, fundamentally altering the relationship as it did (see table 8.1).

Second, the model indicates that as interests diverge, one should expect the principal to resort to more rewards and punishments (H_7). From 2006 to 2008, a resurgent Houthi uprising caused Saleh to turn his attention to the Houthi-held territory in the Northwest. As he did, terrorist attacks in Yemen rose. With Saleh more engrossed in battling the Houthis and less concerned with dismantling al-Qaeda in Yemen, U.S. use of incentives increased.

Finally, the model indicates that when a principal engaged in indirect control becomes sufficiently concerned with a rising level of disturbance due to increased agent effort costs, it will bear the cost of either replacing the agent (H_5) or acting directly on its own behalf (H_1). Direct action is clearly observed in Yemen during 2009–11, the final period under consideration.

Key to the shifts just described are changes in the cost of effort for Saleh. As such, before examining how events unfolded, it is worth detailing the direct and indirect costs that influenced Saleh's behavior.

For the agent, cost of effort can include direct costs of suppressing a disturbance and indirect costs that result from acting to suppress a disturbance. Saleh was charged with preventing Yemen from becoming a safe haven for terrorists. For him, the direct and indirect costs of acting depended first and foremost on how he was expected to deal with terrorists. Saleh preferred to incorporate homegrown, would-be terrorists into the state's patronage system. Doing so was straightforward and cheap, and produced virtually no ancillary (indirect)

TABLE 8.1 Theoretical expectations and summary results, Yemen

PERIOD	KEY PARAMETER(S)	THEORETICAL EXPECTATION	OBSERVED ACTION
2001–5	Principal's and agent's interests are aligned by 9/11 attacks; agent's cost of effort is low.	Principal should reward (H_2). Agent should exert effort to reduce disturbances (H_6).	United States increases aid. Saleh puts pressure on terrorists and terrorist networks operating in Yemen.
2006–8	Interest alignment decreases (raising indirect cost of effort); direct cost of effort begins to rise.	Agent should exert less effort, which should make principal more likely to use indirect tools of control (H_7). Large disturbances are most likely to be responded to with punishments (H_3).	Saleh exerts less effort suppressing terrorists, while exerting minimal effort democratizing and professionalizing Yemen's governance structures. United States punishes in response.
2009–11	Domestic unrest causes agent's cost of effort to rise dramatically at the same time that the level of disturbance (terrorist activity) is rising.	Agent should exert even less effort, which should cause principal to use indirect tools of control more liberally (H_7). Rising disturbances should prompt a similar response (H_{11}). Principal should consider direct action and possibly replacing agent (H_1 and H_5).	United States takes direct action in the form of drone strikes and increases aid to agent in an attempt to build capacity.

costs—Yemen's public never found the act of offering another patronage job in a system built on clientelism to be especially objectionable. Given the option, Saleh always chose this method.

Saleh's cost of effort rose nonnegligibly if the United States required that terrorists be jailed or killed. Always looking to exact the minimal possible punishment on jihadists, as doing so produced the best cost to the (U.S.-provided) reward ratio, Saleh saw trials and imprisonment as his second-best option. Imprisonment varied in terms of how expensive it was for Saleh. The indirect costs of imprisonment were usually quite minimal; none of the big tribal confederations was interested in advocating for politically unimportant actors, which the terrorists generally were, and southern political elites as well as the northern Houthis were happy to see Sunni jihadists rot in dark, poorly regulated Yemeni prisons. Direct costs of imprisonment were higher and greatly depended on where the terrorists happened to be hiding. If they were in the Marib, Shibwa, or al-Jawf Governorates, extracting them could be difficult and expensive. All three zones are outside the area that the central government fully controls and have a reputation for lawlessness.[5] Among these three territories, arresting a terrorist in Marib was the hardest.

Killing a Yemeni citizen on behalf of the United States could carry all the direct costs of less lethal action, such as imprisonment, while always containing the latent possibility of generating manifold more indirect costs. This held true regardless of whether Saleh acted himself or quietly let the United States take action.

When the United States took direct action (in the form of a drone strike), direct costs borne by Saleh were zero. Indirect costs, however, varied wildly depending on how many innocents a U.S. drone strike happened to kill. Surgical strikes such as the one on November 3, 2002, which exclusively killed terrorists, generated rumblings among pockets of the populace. Less accurate strikes that killed civilians, such as the one in al-Majalla at the end of 2009, enraged locals whose friends and relatives were directly impacted. These strikes also created a stir across the nation because, as one tribal leader stated, "The U.S. sees al-Qaeda as terrorism and we consider the drones terrorism."[6]

Saleh incurred additional indirect costs (unrelated to suppressing terrorists) when the Bush administration shifted its interest to corruption and began tasking Saleh with professionalizing Yemen's governance structures. Saleh had a strong interest in maintaining Yemen's prevailing patronage networks, as clientelism was an important element of the country's political system. It kept disparate groups placated and Yemen's political elites on the government's side. When patronage dropped, these groups invariably chafed and began fomenting unrest. Yemen's government, as noted by the RAND Corporation in 2010, "is based on the material cooptation of local tribal leaders, thus permitting GoY [Government of Yemen] sovereignty in the absence of substantive control."[7]

Corruption and ineffective governance also benefited Saleh and his immediate family members. He had placed children and relatives in positions of power, and they (and he) gained substantially from Yemen's exploitative governing system. By tasking Saleh with improving Yemen's government and reducing corruption, the United States was making it harder for Saleh to work with other power brokers, while also hurting his own bottom line.

The last variable that shaped Saleh's cost of effort was domestic unrest. Yemen is different from some of the other cases in this volume because Saleh's cost of effort rose and fell as ambient levels of unrest in the country went up and down. When the Houthis rose in the North and the southerners began to protest in the South, Saleh's indirect and direct costs of effort increased substantially. For Saleh, antigovernment movements were a more pressing concern than counterterrorism and therefore amplified the indirect cost of concentrating on al-Qaeda. Furthermore, quelling unrest required Saleh to channel scarce resources toward fighting for control, which raised his direct cost of conducting counterterrorism in other parts of the country.

Initial Relationship, 2001–5

Our analysis begins under George W. Bush in 2001. Meeting Saleh for the first time in November, Bush impressed on him the importance of conducting an effective counterterrorism policy in Yemen.[8] At the time of their meeting there had already been three serious disturbances in Yemen directly targeting U.S. citizens and assets. In December 1992 the Movenpick and Gold Mohur hotel bombings targeted U.S. marines en route to Somalia. In December 1998 sixteen tourists, some of whom were American, were seized and held as hostages. Finally, in October 2000, seventeen sailors were killed and thirty-nine wounded in the USS *Cole* bombing.

The tenor of Saleh's exchange with Bush was echoed in Saleh's next meeting with George Tenet, then director of the CIA. Tenet gave Saleh a list of al-Qaeda members believed to be residing in Yemen, with the directive that he was to capture or kill them. For his efforts, the Bush administration offered an aid and loan package to Saleh worth about $400 million.[9] Saleh's first meetings with Bush and Tenet made it clear that they were most interested in Saleh's targeting individuals perceived to be dangerous and fundamentally opposed to U.S. interests. They wanted Saleh to target these individuals (the disturbance) and eliminate them.

The Bush administration likely had minimal expectations for Saleh. At the beginning of November the CIA had handed a similar list to the Political Security Organization (PSO), its counterpart in Yemen, only to watch as many of the identified individuals slipped out of the country.[10] This lack of faith in Yemen's government and in Saleh's commitment to capture or kill these individuals undoubtedly contributed to veiled threats that were incorporated into the conversations with him. These included references to possibly sending in U.S. Special Forces if Saleh could not get the job done, and discussing how he needed to demonstrate that he was with the United States, not against it.

Interest Alignment

Bush and Tenet need not have worried, as Saleh's interests were very much aligned with their own. He had no reason to protect al-Qaeda. His country was secure; he faced no threats to the north or south. Moreover, he could be quite certain that countering terrorism mattered to the United States. There could not possibly have been a clearer signal of this than sitting down with the president of the United States to discuss terrorism two and a half months after the September 11 attacks.

Saleh was willing to carry out the wishes of the United States in exchange for substantial rewards, which would strengthen his hold on power and his military's ability to defend him against domestic opponents. It should come as no surprise, therefore, that initial reports on Yemen's efforts were very positive. Many U.S. government officials stationed in Yemen noted a marked change in Yemeni behavior between 2000 and 2001.[11] For example, the USS *Cole* bombing investigation, which had initially been slowed by lackluster effort on the part of Yemeni officials, suddenly became a productive joint operation. The U.S. Department of State described this transformation plainly in its 2001 report on terrorism in Yemen:

> Cooperation was productive, particularly in the aftermath of September 11, and established important linkages between the East Africa U.S. Embassy bombings, the USS *Cole* bombing, and the September 11 attacks. The Yemeni Government's assistance in providing investigators with key documents, allowing evidence to be processed in the United States, and facilitating access to suspects made the discoveries possible.[12]

Over the next several years, interest alignment remained high. Saleh was sure the United States wanted him to capture and kill terrorists and he was very willing to do so. He was being rewarded for his work, and the specter of the United States taking direct action in Yemen was ever present. Interests did not begin to diverge until the end of this period, when the Bush administration unexpectedly changed Saleh's implied contract, throwing their relationship out of equilibrium.

Cost of Effort and Disturbances

During this first period, direct and indirect costs of effort were low. There were no uprisings, Saleh had a secure grasp on power, and the Bush administration was not yet insistent on government reform. This animated Saleh, causing him both to act on behalf of the United States and even to be somewhat public about his support for America. Between 2002 and 2004, Saleh expressed support for the "war on terror" and a commitment to Yemen's role as an active partner in counterterrorism.[13] These statements sometimes accompanied highly visible meetings with prominent U.S. officials, such as that with Vice President Dick Cheney, who visited Yemen in 2002.

With costs of effort low, the model predicts that we should observe high effort and relatively few disturbances. From 2001 to 2005, with the sole exception of

the attack on the MV *Limburg*, a French oil tanker, there were no significant terrorist attacks in Yemen. With the arrest of Muhammed Hamdi al-Ahdal, one of
the terrorists responsible for the attack, at the end of 2003, al-Qaeda-perpetrated
violence virtually disappeared across the country.[14] It would not be until February 2006, when twenty-three terrorists escaped from Sana'a's PSO detention
center, that a major al-Qaeda operation would take place.

Aside from hunting terrorists, the government of Yemen was active in suppressing terrorism in a number of other ways. Religious schools, which had been
an essential cog in the jihad machine, came under greater scrutiny. Foreign visiting students could no longer attend these schools as easily, and some foreign
students with Arab, specifically Islamic, backgrounds were asked to leave the
country.[15] Captured terrorists were run through the court system before ending up in prison.[16] When ten prisoners escaped from a PSO detention center in
Aden, including some believed to be connected to the attack on the USS *Cole*, two
senior prison officers and several prison guards were dismissed and a hunt for the
suspects quickly began.[17]

Saleh's support for U.S. counterterrorism went beyond his own efforts. In
2002, Saleh allowed the United States to use a predator drone to kill Abu Ali
al-Harithi, head of al-Qaeda in Yemen and one of the USS *Cole* bombers, as well
as several other terrorists, as they drove their Humvee through the northern part
of Yemen.[18] When the drone found its target, some members of the Yemeni public, specifically those in the area where the strike took place, suspected that the
United States had been involved. This prompted immediate calls for revenge.[19]
To Yemenis there was a nontrivial difference between Saleh sending the army into
governorates and the United States using a drone to kill locals. As an adviser to
Saleh told the *New York Times* in 2002, "The [Yemenis] don't want Americans to
come in and do the fighting. They feel it is the Yemenis who should fight."[20] Given
that a mentality of confronting and expelling foreigners was still strong in Yemen,
Saleh absorbed some costs on behalf of the principal in allowing a drone strike.

Rewards and Punishments

The model predicts that low cost of effort should lead an agent to comply with
the principal's demands, resulting in material rewards or, if capacity is low, capacity building. Given that Saleh's capacity was demonstrably adequate during this
period, the model would predict rewards. This is more or less what we see.

Prior to 2001, U.S. military aid to Yemen had been insignificant. Yemen
received no foreign military financing and almost nothing from U.S. foreign
military sales.[21] This all changed in 2001when Saleh saw his arms purchases and
military aid begin to rise.

Yemen's armed forces were staffed by members of Saleh's tribe and his imme-diate family.[22] Yemen had a long tradition of deep, often familial and tribal, ties between military and social elites, with just as long a tradition of provid-ing patronage to socially important members of the armed forces.[23] Arms and military aid, which of course went directly to the military, were therefore great rewards. Saleh made a habit of sending the best military resources and equip-ment to units staffed by his son, nephews, and tribal clansmen, so the people closest to him likely received the bulk of the U.S. military assistance.[24] Economic aid, which he almost certainly cared less about as it benefited him less directly, also increased marginally during this period.

Of note is the number of Yemeni fighters the United States trained during this time, which I interpret as both capacity building and reward. From 2001 to 2006, this number rose from 79 to 611 Yemeni fighters per year. A substantial portion of this training went to members of the newly established Central Security Ser-vice's counterterrorism force.[25] This elite unit was built to function alongside, but completely independent of, the PSO, which was an ineffective, bloated, bureau-cratic appendage. This unit undoubtedly helped Saleh carry out counterterror-ism more effectively. Giving this unit exceptional training also likely functioned as a reward, as it was under the purview of Brig. Gen. Yahya Saleh, Saleh's nephew.

The Changing Principal-Agent Relationship, 2006–8

During most of the first period, Saleh was effective at countering terrorism in Yemen. When Bush was reelected in 2004, Saleh immediately sent word through the U.S. embassy that he wanted to meet with the president. Saleh was excited both to continue their relationship and to gather a larger aid bounty, which he anticipated given his work on behalf of the United States. It would be an entire year before Bush would get around to seeing Saleh.[26] When they did meet, things were completely different from how the president of Yemen imagined they would be.

Bush had won in 2000 using the slogan "compassionate conservatism." He promised big tax cuts and major reforms to Social Security and education. In terms of foreign policy, he clearly disavowed nation building. "Maybe I am miss-ing something here," he said. "I mean, are we going to have some nation-building corps from America? Absolutely not."[27] As early as April 2002, Bush's position on state building was already changing. Speaking about Afghanistan at the Virginia Military Institute, he remarked, "We know that true peace will only be achieved when we give the Afghan people the means to achieve their own aspirations.

Peace will be achieved by helping Afghanistan develop its own stable government."[28] A year and a half later, on November 6, 2003, Bush went even further in a foreign policy address to the National Endowment for Democracy, as he explained how important it was to bring democracy to the Middle East: "Our commitment to democracy is also tested in the Middle East, which is my focus today and must be a focus of American policy for decades to come."[29]

Both statements are emblematic of the philosophical position that the Bush administration adopted as it became more deeply involved in the Middle East. In the administration's view, its job was to prevent terrorists from establishing bases from which attacks could be launched. Its evolving theories pushed it to regard building effective governments in Middle Eastern countries where instability and terrorism were rampant as the best way to achieve this. This in turn could only be done by fostering Western-style governance. These nations needed participatory institutions that controlled and legitimized government, efficient markets to dispense goods and services, and formal-legal institutions to create the basis for the rule of law.

The Bush administration's ideology marked an evolution in state-building theory and U.S. foreign policy strategy more generally. It drew both on neoliberal theory on the importance of institutions and on neoconservative theory on the need to take an active role in pushing back oppressive forces that threaten classical liberal values, to create a unique hybrid philosophy. It also drew on democratic exceptionalism theory—the belief that democratic societies are superior to others on a host of fronts. From this amalgam, the Bush administration developed an approach prescribing Western-style institutional designs to foreign nations.[30]

These theories and this approach were applied in Afghanistan and Iraq, the two big state-building projects during the Bush years. They were also exercised in Yemen as the administration's concern with threats from existing terrorists abated and their concern about future terrorism grew. This shift in priorities was apparent to the incoming ambassador, Thomas Krajeski, who replaced Edmund Hull (2001–4) as head of the U.S. embassy in Yemen.

Krajeski warned Saleh about the administration's policy position and how adopting prodemocracy verbiage while doing little more than capturing terrorists was now no longer enough. Saleh was told that he needed to deliver institutional reform if he was to secure the rewards he had been promised.[31] By all accounts Saleh did not grasp how serious Krajeski's remarks were.[32] His inaction, despite his regular affirmations that he was making change, seem to reflect a misunderstanding of the new contractual landscape he was in. The result was a surprise for Saleh when he landed in Washington, DC, in November 2005.

Over the course of two meetings, first with Secretary of State Condoleezza Rice and then with Paul Wolfowitz (then head of the World Bank), Saleh learned that due to Yemen's corruption he would lose his Millennium Challenge Corporation (MCC) funding of $20 million, as well as $140 million in World Bank funds.[33] These punishments had to be nearly impossible for Saleh to swallow, especially as he would have been expecting a reward for effective compliance.

Yemen had been a corrupt dictatorship before Saleh had been tasked with hunting down terrorists, and it remained one during and after his work on behalf of the United States. For Rice and Wolfowitz to act as if corruption was now a serious issue, one standing in the way of further U.S. support, must have seemed to Saleh rather absurd. These charges must have appeared especially outlandish to the Middle Eastern leader given that Yemen had actually improved its governance indicators during the period during which it had worked with the United States.

Starting in 1993, reports regarding electoral institutions in Yemen were mostly positive. The parliamentary election that year was lauded as "free and fair" by international groups monitoring the contest.[34] The same was said of the parliamentary elections of 2003.[35] Yemen's progress in reforming its governance was further corroborated by Freedom House, whose assessments had been previously adopted by the MCC. "Yemen," former ambassador Hull observed, "was the only Middle Eastern country to improve its freedom standing: from 'not free' to 'partly free,' . . . 'because of increased civic participation in the country's political process.'"[36] Some final evidence suggesting that criticism of Yemen's political evolution was, while not contrived, clearly misplaced, can be found in table 8.2, which shows the results from the three most pertinent performance reports by the MCC. From 2004 to 2005, Yemen improved in government accountability and corruption, while maintaining the same rating for government effectiveness and rule of law (both of which improved the following year, postpunishment).[37]

Given the evidence, it seems clear that the goalposts were shifted by the principal. Such a shift is not outside the model, which treats this as an exogenous shock that affects the agent's cost of effort. Saleh saw his reward schedule diminish dramatically during his 2005 trip to the United States, as the expressed interests of his host had shifted. Worse, Saleh, who had taken control of a country built on patronage networks, was now being tasked with undermining a system that benefited him financially and ensured his political survival. Taking steps to achieve his newest directives would be extremely costly, both financially and politically.

Cost of Effort and Disturbances

Given the rise in indirect cost of effort, we should consequently expect to see a rise in level of disturbances, all other variables held equal. This is exactly what we observe.

TABLE 8.2   Yemen's Millennium Challenge Corporation (MCC) performance

INDICATOR	FY04	FY05	FY06
Political rights	5	5	5
Civil liberties	5	5	5
Voice and accountability	−0.32	**−0.19**	*−.30*
Government effectiveness	−0.10	−0.10	**−0.03**
Rule of law	−0.45	−0.45	**−0.26**
Control of corruption	0.12	**0.13**	*0.0*
Primary education completion	58.3	—	—
Girls' primary completion	—	44.8	**48.3**
Primary education spending (% of GDP)	4.40	*3.59*	**6.84**
Health spending (% of GDP)	1.88	*1.44*	**1.59**
Immunization rate	67	66	**77**
Country credit rating	27.7	**29**	—
Cost of starting a business	—	—	240.2
Inflation	9.1	*10.8*	*12.5*
Fiscal policy	0.15	*−.40*	*−3.59*
Trade policy	3.0	3.0	**4.5**
Regulatory quality	0.08	0.08	−0.44
Days to start a business	72	**63**	**63**

Source: Center for Global Development, accessed June 1, 2018, http://www.cgdev.org/page/yemen.

Note: Bold indicates improvement, italics regression.

Three months after Saleh's meetings in Washington, on February 3, 2006, twenty-three al-Qaeda operatives, many connected to very serious attacks (including the *Cole* and *Limburg* bombings), escaped from a PSO detention center in Yemen's capital, Sana'a, where they had been held for several years. The prisoners escaped by digging a fifty-yard tunnel from one cell to a neighboring mosque. None of the prison guards had noticed any suspicious activity as the prisoners dug this long underground tunnel. Furthermore, no prison officers or guards seem to have been fired as a result of this escape. This lack of official response is conspicuously different from what followed the 2003 escape—the only other prison break up to this point.

Five months later, on July 8, a Yemeni Special Penal Court acquitted nineteen individuals charged with "conspiring to attack U.S. and Yemeni interests." While the defendants admitted in court that they had traveled to Iraq to conduct jihad, the court found that they could not be imprisoned, because "jihad was not illegal under Yemeni law." Two Yemeni citizens who had been accused of conspiring to assassinate the U.S. ambassador in 2004 were still sentenced, each receiving five years for their joint plot.[38]

Finally, Saleh failed to suppress Abdul Majeed al-Zindani, a designated terrorist. Al-Zindani is a Yemeni academic and politician who runs his own university (Al-Iman University), and who is known for being a vocal advocate of militant Islam, Osama bin Laden, and al-Qaeda in particular. In 2004, al-Zindani was designated a global terrorist under Executive Order 13224.[39] Yemen was ordered to prevent him from traveling and to freeze his assets. Neither occurred in 2004 or 2005. Interestingly, in 2006, not only did the Yemeni government continue to shirk its responsibility, but Saleh started publicly voicing support for both al-Zindani and his university.[40] Saleh continued to support al-Zindani through 2007.[41]

The divergence of Saleh's interests from those of the Bush administration was by no means Saleh's only concern. Starting in 2004, conflict with the Houthis had begun anew in the Northwest. A sect of Shia Islam whose members inhabited a mountainous region near the border with Saudi Arabia, the Houthis had been in conflict with Saleh and other powerful Hashidi figures in Yemen for some time. During the Yemeni civil war, Hussein Badreddin al-Houthi, then head of the group, had supported southern Yemen separatism. This made him an immediate target of the North Yemen government, and he was forced to flee. He ended up in Iran until the 1990s, returning to Yemen to found the Believing Youth Movement.

The Believing Youth Movement was a political and religious undertaking dedicated to reviving the Zaidi form of Shia Islam in the Saada Governorate occupied by the Houthis. The movement helped shore up support for the Zaidi cause and became a banner under which anti-Saudi, anti-American, and anti-government Yemen sentiments could coalesce. Public lectures criticizing Sunni Arab leaders for supporting the U.S. agenda were given on popular prayer days by Badreddin al-Houthi himself in which he railed against these groups: "Are the leaders of the Islamic world today not Sunni? Are they not the ones who agreed, who hurried to agree, that America is to lead the world against what is referred to as terrorism?"[42] Saleh was often indirectly implicated in these lectures but was hardly ever called out directly.[43]

These were not the only threats that emanated from north of the capital. At least twice, in 1986 and again in 1992, the government of Yemen entered into armed standoffs with far-north factions. Both occasions could have easily turned violent. The first occurred after Houthi fighters forced their way into a government prison to murder Hashidi Confederation tribesmen who had killed two Khwalan bin Amr tribesmen in a disagreement. The army was sent in and apologies and mediation were needed to prevent bloodshed. The second occurred when Hussein Badreddin al-Houthi returned from Iran. Twenty government gun trucks were sent to Sha'ara, where he was rumored to be hiding. Government forces arrived unannounced, running afoul of customary practice. Local sheikhs quickly mobilized, and an armed stalemate ensued until both sides made face-saving gestures and vacated the area.[44]

The multidecade history of unrest north of the capital had made Saleh wary of any outbursts radiating from this region. At the same time, Saleh was now, more than ever, prepared for a fight. U.S. arms and aid that had come into the country helped encourage the belief that the regime's military would be victorious in armed conflict. Furthermore, since a number of regime elites were Salafi or Salafi sympathizers, Saleh could feel confident that conflict with the Houthis would, if anything, generate regime cohesion.[45]

In June 2004, six hundred al-Houthi supporters began demonstrating in front of the Great Mosque of Sana'a. Saleh quickly took action; police were called and protesters arrested.[46] Saleh put a $55,000 bounty on Hussein Badreddin al-Houthi's head, and sent Yemen's military north to crush the Zaidi movement. After a month of fighting in the mountains, the bounty on al-Houthi was raised to $75,000 and more forces were called in to quell the resistance.

For another two months, government forces battled the Houthis while destroying local land and terrorizing local, often unassociated, occupants. By the start of September, al-Houthi and a number of followers had been surrounded and killed. This did not end the resistance, however. Abdul-Malik Badreddin al-Houthi, brother of the slain political and spiritual leader, took over the movement. Abdul-Malik would continue to lead the resistance, which would repeatedly skirmish with government forces in the ensuing years.[47]

From March until June of 2005, months before Saleh headed to Washington, his forces were again drawn into a serious conflict with the Houthis, and a series of expensive battles between the government and the rebels occurred. Saleh, tired of pouring his scarce resources into combating insurgents hiding in mountains, offered a presidential pardon in May 2005, on the condition that everyone who had taken up arms surrender. The Houthis refused. It would take another month of fighting and mediators from Yemeni tribes unconnected to the conflict to finally bring about a temporary peace in June.[48]

Having failed to secure the much-needed funds he had been promised by his principal, Saleh was thrust into an undesirable position when, in January 2007, fighting with the Houthis began again. Houthi militants attacked a series of government fortifications in the North, killing tens of soldiers. Saleh responded by ordering thirty thousand troops north to conduct a massive offensive, which he hoped would end the rebellion once and for all. In the subsequent months, little was decided. The insurgents held out. When peace was brokered in June, nothing more was accomplished than the Houthi leaders agreeing to lay down arms and go into exile in Qatar.

These uprisings in the North were exacerbated in the worst way possible for Saleh by growing unrest in the South. Since the end of the 1994 civil war and coerced reunification, southerners had been stuck in the unhappy position of being treated as quasi-second-class citizens. In addition to a lack of investment and development, and the cancellation of pensions, southerners had to contend with the indignity of having their land and enterprises confiscated by northern elites.[49] None of these policies sat well in the South, and in May 2007 a series of sit-ins and protests were organized by southerners who had been forced into retirement. Over the subsequent months the protests broadened. Southerners representing a variety of different groups joined the protests, as did local parties and politicians. As the movement grew, so too did the demands, which, according to a report by Human Rights Watch, "now included more employment opportunities . . . an end of corruption, and a larger share of oil revenues."[50]

The second period of the U.S.-Yemen relationship under consideration here took place within this increasingly tense environment. Ambient levels of unrest were rising and principal-agent interests diverged. Unlike in the first period, during which Saleh was free to act more or less as he pleased, and his interests were roughly aligned with those of the U.S., Saleh now faced domestic unrest and had to contend with new costs associated with developing Yemen's bureaucracy and democracy, a task that could empower his rivals.

Suppressing Disturbances

Discontent in North and South Yemen posed nonnegligible threats to Saleh's regime. The model predicts that as Saleh's direct cost of effort rose, disturbances would increase, since his ability to control disorder was somewhat muted by his waning resources. Saleh's indirect cost of effort also rose during this period, as the Bush administration's change in directive resulted in Saleh's interests being less aligned with the administration's. This again leads to the prediction that disturbances will grow. One would also expect al-Qaeda to reemerge, as low effort during this period led to less curtailment of terrorism in Yemen. This is what we observe.[51]

Serious disturbances took place in the spring and summer months of 2007. Ali Mahmud Qasaylah, chief investigator in Marib, was assassinated by al-Qaeda in the Arabian Peninsula (AQAP) for assisting the United States in killing Abu Ali al-Harithi in 2002.[52] In July, a member of AQAP drove a vehicle-borne improvised explosive device into a group of Western tourists in Marib. The detonation killed the driver of the vehicle, Abdu Mohamad Sad Ahmad Reheqa, and several of the tourists. In the fall, Jamal Ahmed Badawi, who helped plan the attack on the USS *Cole*, was released by Saleh after promising that he was done with terrorism and aiding AQAP.

This last disturbance, the release of a terrorist as prominent as Badawi, was completely unacceptable to the United States. It triggered an immediate punishment phase from the Bush administration that, through the MCC's CEO, John Danilovich, indefinitely postponed $20.6 million in aid that had been approved a month before. This aid had been earmarked for Yemen to, according to the MCC press release that announced the grant, "**accelerate many positive changes already underway**" (bold text in the original).[53] The October press release announcing the cancellation contained no explanation for why the aid was being terminated. In contrast to the verbose statement from one month earlier, two one-sentence paragraphs were given as explanation. The first simply stated that Yemen had been offered aid in September. The second read, "Originally scheduled to be signed October 31st, MCC's CEO, John Danilovich, has decided to postpone awarding assistance to Yemen and are [sic] currently undertaking a review to determine the country's future status with MCC."[54]

A year later, general disturbances had grown significantly worse. In January, two Belgian tourists were ambushed and killed. In March, four mortars were fired at the U.S. embassy. In April, three mortars hit a residential complex housing U.S. embassy employees and Western workers. Twenty-four days later, two mortars exploded outside the Italian embassy. In September a second attack on the U.S. embassy took place, this time with terrorists using cars, assault weapons, and car bombs. This second attack killed eighteen, including an eighteen-year-old U.S. citizen. Had local guards not raised barriers preventing explosive-filled cars from reaching their target, the attack would have been far more deadly.[55]

Despite contending with greater direct and indirect costs, Saleh's government still made some efforts to curtail disturbances. Saleh responded each time the U.S. embassy was attacked. After the mortars were fired in the first attack, police quickly swarmed the building they originated from, only to find that the terrorists had inadvertently detonated an explosive and were already dead. Saleh ordered mass arrests following the second attack, and security in the area surrounding the embassy was also heightened.[56]

Saleh also tried to stem the tide of fighters heading to Iraq. While jihad had been declared "not illegal" in Yemen's courts, Saleh's government still prosecuted individuals attempting to fight abroad, using lesser charges such as fraudulent documents. Nineteen individuals were charged under this statute, and twenty-one individuals arrested in the previous year remained stuck in Yemen—working their way through the appellate system, hoping for reprieve.[57]

In 2008, Yemen's security forces conducted an assault on an al-Qaeda cell in Tarim, killing five members of the organization and confiscating weapons, car bombs, mortars, and other explosives. This raid was one of the most successful of the period.[58]

Theoretical Expectations and Principal's Behavior

The model predicts that rising direct and indirect costs will lead to less effort by the agent. This in turn should lead to a rise in the number and severity of disturbances. As disturbances grow, the principal must decide whether or not to use larger rewards and punishments to compel the agent to act on its behalf.

Given how disturbances rose during the period of 2006–8, the military aid trend line in figure 8.1 is not surprising. Aid creeps up from 2005 to 2006, rises rapidly from 2006 to 2007, and then plummets from 2007 to 2008, just as one would expect. The trainee trend line (see figure 8.2) somewhat fits with what the model would predict. It skyrockets through 2006 and then drops precipitously for the next two years. Since Saleh's nephew's elite counterterrorism unit was receiving most of the training resources, it is possible that the 2006 prison break was punished via a reduction in the trainee program.

Based on the data, it is also possible that Saleh could have been punished for this breach with a decrease in arms sales. Arms sales to Yemen rise continuously from 2002 to 2008, with only one big dip—in 2006 (see figure 8.3).

Humanitarian aid stays flat throughout this period (see figure 8.4), which fits the model, as humanitarian aid was not a reward for Saleh in the way that military aid, arms transfers, or professionalization of his security forces were. Increasing humanitarian aid or taking it away should therefore not affect his behavior, which is why we see it untouched during the Bush administration's first and second terms.

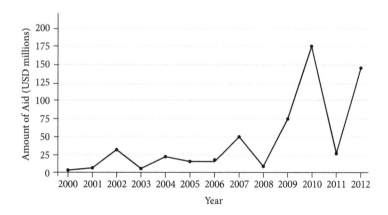

FIGURE 8.1.   U.S. military and security assistance to Yemen, 2001–12 (in constant U.S. dollars). Data from the Center for International Policy, Security Assistance Monitor, http://securityassistance.org/data/

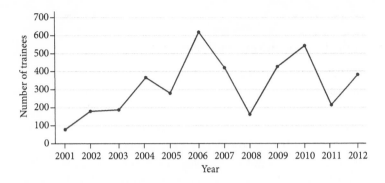

FIGURE 8.2. Yemeni trainees (trained by U.S. government), 2001–12. Data from the Center for International Policy, Security Assistance Monitor, http://securityassistance.org/data/

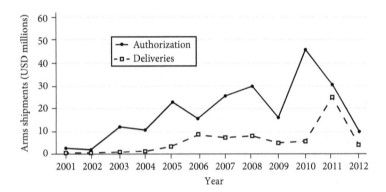

FIGURE 8.3. U.S. arms shipments to Yemen, 2001–12 (in constant U.S. dollars). Data from the Center for International Policy, Security Assistance Monitor, http://securityassistance.org/data/

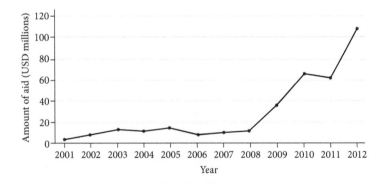

FIGURE 8.4. U.S. humanitarian and development aid to Yemen, 2001–12 (in constant U.S. dollars). Data from the Center for International Policy, Security Assistance Monitor, http://securityassistance.org/data/

Diminished Capacity, 2009–11

When Barack Obama assumed office on January 20, 2009, he was faced with a situation in Yemen that was much worse, and an agent who was far less pliant, than the one his predecessor had encountered in 2001. In January, al-Qaeda united its main branches under Ayman Mohammed Rabie al-Zawahiri, officially forming AQAP in Yemen. In February, reports emerged that Saleh was in discussions with that group to form an alliance against their mutual enemies.[59] Such a move was hardly surprising, as Saleh had made similar agreements with Sunni jihadists in the past. These reports coincided with a release of state prisoners, which Saleh claimed was a necessity due to prison overcrowding.[60]

The new administration's strategy for Yemen materialized in comments to a subcommittee of the Senate Foreign Relations Committee given by Daniel Benjamin, the State Department's coordinator for counterterrorism. "It is important to recognize," Benjamin said, "that our engagement in Yemen was interrupted for many years. Yemen did not have the kind of mentoring programs, the kind of training programs, that many of our other counterterrorism partners had."[61] Simply put, the Obama administration's plan was to provide Yemen with comprehensive governance assistance—both military and civilian—similar to what Afghanistan and Iraq had been receiving.

It is worth noting that U.S. development strategy had transformed substantially between the Bush and Obama administrations. During most of the Bush years, as already detailed, state building revolved around participatory institutions and formal-legal theories of legitimacy. When Obama took office, nation crafting had become premised on social contract theory—the belief that government legitimacy flows from the exchange of public goods and services for compliance and support on the part of the populace. The logic behind this updated state-building theory demands a ramping up of aid to ensure provision of services from local governments that would otherwise be incapable of providing them. This is done to generate local compliance with those governments' dictates. Put in terms of our formal model, states that were exposed to this strategy had their capacity enhanced.

In Yemen we see clear evidence of the application of this updated strategy (see figures 8.1–8.4). Starting in 2009, every single trend line starts to climb steeply. This is especially apparent in figure 8.4, detailing humanitarian aid. Humanitarian and development aid to Yemen never exceeded $15 million during the eight years that the Bush administration was in office. During Obama's first year, Yemen received $36.5 million in aid, a 243 percent increase. This was almost doubled again the following year, as aid rose to $66.2 million.

Cost of Effort and Disturbances

By 2009, levels of unrest in Yemen had become dangerously high. In Houthi territory to the north, Saleh was conducting Operation Scorched Earth—a giant military engagement involving the army, tribal levies, and informal fighters moving
into the mountainous regions to suppress the Houthis and their allies. Operation
Scorched Earth was a very serious attempt to secure a decisive win. Victory would
allow Saleh to reestablish control of Yemen's northernmost region.

The whole affair went poorly. Fighting in the mountains was extremely difficult and prevented Saleh from bringing his full force to bear on the insurgents.
The tribal levies he deployed were unreliable fighters and complicated the situation immensely. Once deployed, they attacked and looted targets unrelated to
the conflict. This raised local ire, drawing supporters to the Houthis' side. It
also precipitated several intertribal skirmishes completely unconnected to the
larger war.[62] The result of this long and costly conflict would ultimately be a
stalemate.

The situation in the South was less bleak but nonetheless contentious. From
2008 until Yemen's Arab Spring in 2011, large protests took place across the
South, particularly in major urban centers such as Mukalla and Aden. These
protests often started out, and at times stayed, peaceful, although some turned
violent when protesters encountered security forces.

While violent confrontations in the North and protests in the South occupied Saleh, AQAP was creating bigger and bigger disturbances in the East. In
March 2009, Korean tourists were attacked and killed. Later that month a Korean
task force, in Yemen to investigate the murders, was assaulted. In August, an
AQAP operative crossed the border into Saudi Arabia and nearly assassinated
Prince Mohammed bin Nayef bin Abdelaziz Al Saud, the Saudi assistant interior
minister and head of intelligence. In November, U.S. Army major Nidal Hasan,
who, it was later revealed, had been in discussions with the Yemen-based cleric
Anwar al-Awlaki, committed the Fort Hood massacre in Texas. In December,
Umar Farouk Abdu Mutallab boarded Northwestern Airlines flight 253, headed
for Detroit, and attempted to detonate an explosive device concealed in his
underwear. This was the first of a series of attacks emanating from Yemen that
would reach far beyond the small Arabian country's borders.[63]

The following year, 2010, saw a continuation of high-level, dangerous terrorist attacks, including one on the British embassy and an attempt on British
ambassador Tim Torlot's life. In October, AQAP tried to ship package bombs to
Jewish sites in Chicago, and in December it tried to plant explosives on a U.S.
embassy vehicle.[64] These accompanied an exponential spike in terrorist attacks
within Yemen (see figure 8.5).

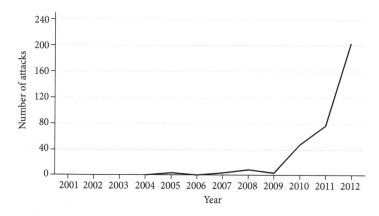

FIGURE 8.5.   Terrorist attacks in Yemen, 2001–12. Data from Global Terrorism Database, National Consortium for the Study of Terrorism and Responses to Terrorism, University of Maryland, https://www.start.umd.edu/gtd/

Principal and Agent

High costs predict low effort. With antiregime forces massing, Saleh's direct and indirect costs of effort would have precluded his attending to disturbances in most cases. While the aid and expertise that the Obama administration started funneling into his country were well received, threats to Saleh's regime were too great to expect substantial effort from him in suppressing AQAP.

This expectation is largely borne out by the record. Saleh exerted substantially less effort in this period than he had in previous ones. During 2009, Yemeni forces conducted three raids on terrorist cells and made a handful of arrests.[65] Saleh's response to terrorist threats that year was described by the State Department as "intermittent," a better assessment than the department's reports in 2010 and 2011, when it described significant political instability and did not bother to consider Saleh's counterterrorism efforts at all.[66]

As an agent becomes unable to suppress disturbances, the model's predictions depend greatly on interest alignment and on the principal's level of concern with those disturbances. If principal-agent interests are aligned, we expect capacity building. If the disturbance concerns the principal enough that it must suppress the disturbance immediately, direct action can occur simultaneously. This might result from the principal's viewing the agent as having a long-term advantage that is worth preserving and investing in, but no advantage in the present moment. If interests have diverged, the model indicates that we should expect to see direct action or replacement with no capacity building whatsoever.

In this case, interests were fairly aligned in the sense that disturbances were of concern. Saleh was most interested in suppressing antiregime forces and

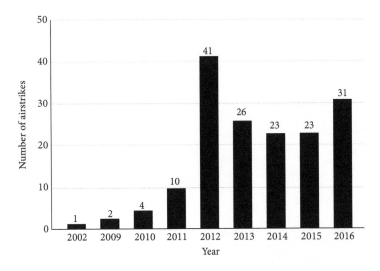

FIGURE 8.6. U.S. drone strikes in Yemen, 2002–16. Bill Roggio and Bob Barry, Charting the Data for U.S. Air Strikes in Yemen, 2002–2017, *Long War Journal,* http://www.longwarjournal.org/multimedia/Yemen/code/Yemen-strike.php, accessed 2016

regaining personal control of Yemen. This overlapped with the United States' interest in ensuring that Yemen remained a governed space with limited transnational terrorism, but their interests were not identical: the U.S. goal was not to keep Saleh in power at all costs. This common ground was ultimately viewed as sufficient to start capacity building after almost a year of intermittent meetings between Obama administration officials and members of Yemen's government.[67]

As the logic of the model suggests, we end up observing both capacity building and direct action. Capacity building has already been discussed. In terms of direct action, as can be seen in figure 8.6, U.S. drone strikes in Yemen (direct action by the principal) rise geometrically from 2009 to 2011. For eight years under Bush (2000–2008), one drone strike took place. Starting in 2009 under Obama, this number doubles, then doubles again in 2010, and then more than doubles a third time in 2011.

The Arab Spring and After

In the first months of 2011, Arab Spring protests broke out across Yemen. Saleh attempted to retain power even as the number of opposition forces arranged against him grew. Some regime elites, members of his tribal confederation and political party, joined already active antiregime groups across the country to press for his resignation. Saleh held out, refusing to step down until the end of his term.[68]

Saleh fired his entire cabinet and, according to the BBC, "vowed to defend his regime 'with every drop of blood.'"[69] He called out his elite force, the Republican Guard, which was headed by his son Ahmed Ali Abdullah Saleh. The Republican Guard clashed with the less trained, more poorly equipped factions of the Yemeni military that were fomenting unrest. Saleh also publicly threatened all who challenged his rule, declaring in no uncertain terms that their actions could lead to civil war. "Those who want to climb up to power through coups," he said, "should know that this is out of the question. The homeland will not be stable, there will be a civil war, a bloody war."[70]

On June 3, the standoff between the well-armed Yemeni government and its own people ended when a bomb attack in the presidential palace injured Saleh, forcing him to seek medical treatment in Saudi Arabia. In the preceding two months, Saleh had been signaling that he would step down peacefully before the end of his term. He had not, however, signed a deal negotiated by the Gulf Cooperation Council that would have had him leave power over a thirty-day period.

We don't know what behind-the-scenes role the United States and Saudi Arabia played during this episode. Ultimately, Saleh would receive medical treatment in both countries before departing for Ethiopia with complete immunity. Saleh's replacement, Vice President Abdrabbuh Hadi, assumed power but did not last long. In the two years that Hadi controlled Yemen before it succumbed to the Houthi uprising, he tried to rework Yemen's military apparatus, which had been a popular arena for elite competition and the center of hard power in Yemen.[71]

Hadi's failure is likely due to two factors. First, he had no tribal base of support in Yemen and therefore had no trusted group of individuals whom he could rely on for political support. The result was anger and resistance on all sides, as Hadi tried to extricate Saleh's supporters from positions of power, while simultaneously trying to prevent the military balance of power from shifting too heavily in favor of Saleh's natural replacement, Ali Mohsen (Saleh's fellow tribesman and ex-compatriot).[72] Second, Hadi did not include the Houthis in any of the power-brokering discussions—a monumental mistake, as it allowed regime-periphery tensions to metastasize. Civil war might have been avoided had Hadi allowed the Houthis to play a more active role in reworking Yemen's political power structures.

Yemen is an interesting case for the theory and formal model. On one hand, it fits extremely well. Initial interest alignment between a U.S. administration looking to stamp out terrorism emanating from the Middle East and a leader who had no qualms about doing it led to perfect compliance on the part of Saleh, and he was rewarded in the process. As interests diverged in 2005, the model continued to fit, as it indicated that we should expect to see lower effort on the part of the agent, and therefore greater disturbances, followed by punishments to induce compliance. This is indeed what we see, as, after a punishment phase, Saleh met the Bush administration's demands for greater democratization by allowing a contentious presidential election with a real opponent.

The model continues to fit well in the period when Obama took office. At this point, Saleh's indirect and direct costs of effort had risen to extreme heights, as he was in serious conflict with antiregime forces. The model predicted capacity building and direct involvement given that interests were relatively aligned. Although this occurred, it was not enough to stabilize Yemen or prevent transnational terrorist cells from taking root.

On the other hand, Yemen as a case study raises questions that are tricky to answer. To begin with, it is unclear why the Bush administration decided to simultaneously shift the goalposts and cut rewards in late 2005. Given that Saleh was quite compliant when it came to fighting terrorism, why not offer him even greater rewards to modernize Yemen's political system and turn Yemen into a noncorrupt democracy? One possibility is that Bush administration officials thought that they were operating under a suboptimal arrangement. They could have believed that Saleh's direct and indirect costs of effort were much lower than they initially anticipated and that they were overpaying for the services rendered. To rectify this, the Bush administration demanded more without offering further compensation.

If this was indeed the case, then one thing that this case study reveals is that the initial contract (implied or otherwise) can set expectations. Principals must be careful with how they establish the first contract, as this will serve as a baseline from which all future developments are judged. If, as in this case, a generous contract is offered and is then replaced with a less favorable one, the agent will be less interested in complying than it would have been had the more frugal contract been offered first.

Another related lesson is the value of carefully monitoring the agent's costs, both direct and indirect. Information gleaned from monitoring may justify shifting some assets away from the disturbance, to direct them instead at the agent.

A second question the case raises is this: given that Saleh started complying less, particularly with his initial task of countering terrorism, why not increase incentives (rewards and punishments) to induce compliance across the board? The most reasonable answer here seems to be that compliance was not important enough to the Bush administration to warrant such actions. All principals must trade off the costs of rewards and punishments against the level of disturbance they are willing to tolerate. The Bush administration was more invested in

Iraq, Afghanistan, and Pakistan, perhaps, than it was in developing Yemen into a model nation. Given that terrorism no longer seemed to be emanating from Yemen, and that the chief concern was now how democratic the country could be, the other three countries were of greater import to the Bush administration and therefore received the type of attention Yemen could have benefited from.[73]

This reveals another lesson from this case study. It is best for principals not to take on arrangements that they are not willing to see through to the end. Had Saleh's contract been left as it was, the Bush administration would have continued to secure its most important objective in Yemen, namely, preventing the establishment of terrorist networks. By changing the contract and not following through, it instead got the worst possible outcome: the undoing of preliminary success, and a failure to achieve either the democratic or the counterterrorism objective.

NOTES

1. In a speech given on the South Lawn six months after the towers were hit, Bush said this plainly as he talked about Yemen: "In Yemen, we are working to avert the possibility of another Afghanistan. Many al-Qaeda recruits come from near the Yemeni-Saudi Arabian border, and al-Qaeda may try to reconstitute itself in remote corners of that region. President Saleh has assured me that he is committed to confronting this danger. We will help Yemeni forces with both training and equipment and to prevent that land from becoming a haven for terrorists" (quoted in Hull 2011, 37).
2. International Crisis Group 2013, 2.
3. Coles 2011.
4. Kambeck 2016, 6.
5. Schanzer 2004, 518.
6. Johnsen 2012, 263.
7. Salmoni, Loidolt, and Wells 2010, 3.
8. Bush 2002.
9. Johnsen 2012, 90.
10. Ibid., 89.
11. U.S. Department of State 2000, 2001.
12. U.S. Department of State 2001, 60.
13. U.S. Department of State 2002, 2003, 2004.
14. National Council on U.S.-Arab Relations 2009, 13.
15. U.S. Department of State 2002.
16. U.S. Department of State 2004, 2005.
17. U.S. Department of State 2003.
18. The choice of direct action by the U.S. was likely due to an absolute advantage its forces had over Yemeni security forces in targeting al-Harithi. It should not be interpreted as a punishment or a symptom of lack of proxy effort.
19. Katz 2003, 42.
20. Gordon 2002.
21. Salmoni, Loidolt, and Wells 2010, 124.
22. International Crisis Group 2013.
23. U.S. Agency for International Development/Yemen 2006, 4.
24. International Crisis Group 2013, 8.

25. Ibid., 9.
26. Bush 2005.
27. *Washington Times* 2008.
28. Quoted in Miller 2010.
29. Bush 2003.
30. Lake 2016.
31. Johnsen 2012, 180.
32. Ibid., 180.
33. Ibid., 184.
34. Human Rights Watch 1994, 5.
35. Hull 2011, 112.
36. Ibid., 88.
37. In 2006, also postpunishment, Yemen held its presidential election. It was contentious and featured a strong opponent, which is unusual for political contests in the Middle East. As Hull (2011, 114) put it, "President Saleh, unlike most of his Arab peers, ran against real opposition." This election should be read as a response to the punishment phase. The Bush administration had made it clear to Saleh that the United States was interested in establishing real democratic politics. This rather anomalously democratic election (for a Middle Eastern ruler) was an acquiescence to those demands.
38. U.S. Department of State 2006.
39. U.S. Department of the Treasury 2004.
40. U.S. Department of State 2006.
41. U.S. Department of State 2007.
42. Salmoni, Loidolt, and Wells 2010, 120.
43. Ibid.
44. Ibid., 111–12.
45. Ibid., 126.
46. Boucek 2010, 5.
47. "Al-Qaeda Organization in the Arabian Peninsula" 2017.
48. Boucek 2010, 6.
49. U.S. Agency for International Development/Yemen 2006, 21.
50. Human Rights Watch 2009, 19.
51. National Council on U.S.-Arab Relations 2009, 13.
52. Johnsen 2012, 209.
53. MCC 2007b.
54. MCC 2007a.
55. U.S. Department of State 2008.
56. Johnsen 2012, 220–34.
57. U.S. Department of State 2007.
58. U.S. Department of State 2008.
59. Novak 2009.
60. Ibid.
61. U.S. Senate 2012, 24.
62. Boucek 2010, 9.
63. U.S. Department of State 2009.
64. U.S. Department of State 2010.
65. U.S. Department of State 2009.
66. U.S. Department of State 2009, 2010, 2011.
67. U.S. Senate 2012, 24.
68. "Yemen President" 2011.
69. Ibid.

70. Quoted in "Yemen President" 2011.

71. International Crisis Group 2013, 14–15. This reworking was specified in detail in the compromise drawn up by the Gulf Cooperation Council.

72. Ibid., 15.

73. This ended up being a mistake. Just six years later, in testimony in a joint intelligence committee hearing, CIA director David Petraeus, who had served in Iraq during the Bush years, would refer to Yemen as "the most dangerous regional node in the global jihad" (Reuters 2011).

9

IRAQ, 2003–11

Principal Failure

David A. Lake

Postwar Iraq is a striking example of the promise and perils of indirect control through proxies. After the overthrow of Saddam Hussein, the United States faced a rising insurgency. It also feared that political instability might create a haven for transnational terrorists, much as in Afghanistan prior to 2001. This fear was later realized by the flood of foreign fighters into Anbar Province. Soon after the initial invasion, the threat of disturbances either in or emanating from Iraq grew quite high. Action was necessary.

After a brief period of direct control under the occupation, the United States moved rapidly to return sovereignty to Iraq and rebuild the Iraqi armed forces. By May 2006, it moved to a strategy of indirect control through its handpicked proxy, Prime Minister Nouri al-Maliki. The prime minister and the United States both sought a stable Iraq with an effective government able to police its territory. At the same time, the United States and al-Maliki differed sharply on the means for obtaining this goal. The United States sought a broad-based coalition of Shia, Sunnis, and Kurds that would—it was hoped—undercut the insurgency and stabilize the state. The United States also placed a priority on ending the war as soon as possible. Concerned first and foremost with consolidating his own political power and position, al-Maliki preferred a Shia-only coalition, and was dependent on support from more radical elements within that community, including those surrounding Muqtada al-Sadr, and later Iran. He was willing to tolerate continued conflict, especially if attacks were primarily directed against Sunnis and his political rivals, if it enabled him to stay in power. Thus, not only did the United States and its proxy differ in their beliefs over who and what kind of government would be best placed to lead the new Iraq, but they also differed fundamentally even on the importance of suppressing disturbances within Iraq of concern to the United States. Given his weak position, the domestic political cost to al-Maliki of following the preferred strategy of the United States was extremely high. To control its proxy in this case would have required high-powered incentives, including substantial rewards and punishments.

Believing that U.S. interests were instead relatively aligned with al-Maliki's, the Bush administration sought to rebuild the capacity of the fractured Iraqi state. Administration officials and military commanders in Iraq, principally Gen. George W. Casey, assumed that the U.S. presence in Iraq was a major driver of the insurgency and that the regime was weak and incapable of defeating the rebels on its own. The plan was to "step up" the Iraqi forces with massive aid and training so that the United States could "stand down," a move that in and of itself was expected to deprive the insurgency of its fuel. The Bush administration also believed, more problematically, that it could work successfully with al-Maliki and, thus, spent billions in military and economic aid to bolster the regime. Much of this aid, however, was redirected by al-Maliki toward partisan and sectarian purposes, including support for Shia militias who attacked both the Sunnis and—even worse—U.S. forces. A brief period of cooperation around the Basra campaign of 2008 was driven not by U.S. sanctions but by a temporary convergence of interests between al-Maliki and the Bush administration. This convergence proved ephemeral, with al-Maliki soon reverting to an even more sectarian strategy as the U.S. role in the country wound down. Losing control of the proxy, as in this case, highlights the perils of indirect control.

Despite al-Maliki's lack of effort in implementing its preferred strategy in Iraq, the United States failed to employ adequate rewards and punishments to change the prime minister's behavior. Al-Maliki's failings were recognized at the time. The Bush administration considered replacing him but anticipated that any other leader would be just as bad or worse. There was, in the words of the administration, no "Plan B." Only during the surge did the newly appointed commander, Gen. David Petraeus, begin to restrict some aid flows to al-Maliki and his allies, producing a slight improvement, most notably in the prime minister's willingness to remove his most sectarian military and police commanders. This modest change in U.S. policy suggests that a strategy of manipulating incentives might have worked in Iraq if it had been embraced earlier and much more extensively. Overall, however, the ability to control its proxy was sharply limited by the Bush administration's unwillingness to recognize its divergent interests and employ adequate rewards and punishments.

This chapter is mostly a cautionary tale of what can happen when proxies are not appropriately rewarded or, especially, punished. It focuses on the period after al-Maliki's appointment as prime minister in June 2006 through the withdrawal of all U.S. military forces in December 2011.

Historical Background

Saddam Hussein, who ruled Iraq from 1979 until he was overthrown by coalition forces in 2003, was used as a proxy by the United States during the Iran-Iraq War. In this period, the interests of the United States and the leader of Iraq were sufficiently aligned in opposing the revolution headquartered in Tehran that Washington relied on indirect control.[1] As Hussein's regional aspirations enlarged, especially in the invasion of Kuwait, the United States came to oppose the Iraqi leader. Washington then punished Hussein through the inspections and sanctions regime enacted in the 1990s, which actually worked in eliminating his WMD programs but not in making him more trustworthy.[2] As concerns about transnational terrorism grew in the United States after 2001, the desire to replace this errant proxy increased as well. Motivations for the war were complicated, but the inability to control Hussein was a primary cause leading to the Bush administration's call for regime change.

The United States expected a relatively easy transition to a new proxy relationship in Iraq. Whether this was simply a function of false hopes or part of a strategy of anointing Ahmed Chalabi as the new agent is unclear.[3] The postwar stabilization effort, though limited, was originally embodied in the minimalist but appropriately named Office for Reconstruction and Humanitarian Affairs (ORHA) headed by Lt. Gen. Jay Garner, who had led the relief effort in northern Iraq in 1991. In keeping with his limited mandate, Garner planned to administer the country through government ministries, which he assumed were intact; remove only senior Baath Party members; and recall the Iraqi Army to rebuild infrastructure and secure the population and borders.[4] Reflecting the initial optimism of the Bush administration, Gen. Tommy Franks, the CENTCOM commander, told subordinates that the Iraqi government would be functioning in thirty to sixty days.[5] Designed largely as a humanitarian effort, ORHA was immediately overwhelmed by the outbreak of violence in Baghdad.[6] As violence swept through the capital, Garner was almost immediately replaced by Ambassador L. Paul Bremer and the new Coalition Provisional Authority (CPA), an announcement that was made public on May 6, 2003.

Bremer rapidly took the occupation in a new direction, creating a brief period of direct control by the United States rarely seen in modern international relations. Whether instructed to do so by President Bush or not—this remains unclear, with conflicting accounts of responsibility—Bremer switched the mission from a humanitarian operation to full-on state building. In Bremer's own vision, he was the head of an occupation authority, albeit one charged with nurturing a Western-style democracy. As he informed the Iraqi Governing Council in his first meeting with the group, the CPA "was the legitimate authority in Iraq in the eyes of the international community under the law of occupation."[7] On May 12, four days after his arrival, Bremer publicly declared the CPA to be the supreme authority in Iraq and assumed sovereignty over its people and territory. Bremer also overturned plans for the creation of a provisional Iraqi government, disbanded the Iraqi Army, and began a purge of Baath Party officials. The latter two actions disproportionately affected Sunnis, especially those previously associated with Hussein, and economic reform threatened established (rent-seeking) interests within the former elite. Although Hussein had long exploited sectarian tensions in Iraq, the CPA did little to bridge gaps between groups and may even have exacerbated the underlying communal conflicts. Along with the failure to provide security to all groups in Iraq after the fall of Hussein, which set off a devastating spiral of violence that destroyed the state, the alienation of the Sunnis from the earliest days of the occupation drove at least some into the insurgency. The belief of Secretary of Defense Donald Rumsfeld that the United States faced an insurgency of "dead enders" was not entirely incorrect, though some of the problem was of the administration's own making.

Soon after his arrival in Baghdad, Bremer outlined a seven-step, 540-day strategy for drafting a new constitution, passing an election law, and holding national, regional, and local elections for a new government.[8] Following this blueprint nearly to the letter, the CPA was dissolved one year later in June 2004, with sovereignty returning to an interim government and ending the period of direct control. A National Assembly, charged with writing a new constitution, was elected in January 2005 (taking office in April 2005), with Ibrahim al-Jaafari as prime minister. A compromise candidate supported because he was expected to be a weak placeholder, al-Jaafari proved as inept and weak as many had feared.[9] The new constitution was approved in a national referendum in October 2005. National elections for the Council of Representatives were held in December 2005, with al-Maliki eventually being asked to form a government only in May 2006.

U.S. and coalition troop deployments embodied the direct involvement of the United States. After an initial decline, the United States and its coalition partners gradually increased troop strength through late 2005 to combat the growing insurgency and violence (see figure 9.1). Reflecting new optimism about the prospects for political accommodation, troop levels then declined once again. U.S. troops remained in Iraq throughout the period covered by this chapter. By

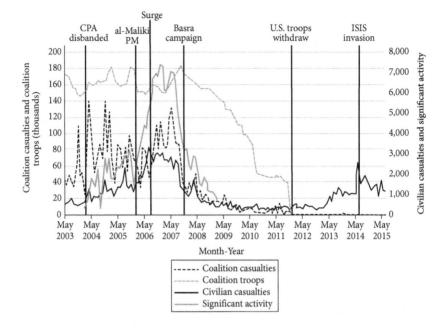

FIGURE 9.1. "Disturbances" in Iraq and coalition troop strength, May 2003–May 2015. Data for coalition casualties from iCasualities, http://icasualities. org/Iraq/index.aspx, accessed July 26, 2015; data for civilian casualties from Iraq Body Count, https://www.iraqbodycount.org/database/, accessed July 26, 2015; data for significant activity from Berman et al. 2011; data for coalition troops from O'Hanlon and Livingston 2011, 13

mid-2006, however, al-Maliki was the effective decision maker in Iraq. Thus, he can be considered a proxy who the principal, the United States, might have wished would suppress disturbances.

Theoretical Expectations

The disturbances at issue in this case, as already indicated, were the insurgent attacks on U.S. and coalition forces in Iraq and the possibility that Iraq might become an "ungoverned space" in which transnational terrorists could hide, train, and initiate attacks against Western targets. As described later in the chapter, actual disturbances in Iraq rose steadily through mid-2007, although there is little evidence that, during this period at least, Iraq was used as a staging platform for external attacks. Although it increased over time, the cost of the disturbance to the United States was high throughout the period examined here.

Direct action by the United States against the insurgency in particular and transnational terrorists in general, in turn, was possible. Unlike in other cases in this volume, the costs of direct action were, in part, "sunk" in the war to overthrow Hussein. The United States did not need to invade Iraq to establish direct control after 2003; the troops were already there for reasons only indirectly related to the subsequent disturbances. The United States strongly preferred that its proxy assume responsibility for counterinsurgency and counterterrorism operations, but it remained involved throughout. The disturbance was, in principle, important enough for the United States to respond unilaterally if required, meeting the most basic scope condition for the application of the theory outlined in the introduction.

Replacement of the proxy was also possible. Due to the deep involvement of the United States in Iraqi politics, and its large role in handpicking al-Maliki as its proxy, Washington could in theory have replaced al-Maliki—if not at will, given its reliance on elections, then certainly with some relatively modest cost. This ability was affirmed in the 2010 election when the United States could have tipped the scales against al-Maliki and again when it helped push him out of office in 2014.

The proxy's cost of effort, in turn, was quite high. As noted and explained in greater detail below, al-Maliki's political strategy centered on building a Shia coalition to support himself in power. Political self-preservation dominated other considerations in the chaos that was the new Iraq. The United States, on the other hand, wanted to build a broad-based coalition and democratic regime that was inclusive of all major groups within Iraqi society. This goal followed from a liberal theory of inclusive peacemaking and a desire to demonstrate that a democratic regime could prosper in the Middle East.[10] This desire for representation of all major groups was critical: if the United States had been content to replace Hussein, a Sunni autocrat, with his Shia equivalent, the conflict of interest between the United States and al-Maliki would have been greatly attenuated. Whether the preferred U.S. strategy would have succeeded is an interesting counterfactual. But al-Maliki clearly calculated that inclusion, especially of Sunnis formerly associated with Hussein's regime, would have lost him necessary support within his own community—perhaps fatally so. Thus, while the United States was concerned with overall levels of violence in Iraq, and especially about the possibility of the country becoming a site from which future attacks against Western interests might arise, al-Maliki was far more tolerant of attacks against Sunnis and even the United States. Equally, the United States, as principal, and its handpicked proxy differed fundamentally in their political strategies for dealing with the possible violence and consolidating the state.

Given the differing interests and high cost of effort by al-Maliki, our theory predicts that he would engage in relatively low levels of effort to control disturbances of concern to the United States and, in turn, focus on building a narrow political coalition against U.S. wishes. Recognizing this, the United States should have offered al-Maliki an implicit contract of high-powered incentives to induce appropriate levels of effort. As explained in the introduction, if disturbances were low, al-Maliki should have been rewarded; if disturbances were moderate, perhaps neither rewards nor punishments should have been offered; but as disturbances increased, al-Maliki should have been punished with more and more severe sanctions. This prediction is summarized in table 9.1. The United States, however, provided *unconditional* capacity-building resource flows for years, and employed only relatively mild sanctions rather late in the game. This might be consistent with the theory if disturbances were too large for rewards but too small relative to the costs of punishments. By late 2006, however, this middling position seems empirically untenable. As both civilian and military casualties rose, the United States should have begun punishing al-Maliki for his lack of effort before it reassumed (partial) leadership of the war through the surge. Although it likely followed from the capacity-building model dominant within the administration and military leadership, this failure to act effectively as a principal remains a puzzle from the point of view of the theory posed in this volume.

TABLE 9.1 Theoretical expectations and summary results, Iraq

PERIOD	KEY PARAMETER(S)	THEORETICAL EXPECTATION	OBSERVED ACTION
2003–6	Disturbances high and increasing	Principal will use larger punishments (H_3)	Principal builds capacity
2007	Disturbances increase through mid-2007, then decline	Principal will use larger punishments while disturbances increase (H_3), then smaller punishments and greater rewards as disturbances decrease (H_2)	Principal engages in direct action (surge) and targeted punishments, but still not at level necessary to induce effective action by proxy
2008	Costs of effort fall as interests converge (temporarily)	Principal will use smaller punishments or rewards and agent will exert greater effort (H_7)	Principal uses neither rewards nor punishments; proxy exerts some effort
2009–11	Disturbances low	Principal will use rewards (H_2)	Principal uses neither rewards nor punishments; proxy exerts less effort

The Principal-Proxy Relationship

The United States was intimately involved in the design of the governance system of Iraq and in the selection of al-Maliki as prime minister in 2006 and again in 2010. Al-Maliki was handpicked by Zalmay Khalilzad, then U.S. ambassador to Iraq, and approved by the White House. For new leadership, many in the U.S. government looked first to the "exiles," especially Chalabi, who was favored by the Department of Defense. Once the violence broke out, and discussions revealed that any exile who had spent most of his life outside Iraq would fail to gain support from Iraqis, attention focused on "internal" candidates. Khalilzad was deeply immersed in the extensive negotiations over the choice of prime minister after the 2005 election. Al-Jaafari was quickly rejected as both incompetent and deeply sectarian. Abd al-Mahdi, another popular and leading contender with good executive skills, was dismissed as too deferential to Adil Abd al-Aziz al-Hakim, leader of the Supreme Council for the Islamic Revolution in Iraq, and too close to Iran. After rejecting several other weak or dark-horse candidates, the ambassador finally settled on al-Maliki, who was a hard-liner on de-Baathification and the Sunni insurgency, reportedly had deep concerns about Iranian influence, and had distanced himself from al-Sadr and the Mahdi Army.[11] Michael Gordon and Bernard Trainor write that "Khalilzad's role in selecting the Iraqi prime minister remained a secret." The Bush administration was interested in fostering the belief that the choice was purely an Iraqi decision, but there was no doubt that "as far as the United States government was concerned, Maliki was fine."[12] Even within the supposedly democratic elections, the United States was heavily involved in selecting Iraq's new leader.[13] Although the proxy relationship between the United States and Iraq began with the return of sovereignty in 2004, the revolving door of leaders before the elections and uncertainty over who exactly would lead Iraq suggest that the proxy relationship really only began in earnest with al-Maliki's appointment as prime minister in May 2006.

The differences in the interests of the United States and al-Maliki were glossed over but still recognized in one form or another by the Bush administration. There was no illusion that al-Maliki would be a perfect proxy (that is, low cost) for the United States. Indeed, al-Maliki was simply the best of a bad lot of possible leaders. He was selected because he was not too close to Iran and was expected to be competent. Without an independent base of political support, moreover, he was expected to be relatively pliable—though this turned out to be shortsighted. Without sufficient attention to the political challenges al-Maliki faced at home, the United States failed to employ sufficient incentives to induce appropriate levels of effort from the prime minister.

Interest Alignment and the Cost of Effort

U.S. interests in postwar Iraq were varied and not necessarily consistent with one another. Just as there were many motivations for invading the country to overthrow Hussein, U.S. goals for postwar Iraq were complex. There is, of course, continuing debate about U.S. motivations in the war. Given that the Bush administration floated many possible arguments in favor of intervention, and focused on those that appeared to resonate with the American public, it is hard to separate the marketing of the war from the "true" motives of the administration and the country more generally. In the postwar period, the United States desired to integrate Iraq into the existing Pax Americana, in which its new partner would (1) give up some control over its own foreign policy in return for U.S. security guarantees; (2) provide forward operating bases in the region, as necessary; and (3) open its economy to international trade and investment. The security and basing relationship was key after U.S. troops withdrew from Saudi Arabia in early 2003. Above all, at least according to the president's public statements, the United States wanted to recruit Iraq as an ally in the war on terror and, for the neoconservatives in his inner circle, create an exemplary liberal and democratic state in the Muslim world. These broad goals would continue to motivate U.S. policy throughout the period examined here. Their realization required a pro-Western leader who would be responsive to U.S. foreign policy concerns. Of the available leaders, al-Maliki was perceived as the most sympathetic, or perhaps the most malleable, on this score.

In pursuit of these goals, however, the United States wanted al-Maliki to build a consolidated state that would integrate the competing communities of the formerly dominant but minority Sunnis, the majority Shia, and the minority and separatist Kurds. With such a consolidated state, Iraq could become the ally in the war on terror that Washington wanted, without challenging its Sunni neighbors, and while still containing Shia Iran. Iraq would also become an exemplar of a new Middle East that was both democratic and Islamic. A joint mission statement negotiated between Casey, commander of U.S. forces in Iraq, and John Negroponte, the first U.S. ambassador to Iraq after the war, identified U.S. goals as "to help the Iraqi people build a new Iraq, at peace with its neighbors, with a constitutional, representative government that respects human rights and possesses security forces sufficient to maintain domestic order, and deny Iraq as a safe haven for terrorists." Operationally, this translated into building an Iraqi state with security forces capable of controlling territory and suppressing violence against all sectarian groups at home and the United States and its allies abroad. Casey adopted the mantra "al-Qaeda out, Sunnis in, Iraqis increasingly in the lead."[14]

Al-Maliki's goals appear to have been more narrowly personal and straight-forwardly political. As a deputy of Dawa, one of several political parties in post-war Iraq, al-Maliki lacked an established base of political support. Plucked from the second rank by the United States, and indeed somewhat incredulous that he was being elevated over senior members of his own party, al-Maliki needed above all to build and consolidate a political coalition to sustain his position as prime minister.[15] This seems to have been his primary ambition throughout the postwar period.

Though a broad-based coalition might have been possible, al-Maliki clearly chose to build a narrow support coalition that depended on immediate fam-ily members and associates, creating an inner circle of trusted supporters—the "Malikiyoun"[16]—as well as more militant Shia, often allied with Iran, who in turn demanded control over important ministries. Most salient, al-Sadr demanded the Interior Ministry as a condition for his support, which allowed him to trans-form the national Iraqi police force into a virtual extension of his Mahdi Army.[17] Al-Sadr also demanded the Transport and Telecommunications Ministry, which controlled major infrastructure projects and the Baghdad airport, and the Health Ministry, which allowed his allies to control access to crucial government ser-vices.[18] Through their control of the airport, Sadrists kept track of the move-ments of people and resources in and out of the country, but also smuggled in weapons and explosives. The Health Ministry guards, in turn, were killing Sunnis in the hospitals, soon causing nearly all to avoid the formal health system under any condition.[19] Al-Sadr's control also extended to some portions of the Iraqi military, with the 3-1-6 Battalion barely distinguishable from his militia except for the uniforms they wore.[20] The Mahdi Army thus effectively captured key ele-ments of the Iraqi state from within. In short, al-Maliki chose to build a highly partisan coalition of formerly disenfranchised Shia who wanted to dominate the Sunnis. That he ceded control over essential ministries indicates the high price he was willing to pay for support from Shia extremists. This reliance on the most extreme elements of the Shia community was challenged only briefly in 2008 when al-Maliki sought to consolidate his political position in advance of elec-tions (see discussion below).

This Shia-only coalition made it difficult (that is, costly) for al-Maliki to com-ply with U.S. wishes, especially the incorporation of the Sunnis into the gov-erning coalition and the creation of truly representative institutions. With the Sunnis now excluded from power, the insurgency grew as the "dead enders" of the former regime engaged in a further spiral of violence with the Shia militias. Al-Qaeda made inroads into Sunni areas (especially Anbar Province), from which it attacked coalition forces and possessed the potential to attack others interna-tionally. With al-Maliki having decided to rely on a strictly Shia coalition, his election did not quell the violence, as the United States had hoped, but appeared to stimulate further fighting and greater casualties (see figure 9.1). Once al-Maliki cast himself as a Shia partisan, however, deviating from this coalition threatened his political survival. Aligning with the rival Sunnis no longer appeared to be an option, despite continuing U.S. pressure. Whether or not a broad-based coalition as preferred by the United States was ever possible, and whether it would have succeeded in dampening the insurgency, will never be known. Nonetheless, having made his choice, al-Maliki faced very high costs for complying with U.S. goals.

The United States, and particularly the Bush administration, seemed unaware of al-Maliki's precarious political position and his domestic political incentives. As President Bush remembers his early relationship with the prime minister,

> Maliki was friendly and sincere, but he was a political novice. I made clear I wanted a close personal relationship. So did he. In the months ahead, we spoke frequently by phone and videoconference. I was careful not to bully him or appear heavy-handed. I wanted him to consider me a partner, maybe a mentor. He would get plenty of pressure from others. From me he would get advice and understanding. Once I had earned his trust, I would be in a better position to help him make tough choices.[21]

This attitude and strategy were shared within the administration, with Condoleezza Rice, the national security adviser at the time, remarking on her first meeting with al-Maliki that her "overwhelming impression was favorable."[22] In terms of structuring al-Maliki's incentives, this desire to be supportive undercut the president's ability to apply appropriate punishments. According to our theory, this was exactly the wrong approach to motivate a proxy.

Some in the military did recognize al-Maliki's dilemma. With tens of thousands of U.S. troops in country throughout the period, some embedded with Iraqi units, the military command was well aware of al-Maliki's actions, and could infer something about his intentions.[23] This substantial U.S. troop presence and monitoring ability had the effect of transforming the agency problem from one of hidden or unobserved action to one of hidden information about al-Maliki's costs of compliance with U.S. wishes. Nonetheless, the political leadership never fully grasped the problem of creating appropriate incentives for their proxy. Maj. Gen. Peter Chiarelli, commander of the Multi-National Corps in Iraq from November 2005 to February 2006, concluded that the United States, as reported by Gordon and Trainor, "needed a plan to deal with the possibility that the Americans and the Iraqi government did not share the same goal: an inclusive, pluralistic Iraq."[24] Chiarelli's secret briefing on this matter for Casey, however, was ignored. Confident of its man in Baghdad, the Bush administration largely sidestepped the need for a political strategy for dealing with the Iraqi leadership. As Linda Robinson describes it, the "strategy was essentially to keep trying to persuade . . . al-Maliki to do the right thing. . . . There was no implicit or explicit 'or else' should he fail to do so."[25]

Disturbances

As noted earlier, the primary disturbances feared by the United States were, in the short run, attacks on its forces, and, in the longer run, transnational terrorists hiding in ungoverned spaces within Iraq. As proxy measures for the disturbance, the United States monitored coalition casualties, civilian casualties (as a measure of the overall level of violence), military engagements (see figure 9.1), and estimates of al-Qaeda fighters in Iraq.[26] On the broadest scale, the disturbance that was of the most immediate concern to the United States by the time al-Maliki assumed office was simply the level of violence in Iraq itself. As figure 9.1 makes clear, violence in Iraq grew steadily from the invasion in 2003 through early 2007, after the surge. The disturbances were also rising, even when the United States was in direct control prior to June 2004 and before al-Maliki's appointment as prime minister in May 2006. Neither the return to sovereignty nor the elections in December 2005 noticeably altered this trend. This suggests that the disturbance was not entirely due to a lack of effort by al-Maliki, a point I return to later. Nonetheless, as disturbances increased in frequency and size, our theory suggests that the United States should have responded with greater punishments directed against al-Maliki.

Capacity Building

The United States, and the Bush administration in particular, initially believed that its interests were relatively aligned with those of the new Iraqi leader and that the primary problem to be solved was a lack of military, political, and economic capacity. Though its views on interest alignment were perhaps naive, the assumption that Iraq lacked capacity was not unreasonable. During the U.S. invasion, the Iraqi military simply dissolved. Though the disbanding of the military and the policy of de-Baathification by the CPA were political moves that frustrated Sunnis who might otherwise have expected some role in the new Iraq, the fact was that the Iraqi military and bureaucracy as organizations were essentially defunct. In the short term, at least, Bremer's acts merely confirmed the facts on the ground.

In turn, the United States quickly learned just how decrepit Iraq's infrastructure and economic foundations were. According to Ali Allawi, Iraq's first postwar minister of defense and minister of finance, the country "was in an advanced state of decay." Under international sanctions and threatened by domestic unrest throughout the 1990s, Hussein had withdrawn from detailed management of the economy, focusing instead on his immediate survival. Large areas of southern Iraq and Kurdistan were deliberately starved of basic services, with Sunni areas north of Baghdad faring only marginally better. Overall, Allawi noted, "the standard of living had precipitously crashed" after the Persian Gulf War.[27] Much of the country's civilian infrastructure, including its oil pipelines, was allowed to deteriorate radically. Whatever residual capacity might have remained evaporated once the violence began to escalate in 2004. Having expected to take over a functioning state, the Bush administration soon discovered that, in fact, it held a failed state in its hands.[28]

Initially focused on capacity building, the United States eventually spent over $59 billion on Iraq reconstruction (as of September 30, 2012, through its period of direct involvement), including $20.86 billion for the Iraq Relief and Reconstruction Fund, $20.19 billion for the Iraq Security Forces Fund, $5.13 billion for the Economic Support Fund, and $4.12 billion for the Commander's Emergency Response Program (CERP). On average, expenditures totaled more than $15 million per day, reaching a peak of $25 million per day in 2005.[29] As predicted by the theory, the spending was front-loaded so that it might do the most good in future years.

Capacity building was also central to U.S. military strategy. Casey, the U.S. military commander in Iraq from June 2004 to February 2007, and Secretary of Defense Donald Rumsfeld shared a strong view that the more the United States did, the less the Iraqis would do for themselves. Understanding the insurgency as a response to the unwanted presence of a foreign invader, rather than a sectarian competition for power, the U.S. goal until the surge was to pull back U.S. troops and involvement, have the Iraqi troops participate in all aspects of all military operations, and withdraw U.S. troops as soon as possible.[30] In November 2005, the White House issued a white paper entitled "National Strategy for Victory in Iraq." In discussing this strategy in a speech in Annapolis, Maryland, President Bush emphasized the capacity-building program then underway and its promising results. "As Iraqi forces increasingly take the lead in the fight against the terrorists," he said, "they're also taking control of more and more Iraqi territory.... As Iraqi forces take responsibility for more of their own territory, coalition forces can concentrate on training Iraqis and hunting down high-value targets.... As the Iraqi security forces stand up, coalition forces can stand down."[31]

Given the devastation of Iraq in the aftermath of the war, capacity building was not—to repeat—an unreasonable strategy. The proxy really did lack the ability to field sufficient troops to deal with the insurgency then facing the new state. Yet despite the flow of resources into Iraq, the increase in capacity had little effect in suppressing the level of violence and improving the political stability of the country. Although the growing Iraqi security forces were plagued by corruption, cronyism, and sectarianism, greatly undermining their effectiveness, responsibility for the expanding violence cannot be placed entirely at the feet of al-Maliki. It is important to remember that military and civilian casualties were growing even during the period of direct control by the United States. Nonetheless, the inflow of resources appeared to have little effect in dampening disturbances in Iraq.

As the United States desired the new Iraqi regime to take a leadership role in fighting the insurgency and stabilizing the country, the number of Iraqi security personnel is one possible indicator of the level of capacity (see figure 9.2). This number was widely reported in the press during the war as a measure of "progress." At the same time, however, the size of these forces was an ambiguous signal. In competition with the Sunni militias and especially the Mahdi Army of his rival, al-Sadr, al-Maliki attempted to use the security forces as his own personal militia. As capacity expanded, this also increased al-Maliki's ability to govern in a sectarian fashion. Both the United States and the prime minister wanted the biggest and most well-equipped forces possible, but they differed in the purposes to which these forces were to be used. Capacity building failed not only because Iraqis lacked ability. Rather, U.S. resource inflows failed due to the sectarian and partisan machinations of the prime minister and other Iraqi leaders. This is consistent with the theory, which posits that when the agent's costs of effort are high, capacity building will have little effect.

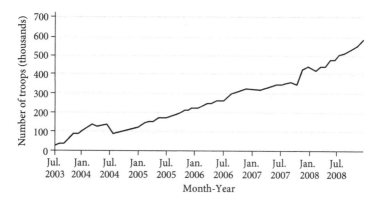

FIGURE 9.2. Total Iraqi security forces, July 2003–December 2008. Data from O'Hanlon and Livingston 2011, 17

Incentives: Phase 1 (2003–7)

Once in power, al-Maliki did not govern as desired by the United States. After a visit to Iraq in October 2006, National Security Adviser Stephen Hadley wrote a confidential assessment for the president. Despite the prime minister's reassuring words, Hadley wrote, there were numerous reports from commanders on the ground of (1) nondelivery of services to Sunni areas, (2) intervention by the prime minister's office to stop military action against Shia targets and to encourage them against Sunni ones, (3) removal of Iraq's most effective commanders on a sectarian basis, and (4) efforts to ensure Shia majorities in all ministries. When combined with the escalation of Mahdi Army killings, substantial evidence suggested "a campaign to consolidate Shia power in Baghdad."[32] During this same time, two brigades promised for the unfortunately named joint U.S.-Iraqi "Operation Forward Together" simply did not show up. Al-Maliki also promised a twenty-four-point national reconciliation plan soon after his inauguration, but never acted on that pledge.[33] Finally, al-Maliki's desire to command his loyal military units directly rather than through the military chain of command further fueled fears about his sectarian intentions.[34] In a visit with al-Maliki in Jordan following Hadley's report, President Bush ran through the list of problems. Yet after seeing al-Maliki, the president concluded that "we could count on his support."[35]

Al-Maliki's failure to act as a "good" proxy was more or less clearly recognized within the Bush administration. Hadley was sanguine, writing in his report to the president that "Maliki is either ignorant of what is going on [or] misrepresenting his intentions." Yet, unable to abandon the optimism about al-Maliki that appears to have pervaded the administration, Hadley still held on to the hope that the prime minister's "capabilities are not yet sufficient to turn his good intentions into action."[36] Condoleezza Rice was ambivalent, blaming all the Iraqi leaders, not just al-Maliki. "They're all at fault," she told the president.[37] Yet she also traveled to Baghdad at one point to tell al-Maliki to shape up. "You're a terrible prime minister," she supposedly told him. "Without progress [toward an inclusive political solution] and without an agreement [to maintain U.S. forces in Iraq], you'll be on your own, hanging from a lamppost."[38]

Yet despite the secretary of state's harsh words, the United States was reluctant to punish al-Maliki. When a senior U.S. official tried to explain to the president how his commitment to stand by al-Maliki no matter what did not help move the prime minister toward necessary compromises, Bush angrily replied, "Are you saying I'm the problem?"[39] The Bush administration's concern about building capacity in the new Iraqi state, and its desperation for the Iraqis to take the lead, made overall U.S. support and the flow of resources to the Iraqi government untouchable.

As the Bush administration grew increasingly frustrated with al-Maliki, however, it did discuss replacing him at several points. After one particularly distressing videoconference, the president mused, "If you dump Maliki, then ensure we get someone we can live with."[40] Several months later, the president repeated the problem: "If not Maliki, who?"[41] Consistent with the theory, without a clearly better alternative, al-Maliki's position was secure. There was no "Plan B."[42] At best, the administration might hope to replace al-Maliki with someone equally partisan but, likely, even more incompetent. Indeed, after his party came in second in the 2010 elections despite widespread voter fraud, the United States still stage-managed al-Maliki's reelection as prime minister.[43] It does not appear that the Bush administration seriously considered even small sanctions for ignoring its wishes (nor did it seriously consider replacing its agent). The very weakness of the Iraqi state and the politically tenuous position of al-Maliki within it appear to have blocked even low-level punishments.

Incentives: Phase 2 (2007)

As figure 9.1 indicates, the number of disturbances increased steadily through mid-2007. This was not unexpected in the surge, as the new counterinsurgency doctrine adopted by the United States required putting forces in harm's way to protect the civilian population. This should have led to either a period of direct control, as observed in the surge, or even greater use of incentives by Washington.

As the disturbance continued to escalate, the United States eventually responded, as predicted, by reestablishing a degree of direct control over Iraq and imposing mild punishments on al-Maliki. The surge reintroduced up to thirty thousand U.S. troops into Iraq and shifted control of the war to Washington. Importantly, the United States once again ran the war in its own way—creating a second period of at least partial direct control that did not retract the sovereignty of Iraq but shifted U.S. troops from a largely advisory role to a combat role. The surge was directed mostly at Baghdad itself and, in turn, the Sunni regions of Iraq. Capitalizing on the Anbar Awakening, begun before the surge, many of the new troops went to the Sunni areas. By supporting the Sunnis, the United States hoped to reduce the presence of al-Qaeda in Anbar, demonstrate its commitment to a more inclusive regime in Baghdad, and bolster the political standing of the Sunnis. Cooperation with the Sunnis in the context of the surge exemplified the political strategy that the United States wished al-Maliki would adopt.

Despite the greater disturbances, U.S. actions during the surge still appear to have been chosen for the purpose of damping down the violence in Iraq rather than manipulating the prime minister's incentives. The surge alone might be interpreted as a punishment against al-Maliki, as it made it somewhat more difficult for him to pursue his sectarian strategy. How costly it was to him, however, is not entirely clear, and in any event is extremely hard to measure. Before the surge was announced, al-Maliki had promised major political reforms, but then in a speech in December 2006 that was supposed to outline a new program, he did not fire any Sadrist officials, announce the formation of a "moderate front," or offer other accommodations to the Sunnis. Yet al-Maliki was clearly worried about bringing additional U.S. troops into the country, leading the new secretary of defense, Robert Gates, to soft-pedal the possible punishment by explaining to the prime minister that Bush planned only a "modest" increase.[44] Indeed, since the additional troops were largely deployed against his political enemies, and not against the militias that supported him, the direct costs to al-Maliki of these U.S. actions—whether or not they were intended as explicit punishments—may not have been that large. However, by encouraging the Sunnis toward a political solution, and increasing their political weight, they did put some political pressure on al-Maliki. At the same time, al-Maliki was able to limit the deployment of new coalition troops in southern Iraq. This region was his base of support, but he faced considerable competition there from other Shia factions and leaders. The last thing he wanted was his American "allies" causing collateral damage in his backyard.[45] He also extracted an agreement from the United States that senior Iraqi officials could be detained only as "a last resort" and with his explicit permission.[46]

As disturbances peaked in mid-2007, the United States for the first time began employing contingent rewards and punishments, using some limited sanctions against al-Maliki to control his behavior. As expected by the theory, these punishments enjoyed a measure of success in altering, if not al-Maliki's behavior, at least that of those close to the prime minister.

Within the surge, Petraeus attempted more targeted punishments of particular Iraqi constituencies and their militias. Picking up on a tactic discussed by the Joint Strategic Assessment Team that helped design the counterinsurgency strategy, which team member Stephen Biddle dubbed "Tony Soprano Goes to Baghdad," Petraeus sought to connect political negotiations in Baghdad to military operations in new ways.[47] Discovering that a national police brigade in southern Baghdad was murdering Sunnis, for instance, he informed the Interior Ministry that he was withholding all support until the killing stopped and the sectarian commanders were replaced. Suddenly, according to Fred Kaplan, the brigade "had no fuel, spare parts, money or equipment; nor were its men allowed into any area controlled by American troops." The brigade backed off, as did similar units—at least temporarily. When al-Maliki complained, Petraeus challenged him to a joint meeting with President Bush, which the prime minister declined.[48] This same threat was used multiple times when al-Maliki proved reluctant to fire sectarian commanders or simply replaced one sectarian commander with another. Under Petraeus, as Biddle, Julia Macdonald, and Ryan Baker observe, "the U.S. presence was so large and Iraqi dependence so great, U.S. threats to withhold support from individual Iraqi units were unusually credible."[49] What proved effective at the brigade level, however, was never tried at the level of the prime minister.

The punishments embodied in the surge, and especially Petraeus's more targeted sanctions, do appear to have had some impact on al-Maliki's behavior, inducing somewhat greater cooperation with the United States. As expected, the increased coalition troops, their dispersal over larger (but not all) areas of the country, and the change in war-fighting tactics to population-centered protection increased the violence in Iraq. Casualties are not, in this sense, a good indicator of the trend in disturbances during this period. More important, however, the direct control exerted by the United States through the surge, in conjunction with the Anbar Awakening, led to a significant reduction in violence in later 2007.[50] This occurred not because al-Maliki became a better agent, but indeed in spite of his efforts. Al-Maliki did not purge the ministries of Sadrists or make any accommodations to the Sunnis. Nor did the surge increase the rate of progress in building Iraqi security forces substantially, although November 2007 did see the largest month-to-month increase in troop deployments since immediately after the war (see figure 9.2). Al-Maliki also continued to resist integrating Sunnis into the military. The sanctions employed in the surge illustrate more the potential of using appropriate rewards and punishments than the reality. Al-Maliki was never going to be the high-quality or low-cost-of-effort agent the United States desired, but had the Bush administration embraced a strategy of incentives earlier and more fully, he might have been induced to be a better agent than he ever was.

Incentives: Phase 3 (2008)

In early 2008, al-Maliki's political interests converged with those of the United States, at least for a limited time, reducing his costs of effort. This was manifested in the prime minister's new willingness to crack down on the extremists in his Shia coalition, a goal long desired by the Bush administration. This convergence in interests—and greater cooperation—appears more the result of changes in al-Maliki's political strategy, however, than of the incentives employed by the United States or the reduction in violence in the wake of the surge. Nonetheless, this new willingness to take on his political allies was interpreted by the Bush administration as a significant success. After years of pressure from U.S. commanders, al-Maliki finally took the fight to al-Sadr's Mahdi Army. Even then, however, al-Maliki shirked in ways that put U.S. forces at considerable risk, forcing them to bail out his troops without adequate preparation and diverting the focus of the war effort away from al-Qaeda and toward the Mahdi Army. Even with the reductions in violence, which might otherwise have generated some rewards for al-Maliki, and with his continued defiance of the administration, which might have produced some punishments, Bush failed to make relations with al-Maliki contingent on his behavior.

As early as December 2004, U.S. intelligence learned that al-Sadr's Mahdi Army had struck a deal with top officials for free movement in and around the city of Basra, a Shia stronghold in the South, provided they attacked only British forces (who had nominal control of the area under the coalition) and not Iraqi soldiers or police.[51] Ineffective in restraining the militias, British troops hunkered down in 2006, and in February 2007 Prime Minister Tony Blair announced planned cuts in strength and base closures, evacuating the city in September and transferring Basra to the Iraqis in December—essentially turning the city over to the Mahdi Army.

Increasingly confident in his personal control over the military, itself the result of his past shirking, al-Maliki announced in March 2007 that the Iraqi Army would drive the militia out of Basra, though the effort did not begin until a year later. U.S. forces had significant doubts about the military plan, and the operation, once begun, went badly. The largest government force, the Fourteenth Iraq Army division, was grossly understaffed and unprepared, and the Fifty-Second Brigade of three thousand soldiers broke under heavy fighting, with half the unit shedding its uniforms and disappearing into the city. Al-Maliki himself, who had flown into the city to lead the attack and claim credit for the expected victory, was holed up in the Basra Palace under heavy shelling. Eventually the Iraqis needed to be reinforced by substantial coalition personnel and resources. Though Petraeus put the best possible face on the operation in public, it was a narrowly averted disaster. With the United States committed to assuring al-Maliki his victory, al-Sadr stood down on March 30.

A major conflict also erupted in Sadr City, a largely Shia area of Baghdad that al-Maliki had previously protected from U.S. operations. As the Mahdi Army was attacked in Basra, it struck back in the capital. As the Basra operation became bogged down, al-Maliki also mobilized an additional Iraqi division to clear Sadr City of the Mahdi Army. When the Iraqi forces crumbled, U.S. troops were again forced join the fight and helped erect a blast wall that bisected Sadr City. As Iraqi troops prepared to continue the fight into the northern portion of Sadr City in May, a deal was finally cut with al-Sadr that allowed his forces (and their Iranian advisers) to slip away once again. Cast as a victory for al-Maliki, the operation in Sadr City was at best a draw and revealed the remarkably poor performance of the Iraqi forces. However, the Basra and Sadr City battles finally broke the back of the Sadrists, reducing the threat from al-Maliki's principal rival within his coalition.

Despite the military failings of the Iraqi Army, the Basra and Sadr City campaigns were interpreted by the United States as demonstrating al-Maliki's willingness to take on the Shia militias for the first time.[52] Al-Maliki's motives for the campaigns remain unclear. One possible explanation is that, faced with new incentives in the context of the surge, al-Maliki finally started to exert greater effort and took on the most sectarian and radical group within his political coalition. There is, however, no evidence that any high-powered sanctions were ever threatened. The Bush administration had not changed its strategy of bolstering al-Maliki no matter what. More likely, the U.S. role produced the opposite problem of moral hazard; that is, the prime minister could take greater risks in opposing his rivals with the foreknowledge that his American backers would come to his aid if needed.

A more reasonable interpretation is that al-Maliki's own political agenda now converged with the military strategy long advocated by the United States. With provincial elections scheduled for October 2008, al-Maliki appears to have wanted to control the Shia stronghold in Basra, where his Dawa Party otherwise held little sway. In addition, within the government a factional plot was brewing with Kurds, Sadrists, and al-Maliki's prime rivals—Chalabi and al-Jaafari—for a no-confidence vote to be taken against the prime minister. In the end, it appears that al-Maliki took on the Shia militias not because he feared U.S. punishment but for his own domestic political reasons.[53] At best, al-Maliki's political interests coincided with the need to demonstrate to the United States that the Iraqi Army was increasingly competent and that he was personally willing to take on his own extremists. As pointed out elsewhere in this volume, the proxy relationship works best when the interests of the principal and those of the proxy are more closely aligned, as they were in early 2008.

Incentives: Phase 4 (2009–11)

By 2009, three trends had converged to allow al-Maliki to revert to his extreme sectarianism. First, the violence in Iraq had fallen dramatically, though not obviously as a result of any effort by al-Maliki. This nonetheless reduced the likelihood, already quite small based on experience, that he would face any punishments from the United States. Second, having consolidated his position in the Shia coalition, al-Maliki had a freer hand politically, which should have reduced his costs of effort and allowed him, if he so chose, to cooperate with the United States in anticipation of greater rewards from Washington. That this greater freedom of action appears to have had the opposite effect reveals something meaningful about al-Maliki's own political preferences. Third, stimulated by the success of the surge, the United States moved quickly to unwind its mission in Iraq, reducing both its ability to monitor al-Maliki's behavior and the likelihood that it would punish him for lack of effort. The net result of these trends was to allow the prime minister to govern in a far more sectarian fashion than he had before.

The temporary alignment of interests in early 2008 may have sent the wrong signal to the Bush administration, with severe long-term consequences. Al-Maliki's new willingness to stand up to al-Sadr was interpreted as a success of the capacity-building strategy long employed by the president. With the Iraqis finally showing some "leadership," the Bush administration began negotiations for a Status of Forces Agreement (SOFA) in fall 2007, which was concluded only in December 2008 after the president became a lame duck. Although Bush wanted to lay a foundation for a relationship with Iraq that would long outlast his fading administration, there was now greater confidence in al-Maliki and the Iraqi military going forward. Events also tipped the balance of power toward al-Maliki. With the success of the surge, American voters wanted the administration to bring the troops home as soon as possible. Having solidified his coalition and expanded ties to Iran as an alternative supplier of military advisers and aid, al-Maliki could simply outwait the United States and its electoral timetable. After tortuous negotiations, the final SOFA committed U.S. forces to withdrawing from all Iraqi cities by mid-2009 and from the country as a whole by the end of 2011.[54]

The withdrawal of U.S. forces essentially gave al-Maliki a free hand politically. He used this freedom, both before and especially after 2011, to govern in an even more partisan and sectarian manner than he had before, including cutting funding for the Awakening Forces in Sunni-dominated provinces, arresting Sunni leaders, turning the Shia militias loose once again, and allying more closely with Iran. His increased partisanship had the predictable effect of further alienating the Sunnis and creating the opening through which ISIS conquered one-third of Iraq in the summer of 2014.

In the end, the alignment of interests—with its lower costs of effort for al-Maliki—proved short lived, though it gave the United States the opportunity it sought to withdraw from Iraq. Greater rewards for less violence might have induced al-Maliki to temper his sectarianism, or greater punishments might have countered his partisanship, but neither was used to any significant extent. The result was, as predicted, that this all-too-ineffective proxy once again pursued his own political interests rather than the goals supported by the United States.

Why Did the United States Not Act as a More Effective Principal?

The theory gets much right about this case. When interests diverge, and punishments are not used effectively, the agent will shirk and act against the principal's interests. When interests converge, however briefly, the agent will exert greater effort. Yet the theory is challenged by the Bush administration's failure to employ sufficiently high-powered incentives to induce al-Maliki to behave in ways desired by Washington, especially in the run-up to the surge and again after 2009 as the U.S. role in the country was unwinding. Although perhaps not sufficiently sensitive to how tenuous al-Maliki's political position was, administration officials were certainly aware of their political and policy differences with the prime minister. The president was urged at various times to punish al-Maliki's lack of effort but chose not to do so. Rather, the administration chose to interpret the problem in Iraq as one of capacity building rather than one of incentives. As noted, given the devastation of Hussein's reign and the war itself, this was not an unreasonable choice. Despite initially optimistic expectations, Iraq was simply not a functioning state or society by the summer of 2003. More curious, though, is why the administration eschewed any use of punishments as casualties among both U.S. forces and Iraqi civilians continued to skyrocket after al-Maliki was appointed prime minister, changing only in very limited ways during the surge. Our cases, this one included, were not chosen to assess alternative explanations for the failure of principals to act according to the theory. Nonetheless, the Iraq case suggests a number of possible reasons worthy of systematic investigation.

One possible explanation for this choice was the massive scale of the U.S. involvement in Iraq, which might have made the contingent use of rewards and punishments impossible. Programs with billions of dollars per year devoted to building infrastructure or training Iraqi troops cannot be easily manipulated as incentives (see chapter 10). The pipeline for large aid projects is simply too long to be turned off and on at the spigot to reward or punish the proxy. This possibility is supported by the finding that the CERP funds—small-scale, local, and, above all, discretionary projects—succeeded in reducing violence in Iraq, while large-scale projects had no effect.[55] Nonetheless, since the possibility of using aid as a strategic tool to reward or punish al-Maliki appears not to have been discussed seriously by the administration, it is difficult to assess just how large a barrier this might have been. It could be that the difficulty of turning the spigot on and off was so enormous that this option never made it onto the agenda. Given the president's refusal to even consider withdrawing his support from al-Maliki, this seems an unlikely reason.

A second possible explanation, suggested by the theory, is that using rewards and punishments might have been too costly for the United States, or insufficient to induce appropriate effort by al-Maliki. If this was the case, the theory implies that the United States either would not become involved at all or would undertake direct action, which it did. Yet the costs do not appear to have been too high or the effectiveness of sanctions too low relative to the goal of stabilizing Iraq. The U.S. effort to stabilize Iraq was one of the largest state-building efforts in history. In turn, the failure of the effort and the breakdown of the Iraqi state in summer 2014 under the assault from ISIS was a major foreign policy disaster for the United States, eventually leading to the reintroduction of U.S. forces under President Barack Obama, one of the most strident opponents of the war from the start. Manipulating incentives would not have cost the United States much in addition to the aid it gave and, if anything, might have achieved a more favorable outcome. The surge and associated punishments carried out by Petraeus were, in turn, gentle rebukes of al-Maliki. Had the full power of the United States been brought to bear on the prime minister, he likely would have been more compliant—or replaceable.

A third possibility, not inconsistent with the theory but not predicted by it either, is that many in the Bush administration simply wore intellectual or ideological blinders that rendered them unable to see the differences in interests between the United States and any likely Iraqi leader. In theoretical terms, the Bush administration had strong "prior beliefs" in the compatibility of its interests and those of the Iraqis. From even before the war, and contributing to it, many believed that regime change in Iraq would be easy in part because Iraqis naturally shared the president's freedom agenda. Embodying this view of the United States as a liberating but not occupying force, former UN ambassador John Bolton later mused that the administration's only mistake was not turning the country over to the Iraqis sooner, saying "here's a copy of the *Federalist Papers*. Good luck."[56] Combined with the very real lack of capacity in the Iraqi regime, this strong set of convictions likely combined to delay any updating of the administration's beliefs about al-Maliki sufficient to bring about a shift from capacity building to incentives until quite late in the war. If so, this explanation implies that the failure in Iraq was a case of self-imposed ideological blindness to the complexities of Iraqi politics.

Finally, in a twist on our theory, the ability of the United States to screen proxies and select a leader who was most likely to support its interests in Iraq may have actually complicated rather than solved the principal-agent relationship. In the other cases in this volume, principals generally "inherit" proxies already in office, and then structure incentives to induce appropriate effort. In Iraq, the United States had greater flexibility to pick a proxy who shared its interests or, at least, might be sympathetic to U.S. goals in the region. This was reflected in the widespread assumption within the administration that al-Maliki was someone the United States could work with. Having selected a sympathetic leader, however, the United States found itself with a proxy who lacked significant domestic support and, indeed, risked being seen at home as a U.S. "puppet." Al-Maliki, in turn, understood that he needed above all to secure his domestic political position and, in fact, to distance himself from the United States, ultimately leading him to push for the withdrawal of U.S. forces by 2011. When proxies are already in office with at least some independent base of support in society, they can possibly explain to their people that they must comply with the demands of the principal or suffer the consequences. Having been installed by the United States and lacking domestic support, however, al-Maliki did not have that option. Al-Maliki himself would have been deeply tarnished had the United States punished him directly or Iraqi society more generally by cutting aid or enacting other sanctions. In this case, the United States felt that it could not push al-Maliki too hard lest he fall. Without proper incentives, however, al-Maliki could not be controlled by the United States. This created, paradoxically, the worst of all possible worlds. Having backed a leader who lacked domestic support in part *because* of their perceived common interests, the United States found itself with a weak proxy it could not punish for fear of weakening him further. Without proper incentives, however, al-Maliki was free to pursue his own political goals at the expense of the United States and its aspirations in the region.

Iraq under al-Maliki should be an ideal case for the theory. The principal, the United States, clearly demonstrated both the importance it placed on Iraqi policy and its willingness to engage in direct action to control disturbances emanating from within the country. Although it preferred indirect control through a local proxy, embodied in its consistent desire to turn responsibility for governance over to the Iraqis, it was willing to exert direct control as necessary early in the occupation. In turn, as the violence in Iraq continued to escalate, the United States did eventually retake de facto control of the war through the surge. While continuing to urge the Iraqis to step up, the United States seized the initiative, sent more troops, and fought the insurgency according to its own strategy for a period of almost two years. The use of direct control by the United States suggests that the disturbance was of sufficient importance that the Bush administration should have employed rewards and punishments to motivate an agent with distinct political interests. Why the administration largely failed to do so, and instead adopted a strategy of capacity building despite its perverse effects, remains a bit of a mystery. What is startlingly clear, however, is that the administration's failure to use the incentives available to it allowed al-Maliki to pursue his own political agenda, often at the expense of the United States.

At the same time, the within-case comparison made possible by increases in the disturbance and (temporary) reductions in al-Maliki's cost of effort supports the theory. Even in this instance, where the United States generally failed to employ appropriate carrots and sticks, small punishments had the effect of inducing somewhat greater cooperation from the Iraqi leader. This shows the promise of strategies of indirect control, with important implications for how the United States and other would-be principals should conduct proxy wars in the future. As suggested in the introduction, indirect control is a political strategy that must be attentive to the interests of both principal and proxy. Rather than assuming that interests are aligned, and therefore that the agent will do the right thing if able, principals must recognize that proxies have their own interests and will not act as desired unless sufficient incentives are applied. This is the sad lesson of the U.S. fiasco in Iraq.

NOTES

1. On U.S. relations with Iraq during the Iran-Iraq War, see Jentleson 1994.

2. On both the WMD programs and Bush's view of Hussein's trustworthiness, see Lake 2010–11, 27.

3. On early CIA interactions with Chalabi, see Filkins 2008, 262–63. On the Pentagon's relations with him, see Ricks 2006, 104.

4. Gordon and Trainor 2013, 11.

5. Ibid., 12.

6. Herring and Rangwala 2006, 12.

7. Gordon and Trainor 2013, 13, 16.

8. Ibid., 14–15.

9. Bolger (2014, 193) describes al-Jaafari as "openly beholden" to al-Sadr and "much tougher to influence" than Ali Allawi.

10. On the liberal theory of state building that was dominant in the United States at this time, see Lake 2016, 88–93.

11. Gordon and Trainor 2013, 183–89. Subsequent reports indicate that the United States actually knew little about al-Maliki at the time, with some administration officials consistently getting his given name wrong until al-Maliki himself corrected them (Baker 2014).

12. Gordon and Trainor 2013, 197–98.

13. Ibid., 183–89.

14. Bolger 2014, 182–83.

15. Gordon and Trainor 2013, 189, 196–98.

16. Dodge 2012, 151–56.

17. Gordon and Trainor 2013, 140–41, 146–48; Cole 2007, 116–17.

18. Herring and Rangwala 2006, 37; Gordon and Trainor 2013, 220–22.

19. Kaplan 2013, 180.

20. Gordon and Trainor 2013, 343. Every ministry was allocated "facilities protection forces," creating over 145,000 officially armed militiamen (Filkins 2008, 322–23).

21. Bush 2010, 362.

22. Rice 2011, 460.

23. On monitoring and security force assistance, see Biddle, Macdonald, and Baker 2018.

24. Gordon and Trainor 2013, 298.

25. Robinson 2008, 36.

26. On the range of metrics, see O'Hanlon and Livingston 2011. Once Gen. David Petraeus assumed command in 2007, this "metrics-oriented" leader monitored dozens of indicators of progress. See Kilcullen 2010, 41.

27. Allawi 2007, 114; see also Pedersen 2007.

28. On the failure of the Iraqi state and U.S. state-building efforts, see Lake 2016, chap. 4.

29. SIGIR 2013, 55–56. Reflecting the initial optimism of the Bush administration, the initial appropriation in 2003 for the Iraq Relief and Reconstruction Fund was $2.48 billion.

30. Gordon and Trainor 2013, 90.

31. Ricks 2009, 14; Robinson 2008, 19.

32. Gordon and Trainor 2013, 291.

33. Robinson 2008, 16.

34. Ibid., 156.

35. Bush 2010, 375.

36. Hadley, quoted in Gordon and Trainor 2013, 291. See also Bush 2010, 373.

37. Rice 2011, 544.

38. Baker 2014. See slightly different version in Rice 2011, 513, 663.

39. Robinson 2008, 11.

40. Gordon and Trainor 2013, 431.

41. Ibid., 456.

42. Ibid., 197–98.

43. Ibid., 631–36, 642, 650–51; Arraf 2010.

44. Gordon and Trainor 2013, 305.

45. Ibid., 445.

46. Ibid., 364.

47. Robinson 2008, 37.

48. Kaplan 2013, 263–64.

49. Biddle, Macdonald, and Baker 2018, 129.

50. Biddle, Friedman, and Shapiro 2012.

51. Gordon and Trainor 2013, 464.

52. Ibid., 503.

53. Ibid., 473.

54. Responsibility for the failure of negotiations surrounding the SOFA is controversial. The U.S. military never expected to withdraw its forces completely. Both the United States and many Iraqis expected follow-on negotiations to produce a different and better agreement that would have allowed for a continued U.S. presence and role. These follow-on negotiations were begun by the Bush administration and continued under the Obama administration, but were then abandoned in frustration. Whether a follow-on agreement was possible is an interesting historical counterfactual, with all parties partly responsible for the unfortunate outcome that was eventually realized. There is lots of blame to spread around. The failure of negotiations, however, left the SOFA in place and allowed the Obama administration, never supportive of the war in the first place, to withdraw U.S. forces on schedule.

55. Berman, Shapiro, and Felter 2011.

56. Luce 2007.

10

POLICY IMPLICATIONS FOR THE UNITED STATES

Stephen Biddle

The chapters in this volume present a principal-agent theory of indirect foreign policy action and proxy warfare, assess it via a series of case studies, and
find important consistency between the theory and the case evidence. This is
not, of course, a proof of validity, but it establishes enough support for the
argument to warrant considering its implications for U.S. national security
policy.

   In this chapter, I address these implications in five steps. First, I discuss the
project's implications for best practices when relying on proxies: When the
United States uses this tool, how can it be done most effectively? Second, I discuss when the tool should be used: What preconditions are needed for successful
employment, where are these most likely to be found, how common are these
preconditions, and how widely applicable a method is proxy reliance? Third,
given this set of preconditions, I examine the overall utility of proxy reliance as
a national security option. How powerful a tool is it, what can it reasonably be
expected to do, and what can it not do? Fourth, what does this imply for U.S.
force structure? To what degree can proxy reliance enable safe reductions in U.S.
ground forces, changes in the design of those forces, or shifts from conventional
end strength toward special operations forces or air power? I conclude with
some summary observations in light of the theory, cases, and policy implications presented.

Best Practices When Relying on Proxies: Focus on Incentives

How, then, can proxies be used most effectively? The theory presented in the introduction suggests two necessary conditions. First, the policy preferences of the principal and proxy cannot be too far apart. The greater the divergence in policy interests, the higher the proxy's cost of effort—since the proxy is being asked to implement policies that run counter to its own interest, the principal must employ larger rewards and sanctions, which may cause the principal to abandon the proxy and deal with the threat itself. Second, and more practically, the principal must use aid strategically to create leverage for maximizing proxies' incentives to suppress threats to U.S. interests.

No two actors have identical interests, and the more the United States depends on another actor, the more vulnerable the United States is to the other actor serving its own interests. In proxy warfare, the proxy's interests are often very different indeed—with results that can radically reduce the utility of aid unless that aid is designed, preferably from the outset, to increase U.S. leverage.

This follows from the adverse selection problem in principal-agent interactions: the very conditions that promote proxy reliance also promote interest misalignment between the proxy and the United States. And because interest alignment is so important for outcomes, this means that U.S. proxy relationships can easily incur major agency losses—performance shortfalls that result from agents pursuing their own interests rather than the principal's—thus limiting the proxy's contribution to U.S. objectives.

Internally stable, economically developed representative democracies rarely serve as U.S. proxies. The United States more typically relies on local proxies in places where internal instability promotes insurgency, terrorism, humanitarian crisis, or subversion—that is, the kinds of real but limited threats to U.S. interests that make the United States want to take some action, but not to devote enough resources to solve the problem through direct action. These kinds of real-but-limited threats, however, are strongly associated with weak states and corrupt, unrepresentative clientelist regimes.[1] Hence, if the United States is considering proxy reliance, it is often *because* the prospective proxy is weakly institutionalized and unrepresentative. Yet such states' interests are often misaligned with those of Americans. In such states, internal political order often requires what North, Wallis, and Weingast have called a "double balance," wherein the distribution of economic spoils matches the distribution of power among potentially violent elites.[2] Regimes that allow the internal balance of power to misalign with the balance of rents risk violent overthrow, and in such systems the threat of violence from armed elites within the state apparatus often exceeds the real threat from foreign enemies, international terrorists, or antigovernment insurgents. Rational leaders of such states thus cannot treat their militaries as disinterested defenders of the state against foreign enemies; the armed forces are natural rivals and potential threats. To defend themselves and maintain an internal balance of power, heads of state in such regimes often resort to some combination of appeasing the officer corps via corruption, replacing technocrats with reliable cronies, or handicapping efficient command and control through multiple overlapping lines of authority and multiple internal security organizations. Such "coup-proofing" techniques systematically reduce the military's effectiveness against foreign enemies, but they also can be highly effective in defending the regime and maintaining internal order.[3] Under the conditions common among U.S. proxies, this is often the first priority: the regime's interests are typically focused less on external enemies than on internal threats from rival elites, and especially the state military itself, which is often seen as a threat at least equal to that of foreign enemies. Such regimes are often willing to tolerate indifferent performance against foreign enemies as the price of maintaining an internal balance of power among armed elites.

In contrast, U.S. interests in such states typically focus on external threats, and especially transnational terrorists or aspiring regional hegemons.[4] U.S. assistance is typically intended to strengthen partner militaries' ability to meet these ostensibly common threats by improving the partners' military proficiency. The assumption that these external dangers threaten the partner in the same way that they threaten the United States, however, is often mistaken. In fact, the kind of powerful, politically independent, technically proficient, and noncorrupt military the United States seeks is often seen by the proxy regime as a far greater threat to its self-interest than foreign invasion or terrorist infiltration. Increased military capability destabilizes the internal balance of power; diminished cronyism and corruption weaken the regime's ability to control the empowered officers.

The result is a commonplace and major divergence in U.S. and partner political interests that derives ultimately from the adverse selection problems inherent in any principal-agent relationship. Under such conditions, proxies have a powerful incentive to use aid not to professionalize their military but to reinforce clientelism. Such regimes often use U.S. aid as a form of largesse, an additional source of benefits to be distributed to buy political loyalty, with limited real impact on military effectiveness against external threats. The interest divergence so common in proxy warfare thus gives rise to a serious potential for agency loss—that is, proxies redirecting U.S. aid to meet the internal threats they care most about at the expense of the external threats the United States prioritizes, reducing the military effectiveness of U.S. assistance and leaving the proxy military unable to realize U.S. objectives.

Proxy warfare is thus not primarily an engineering problem, not a simple matter of identifying capability shortfalls in the allied military and filling them with aid and assistance. What the cases in this volume show is that interests typically differ, so apolitical capacity building of this kind merely empowers the proxy to serve its own interests more effectively, rather than meeting U.S. needs. The analysis in this volume suggests that in such situations, the United States should instead use aid in a politically instrumental way, as leverage to create incentives for local proxies to serve U.S. purposes.

This implies that some combination of conditionality, monitoring, and enforcement will be needed in most cases: without the leverage such tools create, allies' incentives will normally yield large agency losses and frustrating outcomes in which even large assistance budgets fail to solve the U.S. security problem. The most important policy implication is thus to focus more systematically on the proxy's incentives and to reserve apolitical (unconditional) capacity building for conditions of unusual interest alignment with the proxy.

Yet the United States often fails to use its aid to create incentives via conditionality, monitoring, and enforcement, and instead adopts exactly the apolitical capacity-building model that the analysis suggests will rarely succeed. In Afghanistan, Iraq, and Yemen, for example, U.S. assistance was overwhelmingly unconditional, and in each case the result was deeply unsatisfying. The United States spent billions on allied militaries that proved far less effective than was needed to stabilize their countries and defeat the threats the United States most cared about. In contrast, when conditionality was used, outcomes were still imperfect, but proxy action was closer to meeting U.S. preferences, as in South Korea or El Salvador.

Why were U.S. choices so inefficient in so many cases? A complete answer is beyond our scope, but it is worth considering some of the reasons why the United States has so often resorted to unconditional capacity building in the past, and how it might be possible to overcome these problems, at least in part, in the future.

In an important sense, failure in our cases was often a failure of understanding. At the highest levels of government, principals often did not seem to view their options through a principal-agent lens; that is, they did not appear to be trying to reshape their agents' political incentives to comply with goals that the agents would not otherwise share. Too many U.S. heads of state and their advisers appear to have adopted an apolitical capacity-building model in which agents needed only more weapons, more money, or more training and equipment to realize shared goals and defeat an ostensibly common threat. A central purpose of this volume is to demonstrate that such a model is a poor fit with most proxy interactions in the real world, where interest divergence is the norm and where unconditional capacity building typically leads to major agency losses.

There are other, subtler reasons why U.S. policy in particular has often failed to create appropriate incentives for proxy behavior. Four with particular salience for the future are (1) doctrinal assumptions of interest alignment, (2) perceptions of conditionality as self-defeating, (3) perceptions of conditionality as prolonging U.S. commitment, and (4) perceptions of conditionality as destructive to alliance relationships.

Doctrinal Assumptions of Interest Alignment

Conditionality is contrary to the spirit of the doctrine under which most U.S. proxy assistance has been rendered in the last generation. Formal doctrine is essential for success in such projects. Especially for large U.S. engagements such as Iraq or Afghanistan, relations with the proxy are mediated through many thousands of U.S. officials, from the president of the United States and the U.S. ambassador, through the embassy and military staffs in the country, all the way down to the thousands of U.S. soldiers and State Department civilians who interact regularly with allied troops and local officials on the ground. For such sprawling enterprises to be coordinated to a common purpose, common guidelines must be disseminated and followed. Among the most important of these guidelines are the doctrinal manuals and publications produced for this purpose. These, however, have long shared an underlying assumption of interest alignment between the United States and the proxy government. For example, the 2006 edition of *FM 3–24: Counterinsurgency*, perhaps the most celebrated field manual in modern military history, presupposes that both the "host nation" (HN) and the United States seek legitimacy, defined as government in the interest of the governed, and that the U.S. role is chiefly to provide the capacity the host nation lacks for providing the services that underlie such legitimacy.[5] Consistent with this assumption of interest alignment, the manual offers no guidance on creating or using leverage, conditionality, monitoring, or coercive interaction of any kind with the host nation. On the contrary, it counsels U.S. forces to empower and assist the host nation rather than enforce U.S. preferences, overrule allies, or act in their stead if necessary.[6]

Nor is this assumption of interest alignment limited to *FM 3–24*. U.S. military doctrine at all levels has discouraged the use of coercive leverage when interacting with proxies, instead advocating unequivocal rapport building and deference to local preferences. *FM 31–20–3: Foreign Internal Defense Tactics, Techniques, and Procedures for Special Forces,* for example, cautions that advisers should "not use bribery or coercion, since results achieved from these actions are only temporary"; *FM 3–24* itself encourages advisers to be "subtle" and "diplomatic when correcting host-nation forces;" and *FM 3–22: Army Support to Security Cooperation,* which also counsels advisers to be subtle, argues that "foreign units are most receptive to advisor teams that teach unobtrusively."[7]

Of course, leverage should always be used as diplomatically as possible, and few manuals explicitly direct officials to ignore or allow allied misuse of U.S. assistance. But a consistent emphasis on relationship building and the development of rapport, with no explicit discussion of interest divergence or incentive misalignment, encourages officials to see their job as benign, apolitical capacity building. The manuals' consistent, if unstated, assumption of interest alignment offers no concrete guidance for using leverage to change agent behavior even if the reader intuits that this may be needed. When the doctrinal guidance needed to coordinate the actions of thousands of disparate government officials presupposes interest alignment, emphasizes empowering local actors, and presents extensive guidance only for effectively apolitical capacity building, then it should not be surprising that unconditional capacity building plays a large role in U.S. interactions with its proxies.

This, however, suggests an important avenue for improvement: changing published doctrine to reflect a more inherently political, incentive-oriented approach and to provide the guidance needed for large organizations to implement it in the field. In fact, the beginnings of progress on this score are already visible. Recent revisions to the 2006 edition of *FM 3–24* include explicit reference to the problem of misaligned interests; the new edition warns officials to be alert to proxy behavior that reflects the proxy's needs but not those of the United States, and it notes that "behavior modification" may be needed to elicit appropriate action from the proxy.[8] This is a promising start, but more needs to be done. Pertinent doctrine spans a range of manuals aimed at a variety of organizations and levels of command; to bring the entire corpus of official guidance into line with an understanding of proxy interaction as based on incentives will require a consistent, thorough revision of a wide range of official doctrinal material, together with enough practical details on how to go about the necessary "behavior modification" for large organizations to act to this end in a coordinated way.[9]

Perceptions of Conditionality as Self-Defeating

Another barrier to effective conditionality has been the view by many U.S. officials that it would be self-defeating, in that aid withdrawal would undermine the viability of an allied regime. As the special inspector general for Afghan reconstruction recently put it, in Afghanistan, "[imposing] conditions [was] often not credible, as donors were ultimately unwilling to withhold funds that were essential to preventing the collapse of the Afghan government."[10] This is an understandable concern. A major U.S. goal in many such interventions is to defeat insurgencies that threaten proxy governments, and such proxies often have very limited capacity. To threaten deliberate reduction of allied capacity by withholding aid is indeed to risk weakening the very regime one is trying to strengthen.

Yet to fall back on apolitical capacity building in such situations is to court major agency losses and in the process risk a more expensive failure than aid withdrawal would produce. The worst case is not failure—it is *expensive* failure. Apolitical capacity building for an ally whose interests diverge badly from one's own is potentially a recipe for failure despite sometimes massive costs. But the choice need not be framed as simple capacity building versus fatally undermining one's ally. If the United States reconceives its aid in more self-consciously political, incentive-oriented terms, then there are ways to enable a more conditional approach with tolerable risks of proxy collapse. Conditional offers of additional assistance, for example, leave the proxy no worse off if withheld. They give the proxy an incentive to comply with U.S. preferences, but do not compel the United States to reduce a proxy's existing capacity if the proxy resists.

Even unconditional assistance can sometimes change proxy incentives in ways that reduce agency losses without weakening the proxy. As Jacob Shapiro and Oliver Vanden Eynde have shown in the Naxalite insurgency in India, changes in federal tax law and economic regulations in India made mining rights more valuable to local governments, which in turn gave local authorities incentives to extend government control into areas that they had previously been willing to cede to Naxalite rebels. These legal and regulatory changes were not conditional, yet they created incentives for local government proxies to better serve the interests of the federal government principal in its war against the Naxalites.[11] Analogous policies to increase the economic value of mineral resources in Taliban-threatened Northeast Afghanistan or potential petrochemical resources in ISIS-threatened Iraqi Anbar might have similar utility in encouraging better use of U.S. military assistance by reshaping the recipients' incentives.

Conversely, conditional threats of sanction pose lesser threats to regime survival if directed against nonsecurity targets. Proxy elites, for example, often value foreign travel for themselves or their families, foreign education for their children, the status benefits of participation in international political forums, or visits from allied heads of state and other dignitaries. Conditional threats to deny visas, to withhold U.S. support for international conference inclusion, or to cancel official visits can build leverage without risking meaningful reductions in the proxy's ability to resist insurgent attack.

Even threats to withhold security assistance per se can be less self-defeating if metered carefully in discrete, divisible packages. Among the more effective instances of conditionality for leverage in the cases presented here, for example, was in Iraq in 2007, when U.S. general David Petraeus and ambassador Ryan Crocker used the threat to withdraw logistical support from specific Iraqi National Police (INP) brigades to encourage Iraqi prime minister Nouri al-Maliki to replace sectarian brigade commanders (see chapter 9). This threat was credible in part because the sanction was both meaningful and narrow in scope: Petraeus and Crocker were not threatening to leave Iraq altogether, a policy that would risk regime overthrow and undermine the interests it was meant to promote. Instead, an easily revocable threat to immobilize specific brigades could deny al-Maliki a military capability he valued (al-Maliki used the INP to pursue his own Shia political interests) without leaving the Iraqi security forces as a whole unable to defend the country. If al-Maliki refused, pressure could be increased incrementally as needed by sanctioning additional brigades one by one or by extending logistical shutoffs week by week, with limited danger of immediate regime overthrow in the meantime. Of course, any withdrawal of security assistance reduces the proxy's military effectiveness ceteris paribus—but ceteris is rarely paribus here. In exchange for a relatively minor reduction in Iraqi state capacity against insurgent attack, Petraeus and Crocker created incentives for al-Maliki to use his forces in ways that far better suited U.S. needs—as opposed to Shiite partisan political interests.

Effective conditionality, however, will often require deliberate advance planning if it is not to be self-defeating. In fact, it will often require that aid policies be designed for leverage from the outset. It is far harder to create credible conditionality in the middle of a campaign after years of assistance designed instead for apolitical capacity building. Consider military training assistance, for example. In Afghanistan, U.S. assistance to create and field new Afghan National Army (ANA) battalions (or "kandaks") could in principle have offered an important source of leverage for fighting endemic corruption and cronyism. Kandaks are relatively small formations, and these units completed training on a regular basis. The United States could, in theory, have threatened to halt their production as a way to create incentives for reform by halting the force-generation process temporarily if the Afghan government failed to comply, then restarting the process if it cooperated, all with some, but limited and controllable, consequences for Afghan state security. In fact, force-generation processes like this can serve almost as a rheostat, enabling the United States to dial pressure up or down as needed to respond to proxy behavior and maintain continuous incentives. Yet the mechanics of ANA force generation as designed were ill suited to this purpose. Expecting a continuous throughput of new recruits into graduated soldiers, the designers of the system did not build in flexibility to start and stop the process on short notice. A sudden midwar withdrawal of U.S. training or payroll assistance would thus have risked a backlog of recruits entering the service but without the pay, food, uniforms, or housing they had been promised, as troops slightly ahead of them in the pipeline stalled midstream rather than moving through the system into deployment, occupying the resources needed for the incoming recruits. Rather than a continuously manipulable rheostat, the result could easily have been closer to a catastrophic traffic jam without rheostatic flexibility, if a complex system designed for continuous operation was instead turned on and off at short notice. With advance planning, such systems can be engineered for resilience in the face of coercive starts and stops; without it, they can be much less flexible.

Similarly, economic aid programs for large infrastructure projects that have major start-up costs and need sustained multiyear funding streams are ill suited to enable conditionality later. A campaign built around power plant construction and electrical grid development, for example, is hard to start and stop later to maintain incentives—the efficiency loss in a putatively temporary shutdown can threaten the entire project, undermining the credibility of the threat and sacrificing further leverage if the threat is actually carried out. In contrast, similar sums invested in multiple small projects (such as the U.S. Commander's Emergency Response Program, or CERP) may be flimsy tools in a classic economic development program but are better suited to create leverage and manage proxies' incentives—threats to cut off individual projects are more credible, and restoration is a plausible reward for changed behavior.[12]

Intrusive monitoring is another requirement for conditionality that may seem self-defeating but that is actually essential and must be designed into the program early. Conditionality works best when the principal knows whether the agent is actually complying with the principal's demands; however, agents have incentives to conceal shirking, and the circumstances of wartime proxy interaction make concealment easy. Deliberate, intrusive monitoring will usually be necessary to overcome this.[13] Yet monitoring of this kind—like the aid withdrawals it is meant to enable—can easily look like a self-defeating policy. The whole point of proxy reliance is to reduce costs to the principal, after all, and deploying all the personnel needed to oversee a sometimes-sprawling proxy military and its expenditures either increases the U.S. footprint or diverts U.S. soldiers from combat duty, or both.

Effective monitoring often requires intelligence collection on the proxy and its behavior; when the proxy tries to conceal its behavior, monitoring will often require covert collection to overcome proxy concealment. But U.S. soldiers, intelligence analysts, and collection assets are scarce resources normally directed at finding and fighting the enemy. To divert these assets into spying on an ally who is supposed to be fighting a common foe will look to many like a self-imposed reduction in combat power—and a potentially divisive signal of mistrust. Yet without monitoring, incentives must be conditioned on disturbances, which is far less efficient than conditioning on proxy effort, so a large fraction of U.S. assistance may be wasted in agency losses.

In the most successful examples of conditionality in this volume, the U.S. principal did in fact divert important resources to monitoring its ally. In Korea after 1950, U.S. commanders knew which Republic of Korea Army (ROKA) officers needed to be replaced because U.S. advisers were assigned to oversee their units' budgets and report on their advisees' proficiency. For Petraeus and Crocker to know which INP brigade commanders were sectarians in 2007, intelligence information on the INP was needed. In both episodes, a strong case could have been made that scarce intelligence assets were needed to find insurgents rather than monitor allies, or that scarce U.S. soldiers were needed on the front to hold a perilous line.

In the end, the difference between an effective proxy with the right incentives and an ineffective proxy serving other goals will often overwhelm the opportunity costs of intrusive U.S. monitoring. Here, too, however, this is an easier policy to implement if it is designed into the program from the outset. In counterinsurgency campaigns, for example, U.S. doctrine emphasizes persistent population security and discourages the removal of troops whom civilians are relying on to protect them from militants. This reduces flexibility once troops have been committed to population security and makes it harder to adopt a labor-intensive monitoring policy in midcampaign.

In general, aid programs designed from the beginning to provide divisible, reversible, contingent assistance with intrusive monitoring will offer more potential to create leverage for maintaining proxy incentives than will larger programs whose internal efficiency needs are allowed to drive the design in ways that reduce flexibility. Large, apparently efficient, but inflexible or poorly monitored programs for force generation, weapon modernization, logistical support, or economic assistance make sense *if* one assumes perfect interest alignment with the proxy—they provide the greatest raw capacity for the ally at the least cost to the United States. But in the real world of political interest misalignment, where proxies rarely want exactly what the United States wants, nominally efficient but inflexible assistance will often fail to realize its potential, and the approaches with the greatest actual payoff will usually be ones that privilege flexibility and incentive creation over internal efficiency.

Perceptions of Conditionality as Prolonging U.S. Commitment

Another reason why U.S. officials have often been unwilling to use conditionality is that such threats conflict with the U.S. goal of early exit. As one U.S. official in Kabul told me when I proposed that an aid program be made conditional, "What are you talking about? An independent Afghan security force is our ticket home. If we slow them down then we're just stuck here longer." This, too, is an understandable concern. Aside from a soldier's natural desire to go home, domestic political pressures in the United States to avoid unlimited commitments create time pressure to complete the mission on a deadline. Rarely will the U.S. Congress fund perpetual combat operations even if most of the combatants are a proxy's; the campaign in Afghanistan, for example, was fought under a series of calendar deadlines from 2009 through 2017. Conditional assistance, combined with threats to withhold capacity building, creates a deliberate prospect of a longer war even if the sanction does not topple the allied government. This problem can reduce the threat's credibility, since if the proxy knows that the United States is impatient, it may discount threats that flow from conditionality if those threats would prolong the war and delay U.S. departure if implemented.

But just as excessive fear of proxy collapse can merely increase the cost of failure, so an insistence on early exit regardless of proxy behavior can be self-defeating. Conditional threats to withdraw aid—preferably in divisible, revocable packages—can be helpful. But unconditional withdrawal timetables are even worse than unconditional capacity building. As with apolitical capacity building, they give the proxy no incentive to change behavior: Why reform per American preferences when the Americans will leave on a fixed date whether one reforms or not? Unlike apolitical capacity building, however, apolitical withdrawal timetables will leave the proxy materially weaker. This encourages many proxies to worry about regime longevity and to hedge against the risk of regime collapse by maximizing corrupt extraction during the interval before aid withdrawal. This in turn weakens military professionalism and combat motivation, reducing proxy effectiveness against the external threats the United States usually cares most about, even as the proxy builds personal safety nets for individual members of its elite.

Advocates of unconditional-withdrawal timetables sometimes argue that these actually give proxies an incentive to reform: if proxies know they will be on their own soon, they know they must professionalize their military for self-defense lest their regime fall after U.S. withdrawal.[14] But in the divided, weakly institutionalized societies that typically receive such aid, the intra-elite cooperation needed for quick reform on a short deadline is very hard to produce. If the multiple armed power brokers that typically make up the elite in such states all cooperate and reform, then an effective, professionalized security force can be created, often fairly quickly.[15] If any elites defect from this program and default to rent seeking and cronyism, however, then the others can easily be exploited, with potentially lethal consequences. For instance, an Afghan warlord who reforms by demobilizing his militia and relying instead on the state army and police can be arrested and killed if a rival retains his own militia and uses cronies in the state security force to remove a competitor. The result is a dynamic resembling the stag hunt problem in game theory: if all actors cooperate, the result is better for them all, but if any one actor defects, all but that one suffer gravely, and the fear of this unraveling precludes cooperation—unless trust is high across all actors (which it rarely is in divided, weakly institutionalized regimes).[16] In the stag hunt–like environments typical of U.S. proxies, unconditional withdrawal deadlines are much likelier to yield defection in the form of corruption and cronyism rather than cooperation in the form of U.S.-preferred military professionalization and reform. U.S. insistence on early unconditional exit thus creates incentives for the proxy—but the wrong ones.

In fact, some of the most powerful tools for aligning proxies' incentives with ours require the United States to deliberately lengthen, not shorten, its involvement. Consider the example of logistical support. U.S.-provided logistical assistance is a very common form of military aid, and a potentially powerful source of leverage to create incentives for proxy compliance with U.S. interests, as Petraeus and Crocker demonstrated in Iraq in 2007. It is naturally divisible and revocable, and can be provided or withheld in flexible, targetable ways—*if* the proxy is dependent on the United States for its logistics. Yet U.S. security assistance policy normally strives to make the proxy logistically independent as soon as possible, to facilitate U.S. withdrawal. If the proxy becomes logistically independent, then U.S. logistical leverage vanishes. The proxy is then freed to pursue its own objectives, rather than those of the United States, without fear that its sustainment will suffer if it does. An apolitical conception of military aid that seeks only to increase proxy capacity will encourage independence; a more political conception of aid as a tool for establishing incentives for proxies to respect U.S. interests will slow, not hasten, the development of logistical independence, in order to preserve U.S. leverage for reform.

It is thus usually a mistake to prioritize exit over leverage. The result will often be failure following exit, as proxies revert to pursuing their own interests once U.S. assistance is withdrawn. "Offshore" leverage is sometimes possible via sanctions, trade agreements, or arms sales, but many proxies see U.S.-mandated reforms as risking their regime; where this is so, offshore leverage will rarely suffice. If the external threat that the United States cares about continues, then the need for serious leverage will continue, which implies a need for continued onshore engagement to maintain it. Reliance on proxies can reduce U.S. costs, but rarely will it enable a quick departure.

Perceptions of Conditionality as Destructive to Alliance Relationships

A final reason for U.S. reluctance to employ conditionality is the ease with which it can backfire if mishandled, undermining relations with the proxy government. Effective conditionality requires a delicate balance of threats and promises, which can easily be misinterpreted across the cultural divides that often characterize proxy relationships, with results that can weaken diplomats' ability to interact with the proxy effectively in the future. In addition, effective monitoring will often require intrusive intelligence collection on allies in ways that can signal mistrust and encourage wariness.

These problems are exacerbated by the dual moral hazard characteristic of many proxy relationships. The more forcefully the United States threatens an ally with aid withdrawal in the event of shirking, the more a rational ally will doubt the U.S. promise to follow through with its commitment if the ally performs. Threatening an ally with aid withdrawal often undermines U.S. domestic support for the ally (as has been the case with Pakistan, for example). From the ally's perspective, why risk domestic instability by forcing reform on an unwilling military for the sake of a patron whose commitment to your survival is so contingent and domestically controversial?

Conversely, the more the U.S. principal seeks to reassure the agent that U.S. promises are good and that aid will be forthcoming if only the agent accepts the internal risks of professionalizing its military, the greater the risk of moral hazard in the other direction. To build U.S. domestic support for aid, administrations often frame the ally as vital to U.S. national security; a credible promise of aid is normally built on a foundation of American assurance, both to the ally and to the U.S. public and Congress, that the ally's survival is essential to American self-interest. The more forceful these assurances, the more a rational ally will doubt the accompanying U.S. threat to halt aid if the ally shirks. And because conditionality requires both a credible threat and a credible promise, it is very hard in practice to overcome both problems of moral hazard at once. Success with one tends to undermine success with the other, and efforts to balance the two run the risk that neither the threat nor the promise is fully credible.[17] Conditionality thus poses a dual commitment problem: it is difficult for the agent to credibly commit itself to work and not shirk if the principal "pays" the agent, but it is also difficult for the principal to credibly commit itself to pay the agent if the agent works rather than shirks.

The problems of message balancing and dual moral hazard inherent in proxy reliance make conditionality a difficult policy to execute effectively. But doing so is not impossible, and the complexities can be mitigated, at least, with deft diplomacy, careful domestic politics, and sufficient material resources.

In the Korean and Salvadoran cases presented in this volume, the United States issued both threats and promises that the proxy appears to have found credible. In the Korean case in particular (chapter 1), this was facilitated by a policy of combining public support with private threats, where the credibility of the latter was enhanced by discrete, targeted, privately communicated sanctions against particular ROK units found to be lagging in professionalization. In the Salvadoran case (chapter 5), the Bush administration was able to use congressional outrage over Salvadoran rights abuses in a kind of good-cop, bad-cop synthesis: congressional pressure made threats of aid withdrawal more credible without administration officials having to personally position themselves in opposition to their Salvadoran ally.

The Korean and Salvadoran cases also suggest the utility of sweet carrots and big sticks for managing the delicate diplomatic balance of conditionality. In both cases, the scale of aid on offer was unusually large, which gave U.S. diplomats more to work with and helped make the downsides of a more transactional relationship more tolerable to the ally. In Korea, U.S. aid provided the equivalent of almost $1 billion a year in 2016 dollars, hardware sufficient to equip an army of more than fifty thousand troops, and a large U.S. conventional ground force to backstop all that assistance and provide security as the ROKA professionalized. In El Salvador, the United States provided more than $5 billion in assistance to the Salvadoran government between 1979 and 1991, of which more than $1 billion comprised military training and equipment, making El Salvador the eighth-largest recipient of U.S. military aid worldwide at the time.[18] Assistance of this magnitude empowered U.S. diplomats with resources sufficient to provide credible protection to cooperative proxies but to impose real sanctions against others, and made U.S. aid valuable enough to the recipient to make it worth listening carefully to U.S. diplomatic signals. A large U.S. troop presence can also create a safety net to make professionalization less risky to proxy leadership: with more than two hundred thousand U.S. ground troops in South Korea, a ROKA of disinterested technocrats was unlikely to mount a coup d'état against President Syngman Rhee.[19] Leaders such as Rhee may resent the transactional quality of conditionality in U.S. aid, but when the offers are large, the indignity at least comes with substantial compensation. Smaller aid budgets, in contrast, combine the transactional quality of conditionality with smaller consequences for the ally, encouraging would-be partners to look elsewhere for assistance. Of course, large efforts on this scale conflict with the goal of cost saving inherent in proxy reliance. But the less the United States spends, the less wherewithal U.S. diplomats will have at their disposal to maintain partnerships in the face of the transactional quality that conditionality can bring to a relationship. The purpose of proxy reliance is to reduce cost, but an overzealous pursuit of savings can reduce effectiveness even more than it reduces cost.

This is not to suggest that effective conditionality is easy to implement, or that allies cannot be alienated by a relationship that seems to become coldly transactional after an earlier era of apparent unconditional friendship. Maladroit application of conditionality can indeed lead to a downward spiral in relations. But to say it is delicate is not to say it is impossible—and without it, real interest misalignment will often undermine proxy effectiveness.

When and Where to Rely on Proxies: Seek Interest Alignment

Principal-agent theory also has implications for selecting proxies. In particular, it suggests seeking out those whose interests are relatively better aligned with those of the United States.

The utility of interest alignment can be seen most clearly in the Korean War. Of the cases considered in this volume, South Korea presents the most successful experience. By 1952, less than two years after the ROKA's collapse in the North Korean invasion, U.S. assistance had already improved its proxy's military proficiency substantially. By 1954 the ROKA had become a professionalized force capable of holding its own against Chinese regulars in intense combat. In no other case examined here did an assistance mission yield comparable improvement in proxy performance.

Much of this transformation can be attributed to the unusual shift to interest alignment between the U.S. principal and the ROK agent following the invasion of 1950. Prior to the invasion, Rhee was pursuing intraregime internal balancing and vague expansionist ambitions in the North, while the United States sought to counter a growing Communist insurgency in the South. But the existential peril of the invasion brought these interests into alignment in a shared fear of annihilation. This, in turn, enabled a far more efficient use of U.S. aid than in any other case considered here: Rhee accepted U.S. monitoring and removal of crony officers, U.S. control of ROKA budgeting, and even U.S. command of ROKA forces in the field, as the price of survival in a setting where the invaders posed a more immediate threat than coup d'état. With a powerful incentive to improve its military proficiency, and without the kinds of barriers to skill enhancement so often seen in proxies focused on internal balancing, the ROKA could use U.S. training, equipment, and advice to achieve something closer to its full military potential.

Modern warfare is complex and challenging to master, but not impossible. With proper incentives, demanding modern military technique can be learned by mass militaries in a couple of years of intense training and experience. The German Army, for example, was completely retrained in new methods over less than a year in 1917–18; U.S. Army tactical proficiency improved dramatically in the seventeen months between Kasserine Pass and Operation Cobra in 1943–44; and the Soviet Red Army transformed itself into a tactical and operational peer of the German Wehrmacht over the two years leading up to Operation Bagration in 1944.[20] Even Saddam Hussein's Iraqi Army showed itself able to improve dramatically between 1986 and 1988 when the growing threat of Iranian victory gave Saddam an incentive to relax prior coup proofing and pursue military proficiency with real urgency.[21] It does not take twenty years to produce a capable military when its owners are suitably motivated. In most of the cases considered here, they were not. In the Korean case after 1950, Syngman Rhee was.

Of course, there are ways in which principals can seek to mitigate the problems created by interest misalignment, as noted earlier, and such measures can certainly help. But when underlying interests are misaligned, it is difficult for even best-practice policies of monitoring and conditionality to compensate fully. In the Salvadoran case, for example, the United States cut aid repeatedly in an effort to reduce Salvadoran human rights abuses. In 1980, 1983, and 1990, the United States either suspended or reduced aid after the Salvadoran proxy failed to implement U.S.-sought reforms. This combination of aid and conditionality did help—it eventually produced a stronger El Salvador Armed Forces (ESAF) whose human rights abuses became less frequent. But it never produced straightforward Salvadoran cooperation, and there were important limits to its effectiveness. It never created a military strong enough to defeat the Farabundo Martí National Liberation Front (FMLN), and ESAF death squad involvement never went away.

The problem lay in the scale of interest misalignment between the United States and its ally. Salvadoran resistance to reform was rooted in strong requirements for internal power balancing and elite privilege, which U.S. leverage paled in comparison to. Americans could equip ESAF soldiers and train its officers—by 1984, more than half of the entire ESAF officer corps had attended military schools in the United States—and this could improve military performance to a degree.[22] Both sides shared an interest in preventing an FMLN takeover, and the regime was happy to accept proffered firepower to prevent a conventional conquest of San Salvador. But to defeat the FMLN and end the war required reforms that could destabilize the internal balance underlying the agrarian elites' rule; they preferred an indefinite stalemate. Nor could Washington credibly threaten anything worse for them than the destabilization that compliance with U.S. reform demands would risk. Once the ESAF had the firepower to prevent outright collapse, even a total U.S. aid withdrawal would probably have been tolerable. And a total aid cutoff could easily be averted via Salvadoran satisficing and partial compliance—with imperfect U.S. monitoring and the information asymmetries of any principal-agent relationship, Salvadorans could do just enough to restore the aid without fully complying with U.S. demands. In the end, even an unusually aggressive program of monitoring and conditionality failed to fully realize U.S. goals in the presence of significant interest misalignment: U.S. aid produced an ESAF that could avert defeat and impose a brutal stalemate at heavy cost to both sides, but it could not end the war, which continued until outside events enabled a compromise settlement. In general, the cases considered here suggest that it is difficult to fully compensate for misaligned underlying interests—hence an important criterion for effective proxy reliance is to seek proxies whose political interests are aligned with the principal's as closely as possible.

How Much Can One Expect from Proxy Reliance? Real but Limited Results

The importance of interest alignment has other implications as well. It means, especially, that while proxy reliance can be a valuable tool, there are limits to what it can achieve in most cases. In particular, it will more often yield stalemate than victory: it can be a powerful tool for preventing proxies' overthrow, but will rarely suffice to defeat enemies outright.

This is a consequence of adverse selection. U.S.-proxy interest alignment will vary in degree from case to case, and the United States should seek proxies with better-aligned interests wherever possible. This will often not be possible, however. Because the conditions that promote proxy reliance also promote interest misalignment, interest divergence will be the norm, not the exception, in U.S.-proxy relationships. In fact, this has long been the case. If we use UN voting patterns as an indicator of interest congruence, then there is a longstanding, statistically significant negative correlation between U.S.-partner interest alignment and proxy status, operationalized as U.S. security assistance provision: the closer the interest alignment, the less likely the United States is to provide military aid.[23] We see a similar relationship if we consider corruption: a state's rank on the Transparency International list of most-corrupt states correlates directly with its rank on the list of U.S. military aid recipients, with an ability to reject the null hypothesis of no relationship at the 0.1 level.[24]

This does not make interest alignment impossible. As the Korea case shows, proxies sometimes do want what the United States wants, and this can greatly reduce agency losses. But as the Korea case also shows, the stimulus for close interest alignment will often be an acute threat of regime overthrow. On this point, the United States and its proxies are likely to agree: neither side wants the proxy defeated outright, and an acute threat of conquest is among the few perils that will trump coup d'état as an immediate concern for local elites. A credible threat of conquest by actors outside the regime itself will typically align a proxy regime's interests with those of the United States and create the incentives needed for proxies to meet a truly common threat.

In most cases, however, such acute threats are temporary. Either U.S. aid enables the regime to survive and the crisis passes, or the regime falls and the proxy relationship ends altogether. If the regime survives, interest misalignment often reemerges as soon as the immediate crisis is resolved—but long before the war actually ends. In El Salvador, for example, the FMLN posed a credible threat of regime overthrow in the initial phase of the war, which encouraged real ESAF reform to enable it to stabilize the front and protect the capital. Once the ESAF had improved just enough to keep the regime in power, further improvement looked a lot less attractive, as real professionalization would threaten regime privilege and might even risk coup if the U.S.-trained technocrats who would replace incumbent cronies decided to clean house in San Salvador. The regime welcomed enough U.S. arms and training to protect the capital, but then dug in its heels and resisted further change. The result was a long, grinding stalemate, as a partially improved ESAF prevented an FMLN takeover but proved insufficient to defeat the FMLN or to end the war. For the United States, this represented a major disappointment, since an ongoing FMLN insurgency created a persistent threat of Communist insurgency spreading elsewhere in Latin America, a continuing need for U.S. expenditures of aid and deployments of advisers, and ongoing divisiveness in the United States over its participation in an ugly, deadlocked war. Americans wanted victory and an end to the conflict, and were more than willing to risk regime privilege to get this. For the Salvadoran regime, on the other hand, stalemate was not ideal, but it was preferable to the loss of privilege and potential coup at the hands of unreliable military technocrats more beholden to the United States than to the traditional elite. The proxy was willing to tolerate stalemate, and clearly preferred it to the thoroughgoing reforms needed to defeat the FMLN outright and end the war. This postcrisis interest misalignment created persistent agency loss in the form of an ongoing stalemate that ended only when exogenous events left neither the regime nor the FMLN able to continue the war.

In fact, the Salvadoran stalemate dynamic is quite common. Most regimes will accept enough U.S. weapons and training to forestall overthrow at the hands of enemies external to the elite, but few are willing to continue politically destabilizing reforms beyond that point. And because stalemate is far easier to achieve than outright victory in counterinsurgency or counterterrorism, the result will often be long, deadlocked wars in which partially improved U.S. proxies hold the capital and other major urban areas but cannot snuff out persistent guerrilla or terrorist threats in peripheral areas.[25] This does not, however, mean that stalemate is guaranteed. Deeply flawed proxies facing stag hunt incentives may fail to do enough for their own survival (as may yet obtain in Afghanistan), and deeply flawed insurgents may be unable to hold out against even deeply flawed regimes (as has happened to ISIS in its defense of contiguous territory against U.S. proxies in Iraq and Syria). But for many insurgents, terrorist groups, and proxy regimes, adverse selection yields interest misalignment that makes it systematically difficult to get beyond the maintenance of stalemate to full realization of U.S. aims.[26]

Of course, it is important to prevent U.S. proxies from being overthrown and replaced by actors far less aligned with U.S. interests than the incumbent regime. Assistance can often achieve this goal at costs far lower than the unilateral deployment of large numbers of U.S. ground forces. Assisting proxies can thus have real benefits for the United States even without perfect interest alignment. And the greater the interest alignment, the more that can be accomplished. Under typical conditions, however, there will be important limits to the scope of U.S. aims beyond just regime preservation that can be achieved through reliance on proxies.[27] This is a tool that will often be better suited to preserving stalemates than to achieving victories.

Can Proxy Reliance Reshape U.S. Military Posture? Not without Risk

Reliance on proxies can thus be a helpful and important, but limited, tool. To what extent can this tool enable the United States to reduce the ground forces needed for stabilization missions, to shift resources from conventional forces to the special operations forces often considered best suited to work with proxies, or to shift resources from the army and marines to the air forces that Americans often use to support local proxies' infantries?

Any of these changes might—or might not—be advisable, depending on how the United States answers larger grand-strategic and budgetary questions far beyond our scope here. In a time of increasing budgetary austerity for the

U.S. Department of Defense, some real capability may well have to be sacrificed. Perhaps the ability to wage large U.S. ground campaigns to counter insurgencies, deny havens to terrorists, or protect humanitarian aid programs may be the "least bad" choice for capabilities to cut. Or perhaps not: my analysis offers little guidance on how to cast trade-offs across missions for the U.S. military and its associated forces.

One point that can be made on the basis of the analysis in this chapter is that the virtues of small-footprint proxy reliance will not make such cutbacks or resource shifts free of cost or risk. To the extent that the United States is willing to accept stalemates in places such as Syria, Afghanistan, Iraq, or many other parts of the world, increased reliance on local proxies can reduce the risk that accompanies downsizing the U.S. forces needed to address real but limited regional challenges unilaterally. That risk reduction is not unlimited, however, and the ambitions of the policies to which such tools are applied should be kept carefully restrained to avoid promising more than the tools can usually deliver. This restraint will often prove harder in practice than it may seem in principle. The Obama administration's gradual escalation of its troop presence in Iraq and Syria after 2014, for instance, is a cautionary tale about the kind of mission-creep pressures that stalemated proxy wars can create. Whether the result is worth the price is a question beyond our scope. But what the analysis in this chapter can show is that proxy reliance is potentially helpful when implemented correctly and at the right times and places, but that it is neither a panacea for U.S. foreign policy nor a safe means for transforming the U.S. military.

Local proxies are playing an increasingly salient role in U.S. defense policy. After more than a decade of massive U.S. ground force deployments in Iraq and Afghanistan, there is now a powerful demand for less costly ways to address threats to real but limited U.S. interests in places such as Syria, Ukraine, Yemen, Somalia, Libya, Niger, Mali, Nigeria, Pakistan, Colombia, Mauritania, and many other ongoing and prospective conflicts around the world. For many, the solution to that demand is to rely on local proxies to lighten the burden on U.S. forces.

This idea's popularity is not limited to the United States. Many great and regional powers use proxies to pursue real but limited interests abroad. This volume includes examples from Germany and Israel, among the many countries that have used this tool. Reliance on proxies has been extremely common worldwide for at least the last half century. Patrick Regan has documented more than nine hundred individual acts of proxy use globally from 1945 to 1999.[28]

The global ubiquity and increasing salience of reliance on proxies for U.S. national security per se makes it especially important to understand when, where, and how this tool should be best used to advance national interests. In this chapter, I have distilled from the theory and case analyses a series of policy implications to inform the public debate and assist public officials in making the best possible use of this tool for U.S. national security. Among the most important of these are the following:

- Use aid to create incentives, especially via conditionality. Avoid apolitical, unconditional capacity building in all cases except those where an ally's interests align very closely with those of the United States.
- Revise formal doctrine to reflect both the importance of political interest alignment and the ubiquity of misalignment. Provide explicit doctrinal guidance on coercive bargaining with proxies where interests are misaligned, as they usually will be.
- Structure civilian aid with options for increases if proxies comply with U.S. preferences, and decreases if they do not.
- Seek opportunities to increase the economic value to the proxy of controlling territory the United States wants controlled (per the Naxalite example noted earlier).
- Design military assistance programs to be divisible, reversible, and contingent—and do so from the beginning. Avoid large, inflexible, unitary programs, and where necessary accept some inefficiency as the price of the flexibility needed for credible conditionality.
- Monitor intrusively and accept the increased footprint this requires, together with the opportunity cost inherent in using U.S. intelligence resources to monitor proxy compliance with U.S. preferences and proxies' use of U.S. assistance.
- Avoid unconditional deadlines for withdrawal of assistance. Prioritize leverage over exit, and accept longer commitments when necessary to this end.
- Support publicly, threaten privately, and combine threats with promises of aid sufficient to make compliance with U.S. preferences worthwhile to the proxy.
- Seek proxies whose interests align as closely as possible with those of the United States.
- Expect incomplete results. Proxy reliance is potentially much cheaper than large U.S. troop deployments and can be effective in preserving allied governments from overthrow, but it will often be more conducive to a stalemate than to outright victory.
- Do not expect proxy reliance to enable cost- or risk-free reductions in conventional U.S. ground forces, or redesign of U.S. force structure or military posture. Such measures may or may not be needed, but increased reliance on proxies has limited potential to reduce the associated costs and risks.

On balance, proxy reliance is a tool with real—but not unlimited—utility. Its growing popularity puts a premium on carefully observing best practices when using it. In particular, it must be understood as an intrinsically and deeply political process wherein recipients' incentives are critical to the result, and where unconditional, apolitical capacity building usually fails.

Even where used to its maximum potential and when following the best available guidelines for implementation, proxy reliance is still subject to substantial agency losses inherent in the interest misalignments that typically obtain in the places where proxies are actually needed. This creates a serious risk of overuse if policymakers fail to appreciate the limits, as well as the potential, of this tool. Proxies can certainly reduce the footprint of U.S. commitments abroad, and proxy warfare will sometimes be the least-bad option for the United States. But it is not a panacea: even if executed as well as can reasonably be expected, it will rarely yield sweeping policy successes from small U.S. investments.

NOTES

1. Strongly institutionalized, developed industrial democracies with close ties to the United States are typically able to maintain internal order by themselves. Those actors may be threatened by hostile great powers, but those cases are usually seen as direct threats to vital U.S. national security interests warranting direct action (as the United States did on behalf of NATO and Japan during the Cold War). Such cases are closer to external balancing via alliance than to proxy wars, which are much more likely associated with weak states and clientelist regimes.

2. North, Wallis, and Weingast 2009, 20. For a similar analysis, see David 1991.

3. On coup proofing and its military consequences, see Biddle and Zirkle 1996; Brooks 1998; Quinlivan 1999; Talmadge 2015, 15–18; Cohen 1986.

4. Cf. Boutton 2014, which argues that U.S. aid recipients prefer to arm against external rivals, whereas the United States prefers the opposite. Often, however, the recipients' nominal interest in arming against foreign rivals actually serves the internal interest of placating a domestic military that benefits, as in Pakistan; see, for example, Ibrahim 2009 and Siddiqa 2007. Our usage of "internal" and "external" is relative to the government itself: internal threats are those posed to government actors by other factions within the government (such as the military or other rival elites), while external threats are those outside it (such as insurgents or neighboring states).

5. For example, paragraph 5-7 of the field manual (Department of the Army 2006) states that plans must unify "the efforts of joint, interagency, multinational, and HN forces toward a common purpose . . . to establish HN government legitimacy." See also paragraphs 4-1, 5-1, 5-2, 5-5, 5-6, and 5-7. In fact, host nation "legitimacy" is one of the most salient themes in the manual: "legitimate" or "legitimacy" appear no fewer than 121 times in the text, normally in the context of instructions for helping the host nation achieve the shared goal of "legitimate" rule. For a more extensive discussion, see Biddle 2008 and Ladwig 2016, 101–4. For the views of the manual's lead author, see Crane 2016, 114, 122.

6. Note *FM 3–24*'s use of T. E. Lawrence's famous dictum, "Do not try to do too much with your own hands. Better the Arabs do it tolerably than that you do it perfectly. It is their war, and you are to help them, not to win it for them" (Department of the Army 2006, para. 1-154).

7. Department of the Army 1994, I-3; Department of the Army 2006, table 6-5; Department of the Army 2013, 6-6. See also Joint Center for International Security Force Assistance 2008, 6, 40.

8. For example, see Joint Chiefs of Staff 2013, III-6: "In almost all cases, regaining that legitimacy will require a degree of political behavior modification (substantive political reform, anticorruption and governance improvement) to successfully address the root causes that gave rise to insurgency in the first place. Supporting nations may be able to assist the HN in these reforms." See also III-8: "While improving the capacity of the HN government to control its territory and population is key, addressing the core grievances is also necessary to end the insurgency. External counterinsurgents will often have to cajole or coerce HN governments and entrenched elites to recognize the legitimacy of those grievances and address them. Reforms that threaten the political and financial interests of those elites are most likely to generate resistance. Therefore, external counterinsurgents have to put as much effort into understanding and shaping the behavior of their HN partners as they do into countering the insurgents. This typically requires a critical assessment of the motivations and interests of factions and individuals within the HN government."

9. For more detailed suggestions on practical implementation, see the conclusion to this chapter.

10. Quoted in Sopko and Wilder 2016, 12.

11. Shapiro and Vanden Eynde 2014.

12. A separate argument for small, conditional aid programs like CERP is that they incentivize civilians to share information with government forces, as opposed to incentivizing that proxy government to suppress disturbances—perhaps through inclusive, service-providing governance (Berman, Shapiro, and Felter 2011; Berman, Felter, and Shapiro 2018).

13. In many principal-agent relationships, principals combat information asymmetries by sanctioning or rewarding agents based on outcomes rather than by monitoring behavior directly: if the agent delivers a satisfactory product, the principal pays (and vice versa), whether the principal can observe the agent's level of effort or not. In proxy warfare, however, outcome-based monitoring faces major causal attribution challenges: If the agent fails in combat, is this because the agent is shirking or because war is uncertain and outcomes are influenced by a host of exogenous variables beyond the agent's control? (See Feaver 2003, chap. 3.) We thus assume that to overcome information asymmetries in proxy warfare requires direct monitoring of the agent's behavior.

14. Katulis and Korb 2010; Katulis, Lynch, and Juul 2008, 8, 24; Shapiro and Sokolsky 2016.

15. Talmadge 2015, chaps. 4–5.

16. On the stag hunt problem, see Oye 1986.

17. Note that the theoretical model laid out in the introduction makes a simplifying assumption that all contracts presented to the agent are credible. In actual practice, all offers and threats are promises of future action subject to inherent questions of credibility, and these credibility problems can be severe at times. The U.S. withdrawal from Iraq in 2011, for example, was viewed by many Iraqi Sunnis as an abandonment of U.S. promises in 2007–8 to protect them from a hostile Shiite government, and this created serious credibility problems when the United States then tried to recruit Sunni proxies to take action against ISIS in 2014.

18. U.S. GAO 1991b, 9; DeRouen and Heo 2007, 344.

19. A large U.S. presence can also facilitate proxy removal in the event that the proxy falls short, as Ngo Dihn Diem's removal and assassination in Vietnam suggests (see Lewy 1978, 27–28). This, too, can make proxies more attentive to U.S. signaling—but it also makes rational proxies even more wary of limited U.S. assistance that threatens the regime (by

destabilizing internal power balances within the elite, or by facilitating a coup d'état by U.S. allies among officers) but is too small to build a safety net for regime leaders who do cooperate with the United States.

20. On the German Army's retraining program in 1918, see Gudmundsson 1989; Lupfer 1981. On improved proficiency in the U.S. Army from 1943 to 1944, see Mansoor 1999; Doubler 1999; Atkinson 2007, 2014. On improved proficiency in the Soviet Army before Operation Bagration, see especially Glantz and House 1995; also Overy 1998.

21. Talmadge 2015, 207–22.

22. Haggerty 1990, 224.

23. Sullivan, Tessman, and Li 2011.

24. The Spearman's rho is −0.14 with a p-value of 0.09. This calculation assumes that the fifteen countries in NATO at the end of the Cold War received essentially no military proxy assistance from the United States from 2000 to 2010. Data are derived from McNerney et al. 2014; corruption was measured using the Transparency International Corruption Perceptions Index, available at http://www.transparency.org/research/cpi/. The Stata code used is available from the authors upon request.

25. On the prevalence of such long-term stalemates in civil conflict, see Staniland 2012.

26. An interesting feature of the Korea case in this respect is that it displayed an unusual *series* of acute crises that kept U.S. and ROK interests aligned even beyond the war's initial phase. In particular, the Chinese counterinvasion of October 1950 threw the United Nations offensive into disarray and, for Rhee, re-created the early-war danger of overthrow at foreign hands. The continuing Chinese great-power threat after that meant that a credible U.S. threat of withdrawal could create a powerful incentive for Rhee to accept U.S. preferences on issues such as the armistice terms, as even a reformed ROKA would have had a hard time holding the line against a joint Chinese–North Korean foe without U.S. forces. Whereas the Salvadoran armed forces could probably have maintained a stalemate against the nonstate FMLN after 1985 even if the United States had pulled out, leaving the Salvadoran elite unwilling to acquiesce fully to U.S. reform demands, Rhee had no such luxury against the Chinese state military. Such a chronic continuation of acute overthrow risk is unlikely to obtain in most cases.

27. For a related argument on the need to understand the limits, as well as the utility, of proxy reliance for U.S. national security, see Ross 2016.

28. Regan 2002, counting observations where the variable "military" was coded as 1, 2, 3, 4, or 5.

CONCLUSION

Eli Berman and David A. Lake

How can one state, a principal, motivate a second, a proxy, to pursue policies that the former prefers? More specifically, when can the United States compel the leaders of other states to fight insurgents, terrorists, and drug lords within their territories more effectively or, at least, on terms and in ways desired by Washington? Such indirect foreign policies are ubiquitous in international relations, though they are seldom recognized as such. Scholars and policy-makers alike still tend to think of the United States or other great powers acting directly on some problem or "solving" some challenge. Yet across a remarkable range of issues—including transnational violence, our focus in this volume—achieving many policy goals requires working through some foreign proxy, often a national leader. Norms of sovereignty and noninter-vention make direct action more costly, although not unimaginable. How-ever, for many threats and foreign policy goals, ranging from climate change to transnational terrorism, human rights, and gender equality, the United States and others will likely be limited to indirect control. In this concluding chapter, we summarize what we can learn about indirect control from the theory and cases presented, and then discuss what we have learned about the analytical narrative method. The policy implications of our findings for U.S. policy are examined in chapter 10 by Stephen Biddle. Having shown that indirect control can work under specific circumstances when appropriately applied, we close with a brief discussion of how the strategy should be used and toward what ends.

288

Does Indirect Control Work?

The problem in any strategy of indirect control is that foreign proxies rarely if ever have interests identical to those of the principal, even if the United States likes to think of itself as acting in the general welfare according to universally held values of democracy, freedom, and human rights. Local agents often face domestic political challenges quite different from those of the principal. The local leader must be attentive to his own political survival in the face of electoral opponents or extremists willing to use violence to overthrow the regime. In some cases, the leader may even be dependent on political support from the very groups challenging the principal, whether they be drug lords in Colombia or Shia militants in Iraq. Acting against those directing violence against a principal—the disturbance, as we have called these challenges—may threaten the political positions and perhaps even the lives of proxies.

Even when the principal and proxy share common goals, they often prefer to adopt very different strategies for achieving those ends. The United States, for instance, has a template for states plagued by internal violent actors: promote democracy through early and competitive elections; reduce corruption; and train, support, and professionalize the military. These steps are understood to be constructive in building strong states and societies, ones willing and able to support leaders who can suppress violent groups within their countries. At the same time, these very reforms often threaten local leaders as they contemplate their own political futures. This divergence in interests between principal and proxy differs from case to case, but always generates a tension. Israel and the Palestinian Authority may share an interest in security, but they differ on sovereignty, for example. The United States and President Syngman Rhee faced a common enemy but differed dramatically in the importance they attached to the South Korean leader's remaining in political office. This tension creates the "agency problem" at the core of this volume.

Across the range of cases examined here, we find that principals succeed by using rewards and punishments on proxies, calibrated to the latter's domestic political context. Since the principal cannot know exactly what the agent is doing, and because agents always have incentives to misrepresent their actions, rewards and punishments must be used and made contingent on observed disturbances.[1] Reduction in disturbances should be rewarded, while increases in their frequency or severity should be punished. The size of the rewards and punishments, in turn, must reflect the agent's costs of effort in suppressing the disturbance, most often its domestic political costs of complying with the principal's demands. The larger the costs of proxy effort, the more intense these incentives must be. Across all of our cases, summarized in table C.1, indirect control successfully induces

TABLE C.1 Summary of cases and findings

PRINCIPAL-AGENT (PERIOD)	DISTURBANCE	PRIMARY CHANGE OVER TIME	CONCLUSION (ANOMALOUS BEHAVIOR IN ITALICS)
United States–South Korean president (1950–53)	Insurgency/ invasion	Costs of proxy effort decline, then increase (H_6, H_7)	Along with conditionality of aid, expanded capacity building leads to high effort by ROK forces; as interests diverge later in the war, United States uses higher-powered incentives
Germany–Denmark (1940–45)	Insurgents	Costs of proxy effort increase (H_6, H_1)	When costs of effort are relatively low, threat of replacement or direct control sufficient to induce high effort; as costs increase, lack of effort eventually leads Germany to assume direct control
United States–Colombian president (1990–2010)	Drug production and trade	Costs of proxy effort vary across presidents (H_6, H_{12})	When interests are aligned, United States uses rewards conditional on disturbance, and capacity building, producing higher effort
Israel–South Lebanese Army (SLA)/Hamas (1975–2000/2007–14)	Terrorism	Cost of disturbance to principal increases (H_{11})	With SLA, Israel employs conditional rewards and capacity building that produces high effort; ineffective agent abandoned; with Hamas, Israel employs large conditional punishments, producing some effort
United States–El Salvador junta/president (1979–92)	Insurgency	Costs of proxy effort increase (H_6, H_7); cost of disturbance decreases	Low initial cost of effort leads to capacity building and a smaller disturbance; U.S.-backed political reforms eventually threaten regime (increased cost of effort), producing stalemate; end of Cold War reduces threat of disturbance, and renewed threats of punishment eventually lead to political settlement
United States–Pakistani president/military (2001–11)	Terrorism	Costs of proxy effort increase (H_1, H_6)	Few punishments employed due to high punishment cost for principal; as domestic support erodes due to U.S. role in country and costs of effort increase, United States moves to limited direct action; *punishments limited due to ability of Pakistan to retaliate by blocking supply routes into Afghanistan*
Israel–Palestinian Authority (1993–2017)	Terrorism	Costs of proxy effort vary (H_2, H_6)	When interests are relatively aligned after Oslo, Israel focuses on capacity building and rewards that induce effort; when disturbances rise, Israel uses direct control and direct action; *domestic constraints prevent Israel from offering high rewards for continuing effort (sovereignty)*
United States–Yemeni president (2001–11)	Terrorism	Cost of disturbance decreases; costs of proxy effort increase (H_2, H_6)	Initially high effort by agent and shift of U.S. resources to Iraq reduce rewards, leading to lower effort and domestic unrest; increasing cost of effort moves United States to limited direct control; *reduction in rewards violates implicit contract*
United States–Iraqi prime minister (2003–11)	Terrorism/ insurgency	Cost of disturbance increases (H_3)	United States reasserts direct control in Sunni and mixed areas, and imposes weak punishments; *given magnitude of disturbances and apparent lack of effort, underutilizes punishments*

the agent to suppress disturbances when incentives are applied appropriately. Although responsiveness differs according to their costs of effort, in no case are agents impervious to the carrots and sticks used by their respective principals.

Our findings hold at two levels. First, comparing across our nine cases, the greater the divergence in interests between the principal and the proxy, the greater the rewards and incentives must be to induce effective action by the proxy. This finding is somewhat qualified by the lack of a common metric to determine the cost of the disturbance to the principal and the benefit of rewards or cost of punishments to the proxy. This qualification is especially true for the proxy's cost of effort, which is unobserved by the principal and imperfectly observed by us as scholars, even in retrospect. Nonetheless, across our cases and especially in the more disciplined comparison of Israel and two different proxies, the South Lebanese Army and Hamas (chapter 4), the greater the divergence in interests or the greater the costs of effort, the larger incentives must be to induce appropriate action by the agent.

Second, within cases, changes in the disturbance and especially in the agent's costs of effort lead principals to respond by changing the implicit contract of rewards and punishments in the anticipated direction, and that leads proxies to respond by adjusting suppressive effort. Within each case, using t_1 as the best control for that same country at t_2, plausibly exogenous changes in the costs of disturbances or the proxy's costs of effort lead principals and agents to respond in ways predicted by the theory. Even in the most extreme case of Iraq, where the United States otherwise eschewed the use of contingent rewards and punishments, when casualties in Iraq grew too large, the Bush administration eventually responded as predicted with direct action—the surge—and began to punish the prime minister, Nouri al-Maliki, causing him to comply (temporarily at least) with U.S. wishes (chapter 9). Both across-case and within-case comparisons offer strong support for several of the theoretical predictions listed in table 0.1 of the introduction. Proxies cheat unless incentivized, and principals often (but not always) design and adjust incentive contracts accordingly.

Critical to the theory and cases is the cost of effort to the agent, which we interpret as being centrally determined by differences in the policy interests of the principal and those of the proxy. The policy interests of the agent, in turn, are determined largely by domestic political conditions, including the distance between the policies desired by the principal and those preferred by the leader's own supporters, illustrated well by the case of Denmark (chapter 2), and the leader's own political strategy for survival, which varied, for instance, across presidents in the case of Colombia (chapter 3).

Our nonrandom case selection limits generalizations from this study (see below), yet across our cases the principal and agent often agree on basic goals, especially the need for political stability and the survival of the agent, but often disagree about how to achieve those goals. The United States, in particular, has sought to bolster the state—and even its proxy leader—against external or internal threats in South Korea, El Salvador, Yemen, and Iraq, but has insisted that the proxy pursue domestic political reforms that it claims will mitigate the threat but that, from the proxy's point of view, will put his political survival at risk. For example, as seen in chapter 1, South Korean president Syngman Rhee sought to "coup proof" his military, while the United States demanded that he instead professionalize it; the principal prioritized the external threat over the internal one, whereas the agent worried about both. Similarly, in Iraq, Prime Minister al-Maliki sought to build a Shia-based coalition, while the United States demanded a broader government including Sunnis and Kurds, revealing a difference in state-building objectives between principal and agent. The U.S. preference was for an inclusive democracy, while al-Maliki's path to success was best achieved, in his view, by pursuing the very different objective of a Shia-dominated government.

For principals, as discussed in the introduction, knowing the agent's costs of suppressive effort is always difficult. The agent has knowledge about local conditions unavailable to the principal and likely a better idea of what is necessary to survive politically. The principal should remember this, though the United States did not, for instance, appear to do so in the case of Yemen after 2003 (chapter 8). At the same time, a central implication of our theory is that the agent has incentives to lie about these costs, so its explanations for failing to suppress disturbances cannot be taken at face value. Distinguishing the true costs of effort is hard both for principals, as players in this game, and for us, as outside observers. This divergence, however, is the key consideration in determining when a strategy of indirect control is preferred over other strategies and, if indirect control is chosen, in calibrating the size of the rewards and punishments necessary to motivate the agent.

Our cases yield evidence that rejects unequivocally the unconditional capacity-building approach to indirect action currently pursued by the United States and others. Under most circumstances, seeking to build capacity through unconditional transfers of resources to the proxy does not lead to the suppression of violence as desired by the principal. As seen clearly in the case of Iraq, because the principal and agent do not share identical preferences regarding the disturbance, as reflected in the proxy's costs of effort, unconditionally building capacity will result in shirking by the agent, in this instance actually stimulating sectarianism and increasing attacks on U.S. forces (chapter 9). The capacity-building approach by itself is politically naive, as it ignores the incentives of the agent.

At the same time, our theory predicts that capacity building can be a successful strategy when interests are closely aligned and the agent's costs of effort are low. Under these conditions, principals can benefit themselves by making unconditional transfers in the current period that will lower the costs of effort for the agent in the future. U.S. capacity-building aid to Colombia enhanced the government's ability to suppress the drug trade and combat local drug lords, but only when the Colombian president's political constituency made the cost of effort low (chapter 3). Washing away previous tensions, the dovetailing of U.S. interests with President Rhee's after the North Korean invasion allowed for both tremendous capacity building and high effort (chapter 1). In similar ways, Israel, when its interests and those of its proxies were relatively aligned, helped build the South Lebanese Army as an effective fighting force and supported the development of the Palestinian Authority during the Oslo period (1993–2000) and under Prime Minister Salam Fayyad (2007–13) (chapter 7). And in El Salvador, when its interests were relatively aligned with those of the United States (early in its civil war), U.S. assistance considerably expanded the capability and effectiveness of the Salvadoran armed forces in just a few short years (chapter 5). Yet we emphasize that these periods of highly aligned interests are unusual. The United States today appears to assume a harmony of interests with its various proxies, with capacity building as its default one-size-fits-all strategy. Given our theory and empirical findings, however, the United States and other possible principals would do better to assume that available proxies have their own interests, possibly overlapping but distinct, which create significant costs of effort and, thus, temptations to shirk. A strategy of indirect control should be the default, and a strategy of capacity building adopted only after a careful examination of the proxy's interests.

At the same time, rewards and punishments may not always be sufficient, and therefore not optimally chosen. As the theory in the introduction suggests, some disturbances may not be sufficiently costly to the principal to warrant paying the necessary costs to suppress them, either directly or indirectly. These disturbances may be thorns in the sides of the principal's leaders, but provoke neither direct nor indirect action. Conversely, some disturbances may be so salient to the principal, but the necessary costs of rewards and punishments (implied by agent effort costs) so high, that the principal will act directly on the disturbance. Unable to motivate a local agent to do the necessary job, so to speak, the principal must deal with the problem directly, as the United States eventually did in capturing Osama bin Laden despite years of pleading with the Pakistani government for assistance.

Finally, it is important to emphasize that a successful proxy relationship does not imply that disturbances will be reduced to zero. Rewards and punishments can move proxies to act more aggressively against threats, but the disturbances may not be sufficiently costly to the principal to warrant paying the costs necessary to eradicate them entirely. Principals may not get everything they want from their proxy, given the incentives they choose to deploy. Principals trade off the costs of the various rewards and punishments at their disposal against the level of disturbances they believe they can tolerate. Indirect control is not a "magic bullet" that always eliminates disturbances at low cost, a point articulated well in the theory. The right question is this: Does using appropriate carrots and sticks induce a proxy with a local advantage in suppression to exert greater levels of effort to combat disturbances? The evidence from our cases is clearly positive.

Principal Failure

Overall, the theory captures much about the indirect-control relationship as observed in these cases. As noted, agents are responsive to rewards and punishments when implemented, although not always as responsive as the principal would like. Where the theory fails, however, is in predicting how principals, rather than agents, will make choices. Relative to the predictions of the theory, principals are reluctant to withdraw assistance from agents following disturbances (the United States with Iraq and Pakistan, for example) and reluctant to reward success (Israel with the Palestinian Authority). Our set of cases was not designed to diagnose why principals deviate from optimal control of agents, but it does suggest three possible explanations.

First, principals may not be sufficiently powerful relative to their agents to impose effective punishments on subordinates. This challenges the second scope condition of our theory. It also illustrates the problems that arise when the cost of punishment is too high. In Pakistan, the military government and President Pervez Musharraf failed to exert anything close to the effort desired by the Bush administration. The United States was reluctant to impose punishments even when the state was engaging in adverse or "negative" effort by hiding Osama bin Laden. The United States needed Pakistan's cooperation in supplying its troops in Afghanistan and in controlling insurgents along the border, and Pakistan could easily retaliate by cutting off supply lines into Afghanistan (chapter 6). Thus, we can think of this case either as one in which the agent had leverage over the principal and pressed on the scope condition, or as one in which punishing the agent would have been very costly to the principal. Either way, the constraints on the United States in using sanctions against Pakistan's government were sufficiently large that the proxy engaged in very little effort, with the consequence that disturbances threatening the United States went uncontrolled. This suggests that indirect control should only be considered when the power asymmetry between principal and agent is large and can be easily manipulated.

Second, principals may be constrained by their own domestic public in granting rewards for effective effort. In the case of the Palestinian Authority, Prime Minister Fayyad was building an effective state that could control terrorism against Israel; early in his tenure, Israel helped build the capacity of the Palestinian Authority, provided modest rewards for effort, and, more important, promised a future reward of a Palestinian state. Though Fayyad was succeeding, the rightward tilt in Israeli politics and the growing political strength of the settler movement raised the domestic political cost to the Israeli government of granting this final reward—undermining Fayyad, enabling his ouster, and contributing to the deterioration in relations that followed. Although the "prize" was sufficiently important to the Palestinian Authority that it was willing to take the risk of cooperating with Israel, in this case the principal was ultimately willing to renege on the implicit contract. When interests diverge and large rewards are required to induce effort, those rewards may later become too costly for the principal.

In these first two conditions—the weak principal and the cost-constrained principal—the failure of that principal to act effectively is consistent with the theory. Indeed, when rendered in terms of the theory, the anomalous behavior by a principal becomes intuitive and almost obvious. Punishments or rewards are too costly to use, and the proxy relationship is undermined. In other cases, however, the principal simply does not choose to use appropriate incentives, often for what appears to be a third reason: misreading interest alignment.

In Yemen, a compliant agent, President Ali Abdullah Saleh, had been receiving substantial rewards in the form of military aid, which he used to sustain himself in power. He was surprised in 2005 when the United States suddenly began making aid conditional on broader political reforms that threatened his political survival. With the rewards now offered insufficient to justify the greater demands by the principal, Saleh turned his limited resources and attention to fighting his domestic opponents. Why the United States upped the ante, so to speak, appears explicable only as a misreading of the degree of interest alignment between Washington and Saleh, perhaps reinforced by the latter's previously high levels of effort, or as a consequence of the Bush administration's "freedom agenda" and a revision of its counterinsurgency doctrine.

In Iraq, President Bush simply refused to consider contingent punishments and thereby failed to induce high effort from Prime Minister al-Maliki. In this case, the failure of the United States to "act as a principal" was conditioned by the absence of a suitable replacement for al-Maliki, but appears grounded in al-Maliki's very weak domestic political position, the personal relationship the president sought to establish with the prime minister, and a perhaps mistaken belief that U.S. and Iraqi interests were more aligned than they were in reality. During the surge, Gen. David Petraeus did use some mild sanctions, which led to a temporary improvement. That episode suggests support for the theory, and implies that the United States might have achieved greater success in Iraq if it had chosen to use incentives more fully. Overall, the unconditional embrace of al-Maliki by President Bush led the Iraqi leader to ignore many U.S. goals and eventually forced the principal to withdraw.

Although these two cases challenge the theory in that the principal did not act as predicted, the consequence of this failure is entirely consistent with the model's prediction of agent behavior. When rewards and punishments are not well calibrated to the demands made of the proxy, or not used at all, the agent will shirk and engage in very low levels of effort, with a corresponding increase in disturbances. These anomalies suggest the need for a better understanding of the principal's goals and decision making. As Stephen Biddle points out in chapter 10, principal failure has policy implications for the United States.

Analytic Narratives

The conclusions drawn from our cases and the strength of our policy recommendations (chapter 10) flow from the empirical method of analytic narratives, which we have applied to this study. This method is still in its infancy, according to even its originators, and may not be familiar to readers, so it is worth discussing.[2] Analytic narratives seek to explain specific events by combining the usual narrative method of historians with the analytical tools of rational choice theory as developed by economists and political scientists. The primary criterion for evaluation is verisimilitude, or the fit between theory and facts, although we think evaluation can be extended further, to include uncovering "new facts" predicted by theory—as we do in this volume.

Analytic narratives are sometimes described as a conversation between history (as observed or recounted) and theory, which holds true in our case. We began with an intuitive critique of U.S. counterinsurgency strategy—that it was insufficiently sensitive to the needs and incentives of the foreign leaders on whom its success depends. We turned immediately to principal-agent (P-A) theory to help us understand the problem. Principal-agent theory was originally developed in economics to explain the relationship between shareholders, managers, and workers, but it was later applied more broadly to a host of relationships between clients and those with specialized expertise (lawyers, doctors, and so on).[3] It entered political science in the study of relationships between Congress, the president, and bureaucracies, then infiltrated questions of representation (voters and legislators), party structure, and even states and international organizations.[4] The theory identifies a generic problem: one actor delegates to a second with perhaps overlapping but not identical interests, and the latter takes unobserved actions that have somewhat random outcomes. Seeing relations with proxies in international relations as a P-A problem was a short but crucial intellectual step. We turned to existing P-A theories to guide our inquiry, especially a dynamic, game-theoretic version developed by Gerard Padró i Miquel and Pierre Yared.[5] We quickly realized that the theory needed to incorporate capacity building by the principal, a distinct innovation from existing models, and that some of the dynamic machinery originally explored by Padró i Miquel and Yared could be jettisoned in exploring our types of cases. We settled on a relatively simple version of the model summarized in the introduction to guide the project.[6] At this initial stage of selecting and refining the theory, this truly was a conversation with history.

The theory guides our inferential method in four essential ways. First, it identifies scope conditions necessary for a principal-agent relationship to emerge. Perhaps most important here is subordination: the requirement that the principal be able to influence the proxy more than the proxy can influence the principal (i.e., the principal has more carrots and sticks to use and at lower cost than the agent). Strictly speaking, the only way the proxy can affect the principal is by choosing effort or shirking. The case of Pakistan (chapter 6) is one in which the principal-agent relationship breaks down; for instance, this scope condition is violated by Pakistan's ability to hold up supplies to U.S. forces in Afghanistan. The scope conditions also limit the applicability of the theory to situations in which the agent has some natural advantage in suppressing the disturbance, and the principal cannot fully observe what the proxy is doing (or, alternatively, its costs of effort). That condition is often satisfied in general, with the minor exceptions being direct actions at which principals have an immense technological advantage, even abroad, such as surveillance and drone strikes. Importantly, not every international relationship fits these conditions.

Second, the theory captures the core P-A problem but also produces nonobvious predictions. Notable here is the implication that as the cost of the disturbance to the principal increases, the advantage of the proxy in suppressing disturbances becomes ever more important, and the principal will embrace agents from which it might have previously distanced itself. As we write, the use of Kurdish forces by a U.S.-backed coalition to suppress ISIS in Iraq and Syria would be an example. Among our cases, Israel and Hamas provide another example. Where intuition might suggest that greater costs of disturbances lead more often to direct action by the principal, the theory implies that—all else constant—as costs increase, the principal will be more likely to choose indirect control even when it might not have done so when disturbances posed less of a threat.

Third, the theory forces us to specify and consider more fully the alternatives to indirect control, especially the options of doing nothing or taking direct action. This helps us to understand when and where indirect control will be chosen by principals, and when and where it can be used to incentivize agents.[7] In the case of doing nothing, principals may decide to live with low levels of disturbances when the costs of rewards and punishments are relatively large or the costs of effort to available proxies are high. Conversely, principals will choose direct action only when disturbances are large and costly, rewards and punishments are costly, and the proxy's costs of effort are high. These alternatives, especially doing nothing, should not be thought of as "failures" of a proxy relationship, but as core components of our analysis.

Finally, the theory allows us to characterize more precisely the comparative static implications of our analysis, which we then apply to the cases. Within the analytic narrative method, the primary criterion of evaluation is whether the theory captures the essence of the cases. We addressed this in reviewing the findings above; the theory generally does comport with the "facts" of the cases both in cross-case comparisons and, more convincingly, in within-case comparisons over time. To the extent that predictions are falsified, it is with principals who do not employ appropriate incentives, as we have discussed above.

A second criterion for evaluation, however, is whether the theory generates new insights or novel facts beyond what the actors themselves, or close observers, may understand. If the primary criterion is fitting what is *already* known about a particular case, this criterion is somewhat more ambitious: challenging us to see something *new* about cases. Here, we think our theory is particularly successful in tying relations between states to the larger phenomenon of P-A relationships and, especially, in illustrating commonalities across cases that are not otherwise apparent. That relations between the United States and Prime Minister al-Maliki in Iraq are analogous to those between shareholders and managers, or Congress and the bureaucracy, is somewhat surprising. Equally, that Germany's problem of controlling Denmark during World War II, Washington's problem of controlling drugs in Colombia, and Israel's problem of controlling Hamas all share a common structure with U.S. policy toward Pakistan, Yemen, and Iraq today is not well grasped by observers or policymakers—to their detriment, we would add, in the contemporary cases. This common structure highlights that local politicians must, like President Rhee, tend first to their local network of supporters.

Equally important, in our view, are applications of the theory to cases where the actors would never think of themselves as agents or proxies of some foreign power, or admit as much to their citizens. In our era, sovereignty is the highest aspiration of many states, and being cast as a client, puppet, or stooge controlled by Washington is a likely death sentence for at least some foreign leaders. Discretion serves both agent and principal. Therefore, taking almost any case on its own terms, examining only the public record of pronouncements of leaders, and perhaps even examining at some future date the private diaries and thoughts of leaders, would not suggest the importance of the proxy relationship or the use of rewards and punishments to motivate leaders to act for the principal in ways they otherwise would not. As noted in the introduction, one possible objection to our approach is that actors do not think of themselves as agents. True enough, but one strength of the theory is that it sheds new light on cases and identifies commonalities across otherwise disparate events. That foreign leaders are being manipulated by rewards and punishments exercised by a principal—perhaps against their wishes—is an important insight that might not emerge from the historical record alone. Revealing these commonalities may allow both proxies and principals to make better choices in the future. This is a unique advantage of an analytic narrative approach over a narrative based on public statements or even the retrospective accounts of participants.[8]

Three final issues, not directly related to our use of analytic narrative, are worth examining. First, how generalizable is the theory? Can case studies verify its applicability to a broad range of situations that analysts and policymakers will have to confront in the future? Generalizability, of course, is largely a function of the theory itself. Are the scope conditions so narrowly drawn that they apply only to a handful of instances—the "n-of-one" problem that produces a "just so" story—or general enough that the theory can apply to a useful range of cases? Our scope conditions, we believe, are quite encompassing. With the exception of relations with China, Russia, and other major powers, which lack the power asymmetries of P-A relationships, the theory should apply to many U.S. relationships in the world today. Analysts must be careful in coding values of particular variables in the model, of course, but the theory as a whole should apply widely. Empirically, that our cases cover a range of issues (counterinsurgency, counterterrorism, counternarcotics), different principals and agents, and different historical periods (World War II to contemporary cases) suggests the general relevance of the theory.

A second concern is ex post rationalization through coding and interpretation of changing conditions and their effects influenced by an understanding of the theory. In the absence of experimental variation in conditions, this should always be a concern for observational studies, especially with a small number of cases. How then is inference possible? The alternative we chose, as described in the introduction, was ongoing peer review of the coding and interpretation, disciplined by application of precisely the same analytical model to each case. Within the research team, we held a series of meetings to discuss coding, case by case. We also exposed the coding and interpretation to external expert review in our September 2016 conference. For us, that conference provided strong validation of our major findings: proxies cheat unless incentivized, and principals fail to incentivize surprisingly often. Readers of course can judge for themselves, case by case.

A third possible concern is selection bias introduced by our nonrandom choice of cases. As explained in the introduction, we chose cases because they appeared to be salient politically, or driven by disturbances that were sufficiently important to provoke some action by the principal. We did not select cases to systematically vary the proxy's costs of effort, our key independent variable, as would otherwise be advised for qualitative research.[9] Indeed, since assessing effort cost requires considerable context-specific knowledge, our "codings" of this variable often emerged only rather late in the research process. Does this selection rule bias our results in ways that likely favor evidence supporting our theory of proxy relations? If so, this would qualify both our empirical conclusions above and the policy recommendations presented by Stephen Biddle in chapter 10. We think not.

The biggest effect of selecting salient disturbances is to ignore the very large number of everyday events in world politics that do not rise to the attention of policymakers or that are not important enough to require a policy response. There might be a budding insurgency in some foreign country that is too small, or the possibility of an attack on the United States too remote, to provoke U.S. action of any sort. At most, the disturbance might induce some analyst in the government to engage in the equivalent of medicine's "watchful waiting." Such non-events constitute the vast majority of possible "cases" in international relations. They are also likely fully consistent with the theory, which implies that very small disturbances will be ignored as long as there is any cost to rewarding or punishing an agent.[10]

Conversely, very large disturbances should be associated with indirect control or, if the agent's costs of effort are too large, direct action. We do not look at every possible case of large disturbances, but as we have summarized above, the theory is generally supported by the cases we do examine. We do not include cases where the disturbance was so large, or the proxy's costs of effort so high, that the principal jumped immediately to direct action or war, as the United States did in 2001 in Afghanistan when confronted by a devastating attack on its homeland by a terrorist group actively supported by the extant proxy. Although such cases are likely rare, they would also likely support the theory. By truncating the variation in one key parameter of our theory, the cost to the principal of the disturbance, we increase the uncertainty around our findings but do not bias our results. Even so, the across-case comparisons appear to hold reasonably well—better than chance—and the within-case comparisons find strong support for the theory. Had we included a broader range of variation in this key parameter, we might have more confidence in the substantive magnitude of the relationship between disturbances and the choice of strategy, but the direction of the relationship would be the same. It is also the clear predictions of the theory about large disturbances that potentially allow us to falsify the theory, despite our case-based, analytic narrative approach.

Finally, it is worth noting that this team approach to testing using analytical narratives is expensive and time consuming. We could reduce ex post rationalization and selection bias because individual chapters were written by authors who were not necessarily subject experts when the exercise began. This was achieved by recruiting a well-trained team of scholars who, although they sometimes possessed strong background and regional knowledge, then learned the particulars of the cases as they coded them. The effort required ongoing coordination and rounds of peer review on interpretation. We also had the luxury of being able to bring in two theorists who had written a seminal paper in this literature to participate in repeated rounds of the peer review. The ability to focus so much coordinated researcher time on a specific question is rare in social science.

Our methodological conclusion is that the analytical narrative method imposed enough discipline to yield convincing inference. That might be because we got lucky, but even with only nine cases, the data aligned consistently with the predictions of the theory, at least for agent behavior. We believe that our theory is capturing a powerful set of interactions in world politics that both scholars and policymakers ignore at their own expense.

A Final Note

In a nutshell, we have three major findings. First, proxy relationships work well in suppressing political violence when proxies are appropriately incentivized (six or seven of nine cases), but provide disappointing results when incentives are lacking, inconsistent, or absent (two or three of the nine). Second, the United States is surprisingly inconsistent in applying incentives, which accounts for both of the unambiguous disappointments (Yemen and Iraq). Third, the analytical narrative method seems to provide enough discipline to yield conclusions, at least in the fortunate cases where the qualitative data are consistently predicted by theory.

We close with a set of open questions that we hope scholars will address and policymakers will heed. If indirect control can, under some circumstances, be effective in motivating proxies to act in ways desired by the principal, what should the principal ask its agents to do? How can the United States or its proxies best fight counterinsurgencies, or the other disturbances studied here? Are the "asks" that can be made of proxies compatible with their interests, and are the necessary incentives feasible at reasonable cost to the principal? In this volume, we have focused on whether incentives work. In chapter 10, Stephen Biddle examines carefully how the United States can better incorporate the use of contingent rewards and punishments into the conduct of its policy. Here, we reach forward to suggest some preliminary ideas about what principals should ask of their proxies given what we have learned about counterinsurgency warfare in recent years.

The best way to fight counterinsurgencies (the majority of the conflicts in this volume) is still a matter of debate. Asymmetric conflicts, where the proxy and its allies have a coercive advantage over insurgents, are now the dominant form of political violence worldwide. A decade of research now suggests that when adequate security is combined with provision of minimal government services, governments can win asymmetric conflicts against insurgent groups in a cost-effective way by inducing civilians to cooperate with government by sharing information.[11] That line of reasoning provides a prescription for the types of effort that principals might usefully require of agents: a combination of actions that suppress insurgent and terrorist activity (discussed in chapter 10), and basic governance as requested by local civilians (dispute adjudication, security, education, health, and possibly more), which creates the stability necessary for economic development. Some form of institutionalized inclusive governance would make that social compact credible, such as the deal the United States failed to broker between Baghdad and the Sunni-majority areas of Iraq but did manage to help facilitate in Colombia.

These findings on the effectiveness of basic governance are doubly important given a disturbing finding in this volume, namely, that local agents, when not appropriately incentivized, often use foreign military assistance to shore up the opposite of inclusive governance: a patronage security service that threatens political rivals. Proxy relationships are inevitably instruments that will influence some local political bargain between a proxy and its constituency. One hopes that principals will monitor that bargain so that it does not just serve short-term security interests but also contributes to the development of a healthy, inclusive political system that will eventually be sustained, as in South Korea and possibly Colombia, without active intervention by the principal.

NOTES

1. As discussed in chapter 1, the theory is equivalent if we assume the principal lacks information about the proxy's cost of effort rather than the levels of effort exerted.

2. On analytic narratives as a method, see Bates et al. 1998, 2000; Elster 2000; Kiser and Welser 2007; Arias 2011; Mongin 2016.

3. For an initial review and introduction, see Laffont and Martimort 2002.

4. For a political science review and application to international organizations, see Hawkins et al. 2006b.

5. Padró i Miquel and Yared 2012.

6. The model is developed mathematically in Berman, Lake, et al. 2018.

7. Ladwig (2016, 2017) develops a very similar P-A approach to ours. We differ primarily in our explicit theorization of alternative courses of action.

8. We can hardly expect, for instance, that Prime Minister al-Maliki of Iraq would explain to his U.S. principal that he feared suffering the fate of Bashir Gemayel in Lebanon, when the Syrian government perceived him to be unduly influenced by Israel. A single agent influenced by multiple principals is a possible interpretation of the Iraq case.

9. King, Keohane, and Verba 1994.

10. Although we did not select cases on this dimension, an analogous set of non-events is created by proxies with very low costs of effort, or interests that are highly aligned with the principal's. In such instances, the agent does what the principal wants without any need for external rewards or punishments. These non-events would also support the theory.

11. Berman, Felter, and Shapiro 2018.

References

"ABC News/Washington Post Poll: February Monthly—Obama/Taxes/War on Terrorism/2012 Presidential Election, Feb. 2012" [dataset]. 2012. USABCWASH2012–1134, version 2. Produced by Langer Research Associates/ Abt SRBI. Distributed by Cornell University, Roper Center for Public Opinion Research, RoperExpress.

Abrahamsen, Samuel. 1987. "The Rescue of Denmark's Jews." In *The Rescue of the Danish Jews: Moral Courage under Stress*, edited by Leo Goldberger, 3–11. New York: NYU Press.

Abu Amer, Adnan. 2014. "Hamas Denies Role in Kidnapping." Al-Monitor, June 16, 2014. https://www.al-monitor.com/pulse/originals/2014/06/hamas-israel-confrontation-hebron-kidnapping.html.

"Afghanistan War: Closed Pakistan Routes Costing US $100 Million a Month." 2012. ABC News Radio. June 13, 2012. http://abcnewsradioonline.com/world-news/afghanistan-war-closed-pakistan-routes-costing-us-100-millio.html.

Ahmed, Ishtiaq. 2013. *Pakistan the Garrison State: Origins, Evolution, Consequences, 1947–2011.* Karachi, Pakistan: Oxford University Press.

"Airstrike Hits Gaza Ministry Building." 2008. CNN. February 27, 2008. http://edition.cnn.com/2008/WORLD/meast/02/27/mideast/index.html.

Al Waheidi, Majid. 2016. "After Rockets Fired from Gaza, Israelis Strike Hamas Base." *New York Times*, March 12, 2016. http://www.nytimes.com/2016/03/13/world/middleeast/israel-gaza-hamas-airstrike.html.

Al-Ghoul, Asmaa. 2014. "Gaza's Armed Factions Coordinate Response to Israeli Attacks." Al-Monitor, July 7, 2014. http://www.al-monitor.com/pulse/originals/2014/07/gaza-armed-factions-coordinate-response-israel-attacks.html.

Allawi, Ali A. 2007. *The Occupation of Iraq: Winning the War, Losing the Peace.* New Haven, CT: Yale University Press.

Allen, Richard C. 1960. *Korea's Syngman Rhee.* Rutland, VT: Charles E. Tuttle.

Al-Mughrabi, Nidal. 2012. "23 Killed in Israel-Gaza Violence." *Daily Star* (Beirut), March 12, 2012. http://www.dailystar.com.lb/News/Middle-East/2012/Mar-12/166317-2-killed-in-gaza-in-israeli-airstrikes.ashx#axzz38BVN0Pai.

Al-Mughrabi, Nidal. 2016. "Gaza Siblings Killed in Israeli Air Strike after Militant Rockets Hit Israel." Reuters, March 12, 2016. https://www.reuters.com/article/us-israel-palestinians-gaza/gaza-siblings-killed-in-israeli-air-strike-after-militant-rockets-hit-israel-idUSKCN0WE09T.

"Al-Qaeda Organization in the Arabian Peninsula." 2017. Global Security. Last modified March 2, 2017. http://www.globalsecurity.org/military/world/para/al-qaida-arabia.htm.

Andreas, Peter R., Eva C. Bertram, Morris J. Blachman, and Kenneth E. Sharpe. 1991–92. "Dead-End Drug Wars." *Foreign Policy* 85 (Winter): 106–28.

Anwar, Zahid. 2013. "Pakistan and the Geopolitics of Supply Routes to Afghanistan." *Journal of Political Studies* 20 (2): 105–23.

Appleman, Roy E. 1992. *United States Army in the Korean War: South to the Naktong, North to the Yalu (June-November 1950)*. Washington, DC: Center of Military History, U.S. Army.

Arias, Luz Marina. 2011. "Analytic Narratives: The Method." In *International Encyclopedia of Political Science*, edited by Bertrand Badie, Dirk Berg-Schlosser, and Leonardo Morlino, 71–72. Thousand Oaks, CA: Sage.

Arnson, Cynthia J. 1993. *Crossroads: Congress, the President, and Central America, 1976–1993*. 2nd ed. University Park, PA: Pennsylvania State University Press.

Arraf, Jane. 2010. "Allegations of Fraud as Iraq Election Results Trickle In." *Christian Science Monitor*, March 11, 2010. http://www.csmonitor.com/World/Middle-East/2010/0311/Allegations-of-fraud-as-Iraq-election-results-trickle-in.

Atkinson, Rick. 2007. *An Army at Dawn: The War in North Africa, 1942–1943*. New York: Henry Holt.

Atkinson, Rick. 2014. *The Guns at Last Light: The War in Western Europe, 1944–1945*. New York: Picador.

Bacevich, A. J., James D. Hallums, Richard H. White, and Thomas F. Young. 1988. *American Military Policy in Small Wars: The Case of El Salvador*. Washington, DC: Pergamon-Brassey's International Defense Publishers.

Bailey, Cecil E. 2004. "OPATT: The U.S. Army SF Advisers in El Salvador." *Special Warfare* 17 (2): 18–29.

Baker, Peter. 2014. "For 2 U.S. Presidents, Iraqi Leader Proved a Source of Frustration." *New York Times*, August 12, 2014. https://www.nytimes.com/2014/08/12/world/middleeast/for-2-us-presidents-iraqi-leader-proved-a-source-of-frustration.html.

Baldauf, Scott. 2011. "Pakistan Cuts Supply Lines, but U.S. Has Options." *Christian Science Monitor*, November 29, 2011. http://www.csmonitor.com/World/Asia-South-Central/2011/1129/Pakistan-cuts-supply-lines-but-US-has-options.

Bates, Robert H., Avner Greif, Margaret Levi, Jean-Laurent Rosenthal, and Barry R. Weingast. 1998. *Analytical Narratives*. Princeton, NJ: Princeton University Press.

Bates, Robert H., Avner Greif, Margaret Levi, Jean-Laurent Rosenthal, and Barry R. Weingast. 2000. "The Analytic Narrative Project." *American Political Science Review* 94 (3): 696–702.

Becker, Jillian. 1984. *PLO: The Rise and Fall of the Palestine Liberation Organization*. New York: St. Martin's Press.

Belasco, Amy. 2014. *The Cost of Iraq, Afghanistan, and Other Global War on Terror Operations Since 9/11*. Washington, DC: Congressional Research Service.

Berman, Eli. 2009. *Radical, Religious, and Violent: The New Economics of Terrorism*. Cambridge, MA: MIT Press.

Berman, Eli, Joseph H. Felter, and Jacob N. Shapiro. 2018. *Small Wars, Big Data: The Information Revolution in Modern Conflict*. Princeton, NJ: Princeton University Press.

Berman, Eli, David A. Lake, Gerard Padró i Miquel, and Pierre Yared. 2018. Technical Appendix to "Introduction: Principals, Agents, and Indirect Foreign Policies." July 15. https://esoc.princeton.edu/AP1.

Berman, Eli, Jacob N. Shapiro, and Joseph H. Felter. 2011. "Can Hearts and Minds Be Bought? The Economics of Counterinsurgency in Iraq." *Journal of Political Economy* 119 (4): 766–819.

Biddle, Stephen. 2008. "Review of the *US Army/Marine Corps Counterinsurgency Field Manual*." In "Review Symposium: The New US Army/Marine Corps Counterinsurgency Field Manual as Political Science and Political Praxis." *Perspectives on Politics* 6 (2): 347–50.

Biddle, Stephen, Jeffrey A. Friedman, and Jacob N. Shapiro. 2012. "Testing the Surge: Why Did Violence Decline in Iraq in 2007?" *International Security* 37 (1): 7–40.

Biddle, Stephen, Julia Macdonald, and Ryan Baker. 2018. "Small Footprint, Small Payoff: The Military Effectiveness of Security Force Assistance." *Journal of Strategic Studies* 41 (1–2): 89–142. https://doi.org/10.1080/01402390.2017.1307745.

Biddle, Stephen, and Robert Zirkle. 1996. "Technology, Civil-Military Relations, and Warfare in the Developing World." *Journal of Strategic Studies* 19 (2): 171–212.

Birdsall, Nancy, Wren Elhai, and Molly Kinder. 2011. *Beyond Bullets and Bombs: Fixing the U.S. Approach to Development in Pakistan*. Report of the Study Group on a U.S. Development Strategy in Pakistan. Washington, DC: Center for Global Development. http://www.cgdev.org/sites/default/files/1425136_file_CGD_Pakistan_FINAL_web.pdf.

Birtle, Andrew J. 2009. *U.S. Army Counterinsurgency and Contingency Operations Doctrine, 1860–1941*. Washington, DC: Center of Military History, U.S. Army.

"Bitter Retreat for the SLA." 2000. BBC News. May 24, 2000. http://news.bbc.co.uk/2/hi/middle_east/761817.stm.

Blomstedt, Larry. 2016. *Truman, Congress, and Korea: The Politics of America's First Undeclared War*. Lexington: University Press of Kentucky.

Bolger, Daniel P. 2014. *Why We Lost: A General's Inside Account of the Iraq and Afghanistan Wars*. Boston: Houghton Mifflin Harcourt.

Bolton, John. 2007. "Iraq 4 Years On." Interview by Jeremy Paxman. *Newsnight*, BBC. March 21, 2007.

Boot, Max. 2013. *Invisible Armies: An Epic History of Guerrilla Warfare from Ancient Times to the Present*. New York: Liveright.

Boucek, Christopher. 2010. *War in Saada: From Local Insurrection to National Challenge*. Yemen on the Brink: A Carnegie Paper Series. Middle East Program no. 110. April 2010. Washington, DC: Carnegie Endowment for International Peace.

Boutton, Andrew. 2014. "U.S. Foreign Aid, Interstate Rivalry, and Incentives for Counterterrorism Cooperation." *Journal of Peace Research* 51 (6): 741–54.

Brooks, Risa. 1998. *Political-Military Relations and the Stability of Arab Regimes*. New York: Oxford University Press.

B'Tselem. 2013. "Human Rights Violations during Operation Pillar of Defense, 14–21 November 2012." May 9, 2013. http://www.btselem.org/press_releases/20130509_pillar_of_defense_report.

B'Tselem. n.d. "Fatalities during Operation Cast Lead." Accessed April 26, 2017. http://www.btselem.org/statistics/fatalities/during-cast-lead/by-date-of-event.

Bueno de Mesquita, Ethan, C. Christine Fair, Jenna Jordan, Rasul Bakhsh Rais, and Jacob N. Shapiro. 2013. *Codebook for BFRS Dataset of Political Violence in Pakistan*. https://esoc.princeton.edu/files/bfrs-political-violence-pakistan-dataset.

Bueno de Mesquita, Ethan, C. Christine Fair, Jenna Jordan, Rasul Bakhsh Rais, and Jacob N. Shapiro. 2015. "Measuring Political Violence in Pakistan: Insights from the BFRS Dataset." *Conflict Management and Peace Science* 32 (5): 536–58.

Bush, George W. 2002. "Remarks following a Roundtable Discussion on Retirement Savings and an Exchange with Reporters in Des Moines, Iowa." American Presidency Project. March 1, 2002. http://www.presidency.ucsb.edu/ws/?pid=63306.

Bush, George W. 2003. "President Bush Discusses Freedom in Iraq and Middle East: Remarks by the President at the 20th Anniversary of the National Endowment for Democracy." The White House (website). November 6, 2003. https://georgewbush-whitehouse.archives.gov/news/releases/2003/11/20031106-2.html.

Bush, George W. 2005. "President Welcomes President Saleh of Yemen to the White House." The White House (website). November 10, 2005. https://georgewbush-whitehouse.archives.gov/news/releases/2005/11/20051110-2.html.

Bush, George W. 2010. *Decision Points.* New York: Crown.

Carney, Christopher P. 1989. "International Patron-Client Relationships: A Conceptual Framework." *Studies in Comparative International Development* 24 (2): 42–55.

Casey, Nicholas. 2016. "Colombia and FARC Sign New Peace Deal, This Time Skipping Voters." *New York Times,* November 24, 2016. http://www.nytimes. com/2016/11/24/world/americas/colombia-juan-manuel-santos-peace-deal-farc.html.

Cha, Victor. 2009/10. "Powerplay: Origins of the U.S. Alliance System in Asia." *International Security* 34 (3): 158–96.

Chavez, Lydia. 1983. "El Salvador Loses Ground, Not Least in Washington." *New York Times,* February 6, 1983.

"The Chicago Council on Global Affairs Poll: 2014 Chicago Council Survey of American Public Opinion and US Foreign Policy, May 2014" [dataset]. 2014. USMISC2014-CCGA, version 2. Produced by GfK Knowledge Networks. Distributed by Cornell University, Roper Center for Public Opinion Research, RoperExpress.

Christensen, Claus, Niels Poulsen, and Peter Smith. 1997. "The Danish Volunteers in the Waffen SS and Their Contribution to the Holocaust and the Nazi War of Extermination." In *Denmark and the Holocaust,* edited by Mette Bastholm Jensen and Steven L. Bjerregard Jensen, 62–101. Berkeley, CA: Institute for International Studies.

Clemente, Dave, and Ryan Evans. 2014. *Wartime Logistics in Afghanistan and Beyond: Handling Wicked Problems and Complex Adaptive Systems.* January 2014. London: Royal Institute of International Affairs. https://www.chathamhouse. org/sites/files/chathamhouse/home/chatham/public_html/sites/default/files/ afghanistan_clemente.pdf.

Clemmesen, Michael H. 2010. "The Army in Positional Defense against the Developing Political Reality." In *The Danish Straits and German Naval Power, 1905–1918,* edited by Michael Epkenhans and Gerhard Paul Gross, 167–88. Potsdam: Militärgeschichtliches Forschungsamt.

Clines, Francis X. 1981. "President Doubtful on U.S. Intervention." *New York Times,* March 4, 1981.

Clodfelter, Michael. 2002. *Warfare and Armed Conflicts.* New York: McFarland.

CNN Wire Staff. 2012. "Pakistan Reopens NATO Supply Routes to Afghanistan." July 3, 2012. http://www.cnn.com/2012/07/03/world/asia/us-pakistan-border-routes/ index.html.

"Coca Clashes: Colombia." 1996. *Economist,* August 17, 1996. Gale Business Insights: Global database.

Cohen, Eliot. 1986. "Distant Battles: Modern War in the Third World." *International Security* 10 (4): 143–71.

Cole, Juan. 2007. "Shia Militias in Iraqi Politics." In *Iraq: Preventing a New Generation of Conflict,* edited by Markus E. Bouillon, David M. Malone, and Ben Rowswell, 109–23. Boulder, CO: Lynne Rienner.

Coles, Isabel. 2011. "Newsmaker: Yemen's Saleh, 'Dancing on the Heads of Snakes.'" Reuters, September 23, 2011. http://www.reuters.com/article/us-yemen-saleh-idUSTRE78M20X20110923.

Comisión Nacional de Reparación y Reconciliación, Grupo de Memoria Histórica (Colombia). 2013. *Basta ya! Colombia: Memorias de guerra y dignidad.* Bogotá: Centro Nacional de Memoria Histórica.

Cordesman, Anthony H., with George Sullivan and William D. Sullivan. 2007. *Lessons of the 2006 Israeli-Hezbollah War.* Washington, DC: Center for Strategic and International Studies.

Crandall, Russell. 2002. *Driven by Drugs: U.S. Policy toward Colombia.* Boulder, CO: Lynne Rienner.

Crandall, Russell. 2016. *The Salvador Option: The United States in El Salvador, 1977–1992.* Cambridge: Cambridge University Press.

Crane, Conrad. 2016. *Cassandra in Oz: Counterinsurgency and Future War.* Annapolis, MD: Naval Institute Press.

Cumings, Bruce. 2005. *Korea's Place in the Sun: A Modern History.* New York: W. W. Norton.

Cumings, Bruce. 2010. *The Korean War: A History.* New York: Modern Library.

Daggett, Stephen. 2010. *Costs of Major U.S. Wars.* Washington, DC: Congressional Research Service.

Dale, Catherine. 2012. *In Brief: Next Steps in the War in Afghanistan? Issues for Congress.* CRS Report for Congress. December 6, 2012. Washington, DC: Congressional Research Service.

Danin, Robert. 2011. "A Third Way to Palestine." *Foreign Affairs* 90 (1): 94–109.

David, Stephen. 1991. *Choosing Sides: Alignment and Realignment in the Third World.* Baltimore, MD: Johns Hopkins University Press.

Dayton, Keith. 2009. "Michael Stein Address on U.S. Middle East Policy." Lecture delivered at the Washington Institute for Near East Policy, Soref Symposium, Washington, DC. May 7, 2009. https://www.washingtoninstitute.org/html/pdf/DaytonKeynote.pdf.

Department of the Army. 1994. *FM 31-20-3: Foreign Internal Defense Tactics, Techniques, and Procedures for Special Forces.* September 20, 1994. Washington, DC: U.S. Government Printing Office.

Department of the Army. 2006. *FM 3-24 and MCWP 3-33.5: Counterinsurgency.* Washington, DC: Government Printing Office.

Department of the Army. 2013. *FM 3-22: Army Support to Security Cooperation.* Washington, DC: U.S. Government Printing Office.

Department of the Army. 2014. *FM 3-24 and MCWP 3-33.5: Insurgencies and Countering Insurgencies.* Washington, DC: Government Printing Office.

DeRouen, Karl R., and Uk Heo, eds. 2007. *Civil Wars of the World: Major Conflicts since World War II.* Santa Barbara, CA: ABC-CLIO.

Dethlefsen, Henrik. 1990. "Denmark and the German Occupation: Cooperation, Negotiation, or Collaboration?" *Scandinavian Journal of History* 15 (3): 193–206.

Dethlefsen, Henrik. 1996. "Denmark: The Diplomatic Solution." In *Anpassung, Kollaboration, Widerstand: Kollektive Reaktionen auf die Okkupation*, edited by Wolfgang Benz, Johannes Houwink ten Cate, and Gerhard Otto, 25–41. Berlin: Metropol.

Dodge, Toby. 2012. "Iraq's Road Back to Dictatorship." *Survival* 54 (3): 147–68.

Doubler, Michael. 1999. *Closing with the Enemy: How GIs Fought the War in Europe.* Lawrence: University Press of Kansas.

Dunkerley, James. 1982. *The Long War: Dictatorship and Revolution in El Salvador.* London: Junction Books.

El Kurd, Dana. 2017. "Hamas and Fatah's Step Forward Takes Palestine a Step Back." *Foreign Affairs*, October 16, 2017. https://www.foreignaffairs.com/articles/israel/2017-10-16/hamas-and-fatahs-step-forward-takes-palestine-step-back.

Elster, Jon. 2000. "Rational Choice History: A Case of Excessive Ambition." *American Political Science Review* 94 (3): 685–95.

Ephron, Dan. 2015. *Killing a King: The Assassination of Yitzhak Rabin and the Remaking of Israel.* New York: W. W. Norton.

Epstein, Susan B., and K. Alan Kronstadt. 2011. *Pakistan: U.S. Foreign Assistance.* CRS Report for Congress. July 28, 2011. Washington, DC: Congressional Research Service.

Epstein, Susan B., and K. Alan Kronstadt. 2013. *Pakistan: U.S. Foreign Assistance.* CRS Report for Congress. July 1, 2013. Washington, DC: Congressional Research Service.

Fair, C. Christine. 2012. "Pakistan in 2011." *Asian Survey* 52 (1): 100–113.

Fair, C. Christine. 2014a. *Fighting to the End: The Pakistan Army's Way of War.* Oxford: Oxford University Press.

Fair, C. Christine. 2014b. "Insights from a Database of Lashkar-e-Taiba and Hizb-ul-Mujahideen Militants." *Journal of Strategic Studies* 37 (2): 259–90.

Fair, C. Christine. 2018. "Pakistan Has All the Leverage over Trump." *Foreign Policy*, January 3, 2018. http://foreignpolicy.com/2018/01/03/pakistan-has-all-the-leverage-over-trump/.

Fair, C. Christine, and Seth G. Jones. 2009. "Pakistan's War Within." *Survival* 51 (6): 161–88.

Fair, C. Christine, and Sarah J. Watson. 2015. "Introduction: Pakistan's Enduring Challenges." In *Pakistan's Enduring Challenges*, edited by C. Christine Fair and Sarah J. Watson, 1–24. Philadelphia: University of Pennsylvania Press.

Falk, Richard. 2012. "Understanding Hamas after Khaled Meshaal's Gaza Speech." Al Jazeera, December 16, 2012. http://www.aljazeera.com/indepth/opinion/2012/12/20121215135432787820.html.

Feaver, Peter D. 2003. *Armed Servants: Agency, Oversight, and Civil-Military Relations.* Cambridge, MA: Harvard University Press.

Filkins, Dexter. 2008. *The Forever War.* New York: Vintage.

Fisk, Robert. 1990. *Pity the Nation: The Abduction of Lebanon.* New York: Nation Books.

Fox, Anette Baker. 1959. *The Power of Small States: Diplomacy in World War II.* Chicago: University of Chicago Press.

Friedman, Thomas L. 1995. *From Beirut to Jerusalem.* New York: Doubleday.

Frisch, Hillel. 2010. *The Palestinian Military: Between Militias and Armies.* London: Routledge.

Gall, Carlotta. 2014. *The Wrong Enemy: America in Afghanistan, 2001–2014.* New York: Houghton Mifflin Harcourt.

George, Alexander L., and Andrew Bennett. 2005. *Case Studies and Theory Development in the Social Sciences.* Cambridge, MA: MIT Press.

Gerges, Fawaz A. 2009. *The Far Enemy: Why Jihad Went Global.* 2nd ed. New York: Cambridge University Press.

Getmansky, Anna, and Thomas Zeitzoff. 2014. "Terrorism and Voting: The Effect of Rocket Threat on Voting in Israeli Elections." *American Political Science Review* 108 (3): 588–604.

Gettleman, Marvin E., Patrick Lacefield, Louis Menashe, and David Mermelstein. 1986. "El Salvador: A Political Chronology." In *El Salvador: Central America in the New Cold War*, 2nd ed., edited by Marvin E. Gettleman, Patrick Lacefield, Louis Menashe, and David Mermelstein, 53–64. New York: Grove.

Ghani, Ashraf, and Clare Lockhart. 2009. *Fixing Failed States: A Framework for Rebuilding a Fractured World.* Oxford: Oxford University Press.

Gibby, Bryan. 2004. "Fighting in a Korean War: The American Advisory Mission from 1946–53." PhD diss., Ohio State University.

Gibby, Bryan. 2012. *Will to Win: American Military Advisors in Korea, 1946–53.* Montgomery: University of Alabama Press.

Giltner, Phil. 2001. "The Success of Collaboration: Denmark's Self-Assessment of Its Economic Position after Five Years of Nazi Occupation." *Journal of Contemporary History* 36 (3): 485–506.

Glantz, David, and Jonathan House. 1995. *When Titans Clashed: How the Red Army Stopped Hitler*. Lawrence: University Press of Kansas.

Glanville, Luke. 2014. *Sovereignty and the Responsibility to Protect: A New History*. Chicago: University of Chicago Press.

Goertz, Gary, and James Mahony. 2012. *A Tale of Two Cultures: Qualitative and Quantitative Research in the Social Sciences*. Princeton, NJ: Princeton University Press.

Gordon, Michael R. 2002. "Cheney Asks Yemen to Join the Pursuit of Al Qaeda's Remnants." *New York Times*, March 15, 2002. http://www.nytimes.com/2002/03/15/world/nation-challenged-vice-president-cheney-asks-yemen-join-pursuit-al-qaeda-s.html.

Gordon, Michael R., and Bernard E. Trainor. 2013. *The Endgame: The Inside Story of the Struggle for Iraq, from George W. Bush to Barack Obama*. New York: Vintage.

Greentree, Todd. 2008. *Crossroads of Intervention: Insurgency and Counterinsurgency Lessons from Central America*. Westport, CT: Praeger Security International.

Gregory, Derek. 2012. "Supplying War in Afghanistan: The Frictions of Distance." openDemocracy. June 11, 2012. http://www.opendemocracy.net/derek-gregory/supplying-war-in-afghanistan-frictions-of-distance.

Gudmundsson, Bruce. 1989. *Stormtroop Tactics: Innovation in the German Army, 1914–1918*. New York: Praeger.

Haestrup, Jorgen. 1976. *Secret Alliance: A Study of the Danish Resistance Movement, 1940–45*. Vol. 1. Odense: Odense University Press.

Haggerty, Richard. 1990. *El Salvador: A Country Study*. Washington, DC: Library of Congress.

Hamas. 1988. *The Covenant of the Islamic Resistance Movement*. Avalon Project, Yale Law School. http://avalon.law.yale.edu/20th_century/hamas.asp.

"Hamas Accepts Palestinian State with 1967 Borders." 2017. Al Jazeera. May 2, 2017. http://www.aljazeera.com/news/2017/05/hamas-accepts-palestinian-state-1967-borders-170501114309725.html.

Hamizrachi, Beate. 1988. *The Emergence of the South Lebanon Security Belt: Major Saad Haddad and the Ties with Israel, 1975–1978*. New York: Praeger.

Hammes, T. X. 2012. "Counterinsurgency: Not a Strategy, but a Necessary Capability." *Joint Forces Quarterly* 65 (2): 48–52.

Handel, Michael I. 1990. *Weak States in the International System*. London: Frank Cass.

Harel, Amos, and Avi Issacharoff. 2008. *34 Days: Israel, Hezbollah, and the War in Lebanon*. New York: Palgrave Macmillan.

Harik, Judith Palmer. 2004. *Hezbollah: The Changing Face of Terrorism*. London: I. B. Tauris.

Hastings, Max. 1987. *The Korean War*. New York: Simon and Schuster.

Hawkins, Darren G., David A. Lake, Daniel L. Nielson, and Michael J. Tierney. 2006a. *Delegation and Agency in International Organizations*. New York: Cambridge University Press.

Hawkins, Darren G., David A. Lake, Daniel L. Nielson, and Michael J. Tierney, eds. 2006b. "Delegation under Anarchy: States, International Organizations, and Principal-Agent Theory." In *Delegation and Agency in International Organizations*, edited by Darren G. Hawkins, David A. Lake, Daniel L. Nielson, and Michael J. Tierney, 3–38. Cambridge: Cambridge University Press.

Hennelly, Michael J. 1993. "U.S. Policy in El Salvador: Creating Beauty or the Beast?" *Parameters* 23 (1): 59–69.

Hermes, Walter G. 1966. *Truce Tent and Fighting Front*. Washington, DC: Center of Military History, U.S. Army.

Herring, Eric, and Glen Rangwala. 2006. *Iraq in Fragments: The Occupation and Its Legacy*. Ithaca, NY: Cornell University Press.

Herring, George C. 1986. "Vietnam, El Salvador, and the Uses of History." In *El Salvador: Central America in the New Cold War*, 2nd ed., edited by Marvin E. Gettleman, Patrick Lacefield, Louis Menashe, and David Mermelstein, 369–79. New York: Grove.

Hilal, Jamil. 1977. "Class Transformation in the West Bank and Gaza." *Journal of Palestine Studies* 6 (2): 167–75.

Hodgkins, Allison Beth. 2014. "Why Hamas Escalated, When Before They Didn't." *Political Violence at a Glance* (blog). July 15, 2014. http://politicalviolenceataglance. org/2014/07/15/why-hamas-escalated-when-before-they-didnt/.

Holbrooke, Richard. 2009. "Prepared Statement of Ambassador Richard Holbrooke." In *U.S. Strategy toward Pakistan: Hearing before the Committee on Foreign Relations, United States Senate, May 12*, 8–10. Washington, DC: U.S. Government Printing Office.

Hollander, Ethan. 2006. "Swords or Shields? Implementing and Subverting the Final Solution in Nazi-Occupied Europe." PhD diss., University of California San Diego.

Hollander, Ethan. 2013. "The Banality of Goodness: Collaboration and Compromise in the Rescue of Denmark's Jews." *Journal of Jewish Identities* 6 (2): 41–66.

Hollander, Ethan. 2016. *Hegemony and the Holocaust: State Power and Jewish Survival in Occupied Europe*. New York: Palgrave Macmillan.

Hong, Nathaniel. 2012. *Occupied: Denmark's Adaptation and Resistance to German Occupation, 1940–1945*. Copenhagen: Frihedsmuseets Venner.

Hotolevy, Tzipi. 2016. "Where Does All That Aid for Palestinians Go?" *Wall Street Journal*, January 24, 2016.

HQ Eighth US Army Korea. 1952. *Special Problems in the Korean Conflict*. Carlisle, PA: Army War College.

Hull, Edmund J. 2011. *High Value Target: Countering Al Qaeda in Yemen*. Dulles, VA: Potomac Books.

Human Rights Watch. 1994. *Yemen: Human Rights in Yemen During and After the 1994 War*. October 1, 1994. https://www.hrw.org/sites/default/files/reports/ YEMEN94O.PDF.

Human Rights Watch. 2009. *In the Name of Unity: The Yemeni Government's Brutal Response to Southern Movement Protests*. December 15, 2009. https://www.hrw. org/report/2009/12/15/name-unity/yemeni-governments-brutal-response-southern-movement-protests.

Ibrahim, Azeem. 2009. "How America Is Funding Corruption in Pakistan." *Foreign Policy*, August 11, 2009. http://foreignpolicy.com/2009/08/11/how-america-is-funding-corruption-in-pakistan/.

Inbar, Efraim. 2007. "How Israel Bungled the Second Lebanon War." *Middle East Quarterly* 14 (3): 57–65.

International Crisis Group. 2010. *Squaring the Circle: Palestinian Security Reform under Occupation*. Middle East Report no. 98. September 7, 2010. https:// d2071andvip0wj.cloudfront.net/98-squaring-the-circle-palestinian-security-reform-under-occupation.pdf.

International Crisis Group. 2013. *Yemen's Southern Question: Avoiding a Breakdown*. Middle East Report no. 145. September 25, 2013. https://d2071andvip0wj. cloudfront.net/yemen-s-southern-question-avoiding-a-breakdown.pdf.

International Republic Institute. 2008. "IRI Releases Survey of Pakistan Public Opinion." February 11, 2008. http://www.iri.org/resource/iri-releases-survey-pakistan-public-opinion-3.

"In the Fight against Islamic Extremists, Do You Favor or Oppose . . . Using Drone Strikes?" 2015a. Fox News Poll, USASFOX.030415.R27, March 2015. Produced by Anderson Robbins Research/Shaw and Co. Research. Distributed by Cornell University, Roper Center for Public Opinion Research, iPOLL.

"In the Fight against Islamic Extremists, Do You Favor or Oppose . . . Using Drone Strikes?" 2015b. Fox News Poll, USASFOX.060415.R11, May 2015. Produced by Anderson Robbins Research/Shaw and Co. Research. Distributed by Cornell University, Roper Center for Public Opinion Research, iPOLL.

Isacson, Adam. 2010. "Uribe Checks Out." *Foreign Policy*, March 4, 2010. https://foreign policy.com/2010/03/04/uribe-checks-out/.

"Israel Launches Strikes on Gaza after Attacks." 2011. Al Jazeera. August 19, 2011. http://www.aljazeera.com/news/middleeast/2011/08/201181893519247218.html.

Jackson, Robert H. 1990. *Quasi-states: Sovereignty, International Relations, and the Third World*. New York: Cambridge University Press.

Jalal, Ayesha. 2014. *The Struggle for Pakistan: A Muslim Homeland and Global Politics*. Cambridge, MA: Harvard University Press.

Jamal, Amaney A. 2012. *Of Empires and Citizens: Pro-American Democracy or No Democracy at All?* Princeton, NJ: Princeton University Press. Kindle.

Jentleson, Bruce. 1994. *With Friends Like These: Reagan, Bush, and Saddam, 1982–1990*. New York: W. W. Norton.

Jespersen, Knud. 2002. *No Small Achievement: Special Operations Executive and the Danish Resistance, 1940–1945*. Odense: University Press of Southern Denmark.

JMCC (Jerusalem Media and Communications Center). 1993. *JMCC Public Opinion Poll No. 3 on Palestinian Attitudes on PLO-Israel Agreement*. http://www.jmcc.org/documents/no4.pdf.

JMCC (Jerusalem Media and Communications Center). 1999. *JMCC Public Opinion Poll No. 35 on Palestinian and Israeli Attitudes towards the Future of the Peace Process*. http://www.jmcc.org/Documentsandmaps.aspx?id=466.

JMCC (Jerusalem Media and Communications Center). 2011. *Tracking Palestinian Public Support for Armed Resistance during the Peace Process and Its Demise*. http://www.jmcc.org/Documentsandmaps.aspx?id=850.

Johnsen, Gregory D. 2012. *The Last Refuge: Yemen, Al-Qaeda, and America's War in Arabia*. New York: W. W. Norton.

Johnson, Chalmers. 2000. *Blowback: The Costs and Consequences of American Empire*. Boston: Little, Brown.

Johnston, Patrick B., and Anoop K. Sarbahi. 2016. "The Impact of U.S. Drone Strikes on Terrorism in Pakistan." *International Studies Quarterly* 60 (2): 203–19.

Joint Center for International Security Force Assistance. 2008. *Commander's Handbook for Security Force Assistance*. July 14, 2008. Washington, DC: U.S. Government Printing Office.

Joint Chiefs of Staff. 2013. *Joint Publication 3-24: Counterinsurgency*. November 22, 2013. Washington, DC: U.S. Government Printing Office.

Kambeck, Jens. 2016. *Returning to Transitional Justice in Yemen: A Backgrounder on the Commission on the Forcibly Retired in the Southern Governorates*. Bonn: Center for Applied Research in Partnership with the Orient. http://carpo-bonn.org/wp-content/uploads/2016/07/carpo_policy_report_03_2016.pdf.

Kane, Tim. 2006. "Global U.S. Troop Deployment, 1950–2005." Heritage Foundation (website). May 24, 2006. http://www.heritage.org/research/reports/2006/05/global-us-troop-deployment-1950-2005.

Kaplan, Fred. 2013. *The Insurgents: David Petraeus and the Plot to Change the American Way of War*. New York: Simon and Schuster.

Karl, Terry Lynn. 1992. "El Salvador's Negotiated Revolution." *Foreign Affairs* 71 (2): 147–64.

Karlin, Mara E. 2017a. *Building Militaries in Fragile States: Challenges for the United States*. Philadelphia: University of Pennsylvania Press.

Karlin, Mara E. 2017b. "Why Military Assistance Programs Disappoint: Minor Tools Can't Solve Major Problems." *Foreign Affairs* 96:111–20.

Katulis, Brian, and Lawrence Korb. 2010. "Today's Iraq Redeployment Made Possible by Our Deadline." *Foreign Policy*, August 31, 2010. http://foreignpolicy.com/2010/08/31/todays-iraq-redeployment-made-possible-by-our-deadline/.

Katulis, Brian, Marc Lynch, and Peter Juul. 2008. *Iraq's Political Transition after the Surge: Five Enduring Tensions and Ten Key Challenges*. Washington, DC: Center for American Progress.

Katz, Mark. 2003. "Breaking the Yemen-Al Qaeda Connection." *Current History* 102 (660): 40–44.

Kaufman, Burton I. 1986. *The Korean War: Challenges in Crisis, Credibility, and Command*. New York: Alfred A. Knopf.

Keohane, Robert O. 1969. "Lilliputians' Dilemmas: Small States in International Politics." *International Organization* 23 (2): 291–310.

Keohane, Robert O. 1971. "The Big Influence of Small Allies." *Foreign Policy* 2:161–82.

Kerr, Paul K., and Mary Beth Nikitin. 2016. *Pakistan's Nuclear Weapons*. CRS Issue Brief for Congress. August 1, 2016. Washington, DC: Congressional Research Service.

Kerry, John. 2016. "Getting the Endgame Right in Colombia." *Miami Herald*, January 30, 2016. http://www.miamiherald.com/opinion/op-ed/article57352418.html.

Khalidi, Rashid. 2013. *Brokers of Deceit: How the United States Has Undermined Peace in the Middle East*. Boston: Beacon.

Khattak, Daud. 2012. "Reviewing Pakistan's Peace Deals with the Taliban." *CTC Sentinel* 5 (9): 11–13.

Kilcullen, David. 2010. *Counterinsurgency*. New York: Oxford University Press.

King, Gary, Robert O. Keohane, and Sidney Verba. 1994. *Designing Social Inquiry: Scientific Inference in Qualitative Research*. Princeton, NJ: Princeton University Press.

Kirkpatrick, Jean. 1979. "Dictatorships and Double Standards." *Commentary*, November 1, 1979.

Kiser, Edgar, and Howard T. Welser. 2007. "The Microfoundations of Analytic Narratives." *Sociologica* 3:1–19. https://doi.org/10.2383/25957.

Krasner, Stephen D. 1999. *Sovereignty: Organized Hypocrisy*. Princeton, NJ: Princeton University Press.

Kronstadt, K. Alan. 2006. "Pakistan-U.S. Relations." CRS Issue Brief for Congress. May 9, 2006. Washington, DC: Congressional Research Service.

Kronstadt, K. Alan. 2012. *Pakistan-U.S. Relations*. CRS Report for Congress. May 24, 2012. Washington, DC: Congressional Research Service.

Kronstadt, K. Alan. 2015. *Pakistan-U.S. Relations: Issues for the 114th Congress*. CRS Report for Congress. May 14, 2015. Washington, DC: Congressional Research Service.

Kurtzer, Daniel C., Scott B. Lasensky, William B. Quandt, Steven L. Spiegel, and Shibley Z. Telhami. 2012. *The Peace Puzzle: America's Quest for Arab-Israeli Peace, 1989–2011*. Ithaca, NY: Cornell University Press.

Kydd, Andrew, and Barbara F. Walter. 2002. "Sabotaging the Peace: The Politics of Extremist Violence." *International Organization* 56 (2): 263–96.

Kydd, Andrew H., and Barbara F. Walter. 2006. "The Strategies of Terrorism." *International Security* 31 (1): 49–80.

Ladwig, Walter C., III. 2016. "Influencing Clients in Counterinsurgency: U.S. Involvement in El Salvador's Civil War, 1979–92." *International Security* 41 (1): 99–146.

Ladwig, Walter C., III. 2017. *The Forgotten Front: Patron-Client Relations in Counterinsurgency*. New York: Cambridge University Press.

Laffont, Jean-Jacques, and David Martimort. 2002. *The Theory of Incentives: The Principal-Agent Model*. Princeton, NJ: Princeton University Press.

Lake, David A. 2010–11. "Two Cheers for Bargaining Theory: Rationalist Explanations of the Iraq War." *International Security* 35 (3): 7–52.

Lake, David A. 2016. *The Statebuilder's Dilemma: On the Limits of Foreign Intervention*. Ithaca, NY: Cornell University Press.

Lambert, Andrew. 2010. "The German North Sea Islands, the Kiel Canal, and the Danish Narrows in Royal Navy Thinking and Planning, 1905–1918." In *The Danish Straits and German Naval Power, 1905–1918*, edited by Michael Epkenhans and Gerhard Paul Gross, 35–62. Potsdam: Militärgeschichtliches Forschungsamt.

Lambeth, Benjamin S. 2011. *Air Operations in Israel's War against Hezbollah: Learning from Lebanon and Getting It Right in Gaza*. Santa Monica, CA: RAND.

Lee, Rensselaer W., III, and Patrick L. Clawson. 1998. *The Andean Cocaine Industry*. New York: St. Martin's.

Lejenäs, Harald. 1989. "The Severe Winter in Europe, 1941–42: The Large-Scale Circulation, Cut-Off Lows, and Blocking." *Bulletin of the American Meteorological Society* 70:271–81.

LeoGrande, William M. 1998. *Our Own Backyard: The United States in Central America, 1977–1992*. Chapel Hill: University of North Carolina Press.

LeoGrande, William M., and Carla Anne Robbins. 1980. "Oligarchs and Officers: The Crisis in El Salvador." *Foreign Affairs* 58 (5): 1084–1103.

Lewy, Guenter. 1978. *America in Vietnam*. New York: Oxford University Press.

Lowe, Peter. 1986. *The Origins of the Korean War*. New York: Longman.

Lowe, Peter. 2000. *The Korean War*. New York: St. Martin's.

Lowenthal, Abraham F. 1995. *The Dominican Intervention*. Baltimore, MD: Johns Hopkins University Press.

Luce, Edward. "Lunch with the FT: John Bolton." *Financial Times*, October 19, 2007. Accessed July 5, 2018. https://www.ft.com/content/7a2140c6-7b7c-11dc-8c53-0000779fd2ac.

Lupfer, Timothy. 1981. *The Dynamics of Doctrine: The Changes in German Tactical Doctrine during the First World War*. Fort Leavenworth, KS: U.S. Army Combat Studies Institute.

Lyall, Jason, and Isaiah Wilson. 2009. "Rage against the Machines: Explaining Outcomes in Counterinsurgency Wars." *International Organization* 63 (1): 67–106.

Macdonald, Douglas J. 1992. *Adventures in Chaos: American Intervention for Reform in the Third World*. Cambridge, MA: Harvard University Press.

Maier, Clemens. 2007. "Making Memories: The Politics of Remembrance in Postwar Norway and Denmark." PhD diss., European University Institute.

"The 'Majors List' Presidential Determination." n.d. U.S. Department of State (website). Accessed May 25, 2018. https://www.state.gov/j/inl/rls/rpt/c11766.htm.

Malkasian, Carter. 2001. *The Korean War*. Chicago: Osprey.

Malkasian, Carter, and J. Kael Weston. 2012. "War Downsized: How to Accomplish More with Less." *Foreign Affairs* 91 (2): 111–21.

Mansoor, Peter. 1999. *The GI Offensive in Europe: The Triumph of American Infantry Divisions, 1941–1945*. Lawrence: University Press of Kansas.

Manwaring, Max G., and Court Prisk, eds. 1988. *El Salvador at War: An Oral History of Conflict from the 1979 Insurrection to the Present*. Washington, DC: National Defense University Press.

Markey, Daniel S. 2013. *No Exit from Pakistan: America's Tortured Relationship with Islamabad*. Cambridge: Cambridge University Press.

"Mashal: Hamas Was Behind Murder of Three Israeli Teens." 2014. Ynetnews. August 23, 2014. http://www.ynetnews.com/articles/0,7340,L-4562328,00.html.

Masood, Salman, and Eric Schmitt. 2011. "Tensions High after NATO Air Strikes Kill Pakistani Soldiers." *New York Times*, November 27, 2011. http://www.nytimes.com/2011/11/27/world/asia/pakistan-says-nato-helicopters-kill-dozens-of-soldiers.html.

Mazower, Mark. 2009. *Hitler's Empire: How the Nazis Ruled Europe*. New York: Penguin.

MCC (Millennium Challenge Corporation). 2007a. "Assistance to Yemen." Press release. October 26, 2007. https://www.mcc.gov/news-and-events/release/release-102607-yemen.

MCC (Millennium Challenge Corporation). 2007b. "MCC Approves Threshold Program Grant to Fight Corruption and Improve Governance in Yemen." Press release. September 12, 2007. https://www.mcc.gov/news-and-events/release/release-091207-yementhreshold.

McDermott, Jeremy. 2010. "How President Alvaro Uribe Changed Colombia." BBC News. August 4, 2010. http://www.bbc.com/news/world-latin-america-10841425.

McNerney, Michael, Angela O'Mahony, Thomas Szayna, Derek Eaton, Caroline Baxter, Colin Clarke, Emma Cutrufello, Michael McGee, Heather Peterson, and Leslie Payne. 2014. *Assessing Security Cooperation as a Preventive Tool*. Santa Monica, CA: RAND.

Mejia, Daniel. 2016. *Plan Colombia: An Analysis of Effectiveness and Costs*. Washington, DC: Brookings Institution. https://www.brookings.edu/wp-content/uploads/2016/07/Mejia-Colombia-final-2.pdf.

Menzel, Sewall H. 1997. *Cocaine Quagmire: Implementing the U.S. Anti-Drug Policy in the North Andes-Colombia*. New York: University Press of America.

Miller, Paul. 2010. "Bush on Nation Building and Afghanistan." *Foreign Policy*, November 17, 2010. https://foreignpolicy.com/2010/11/17/bush-on-nation-building-and-afghanistan/.

Millett, Alan R. 2005. *The War for Korea, 1945–1950*. Lawrence: University Press of Kansas.

Millett, Alan R. 2007. *The Korean War*. Washington, DC: Potomac Books.

Milton-Edwards, Beverley, and Stephen Farrell. 2010. *Hamas: The Islamic Resistance Movement*. Malden, MA: Polity.

Miyoshi Jager, Sheila. 2013. *Brothers at War: The Unending Conflict in Korea*. New York: W. W. Norton.

Mongin, Philippe. 2016. "What Are Analytic Narratives?" HEC Paris Research Paper No. ECO/SCD-2016-1155. June 16, 2016. http://dx.doi.org/10.2139/ssrn.2796567.

Montgomery, Tommie Sue. 1995. *Revolution in El Salvador: From Civil Strife to Civil Peace*. 2nd ed. Boulder, CO: Westview.

Moreh, Dror, dir. 2012. *The Gatekeepers.* Culver City, CA: Sony Pictures Classics. DVD.

Moroni Bracamonte, José Angel, and David E. Spencer. 1995. *Strategy and Tactics of the Salvadoran FMLN Guerrillas: Last Battle of the Cold War, Blueprint for Future Conflicts.* Westport, CT: Praeger.

Mueller, John E. 1971. "Trends in Popular Support for the Wars in Korea and Vietnam." *American Political Science Review* 65 (2): 358–75.

Muñoz, Carlo. 2012. "Loss of Supply Lines in Pakistan Costs $100M a Month, Says Panetta." *The Hill.* June 13, 2012. http://thehill.com/policy/defense/232609-loss-of-pakistan-routes-costing-dod-100-million-a-month-.

Musharraf, Pervez. 2006. *In the Line of Fire: A Memoir.* New York: Simon and Schuster.

Myre, Greg, and Steven Erlanger. 2006. "Israelis Enter Lebanon after Attacks." *New York Times,* July 13, 2006. http://www.nytimes.com/2006/07/13/world/middleeast/13mideast.html.

Na, Jongnam. 2006. "Making Cold War Soldiers: The Americanization of the South Korean Army, 1945–1955." PhD diss., University of North Carolina at Chapel Hill.

Nanes, Matthew J. 2017. "Political Violence Cycles: Electoral Incentives and the Provision of Counterterrorism." *Comparative Political Studies* 50 (2): 171–99.

NARA (National Archives and Records Administration). 1949. *U.S. Military Advisory Group to the Republic of Korea, Semi-Annual Report.* Washington, DC: NARA.

National Bipartisan Commission on Central America. 1984. *Report of the National Bipartisan Commission on Central America.* Washington, DC: Government Printing Office.

National Council on U.S.-Arab Relations. 2009. *Yemen Headlined: Contemporary Myths and Empirical Realities.* Congressional Briefing Series. https://ncusar.org/programs/09-transcripts/09-12-10-yemen-headlined.pdf.

National Security Council. 1950. National Security Council Report, NSC 81/1, *United States Courses of Action with Respect to Korea.* History and Public Policy Program Digital Archive, Truman Presidential Museum and Library. September 9, 1950. http://digitalarchive.wilsoncenter.org/document/116194.

"A New Dawn for South Lebanon." 2010. Al Jazeera. August 3, 2010. Video, 45:54. http://www.aljazeera.com/programmes/2010/05/20105246457594391.html.

Newport, Frank. 2014. "More Americans Now View Afghanistan War as a Mistake." Gallup. February 19, 2014. http://news.gallup.com/poll/167471/americans-view-afghanistan-war-mistake.aspx.

Nielsen, Finn Årup. 2011. "A New ANEW: Evaluation of a Word List for Sentiment Analysis in Microblogs." In *Making Sense of Microposts 2011: Proceedings of the ESWC2011 Workshop on "Making Sense of Microposts"; Big Things Come in Small Packages,* edited by Matthew Rowe, Milan Stankovic, Aba-Sah Dadzie, and Mariann Hardey. *CEUR Workshop Proceedings* 718:93–98.

North, Douglass C., John Joseph Wallis, and Barry R. Weingast. 2009. *Violence and Social Orders: A Conceptual Framework for Interpreting Recorded Human History.* Cambridge: Cambridge University Press.

Novak, Jane. 2009. "Yemen Strikes Multifaceted Deals with Al-Qaeda." *Long War Journal,* February 11, 2009. http://www.longwarjournal.org/archives/2009/02/yemens_multifaceted.php.

Obama, Barack. 2009. "Remarks by the President in Address to the Nation on the Way Forward in Afghanistan and Pakistan." The White House (website). December 1, 2009. https://obamawhitehouse.archives.gov/the-press-office/remarks-president-address-nation-way-forward-afghanistan-and-pakistan.

Obama, Barack, and Nawaz Sharif. 2013. "Remarks by President Obama and Prime Minister Nawaz Sharif of Pakistan after Bilateral Meeting." The White House (website). October 23, 2013. https://obamawhitehouse.archives.gov/the-press-office/2013/10/23/remarks-president-obama-and-prime-minister-nawaz-sharif-pakistan-after-b.

O'Hanlon, Michael E., and Ian Livingston. 2011. *Iraq Index: Tracking Variables of Reconstruction and Security in Post-Saddam Iraq*. January 31, 2011. Washington, DC: Brookings Institution. https://www.brookings.edu/wp-content/uploads/2016/07/index20110131.pdf.

Oñate, Andrea. 2011. "The Red Affair: FMLN-Cuban Relations during the Salvadoran Civil War, 1981–92." *Cold War History* 11 (2): 133–54.

Onuf, Nicholas. 1998. *The Republican Legacy in International Thought*. New York: Cambridge University Press.

Osiander, Andreas. 2001. "Sovereignty, International Relations, and the Westphalian Myth." *International Organization* 55 (2): 251–87.

Overy, Richard. 1998. *Russia's War: A History of the Soviet Effort: 1941–1945*. New York: Penguin.

Oye, Kenneth A. 1986. "Explaining Cooperation under Anarchy: Hypotheses and Strategies." In *Cooperation under Anarchy*, edited by Kenneth Oye, 1–24. Princeton, NJ: Princeton University Press.

Padró i Miquel, Gerard, and Pierre Yared. 2012. "The Political Economy of Indirect Control." *Quarterly Journal of Economics* 127 (2): 947–1015.

Paul, Christopher, Colin P. Clarke, and Beth Grill. 2010. *Victory Has a Thousand Fathers: Detailed Counterinsurgency Case Studies*. Santa Monica, CA: RAND.

Paulsson, Gunnar. 1995. "The 'Bridge over the Oresund': The Historiography on the Expulsion of the Jews from Nazi-Occupied Denmark." *Journal of Contemporary History* 30:431–64.

PCPSR (Palestinian Center for Policy and Survey Research). 2004. *PCPSR Public Opinion Poll No. 13*. http://www.pcpsr.org/en/node/242.

PCPSR (Palestinian Center for Policy and Survey Research). 2005. *PCPSR Public Opinion Poll No. 15*. http://www.pcpsr.org/en/node/240.

PCPSR (Palestinian Center for Policy and Survey Research). 2017. *PCPSR Public Opinion Poll No. 65*. http://www.pcpsr.org/en/node/711.

Peceny, Mark, and William D. Stanley. 2010. "Counterinsurgency in El Salvador." *Politics and Society* 38 (1): 67–94.

Pedersen, Jon. 2007. "Three Wars Later . . . Iraqi Living Conditions." In *Iraq: Preventing a New Generation of Conflict*, edited by Markus E. Bouillon, David M. Malone, and Ben Rowswell, 55–70. Boulder, CO: Lynne Rienner.

Pew Research Center. 2011. *U.S. Image in Pakistan Falls No Further following Bin Laden Killing*. Global Attitudes Project. June 21, 2011. Washington, DC: Pew Research Center.

Pew Research Center. 2012. *Pakistani Public Opinion Ever More Critical of U.S.* Global Attitudes Project. June 27, 2012. Washington, DC: Pew Research Center.

Pollard, Ruth. 2011. "Hezbollah Cited in Deadly Hit on Israel." *Sydney Morning Herald*, August 20, 2011. http://www.smh.com.au/world/hezbollah-cited-in-deadly-hit-on-israel-20110819-1j2d3.html.

Prevost, Gary, Harry E. Vanden, Carlos Olivia Campos, and Luis Fernando Ayerbe, eds. 2014. *US National Security Concerns in Latin America and the Caribbean*. New York: Palgrave Macmillan.

"Q&A: Gaza Conflict." 2009. BBC News. January 18, 2009. http://news.bbc.co.uk/2/hi/middle_east/7818022.stm.

Quinlivan, James. 1999. "Coup-Proofing: Its Practice and Consequences in the Middle East." *International Security* 24 (2): 131–65.

Ramos, Jennifer M. 2013. *Changing Norms through Actions: The Evolution of Sovereignty.* New York: Oxford University Press.

Ramsey, Robert D., III. 2006. *Advising Indigenous Forces: American Advisors in Korea, Vietnam, and El Salvador.* Global War on Terrorism Occasional Paper 18. Fort Leavenworth, KS: Combat Studies Institute Press.

Rashid, Ahmed. 2008. *Descent into Chaos: The U.S. and the Failure of Nation Building in Pakistan, Afghanistan, and Central Asia.* New York: Penguin.

Ravid, Barak, and Chaim Levinson. 2016. "Shin Bet Opposes Plan to Limit Israeli Army's Operations in Palestinian Cities." *Ha'aretz*, April 18, 2016. http://www.haaretz.com/israel-news/.premium-1.714914.

Reagan, Ronald. 1981. "The President's News Conference." American Presidency Project. March 6, 1981. http://www.presidency.ucsb.edu/ws/index.php?pid=43505.

Reagan, Ronald. 1983. "Remarks on Central America and El Salvador at the Annual Meeting of the National Association of Manufacturers." Ronald Reagan Presidential Library & Museum (website). March 10, 1983. https://reaganlibrary.archives.gov/archives/speeches/1983/31083a.htm.

Rearden, Stephen L. 1984. *History of the Office of the Secretary of Defense: The Formative Years, 1947–50.* Washington, DC: Historical Office, Office of the Secretary of Defense.

Regan, Patrick M. 2002. "Third-Party Interventions and the Duration of Intrastate Conflicts." *Journal of Conflict Resolution* 46 (1): 55–73.

Reiter, Dan. 2009. *How Wars End.* Princeton, NJ: Princeton University Press.

Reuters. 2011. "CIA Chief: Yemen Qaeda Affiliate Most Dangerous." September 13, 2011. https://www.reuters.com/article/us-usa-security-qaeda/cia-chief-yemen-qaeda-affiliate-most-dangerous-idUSTRE78C3G720110913.

Reuters. 2018. "U.S. Suspends at Least $900 Million in Security Aid to Pakistan." *New York Times*, January 5, 2018. https://www.nytimes.com/reuters/2018/01/05/world/asia/05reuters-usa-pakistan-aid.html.

Reynolds, Phillip W. 2014. "Persistent Conflict and Special Operations Forces." *Military Review* 94 (3): 62–69.

Rice, Condoleezza. 2011. *No Higher Honor: A Memoir of My Years in Washington.* New York: Crown.

Ricks, Thomas E. 2006. *Fiasco: The American Military Adventure in Iraq.* New York: Penguin.

Ricks, Thomas E. 2009. *The Gamble: General David Petraeus and the American Military Adventure in Iraq, 2006–2008.* New York: Penguin.

Riedel, Bruce. 2012. *Deadly Embrace: Pakistan, America, and the Future of the Global Jihad.* Washington, DC: Brookings Institution Press.

Risse, Thomas, ed. 2011. *Governance without a State? Policies and Politics in Areas of Limited Statehood.* New York: Columbia University Press.

Robinson, Linda. 2008. *Tell Me How This Ends: General David Petraeus and the Search for a Way out of Iraq.* New York: PublicAffairs.

"Rockets Fired from Gaza at Southern Israel." 2015. Al Jazeera. June 4, 2015. http://www.aljazeera.com/news/2015/06/rockets-fired-gaza-southern-israel-150603230355923.html.

Rollins, John. 2011. *Osama bin Laden's Death: Implications and Considerations.* CRS Report for Congress. May 5, 2011. Washington, DC: Congressional Research Service.

Rose, David. 2008. "The Gaza Bombshell." *Vanity Fair*, April 2008. https://www.vanityfair.com/news/2008/04/gaza200804.

Ross, Alice, and Jack Serle. 2014. "Get the Data: What the Drones Strike." Bureau of Investigative Journalism. May 23, 2014. https://www.thebureauinvestigates.com/stories/2014-05-23/get-the-data-what-the-drones-strike.

Ross, Tommy. 2016. "Leveraging Security Cooperation as Military Strategy." *Washington Quarterly* 39 (3): 91–103.

Rothstein, Robert L. 1968. *Alliances and Small Powers*. New York: Columbia University Press.

Roy, Sara. 2013. *Hamas and Civil Society in Gaza: Engaging the Islamist Social Sector*. Princeton, NJ: Princeton University Press.

Rudoren, Jodi, and Isabel Kershner. 2014. "Israel's Search for 3 Teenagers Ends in Grief." *New York Times*, June 30, 2014. http://www.nytimes.com/2014/07/01/world/middleeast/Israel-missing-teenagers.html.

Sahliyeh, Emile F. 1986. *The PLO after the Lebanon War*. Boulder, CO: Westview.

Sales, Marcus. 2013. "Plan Colombia: A Success?" *Colombia Politics* (blog). May 14, 2013. http://www.colombia-politics.com/tag/pastrana/.

Salmoni, Barak, Bryce Loidolt, and Madeleine Wells. 2010. *Regime and Periphery in Northern Yemen: The Huthi Phenomenon*. Santa Monica, CA: RAND.

Sanger, David E. 2012. *Confront and Conceal: Obama's Secret Wars and Surprising Use of American Power*. New York: Crown.

Savage, Charlie, and Scott Shane. 2016. "U.S. Reveals Death Toll from Airstrikes outside War Zones." *New York Times*, July 2, 2016. http://www.nytimes.com/2016/07/02/world/us-reveals-death-toll-from-airstrikes-outside-of-war-zones.html.

Savir, Uri. 2015. "Israel, Hamas Negotiate, but Truce Still Far Off." Al-Monitor, June 30, 2015. http://www.al-monitor.com/pulse/en/originals/2015/06/israel-hamas-truce-negotiations-egypt-netanyahu.html.

Sawyer, Robert K. 1962. *Military Advisors in Korea: KMAG in Peace and War*. Washington, DC: Center of Military History, U.S. Army.

Schanzer, Jonathan. 2004. "Yemen's War on Terror." *Orbis* 48 (3): 517–31.

Schanzer, Jonathan. 2008. *Hamas vs. Fatah: The Struggle for Palestine*. New York: Palgrave Macmillan.

Schelling, Thomas C. 1966. *Arms and Influence*. New Haven, CT: Yale University Press.

Schiff, Ze'ev, and Ehud Ya'ari. 1985. *Israel's Lebanon War*. New York: Simon and Schuster.

Schirman, Nadav, dir. 2014. *The Green Prince*. Chicago: Music Box Films. DVD.

Schnabel, James F., and Robert J. Watson. 1998. *History of the Joint Chiefs of Staff: The Joint Chiefs of Staff and National Policy, 1950–1951*. Washington, DC: Office of Joint History.

Schwarz, Benjamin C. 1991. *American Counterinsurgency Doctrine and El Salvador: The Frustrations of Reform and Illusions of Nation Building*. Santa Monica, CA: RAND.

Shah, Aqil. 2014. *The Army and Democracy: Military Politics in Pakistan*. Cambridge, MA: Harvard University Press.

Shapiro, Jacob N., and C. Christine Fair. 2010. "Understanding Support for Islamist Militancy in Pakistan." *International Security* 34 (3): 79–118.

Shapiro, Jacob N., and Oliver Vanden Eynde. 2014. "Suppression of Naxalites by State Governments." PowerPoint presentation, slides 96–124. Deterrence with Proxies, kickoff meeting, September 9, 2014, Washington, D.C.

Shapiro, Jeremy, and Richard Sokolsky. 2016. "How America Enables Its Allies' Bad Behavior." Vox.com. April 27, 2016. http://www.vox.com/2016/4/27/11497942/america-bad-allies.

Sharpe, Kenneth. 1988. "The Drug War: Going after Supply." *Journal of Interamerican Studies and World Affairs* 30 (2/3): 77–85.

Shifter, Michael. 2012. "Plan Colombia: A Retrospective." *Americas Quarterly*, Summer 2012. http://www.americasquarterly.org/node/3787.

Shikaki, Khalil. 2016. *The End of the "Abbas Decade": The Crumbling of the Post-Intifada Status-Quo.* January 2016. Brandeis University, Crown Center for Middle East Studies, Middle East Brief no. 97. http://www.brandeis.edu/crown/publications/meb/meb97.pdf.

Shuttleworth, Kate. 2015. "Israeli Airstrikes Target Hamas after Rocket Attacks." *Guardian* (US edition), September 19, 2015. http://www.theguardian.com/world/2015/sep/19/israeli-aircraft-hit-targets-in-gaza-after-rockets-are-fired-on-town.

Siddiqa, Ayesha. 2007. *Military Inc.: Inside Pakistan's Military Economy.* London: Pluto.

SIGIR (Special Inspector General for Iraq Reconstruction). 2013. *Learning from Iraq: A Final Report from the Special Inspector General for Iraq Reconstruction.* http://www.globalsecurity.org/military/library/report/2013/sigir-learning-from-iraq.pdf.

Simons, Geoff. 2004. *Colombia: A Brutal History.* London: SAQI.

"Sixty Years of U.S. Aid to Pakistan: Get the Data." 2011. *Datablog, Guardian* (UK edition). July 11, 2011. http://www.theguardian.com/global-development/poverty-matters/2011/jul/11/us-aid-to-pakistan.

Sofer, Roni. 2008. "Israel in Favor of Extending Gaza Lull." Ynetnews, December 13, 2008. http://www.ynetnews.com/articles/0,7340,L-3637877,00.html.

Sopko, John, and Andrew Wilder. 2016. *Conference Report: Lessons from the Coalition.* Product no. SIGAR-16–59-LL. Washington, DC: SIGAR and USIP.

"Standing Guard for Uncle Sam: Colombia." 1995. *Economist*, January 14, 1995. Gale Business Insights: Global database.

Staniland, Paul. 2012. "States, Insurgents, and Wartime Political Orders." *Perspectives on Politics* 10 (2): 243–64.

Stanley, William. 1996. *The Protection Racket State: Elite Politics, Military Extortion, and Civil War in El Salvador.* Philadelphia: Temple University Press.

Steele, Abbey. 2017. *Democracy and Displacement in Colombia's Civil War.* Ithaca, NY: Cornell University Press.

Steward, Richard W., ed. 2005. *American Military History.* Vol. 2, *The United States Army in a Global Era, 1917–2003.* Washington, DC: Center of Military History, U.S. Army.

Stokes, Doug. 2005. *America's Other War: Terrorizing Colombia.* New York: Zed Books.

Sullivan, Patricia L., Brock F. Tessman, and Xiaojun Li. 2011. "U.S. Military Aid and Recipient State Cooperation." *Foreign Policy Analysis* 7:275–94.

Sylvan, David, and Stephen Majeski. 2009. *U.S. Foreign Policy in Perspective: Clients, Enemies, and Empire.* New York: Routledge.

Talmadge, Caitlin. 2015. *The Dictator's Army: Battlefield Effectiveness in Authoritarian Regimes.* Ithaca, NY: Cornell University Press.

Tartir, Alaa. 2015. "Securitized Development and Palestinian Authoritarianism under Fayyadism." *Conflict, Security and Development* 15 (5): 479–502.

Tate, Winifred. 2015. *Drugs, Thugs, and Diplomats: U.S. Policymaking in Colombia.* Redwood City, CA: Stanford University Press.

Taubman, Philip. 1983. "Salvador's Ability to Win Doubted in Report." *New York Times*, April 22, 1983.

"Terrorist Attacks in Israel." 2011. Global Security. Last modified November 7, 2011. http://www.globalsecurity.org/military/world/war/israel-terror.htm.

Thomas, John. 1976. *The Giant-Killers: The Story of the Danish Resistance Movement, 1940–1945.* New York: Taplinger.

Thomson, Janice E. 1994. *Mercenaries, Pirates, and Sovereigns: State-Building and Extraterritorial Violence in Early Modern Europe.* Princeton, NJ: Princeton University Press.

Thrall, Nathan. 2010. "Our Man in Palestine." *New York Review of Books,* October 14, 2010. http://www.nybooks.com/articles/2010/10/14/our-man-palestine/.

Times of Israel. 2015. "Israel Strikes Gaza in Response to Rocket Fire." September 30, 2015. http://www.timesofisrael.com/idf-launches-air-strikes-in-gaza-in-response-to-rocket-fire/.

Tokatlian, Juan Gabriel. 1994. "Latin American Reaction to U.S. Policies on Drugs and Terrorism." In *Security, Democracy, and Development in U.S.-Latin American Relations,* edited by Lars Schoultz, William C. Smith, and Augusto Varas. Miami, FL: University of Miami North-South Center Press.

Trendle, Giles. 2010. "The Cost of Collaboration." Al Jazeera, May 26, 2010. http://www.aljazeera.com/focus/2010/05/201051992011673189.html.

Ucko, David H. 2013. "Counterinsurgency in El Salvador: The Lessons and Limits of the Indirect Approach." *Small Wars and Insurgencies* 24 (4): 669–95.

United Nations Human Rights Committee. 2015. *Report of the Detailed Findings of the Independent Commission of Inquiry Established Pursuant to Human Rights Council Resolution S-21/1.* June 23, 2015. https://digitallibrary.un.org/record/800872/files/A_HRC_29_CRP-4-EN.pdf.

"United States Objectives, Policies, and Courses of Action in Asia." (1951) 1977. NSC 48/5, May 17, 1951. In *Foreign Relations of the United States, 1951,* Vol. 6, *Asia and the Pacific,* Part 1, edited by Paul Claussen, John P. Glennon, David W. Mabon, Neal H. Petersen, and Carl N. Raether, 33–63. Washington, DC: U.S. Government Printing Office.

UNODC (United Nations Office on Drugs and Crime). 2007. *World Drug Report 2007.* https://www.unodc.org/pdf/research/wdr07/WDR_2007.pdf.

UNODC (United Nations Office on Drugs and Crime). 2010. *World Drug Report 2010.* https://www.unodc.org/documents/wdr/WDR_2010/World_Drug_Report_2010_lo-res.pdf.

UNODC (United Nations Office on Drugs and Crime). 2013. *World Drug Report 2013.* https://www.unodc.org/unodc/secured/wdr/wdr2013/World_Drug_Report_2013.pdf.

U.S. Agency for International Development/Yemen. 2006. *Yemen Corruption Assessment.* September 25, 2006. https://yemen.usembassy.gov/root/pdfs/reports/yemen-corruption-assessment.pdf.

U.S. CIA (U.S. Central Intelligence Agency). 1984. *Military Commanders' Resentment and Opposition to U.S. Government Pressure to Detain Captain Eduardo Avila.* https://www.cia.gov/library/readingroom/docs/DOC_0000049079.pdf.

U.S. CIA (U.S. Central Intelligence Agency). 1990. *El Salvador's Insurgents: Key Capabilities and Vulnerabilities.* https://www.cia.gov/library/readingroom/docs/DOC_0000808521.pdf.

U.S. CIA (U.S. Central Intelligence Agency). 1991. *El Salvador: Assessing the Impact of Rebel Surface-to-Air Missiles.* June 7, 1991. https://www.cia.gov/library/readingroom/docs/DOC_0000808523.pdf.

U.S. Congressional Budget Office. 1994. *The Andean Initiative: Objectives and Support.* March 1994. https://www.cbo.gov/sites/default/files/103rd-congress-1993-1994/reports/doc10.pdf.

U.S. Department of State. 1983. *Foreign Relations of the United States, 1951.* Vol. 7, *Korea and China,* Part 1, edited by John P. Glennon, Harriet D. Schwar, and Paul Claussen. Washington, DC: U.S. Government Printing Office.

U.S. Department of State. 1984. *Foreign Relations of the United States, 1952–1954.* Vol. 15, *Korea,* Part 2, edited by Edward C. Keefer. Washington, DC: U.S. Government Printing Office.

U.S. Department of State. 1990. "ESAF Compliance Unsatisfactory on Jesuit Investigation." Telegram 12056. October 17, 1990. El Salvador: War, Peace, and Human Rights, 1980–1994 Collection. Washington, DC: Digital National Security Archive.

U.S. Department of State. 2001. *Patterns of Global Terrorism 2001.* https://www.state.gov/j/ct/rls/crt/2001/html/index.htm.

U.S. Department of State. 2002. *Patterns of Global Terrorism 2002.* https://www.state.gov/j/ct/rls/crt/2002/html/index.htm.

U.S. Department of State. 2003. *Patterns of Global Terrorism 2003.* https://www.state.gov/j/ct/rls/crt/2003/c12108.htm.

U.S. Department of State. 2004. *Country Reports on Terrorism 2004.* https://www.state.gov/j/ct/rls/crt/c14818.htm.

U.S. Department of State. 2005. *Country Reports on Terrorism 2005.* https://www.state.gov/j/ct/rls/crt/2005/.

U.S. Department of State. 2006. *Country Reports on Terrorism 2006.* https://www.state.gov/j/ct/rls/crt/2006/.

U.S. Department of State. 2007. *Country Reports on Terrorism 2007.* https://www.state.gov/j/ct/rls/crt/2007/index.htm/.

U.S. Department of State. 2008. *Country Reports on Terrorism 2008.* https://www.state.gov/j/ct/rls/crt/2008/index.htm.

U.S. Department of State. 2009. *Country Reports on Terrorism 2009.* https://www.state.gov/j/ct/rls/crt/2009/index.htm.

U.S. Department of State. 2010. *Country Reports on Terrorism 2010.* https://www.state.gov/j/ct/rls/crt/2010/index.htm.

U.S. Department of State. 2011. *Country Reports on Terrorism 2011.* https://www.state.gov/j/ct/rls/crt/2011/index.htm.

U.S. Department of State. 2018. "Department Press Briefing." U.S. Department of State (website). January 4, 2018. https://www.state.gov/r/pa/prs/dpb/2018/01/276852.htm#PAKISTAN.

U.S. Department of State, Bureau of International Narcotics and Law Enforcement Affairs. 1996. *International Narcotics Control Strategy Report.* March 1997. https://1997-2001.state.gov/global/narcotics_law/1996_narc_report/index.html.

U.S. Department of State, Bureau of International Narcotics and Law Enforcement Affairs. 1997. *International Narcotics Control Strategy Report.* March 1998. https://1997-2001.state.gov/global/narcotics_law/1997_narc_report/index.html.

U.S. Department of State, Bureau of International Narcotics and Law Enforcement Affairs. 1998. *International Narcotics Control Strategy Report.* February 1999. https://1997-2001.state.gov/global/narcotics_law/narc_reports_mainhp.html.

U.S. Department of State, Bureau of International Narcotics and Law Enforcement Affairs. 1999. *International Narcotics Control Strategy Report.* March 1, 2000. https://www.state.gov/j/inl/rls/nrcrpt/1999/index.htm.

U.S. Department of State, Bureau of International Narcotics and Law Enforcement Affairs. 2000. *International Narcotics Control Strategy Report.* March 1, 2001. https://www.state.gov/j/inl/rls/nrcrpt/2000/index.htm.

U.S. Department of State, Bureau of International Narcotics and Law Enforcement Affairs. 2002. *International Narcotics Control Strategy Report.* March 1, 2003. https://www.state.gov/j/inl/rls/nrcrpt/2002/index.htm.

U.S. Department of State, Bureau of International Narcotics and Law Enforcement Affairs. 2005. *International Narcotics Control Strategy Report.* Washington DC: U.S. Government Printing Office. https://www.state.gov/j/inl/rls/nrcrpt/2005/index.htm.

U.S. Department of the Treasury. 2004. "United States Designates bin Laden Loyalist." Press release, Office of Public Affairs. February 24, 2004. https://www.treasury.gov/press-center/press-releases/Pages/js1190.aspx.

U.S. Director of Central Intelligence. 1983. *Special National Intelligence Estimate: Near-Term Prospects for El Salvador.* SNIE 83.1–2–83. https://www.cia.gov/library/readingroom/docs/DOC_0001016744.pdf.

U.S. Director of Central Intelligence. 1989. *Special National Intelligence Estimate: El Salvador; Government and Insurgent Prospects.* February 1989. https://www.cia.gov/library/readingroom/docs/DOC_0000049407.pdf.

"US Enters the Korean Conflict." n.d. U.S. National Archives and Records Administration (website). Accessed May 20, 2018. https://www.archives.gov/education/lessons/korean-conflict.

U.S. GAO (U.S. General Accounting Office). 1990. *El Salvador: Extent of U.S. Military Personnel in Country.* July 9, 1990. GAO/NSIAD-90–227FS. http://www.gao.gov/products/NSIAD-90-227FS. Washington, DC: U.S. Government Printing Office.

U.S. GAO (U.S. General Accounting Office). 1991a. *The Drug War: Observations on Counternarcotics Aid to Colombia.* GAO/NSIAD-91–296. September 30, 1991. Washington, DC: U.S. Government Printing Office.

U.S. GAO (U.S. General Accounting Office). 1991b. *El Salvador: Military Assistance Has Helped Counter but Not Overcome the Insurgency.* NSIAD-91–166. April 23, 1991. http://www.gao.gov/products/NSIAD-91-166. Washington, DC: U.S. Government Printing Office.

U.S. GAO (U.S. General Accounting Office). 1992. *Foreign Assistance: Promising Approach to Judicial Reform in Colombia.* GAO/NSIAD-92–296. September 24, 1992. Washington, DC: U.S. Government Printing Office.

U.S. GAO (U.S. General Accounting Office). 1993. *The Drug War: Colombia Is Undertaking Anti-Drug Programs, but Impact Is Uncertain.* GAO/NSIAD-93–158. August 10, 1993. Washington, DC: U.S. Government Printing Office.

U.S. GAO (U.S. General Accounting Office). 1995a. *The Drug War: Observations on U.S. International Drug Control Efforts.* GAO/NSIAD-95–194. August 1, 1995. Washington, DC: U.S. Government Printing Office.

U.S. GAO (U.S. General Accounting Office). 1995b. *Review of Assistance to Colombia.* GAO/NSIAD-96–62R. December 12, 1995. Washington, DC: U.S. Government Printing Office.

U.S. GAO (U.S. General Accounting Office). 1998. *Drug Control: U.S. Counternarcotics Efforts in Colombia Face Continuing Challenges.* GAO/NSIAD-98–60. February 12, 1998. Washington, DC: U.S. Government Printing Office.

U.S. GAO (U.S. General Accounting Office). 1999. *Drug Control: Narcotics Threat from Colombia Continues to Grow.* GAO/NSIAD-99–136. June 22, 1999. Washington, DC: U.S. Government Printing Office.

U.S. GAO (U.S. General Accounting Office). 2000. *Drug Control: Challenges in Implementing Plan Colombia.* GAO/NSIAD-02–291. October 12, 2000. Washington, DC: U.S. Government Printing Office.

U.S. GAO (U.S. General Accounting Office). 2002. *Drug Control: Efforts to Develop Alternatives to Cultivating Illicit Crops in Colombia Have Made Little Progress and Face Serious Obstacles.* GAO/NSIAD-01–79T. February 2002. Washington, DC: U.S. Government Printing Office.

U.S. ONDCP (U.S. Office of National Drug Control and Policy). 1999. *1999 National Drug Control Strategy.* https://www.ncjrs.gov/ondcppubs/publications/policy/99ndcs/ii-e.html.

U.S. Senate. 2012. *U.S. Policy in Yemen: Hearing before the Subcommittee on Near Eastern and South and Central Asian Affairs of the Committee on Foreign Relations.* 112th Cong., First Session. July 19, 2011. Washington, DC: U.S. Government Printing Office. https://www.gpo.gov/fdsys/pkg/CHRG-112shrg73916/pdf/CHRG-112shrg73916.pdf.

von Neumann, John. 1928. "Zur Theorie der Gesellschaftsspiele." *Mathematische Annalen* 100 (1): 295–320. https://doi.org/10.1007/BF01448847.

von Neumann, John. 1959. "On the Theory of Games of Strategy." In *Contributions to the Theory of Games* (AM-40), vol. 4, edited by A. W. Tucker and R. D. Luce, 13–42. Princeton, NJ: Princeton University Press.

Wainstock, Dennis D. 1999. *Truman, MacArthur, and the Korean War.* Westport, CT: Greenwood.

Warrick, Joby. 2008. "CIA Places Blame for Bhutto Assassination." *Washington Post,* January 18, 2008. http://www.washingtonpost.com/wp-dyn/content/article/2008/01/17/AR2008011703252.html.

Washington Times. 2008. "Bush a Convert to Nation Building." April 7, 2008. http://www.washingtontimes.com/news/2008/apr/7/bush-a-convert-to-nation-building/.

Watts, Stephen. 2015. *Identifying and Mitigating Risks in Security Sector Assistance for Africa's Fragile States.* Santa Monica, CA: RAND.

Watts, Stephen, Jason H. Campbell, Patrick B. Johnston, Sameer Lalwani, and Sarah H. Bana. 2014. *Countering Others' Insurgencies: Understanding U.S. Small-Footprint Interventions in Local Context.* Santa Monica, CA: RAND.

Webb, William J. 2006. *The Korean War: The Outbreak 27 June–15 September 1950.* CMH Publication 19–6. Washington, DC: Center of Military History, U.S. Army.

Weitz, Gidi, and Jack Khoury. 2016. "Will Marwan Barghouti Be the Palestinian Nelson Mandela?" *Ha'aretz,* July 5, 2016. http://www.haaretz.com/israel-news/1.728135.

Whitelaw, Kevin. 2008. "Inside Colombia's War on Kidnapping." *U.S. News and World Report,* February 27, 2008. http://www.usnews.com/news/world/articles/2008/02/27/inside-colombias-war-on-kidnapping.

Wike, Richard. 2007. "Musharraf's Support Shrinks, Even as More Pakistanis Reject Terrorism . . . and the U.S." Pew Research Center, Global Attitudes and Trends. August 8, 2007. http://www.pewglobal.org/2007/08/08/pakistanis-increasingly-reject-terrorism-and-the-us/.

Williams, Brian Glyn. 2010. "The CIA's Covert Predator Drone War in Pakistan, 2004–2010: The History of an Assassination Campaign." *Studies in Conflict and Terrorism* 33 (10): 871–92.

Woerner, Fred E. 1981. *Report of the El Salvador Military Strategy Assistance Team (Draft).* Accession Number EL00383. El Salvador: War, Peace, and Human Rights, 1980–1994 Collection. Washington, DC: Digital National Security Archive.

Wood, Elizabeth Jean. 2003. *Insurgent Collective Action and Civil War in El Salvador.* Cambridge: Cambridge University Press.

Yahil, Leni. 1969. *The Rescue of Danish Jewry.* Philadelphia: Jewish Publication Society.

Yared, Pierre. 2010. "A Dynamic Theory of War and Peace." *Journal of Economic Theory* 145:1921–50.

"Yemen President Ali Abdullah Saleh Warns of Coup." 2011. BBC News. March 22, 2011. http://www.bbc.com/news/world-middle-east-12819003.

You, Jong-Sung. 2013. "Transition from a Limited Access Order to an Open Access Order: The Case of South Korea." In *In the Shadow of Violence: Politics, Economics, and the Problems of Development*, edited by Douglass North, John Wallis, Steven Webb, and Barry Weingast, 293–327. Cambridge: Cambridge University Press.

Zitun, Yoav. 2014a. "Operation Bring Back Our Brothers: IDF Arrest 200, Shift Focus to Nablus." Ynetnews. June 17, 2014. http://www.ynetnews.com/articles/0,7340,L-4531266,00.html.

Zitun, Yoav. 2014b. "Terror Persists, but West Bank Fence Still Porous." Ynetnews. May 1, 2014. http://www.ynetnews.com/articles/0,7340,L-4473355,00.html.

About the Contributors

Alexei S. Abrahams is a postdoctoral researcher of regional political economy at the Niehaus Center of the Woodrow Wilson School of Public and International Affairs, Princeton University.

Ryan T. Baker is a PhD candidate in public policy at George Washington University.

Eli Berman is professor of economics at the University of California, San Diego and research director for international security studies at the UC Institute on Global Conflict and Cooperation.

Stephen Biddle is professor of international and public affairs at Columbia University and adjunct senior fellow for defense policy at the Council on Foreign Relations.

Ben Brewer is a PhD candidate in political science at the University of California, San Diego.

David A. Lake is Gerri-Ann and Gary E. Jacobs Professor of Social Sciences and Distinguished Professor of Political Science at the University of California, San Diego.

Julia M. Macdonald is assistant professor at the Josef Korbel School of International Studies, University of Denver.

Brandon Merrell is a PhD candidate in political science at the University of California, San Diego.

Matthew J. Nanes is assistant professor of political science at Saint Louis University.

Gerard Padró i Miquel is professor of economics and political science at Yale University.

Clara H. Suong is a PhD candidate in political science at the University of California, San Diego.

Abigail Vaughn is a PhD candidate in political science at the University of California, San Diego.

Pierre Yared is professor of business at Columbia Business School and codirector of the Richard Paul Richman Center for Business, Law, and Public Policy at Columbia University.

Index